THE NAQSHB

GUIDEBOOK

OF DAILY PRACTICES AND DEVOTIONS

Shaykh Muhammad Hisham Kabbani

ISLAMIC SUPREME COUNCIL OF AMERICA

Library of Congress Publication Control Number: 2004013090
ISBN: 1-930409-22-2

Published and Distributed by:
Islamic Supreme Council of America (ISCA)
1400 Sixteenth Street NW, #B112, Washington, DC 20036 USA
Tel: (202) 939-3400
Fax: (202) 939-3410
Email: staff@islamicsupremecouncil.org
Web: http://www.islamicsupremecouncil.org

Publishing Office:
17195 Silver Parkway, #201
Fenton, MI 48430 USA
Tel: (888) 278-6624
Fax: (810) 815-0518

Printed in Canada

بِسْمِ اللَّهِ الرَّحْمَنِ الرَّحِيمِ

وَاتَّقُوا اللَّهَ وَيُعَلِّمُكُمُ اللَّهُ

Observe your duty to God and God will teach you. (2:283)

يَا أَيُّهَا الَّذِينَ آمَنُوا اتَّقُوا اللَّهَ وَكُونُوا مَعَ الصَّادِقِينَ

*O ye who believe! Fear God and be with those who are true (in word and deed).
(9:119)*

وَاذْكُر رَّبَّكَ فِي نَفْسِكَ تَضَرُّعاً وَخِيفَةً وَدُونَ الْجَهْرِ مِنَ الْقَوْلِ بِالْغُدُوِّ وَالآصَالِ وَلاَ تَكُن مِّنَ الْغَافِلِينَ

*And do thou (O Muhammad!) Bring thy Lord to remembrance in thy (very) soul,
with humility and in reverence, without loudness in words, in the mornings and
evenings; and be not thou of those who are unheedful. (7:205)*

وَاذْكُر رَّبَّكَ كَثِيراً وَسَبِّحْ بِالْعَشِيِّ وَالإِبْكَارِ

*Then celebrate the praises of thy Lord again and again, and glorify Him in the
evening and in the morning. (3:41)*

يَا أَيُّهَا الَّذِينَ آمَنُوا اذْكُرُوا اللَّهَ ذِكْراً كَثِيراً

O ye who believe! Remember Allah with much remembrance. (33:41)

يَا أَيُّهَا الَّذِينَ آمَنُوا اتَّقُوا اللَّهَ وَابْتَغُوا إِلَيْهِ الْوَسِيلَةَ وَجَاهِدُوا فِي سَبِيلِهِ لَعَلَّكُمْ تُفْلِحُونَ

*O ye who believe! Be mindful of your duty to Allah, and seek the way of approach
unto Him, and strive in His way in order that ye may succeed. (5:35)*

إِنَّ اللَّهَ وَمَلائِكَتَهُ يُصَلُّونَ عَلَى النَّبِيِّ يَا أَيُّهَا الَّذِينَ آمَنُوا صَلُّوا عَلَيْهِ وَسَلِّمُوا تَسْلِيماً

*Lo! Allah and His angels shower blessings on the Prophet. O ye who believe! Ask
blessings on him and salute him with a worthy salutation. (33:56)*

هُوَ الَّذِي يُصَلِّي عَلَيْكُمْ وَمَلائِكَتُهُ لِيُخْرِجَكُم مِّنَ الظُّلُمَاتِ إِلَى النُّورِ وَكَانَ بِالْمُؤْمِنِينَ رَحِيماً

*He it is Who sends blessings on you, as do His angels, that He may bring you out
from the depths of Darkness into Light: and He is Full of Mercy to the Believers.
(33:43)*

Shaykh Muhammad Nazim Adil al-Haqqani with his son-in-law, Shaykh Muhammad Hisham Kabbani (right), and his brother, Shaykh Muhammad Adnan Kabbani (left).

Contents

Exordium

The most distinguished Naqshbandi Order is the way of the Companions of the Prophet ﷺ and those who follow them. This Way consists of continuous worship in every action, both external and internal, with complete and perfect discipline according to the *Sunnah* of the Prophet ﷺ. It consists in maintaining the highest level of conduct and leaving absolutely all innovations and all free interpretations in public customs and private behavior. It consists in keeping awareness of the Presence of God, Almighty and Exalted, on the way to self-effacement and complete experience of the Divine Presence. It is the Way of complete reflection of the highest degree of perfection. It is the Way of sanctifying the self by means of the most difficult struggle, the struggle against the self. It begins where the other orders end, in the attraction of complete Divine Love, which was granted to the first friend of the Prophet ﷺ, Abu Bakr as-Siddiq ؓ.

Preface

Praise be to God who has revealed to the purest of mankind, our master Muhammad the Messenger of God ﷺ, the wonderful signs of His Wisdom, bestowed on him the goodness of His knowledge and love, and honored him with the stewardship of this life and the next.

The Prophet of God ﷺ is like a hidden treasure to which all seekers are drawn. His name is mentioned on every tongue, his remembrance rejoiced in every meeting. Nothing can contain his wisdom, and yet he contains everything with his heart.

And praise yet again to God, who has inspired His Beloved Prophet ﷺ to bestow from the Oceans of Knowledge which God has gifted him to those devoted and sincere seekers in every age, the ones chosen by God to be of God, by God, with God and for God and who sought nothing but God and for whom God was sufficient as recompense. Their days were spent in working for God and their nights were spent in crying before His Divine Court. The eyes of their bodies, like those of their hearts, were continually dimmed by the outpouring of tears in soliciting God to shower mankind from His overflowing mercy.

Sainthood's azimuth was manifest distinctly in the Naqshbandi spiritual path. As a school whose graduate saints were the epitome of piety in every century, it represents the highest path of safety for mankind. When evil was first created, prophets, messenger and angels were aghast. When God showed them how the Naqshbandi saints would stand forth firmly for truth against evil, their hearts were calmed.

Naqshbandi saints are proven experts in every field, encompassing both hidden and manifest knowledge. They can see without the necessity to look. They are the guardians of faith and the sentries on the watchtower of sincerity. They are utterly powerful against evildoers.

In particular this century has been blessed, for in this time of flagrant materialism and unlimited freedom for the rampant extremes of the ego, there yet lives a man who brings to bear a miracle in every encounter: Shaykh Muhammad Nazim Adil al-Haqqani, may God sanctify his secret.

The living inheritor of the *warith al-Muhammadiyya,* the Muhammadan Inheritance, sincere seekers of the 21st century aspire to emulate his inimitable example. As prime upholder of the *Sunnah* of the Prophet ﷺ in this age, Mawlana Shaykh Muhammad Nazim Adil al-Haqqani stands as an extraordinary symbol for all lovers of peace, seekers of truth, and healers of humankind's injuries. Shaykh Nazim is an unparalleled saint of boundless potential, possessing a candid, calm and dignified approach, as well as the rare ability to heal, serve, console, and express the compassion which is the hallmark of all persons of true faith. With his example, and his beloved ever-familiar smile as inspiration in their hearts, the seekers on the path to God have been empowered to achieve the vast vision set before them by his guiding words.

The extraordinary vision of the Naqshbandi saints was manifest in their establishment of the Naqshbandi devotions. These practices enable in devout seekers an awakening of belief in the unseen world around us, and then, as they ascend through stages of enlightenment, empower them to attain supreme heights of proximity to the Divine Presence. The renewed prominence of these practices at the turn of the 21st century, signal an impending change to our society in which the aspirants to divine service will be granted to transcend the bounds of the physical senses in order to fulfill the unexplored potential in every human heart.

The Naqshbandi devotions are a source of light and energy, an oasis in a worldly desert. They are the secret behind the motion of every living cell. The lights bestowed on seekers, who hold fast to the perfect conduct and who stand forth on the platform of the duties of divine service appear like stars, suns and moons in every firmament. Through the manifestations of Divine Blessings bestowed on the practitioners of these magnificent rites, they will be granted the power of magnanimous healing, by which they seek to cure the hearts of mankind darkened by the gloom of spiritual poverty and materialism and scorched in the flames of iniquity and heedlessness.

We present this volume of select and spiritual devotions with the prayer that each person who picks it up with sincere intention to observe any of its efficacious practices receive the blessings and manifestations bestowed on the greatest saints of earlier times. As with any method of approach to the Divine Presence, proper conduct must be observed in its performance. May God support and guide the seeker to the best conduct in observing these devotions; in every step, in every breath, and in every heartbeat.

Shaykh Muhammad Hisham Kabbani
Chairman, Islamic Supreme Council of America
Washington, D.C.
Jumada al-Awwal 4, 1425/June 21, 2004

Publisher's Notes

References from the Quran and the *hadith* (holy traditions) are most commonly italicized and offset. References from the Quran are noted in parenthesis, i.e. (3:127), indicating the third chapter, verse 127. References from *hadith* are attributed to their transmitter, i.e. Bukhari, Muslim, Ahmed, etc. Quotes from other sources are offset without italics.

Dates of events are characterized as "AH/CE," which infers "after Hijrah (migration)" on which the Islamic calendar is based, and "Christian Era," respectively. A table of Islamic months and holy days is provided.

Muslims around the world typically offer praise upon speaking, hearing, or reading the name "*Allah*" and any of the Islamic names of God. Muslims also offer salutation and/or invoke blessing upon speaking, hearing or reading the names of Prophet Muhammad, other prophets, his family, his companions, and saints. We have applied the following international standards, using Arabic calligraphy and lettering:

ﷺ *sall-Allahu 'alayhi wa sallam* (God's blessings and greetings of peace be upon him) following the names of the Prophet.

عليه السلام *'alayhi 's-salām* (peace be upon him) following the names of other prophets, angels, and Khidr.

عليها السلام *'alayhā s-salām* (peace be upon her) following the name of Mary, Mother of Jesus.

رضي الله عنه/عنها *rady-Allahu 'anhu/'anhā* (may God be pleased with him/her) following the name of a male or female companion of the Prophet.

ق *qaḍḍas-Allāhu sirrah* (may God sanctify his secret) following the name of a saint.

Transliteration

To simplify reading the Arabic names, places and terms are not transliterated in the main text. Transliteration is provided in the glossaries and in the section on the spiritual practices to facilitate correct pronunciation and is based on the following system:

Symbol	Transliteration	Symbol	Transliteration	Vowels:	
				Long	
ء	ʼ	ط	ṭ	آ ى	ā
ب	b	ظ	ẓ	و	ū
ت	t	ع	ʻ	ي	ī
ث	th	غ	gh	**Short**	
ج	j	ف	f	َ	a
ح	ḥ	ق	q	ُ	u
خ	kh	ك	k	ِ	i
د	d	ل	l		
ذ	dh	م	m		
ر	r	ن	n		
ز	z	ه	h		
س	s	و	w		
ش	sh	ي	y		
ص	ṣ	ة	ah; at		
ض	ḍ	ال	al-/'l-		

Introduction

Stepping Forth on the Path of Wayfaring to the Divine Presence

The Station of Extinction

The station of extinction, *maqam al-fana,* is one of the primary stations on the Path of the Sufi towards the state of perfection, *maqam al-Ihsan*. This station in fact is the first target of the seeker as he moves on the way of spiritual wayfaring, and while not the ultimate final destination, it attainment is considered the first foothold into the Garden of Sainthood—for one who reaches this has become of the Elect. It is for this reason that many identified this station as the final goal and declared that one who attained it had in fact achieved ultimate felicity, complete nothingness. Whereas in reality, this station, while of immense magnitude, is still a waystation on the ascent towards the Divine. For this reason the Naqshbandi Saints said, "Our Way begins where others leave off."

In the station of extinction, the servant of God leaves his very self behind, and in abandonment of all that pertains to selfhood is cut adrift in the oceanic realm of God's Reality. At that station, self-realization is achieved for the seeker has achieved the vision of Witnessing, *aynu 'l-mushahadah,* and is thus able to testify with true vision, as a witness of the One. When that is attained, the seeker is unable to identify him or herself as existent and sees all existence as a manifestation of the Oneness of God.

The Prophet Muhammad ﷺ, who was the leader of humanity in seeking the Divine Presence, said, *"I am the City of Knowledge and Ali is its gate."*[1] In this statement is an affirmation of two realities:

- The Prophet ﷺ encompasses all knowledge granted to creation from the Lord of Creation.
- Ali ibn Abi Talib ؓ, the Lion of God, was chosen as the one through whom access to that knowledge was made possible.

As regards the first point, God said:

---

[1] Narrated by al-Hakim and rigorously authenticated (*sahih),* also from at-Tirmidhi with chains from Jabir and Ali; at-Tirmidhi and as-Suyuti declared it to be good (*hasan*).

He discloses not His unseen (ghayb) to anyone, except only to such a Messenger as He is well-pleased with. (72:26)

Muhammad ﷺ is the Crown of those messengers with whom God is well-pleased. As a prophet who brought reports from His Lord; as the one who ascended above the seven heavens and the seven Paradises to His Lord's Presence by *"two bows' length or even nearer"* (53:9); as the one who told of the events that attended the creation of all existent beings; as the one who saw the events after resurrection and Judgment Day, and as the one to whom was revealed the inimitable Qur'an, who is more deserving of such a boundless gift—the gift of Knowledge from the Divine Presence? If about a saint, as our master Khidr ﷺ is regarded by many scholars, (while others assert he was a prophet), about whom God said, *"We had taught knowledge from Our own Presence,"* (18:65) how would it not be befitting that the All-wise Creator grant the entire body of heavenly knowledge to His Beloved ﷺ. For the Lord of the heavens and the earth said of him:

And We granted you knowledge of what you knew not, and the bounty of Allah for you has been infinite. (4:113)

And He, the Almighty said:

This is of the tidings of the Unseen which we reveal to you. You did not know it before this, nor your people. (11:49)

Also regarding the knowledge granted him by His Lord, the Prophet ﷺ said:

My Lord came to me in the best image and asked me over what did the angels of the higher heaven vie, and I said I did not know, so He put His hand between my shoulders, and I felt its coolness in my innermost, and the knowledge of all things between the East and the West came to me.[2]

---

[2] Related on the authority of Muadh ibn Jabal by Tirmidhi (*hasan sahih*) and Baghawi in *Sharh al-Sunnah*. About the wording, "My Lord came to me in the best image (*surah*)," Ali al-Qari observed, "God is exalted from possessing a body, a form (*surah*), and directions with regard to His essence." when wrote about this hadith in the chapter on the Prophet's turban in his book *Jam al-wasail fi sharh al-shamail*, a commentary on Tirmidhi's *Shamail* or Characteristics of the Prophet. He also said:

> Whether the Prophet saw his Lord during his sleep or whether Allah the Glorious and Exalted manifested Himself to him with a form (*bi al-tajalli al-suwari*), this type of

In this regard, a man from Banu Amir, asked the Prophet ﷺ, "Is there any knowledge left which you do not know?" whereupon the Prophet ﷺ said, "God has taught me a great good, and there is a kind of Unseen knowledge which God alone knows..."[3]

The statement *"I am the City of Knowledge and Ali is its gate"* means that Muhammad was the essence of the heavens itself; the fabric of creation itself in its entirety. The evidence of this is the famous hadith of Jabir ؓ, where it is related that Jabir ibn Abd Allah ؓ said to the Prophet ﷺ, "O Messenger of God, may my father and mother be sacrificed for you, tell me of the first thing God created before all things." He said:

> *O Jabir, the first thing God created was the light of your Prophet from His light, and that light remained[4] in the midst of His Power for as long as He wished, and there was not, at that time, a Tablet or a Pen or a Paradise or a Fire or an angel or a heaven or an earth. And when God wished to create creation, he divided that Light into four parts and from the first made the Pen, from the second the Tablet, from the third the Throne, then He divided the fourth into four parts [and from them created everything else].[5]*

The light of the First Creation was the Muhammadan Reality and from that Light all other creation came into existence. It was in truth the creation of Muhammad which is the reason for the existence of all things, as God said, "If not for you [O Muhammad] I would not have created the cosmos."[6]

All that is conveyed in the first revelation, *Iqra – "Read!"* for from its outwardly apparent meaning, *"Read in the name of thy Lord who created"* the mention of the Lord's creation is first. This means, "I order you to

---

manifestation is known among the masters of spiritual states and stations (*arbab al-hal wa al-maqam*), and it consists in being reminded of His qualities (*hayatihi*) and reflecting upon His vision (*ruyatihi*), which is the outcome of the perfection of one's inner detachment (*takhliyatihi*) and self-adornment (*tahliyatihi*).

[3] Ahmad narrated it and Ibn Kathir mentions it in his exegesis of Surat Luqman. Al-Haythami said in *Majma al-zawaid* (#116): "Abu Dawud narrates part of it, and all of the sub-narrators in Ahmad's chain are trustworthy and they are Imams."

[4] Literally: "turned"

[5] Abd ar-Razzaq (d. 211) narrates it in his *Musannaf*. Bayhaqi (d. 458) narrates it with a different wording in *Dalail al-nubūwwa* according to Zurqani in his *Sharh al-mawahib* (1:56 of the Matbaa al-amira in Cairo) and Diyarbakri in *Tarikh al-khamis* (1:20).

[6] al-Ajlouni, *Kashf al-Khafa*, ii, 164; Ali al-Qari, *Sharh al-Shifa*, i, 26.

read, O Muhammad, in My name, for I am the one Who created You, and from you all creation emerged."

God's Order for creation proceeded from the Divine Essence and resulted in the creation of the Muhammadan Reality, *al-haqiqat al-muhammadiyyah.* God is the One who caused it to emerge in the way that He liked. Thus the Prophet's light exists in everything for which God said:

And know that within you is Allah's Messenger. (49:7)

Gabriel ﷺ did not say, "Recite!" for recitation comes from what is already known and held in the mind, but reading refers to something that must first be seen in order to be read. If God was ordering Prophet Muhammad to read, it means before him was something which could be read – from it he was looking and reading. What was he reading? He was reading *bismi rabbika alladhee khalaq - "in the name of your Lord Who Created."* It means, "O Muhammad! I am granting and then opening to you knowledge of the secret of creation; the secret of which was never opened before."

Even today's scientists still do not know the secret of when the soul reaches the embryo in the womb of the mother. God gave that secret to Muhammad ﷺ when He said, "Read!" where it means "see for I am showing you, so read and learn, and know that in My Name I am showing you My Creation."

Creation of the universe is easy. But as God said, to create one human being is not easy. He said, *"Who created the human being from a clot."* That clot has been identified today by scientists as the female's egg fertilized by one sperm.

A woman normally produces three or four eggs at one time and at most eight. But the man gives forth 500 million sperm at one time. From that huge number God allows only one sperm to connect with the single egg. This secret and further secrets which have yet to be disclosed to mankind, were granted to the Prophet ﷺ in that first revelation.

When Gabriel ﷺ said "read!" the Prophet ﷺ was unlettered (*umiyyun*), he did not know how to handle a pen, yet God ordered him to "Read!" The secret of this comes in the second repetition of the order to "read!" - *"Read and your Lord is most Generous who taught humankind by means of the pen; taught humankind what it knew not."*

It means, "Read in the name of thy Lord who taught You O Muhammad, the original man, by means of the Pen."

It was no ordinary pen that God mentioned to Prophet Muhammad ﷺ such as those carried by people today. "*Who taught humankind by means of the pen*" refers to the Pen of Power (*Qalam al-Qudrah),* the Pen by the Beautiful Names of God were inscribed on the Preserved Tablet (*al-lawh al-mahfudh*). It is the Pen that wrote the destinies of all created beings before God brought them from the world of possibilities into the world of existence. About it, the Prophet ﷺ said:

> *Allah inscribed the destinies of all created things before creating the heavens and the earth by fifty thousand years, while His Throne stood upon the water.*[7]

> It is narrated:

> Before creating any of the cosmos God ordered the Pen to write, and it said, "What should I write?" and He said, "Write: there is no god except God (*la ilaha ill-Allah.*)" So for 70,000 years the Pen wrote *la ilaha ill-Allah.*

> And then God said again, "Write!" And the Pen asked, "What should I write?" He said, "Write Muhammad is the Prophet of God (*Muhammadun Rasulullah.*)"

> And so for 70,000 years the Pen wrote *Muhammadun Rasulullah.* The Pen asked, "Who is that Muhammad that you put his name with Your Name?" God said, "Silence! If not for Muhammad I would not have created creation."[8]

---

[7] Narrated from Abd Allah ibn Amr ibn al-As by *Muslim* in his *Sahih.*

[8] A version similar to this is related in *Lore of Light*, Vol. 1, Hajjah Amina Hattun, and yet another version is related by as-Sufuri in *Nuzhat al-Majalis* as:

> When God created the Pen, He said, "Write My Oneness: 'There is no god except God.'" Then He said: "Write, 'Muhammad is the Messenger of God.'"

> When the Pen heard the name "Muhammad," it prostrated and said in its prostration, "Glory to the One Who is characterized with generosity; Glory be to the Gracious, the Most Compassionate. I have known your Greatest Name, so who is this Muhammad whose name You have joined with Yours?" Then God said, "Keep good manners O Pen! For by My Glory and My Majesty, I did not create My creation except for the love of Muhammad ﷺ." The Pen then split due to the sweetness of

Whatever God has created emerged from His Ocean of Power (*bahr al-qudrah*), and whatever exists in this universe is under the power and authority of Sayyidina Muhammad ﷺ and all of that is contained in the Muhammadan Reality. Now whereas the Muhammadan Reality is in fact the essence and source of all created beings, therefore within himself our master Muhammad ﷺ holds knowledge of all creation:

Say: "If the ocean were ink (wherewith to write out) the words of my Lord, sooner would the ocean be exhausted than would the words of my Lord, even if we added another ocean like it, for its aid." (36:109)

And this is followed by a reference to the Prophet ﷺ himself, indicating that the Oceans of God's Knowledge described in the preceding verse are in fact in his possession, despite his tremendous humility and sense of non-existence before the Greatness of His Lord:

Say: "I am but a man like yourselves, (but) the inspiration has come to me, that your Allah is one Allah: whoever expects to meet his Lord, let him work righteousness, and, in the worship of his Lord, admit no one as partner. (36:110)

And as the Prophet ﷺ is the holder of the Oceans of Divine Knowledge, Sayyidina Ali ؓ is the link one crosses to ascertain that reality.

Thus those who seek to traverse in the Paths of God, must seek the means in our master Ali ؓ and his teachings. Where are such teachings to be found? It is a truism that "who seeks finds" and thus the sincere seeker, immediately upon setting out with firm intention, will be guided to the Door of Knowledge and River of Truth which stems from the heart of Sayyidina Ali ؓ and the hearts of the other three rightly-guided caliphs of the Prophet ﷺ.

When the Prophet ﷺ described Ali ؓ as the Door of the City of Knowledge it means, "I am the one carrying the secrets that God has given to humanity because I am the one from whose light God created creation. I am but a servant, but He gave me that honor." So he ﷺ told our master Ali, "Explain to them from those realities."

Muhammad ﷺ and said, "Peace be upon you, O Messenger of God." But it found no one to respond to its greeting, upon which God said, "And peace be unto you, and My mercy and My blessings."

From these wisdoms we know that even the Companions, despite all their high levels of spiritual attainment, none of them could understand the reality of Sayyidina Muhammad ﷺ except two: Abu Bakr as-Siddiq ؓ and Ali ibn Abi Talib ؓ. Sayyidina Ali ؓ was given the task of explaining from these realities to the Companions. An example of that is:

> It is reported that when Umar ibn al-Khattab ؓ performed pilgrimage and embraced the (Black) Stone, he said, "I know by God that you are a stone which neither harms nor benefits, and had I not seen God's Messenger embrace you, I would not have embraced you."
>
> However, Alī ibn Abi Talib ؓ said to him, "Abu Hafs, do not say this, for God's Messenger ﷺ did not embrace it (the Black Stone) save for wisdom he knew: It has two eyes and two lips and possesses a keen tongue that testifies for those who fulfill their obligations to it."[9]

So in fact Sayyidina Ali ؓ was explaining to Sayyidina Umar ؓ, reminding him of the hadith which he had forgotten. Both the modern scholars (*al-mutaqqadimeen)* and the scholars of old, whoever wants to understand the reality of this life must look at the vision of Sayyidina Ali ؓ to Sayyidina Muhammad ﷺ, that is how the Prophet ﷺ appeared to him. You want to understand the reality of eternal life you have to go thru the heart of Sayyidina Ali ؓ and the heart of the family of the Prophet ﷺ for God told the Prophet ﷺ: *"Say, I ask of you no payment except love of my relatives."*

It means, "Love my near of kin in order to be granted from the Divine realities and secrets, for they are the vehicles of my light and carriers of my knowledge. They are the means by which to know what God has dressed me on the Day of Promises."

While the door to Sayyidina Muhammad's ﷺ city is Sayyidina Ali ؓ, and there is only one door, but inside the city is what the Prophet ﷺ has given to the Veracious One, Abu Bakr as-Siddiq ؓ. He is inside that city watching over the jewels that are within its most valued treasure

---

[9] Reported by Imam Ghazali, *Ihya ulum ad-din,* and, Hajjah Amina Adil, *Lore of Light,* volume 1, p.24, with additional wording.

chest. The Prophet ﷺ is the knowledge itself. There is someone receiving and keeping that treasure and that is Sayydina Abu Bakr as-Siddiq ﵁.

Speaking of the station of extinction, Sayydina Ali ﵁ said in verse:

Ra'āitu rabbī bi 'aini qalbī رأيت ربي بعين قلبي

Fa-qultu la shakka anta anta فقلت لا شك أنت أنت

I saw my Lord with the eye of my heart

I said no doubt it's You! It's You!

Anta-ladhī hizta kula aynin أنت الذي حزت كل أين

Bi haythu lā ayna thamma anta بحيث لا أين ثَمّ أنت

You are the One who encompassed every "where"

so that there is no "where," except You are there

Fa laysa li 'l-ayni minka aynun فليس للأين منك أين

Fa y'alamu al-aynu ayna anta فيعلم الأين أين أنت

"Where" has no "where" in regards to You

for "where" to know where You are

Wa laysa li 'l-wahmi fīka wahmun وليس للوهم فيك وهم

Fa y'alamul wahmu ayna anta فيعلم الوهم أين أنت

nor can imagination, imagine You

for imagination to know where You are

Aḥatta 'ilman bi kulli shayin أحطت علما بكل شيء

Fa kullu shayin arāhu anta فكل شيء اراه أنت

Your knowledge encompasses everything

so that everything I see is You

Wa fī fana-iī fanā fanā'ī	وفي فنائي فنا فنائي
Wa fī fana'ī wajadtu anta	وفي فنائي وجدت أنت

and in my annihilation, is the annihilation of my annihilation

and in my annihilation, I found You.[10]

So when we see this kind of poetry and this kind of love, this description of the state of *fana*, annihilation, we see this kind of relationship between the human being and His Lord where then is room for human beings to spend on this worldly life? It is in that state of awe, and non-existence that the Lovers and Friends of God find themselves. And when they are in this state, no one can approach them.

Al-Hasan ibn al-Mansour said:

> The identity of God's elect servant becomes extinguished in the Divine Presence. No one bears such a person nor does that person put up with [standards of behavior] others [tolerate]. Still, the elect one among God's servants is like unto the earth; it accepts every type of refuse and yet nothing issues from it but sweetness. Both the good and the sinner walk over and step on the servant of God. And the vilest of creation are they who pretend to be the elect of God when in fact they are stingy.

Ash-Shibli said, "the elect servant of God is cut off from creatures and connected to the Truth."[11] Ibn Ajiba relates that it has been said, "Whoever owns states whose character indicates proximity to God is insupportable. The mountains carry him not." Such is the aspect of whoever realizes the station of extinction, *maqam al-fana*. Al-Hasan ibn al-Mansour wrote of the one who became extinguished (*fani*) in the love of God [12]:

---

[10] From *The Commentary of the Hikam of Ibn Ataillah as-Sakandari* by Ibn Ajiba. (*Ikaz al-himmam fee sharhi al-hikam li Ahmad bin Muhammad bin Ajiba al-Hasani*).

[11] From *The Commentary of the Hikam of Ibn Ataillah as-Sakandari* by Ibn Ajiba, (*Ikaz al-himmam fee sharhi al-hikam li Ahmad bin Muhammad bin Ajiba al-Hasani*, p. 4.)

[12] *maqam*—what the servant realizes in his station in terms of spiritually-perfected manners, *adab*, and what is communicated... [al-Qushayri]

People find it difficult to tolerate the one who has lost any sense of self and who stands in awe stunned before God's Absolute Existence. Whoever reaches that station (*maqam*) and would in any way divulge its secret, will act differently from the commonality of humankind.

For that reason, the Friends of God (*awliyaullah*) who reach that *maqam* hide themselves. The story in the Holy Quran about al-Khidr عليه السلام illustrates this truth. He did things people do not usually do; things that even the Prophet Moses عليه السلام found difficult to accept. God instructs us by means of that example, to learn, not because Moses عليه السلام is lower in station for after all, he is one of the five greatest Prophets. No one attains the level of the prophets and the Prophet's Companions (*Sahaba*). By informing us of Moses' عليه السلام relation to Khidr عليه السلام, the Qur'an wishes to give us the example of one brought near to God, one of His saints. Such individuals are just as the hadith *qudsi* describes them, "My saints are under My domes; no one knows them except Me." God Himself hides saints, since they are exceedingly precious to Him. Another hadith illustrates this, "Whoever comes against a Friend of Mine I declare war on him."[13]

In the midst of people, God's Friends say and do things that others do not accept. That is the meaning of Ibn Ajiba's words, "No one bears such a person." For the same reason, when the Prophet Sayyidina Muhammad ﷺ came forth, his people rejected him. All prophets were rejected by their people. Since that is the case of the prophets what then can be expected for *awliya*? It is natural that they will be rejected completely by common people, because *awliya* are ordinary human beings upon whom God has bestowed heavenly power.

Today's religious scholars (*ulama*) say there no longer remain any *awliya*. This is not true. Rather, these people have become blind so that they cannot see them. Why have they become blind? Because *awliya* have hidden themselves, especially in the present era. They know that no one will accept them and the power granted them by the Lord. If they display anything of what they have been empowered with, people come against them.

---

[13] Even the rigorous Ibn Taymiyya verified this hadith.

Thus the highest level of *wali,* is one who acts like normal people and does not appear different from them in aspect or behavior. Thus one of God's friends (*awliya*) behaves like others to the extent that people say about him, "He is like us. What is different?" What they don't know about him is that he has been tested by *awliya*; by the Prophet ﷺ, and finally by God the Exalted. He passed his tests and was given his spiritual trusts (*amanat*).

Ibn Ajiba continues: *Wa la yaqbalu ahad*—"nor does that person put up with [standards of behavior] others tolerate." This means he watches as they go astray, calling them to return to the Path, but they do not listen. After a while, the saint leaves them. Bayazid al-Bistami, one of the greatest saints of Islam, was constantly worshipping God, ascending in closeness, until he could even hear the angels. He arrived at a station where he sought the Divine Presence saying, "O my Lord! Open for me the gate to Your Divine Presence." He heard a voice in his heart saying, "O Bayazid! If you want to enter My Presence, you must become people's refuse pile." Hence, al-Hasan ibn Mansour says here, "The elect servants of God are like the earth. They accept every type of refuse to be cast upon them and yet nothing issues from them but sweetness. Both the good and the sinner walk upon it."

The "earth" is characterized by strength. Whatever God Wills the earth accepts. It has no will of its own. In this respect *awliyaullah* resemble the earth: "every vile and ugly thing is cast upon it," and it accepts. The Arabic word used, *qabih* does not means just "vile" or "ugly" but rather, "rank" and "putrid" suggesting the worst refuse thrown on the earth. Yet, after he accepts it, the verse continues, "nothing comes from him except goodness."

The Friend of God (*wali*) does not treat you the same way you treat him. Rather he returns good for evil. It is related that Bayazid tested the *ulama,* with extreme ecstatic utterances, until at last they elected to stone him. This was due to their lack of understanding the station from which he was speaking. Bayazid was not someone inclined to commit heresy, for even Ibn Taymiyya praises his piety. But his intention was to test them, for they in fact had tried to test him.

Finally, when they had stoned Bayazid and left him for dead, his inert body was thrown in a garbage dump. Actually, he was still alive, but very weak. Eventually after lying injured in the dump seven days, he revived slightly and was able to move. He began searching about for something to eat. He found a bone, with a bit of fetid meat on it, probably thrown out one week before. When he took it a dog appeared growling and spoke to him, saying, "This is my territory, and this my food. You cannot touch it." Thus did God reveal to him the understanding of animal speech.

Bayazid relates, "I was beseeching God and saying, 'O God! O my Lord! What I have sought I sought only for the sake of Thy love. I willed for them to kill me but Thou quickened me and caused me to live. And once I regained my life I wished them to put me to death yet again; and that then Thou wouldst quicken me once more, and they would stone me yet another time. And again wouldst Thou revive me, over and over, because each time they stone me I would pray for them that Thou, My God, wouldst forgive them of their sins. So whatever Thou hast granted me of rewards for prayer and spiritual struggle, do Thou, O Lord, cause them to share in that same reward with me." This shows how much the Saint (*wali*) will love God's servants when he enters into His love.

Today many Muslim scholars say, "There are no more *awliya*." In reality, they exist, but since only a few will understand their states, they are hidden. Another saying of today's scholars is, "Every *mumin* (believer) is a *wali*." If that is the case, God would not differentiate between *mumin* and *wali*.

In any case, who can truly say he is a believer (*mumin*)? Do these scholars not recall God's saying:

> *The Arabs say, "We believe." Say, "Ye have no Faith; but ye (only) say, 'We have submitted our wills to Allah,' For not yet has Faith entered your hearts. But if ye obey Allah and His Messenger, He will not belittle aught of your deeds: for God is Oft-Forgiving, Most Merciful."* (49:14)

Who can grant one the certification that faith (iman), has entered his heart? Such certification is not given from one Muslim to another; it is given from God to the believer.

Wherever they find themselves, *awliya* build places of prayer, *zawiyas, khaniqas* or *ribats* (gathering places for spiritual training and practice). Once raised, people come from far and wide to visit them and they receive all in their meetings. They do not say, "We will not meet this one or that one." Today people say, "These individuals are enemies. We cannot meet them. These people cursed us, we cannot meet them." But the Prophet ﷺ came to all humankind—enemy or not.

> *We have not sent thee but as a universal (Messenger) to men, giving them glad tidings, and warning them (against sin), but most men understand not.* (34:28)

If an enemy came to him ﷺ he was obliged to open his door. As *awliyaullah,* are inheritors of the Prophet's states and character, their doors must always be open. Else what is the benefit of *wilayat* (sainthood)? God bestowed *wilayat* upon them in order to hear people out, to deal with them and to bring them to Islam. When you close your door and say, "I don't work with those people," you have isolated yourself and become a barrier to the Way. You have to work with people of any faith, any religion, and any group to convey them to *Haqq* (Truth). That is why Grand Shaykh Abd Allah al-Faiz ad-Daghestani met with everyone, and we seek to follow in his footsteps. You cannot close the door saying, "You are not a member." Now everything is based membership—for money. They tell you, "Pay fifty dollars and become a member." Nothing is done purely for God's sake any longer.

"Both good people and the ugliest of sinners walk over and step on the elect servant of God." That means he will carry burdens—he is everyone's garbage disposal. And in return, he offers prayers for people; in order to turn their hearts round to God. The elect servants of God try to do their best for people although people do their worst for them. That is why the good and the bad step on them and walk all over them.

Ibn Ajiba said, "And the vilest ones are they who pretend that they are an elect servant of God while failing in generosity." An elect servant of God does not fail in generosity. He is not stingy. A servant of God is always generous with the gifts his Lord has granted him or her, by not withholding it. God is the Most Generous of the generous (*Akram al-akramin).*

Similarly, the Prophet ﷺ is described by God as:

> *to the Believers is he most kind and merciful.* (9:128)

and

> *We sent thee not, but as a Mercy for all creatures.* (21: 107)

This verse means that Prophet Muhammad ﷺ will ask God's forgiveness on everyone's behalf. In short, a servant of God cannot be stingy. The worst person is someone who pretends to be an elect servant of God and is stingy. Not stingy with his money, but stingy in carrying the difficulties of people and taking back for himself, whatever God gave him of *hasanat* (rewards), as gifts to them.

Worse yet, are those of God's servants on whom he has bestowed the gifts of knowledge of the religion and its inner meanings and who withhold this knowledge from those who are capable of receiving it. These are the *ulama* that tell lies about God and pronounce permitted what He has prohibited. Of these, we have many examples today. They say, for example, that God wills people to lay down their lives in support of the corrupt or, serve false causes or to propagate wrong doctrine. These servants are the spiritually stingy. Such persons never succeed and on the Day of Judgment, they will be reckoned among the losers. They are like a tree covered with beautiful blossoms in spring, but which is infertile and fails to yield fruits in autumn.

To be perfectly clear, the true authorized servant of God carries the sins of those who are under his authority by asking God's forgiveness for those under him and by requesting God bestow whatever he received of rewards on them from whatever levels God has raised him to. That is for whoever comes to visit him.

The Prophet ﷺ said:

> *God has angels roaming the roads seeking the people of His Remembrance (dhikr), and when they find a group of people reciting dhikr, they call each other and encompass them in layers until the first heaven .... And someone not from them, but who came only for a certain issue, sits with them. God said, "no regrets will come to whoever sits with them*—la yashqa jalisahum.*"*[14]

That means that anyone coming for only a few minutes, even if he is not one of them, will be rewarded for being with them. Anyone who comes to the *wali*, the *wali* will give to him from what God and the Prophet ﷺ gave him. That is what it means—the opposite of stingy. It means giving what God adorned him with in the way of mercy. It means

---

[14] *Sahih Bukhari* and *Sahih Muslim*.

taking on and carrying the difficulties and problems of people who came to see him.

Now Ash-Shibli goes on to say, "The elect servant of God is disconnected from creation and connected to the Truth, al-Haqq." He continues, "Munqati an il-khalq," meaning "his heart is cut off from people and connected with the Divine." At the most literal level, it means he severs himself from the creatures and connects himself spiritually with God's Love. But at a deeper level it also means that he rejects all that is false and loves all that is true. The servant of God does not involve himself in issues that do not concern him or in what people do and say contrary to the Truth. He is connected with Truth. He likes everything about Truth and dislikes whatever is false. When he disconnects himself from falsehood, he veils it, as if he is not seeing it, even while being perfectly aware of it. At the same time, he does not backbite and draw attention to the falsehood and wrongdoing perpetrated by people.

He connects himself to Truth and disconnects himself from falsehood. He does this in order to balance their falsehood by bringing Truth to the other side of the balance. Otherwise, if falsehood goes unchecked, it will cause disaster both in the Ummah and in the world. Thus the *awliya* are like mountains in the Ummah; they balance everything, as the mountains keep the earth in balance:

And the mountains as pegs (78:7)

If falsehood were to increase unchecked there would no longer be any balance in the world and it would turn upside down. Thus, the *awliya* bring everything into balance. For this reason God said:

In order that ye may not transgress (due) balance. So establish weight with justice and fall not short in the balance. (55:8-9)

These verses mean, "Make everything balanced in the scale." If the *awliya* do not balance falsehood by means of worship, if they do not balance what the workers of iniquity perpetrate in the way of falsehood with truth, this *dunya* (world, material life) would have disappeared long ago.

Among the Signs of Last Days, Abd Allah bin Amr Ibn al-As 🙏 related that the Prophet ﷺ said:

God will not take knowledge from the hearts of the scholars but he takes the scholars (they die). There will be no more scholars to take their place so people will take extremely ignorant leaders. They will be asked questions and will give fatwas (legal rulings) without knowledge. They are misguided and they misguide others.[15]

The pious servants (*salihin)* have been balancing everything from the time of the Prophet ﷺ. Indeed, throughout all ages, they are balancing falsehood with truth. But now that balance they have brought to the worlds is reaching its end so that there is no longer a balance. Indeed, the lack of a sense of proportion has become the dominant characteristic of our epoch. That is why today one sees so much killing. And while everyone speaks of peace, peace, peace, in fact everywhere people are dying. May God keep us under the wings of His pious servants whom He has endowed with knowledge and entrusted with the guidance of the community of Muhammad ﷺ and balance our deeds to be in a good way.

Balancing the Self

Balance begins with the self, for the self is the root of all spiritual troubles. In the approach to the Divine Presence, the seeker must build his or her divine aspect based on the spirit of the holy hadith:

...My servant draws not near to Me with anything more loved by Me than the religious duties I have enjoined upon him, and My servant continues to draw near to Me with supererogatory works so that I shall love him. When I love him I am his hearing with which he hears, his seeing with which he sees, his hand with which he strikes and his foot with which he walks...[16]

One may be fastidious in observing the obligations and in practicing supererogatory worship: making all the voluntary prayers and fasts, paying extra charity and practicing the *Sunnah* to excess. However, in the search for realities, even that is not enough. This is because often the worshipper will miss a critical step: that of self-examination - *al-muhasabah*.

---

[15] *Sahih Bukhari* 1:33, "Kitab al-ilm." *Sahih Muslim* #157, "Kitab al-ilm".

[16] Related by Abu Hurayrah in *Sahih al-Bukhari*.

Without this aspect, the very worship we do in the belief we are attaining higher levels can in fact become an obstacle to progress. How? When that worship is not absolutely pure, done for the sake of God Alone, and we continue to do it under the self-satisfied notion that we are doing all that is humanly possible to achieve spiritual progress. At that time, the self will have held sway for it relishes its "success" in spiritual work and discipline.

The House of Illness

Therefore, as with all illnesses there is a cure. In entering this discussion, we note the relevance of the Prophetic saying:

> *The stomach is the house of all illnesses* and the source of all cures is diet.[17]

Dieting means to be fully ware of what enters one's mouth and arrives at the stomach. The first step in dieting is to impose controls on the ego's desire to eat. This is found in implementing the hadith where the Prophet ﷺ said,*"We are a people who don't eat until we are hungry and when we eat we don't eat our fill."*[18]

True cleverness is possessed by the one who can prevent his hand from reaching out to eat more, such a person truly controls his ego. Egos always desire more - they are endlessly greedy. If God granted us a house, and the ego sees someone who owns a bigger house, it wants that house. The ego never says, "All praise be to God, we have a place to stay."

If someone has one million dollars the ego wants two million; if he has two million, it wants three million.

---

[17] The first part is a hadith, but the second, while often attributed to the Prophet is in fact as as-Sakhawi noted in his *Maqasid*, "not attributed to the Prophet ﷺ, rather it is the words of Harith bin Kaldah, a physician of the Arabs or from someone else." Al-Hafiz as-Suyuti said the same in his *al-Hawi* and his own commentary of the hadiths he used in his exegesis *ad-Durar*, attributed it to a Tabi or a *hakim* (physician) or an Israelite tradition and he added at the end of the saying, *"and the head of every fault is the love of the world."* Ibn Arabi mentioned it in his *Futuhat*, Ibn Ata-Allah in his *Hikam*.

[18] Related from Umar bin al-Khattab. Ibn Kathīr says its chain is weak, but the meaning is true.

Yahya bin Yahya, a student of Imam Malik, asked him for advice. Imam Malik gave him three recommendations, each of which comprises a treasure. He said:

> I will compose all the medicine of the physicians, and the entire fruit of the science of medicine in one sentence: withdraw your hand from eating as long as you have desire to eat.[19]

Following such advice one will never see sickness in his life. More importantly that is training the ego to listen to and accept to say the truth. For the battle with the ego begins with a conversation, a debate between the soul, which yearns for spiritual attainment, and the ego, *nafs*, which always seeks satisfaction in the basest desires. The soul will ask the ego, "Are you done eating?" To which it replies, "No, I want another bite, for this food is so tasty." At that time the reproachful-self (*an-nafs al-lawwāmah*) will say, "But you are not keeping the *Sunnah* of eating." That is the decision point: to observe the *Sunnah*, or not; to keep discipline or not; to control the ego or not.

It is for this reason that the Prophet ﷺ said:

Contemplation for one hour is better than seventy years of worship.[20]

What you achieve by contemplation *tafakkur*, also known in Arabic as *muraqabah,* is to achieve what you cannot achieve even if you are performing voluntary worship for seventy years. It means that what is gained by meditation is unattainable through worship alone, for even Iblis, the condemned, busied himself with worship constantly such that not one handspan in heavens and earth remained without the traces of his prostration. Yet in the end he failed due to his rebellious ego, and spurred on by self-conceit he disobeyed a single order of His Lord and thus fell from grace.

Shaykh Abul Hasan ash-Shadili said, "The fruits of meditation (*muraqabah*) are the Divinely-gifted talents." But meditation cannot be

---

[19] *An tarfa yadak ani t-taam*

[20] As-Sufuri in *Nuzhat al-majalis* from both Ibn Abbas and Abu Hurayrah through Miqdad ibn al-Aswad. Another version is: Contemplation for one hour on the alteration of the night and day is better that eighty years of worship. (ad-Daylamī related it from Anas) Yet another version is related: "Contemplation for one hour is better than sixty years of worship." (Abu ash-Shaykh in his Azamah from Abu Hurayrah.)

done amongst the people, it must be done in isolation (*al-uzlah*). That in fact, is the primary reason people sit in isolation: to do meditation.

Such meditation, completely secluded away from all other eyes and ears, will allow you train the ego, to ride it, as a horseman rides his mount. Then once you ride the ego, it can no longer control you. When you say, "I am not eating," it will say, "I hear and I obey." On the other hand, if you have not trained it you will be overcome by your ego.

That is why a master may try his students by giving them excess food to eat. Such a trial is actually to combat the ego's desires to **not eat**, which comes about when the stomach is full and the food is not particularly delicious. In keeping the ways of Sufism nothing must accord with the ego's desires. So should the Shaykh order you to eat an entire pot of bland and tasteless food, you must do so willingly, for it is in obedience to the order that he will raise you.

However, if the Shaykh dispenses more food to you—food which is blessed by his hands, his prayers and his preparing it while invoking God and praising His Prophet ﷺ—and you indicate in even the slightest way, "That is enough," you are displaying your disobedience, struggling in fact to say, "No, I will not eat any more." Consider, if that is your reaction to something that cannot harm you what do you think if the Shaykh puts you to a more difficult trial?

This is all in regard to physical nourishment. If we observe dieting in regard to our physical constitution, what are we doing in regards to our spirit, for it too is nourished and it too has its source of food?

Dieting for the Soul

Dieting for the soul means to prevent oneself from doing anything originating in bad desires; it will be a cure for one's spiritual dimension and a preparation for the afterlife.

People today do not diet for the soul. They are not examining the desires of the self and asking "How am I going to face God the Almighty and Exalted, on the Day of Examination, where He is going to ask us, 'Did you stop yourself from being greedy, from jealousy and from envy?'"

If someone is receiving his provision from God, then no one can prevent him from receiving his destined portion. If God has granted you one thousand of something then you will get your one thousand, even if one thousand others are seeking it; and if God has written for you ten, then it may be that someone else will get one thousand and you will get your destined ten. Never worry that someone else will eat your provision. With that in mind, jealousy and envy can never arise.

Thus it is said, "Dieting is the head of all cures."[21]

Himyah means dieting but in this context it means preventing yourself from doing anything outside the bounds of Islam. Whatever you are doing that contravenes the Divine Law you must stop doing, else you will end up in a situation that you are happy in this life but in the afterlife you are full of regret.

The heart is an organ but its nourishment is not through eating, Rather the heart uploads and downloads. Its food is gossips, dark whisperings, and evil promptings with which you fill it up. If you give it bad spiritual food, it will be demolished, but if you are giving it healthful spiritual food, it will flourish, and each person must choose.

Just as the stomach is the house of physical maladies, the heart is the house of spiritual malaises. So just as one diets as a cure for the physical body so to will observing the nourishment intake of the heart enable one to receive God's light.

It is related that God said:

> Neither My heaven nor My earth could contain Me, but the soft, humble heart of my believing servant can contain Me.[22]

There cannot be two within the heart. God does not accept association, though He may forgive anything less than that. What does He accept? Oneness. God does not accept that anyone share with Him, for He is the Ultimate Sovereign King. God wants Absolute Oneness to be attributed to Himself. If there is even the slightest aspect of filth or impurity in the heart then no light will penetrate into your heart from

---

[21] *Al-himyatu ras ad-daw.*

[22] Al-Ajlouni says, "Al-Ghazali mentioned it in *Ihya Ulum al-Din.*" Al-Sakhawi said in *al-Maqasid,* following his shaykh al-Suyuti in *al-Laali,* "There is no known chain from the Prophet for it, and its meaning is that his heart can contain belief in Me, love of Me and gnosis of Me." And it is similar to the Israelite tradition Ahmad has related in *al-Zuhd* from Wahb bin Munabbih who said that God opened the heavens for Ezekiel until he saw the Throne, so Ezekiel said, 'How Perfect are You! How Mighty are You, O Lord!' So God said, 'Truly, the heavens and the earth were too weak to contain Me, but the soft, humble heart of my believing slave contains Me'."

God's lights. That would be unacceptable for God's lights can only be for Himself.

For this reason, the dieting of the heart consists of listening to a guided and guiding master, a *murshid,* who has the skill to disconnect the seeker from his own self-aggrandizing self and then, like a heart surgeon, carefully reconnect the seeker to his reality in the Divine Presence.

Breaking the Ego's Pride

As we said earlier, the seeker may make great strides of progress in attainment by means of voluntary worship. However, he or she will reach a limit that cannot be crossed, and that is the blockage of the self, for the self will use any means at its disposal to intercept the upward progress of the seeker. The cause of this is arrogance, for the self does not allow the soul to take precedence, claiming, on the pattern of Pharoah, *"I am your Lord most high!"*(79:24). For this the guide must use drastic means, like emergency surgery, to eliminate the tyrannical self. This is illustrated in another story about Bayazid:

> There was a man in Bistam who was always in Bayazid's assembly and he never separated from him. At the same time the man was a renowned scholar of the region. Once he said to Bayazid, "O master! For thirty years I have been fasting in the daytime and remained standing at night in prayers. I have left all my passions. But I feel in my heart nothing at all of what you are talking about, although I believe in what you say and I know that you are telling the truth."
>
> Bayazid replied, "Even if you fast for three hundred years and keep standing in night prayers for three hundred years while you are (in the state in which) I see you, you will not experience one atom of this knowledge." The man asked, "Why, O master?" Bayazid answered, "Because you are veiled by your own self."
>
> He asked, "Is there any medicine by which to remove this veil?" Bayazid told him, "Remove the clothes (of the scholar) that you are wearing, put on this (ragged) cloak, attach a bag around your neck and fill it with chestnuts. Then gather children around you and say at the top of your voice, 'O children! Whoever will slap me once I

will give one chestnut. And whoever slaps me twice I will give two chestnuts. And whoever will push me so I fall down I will give three chestnuts." Go the place where you are most respected and let everyone who knows you see you like this. Begin with this before all else, so that first you fall from prestige (*jah*) and cause your self to be humiliated."

That man (who was a scholar of renown) said, "*Ya Subhanallah! Ali mithli yuqalu hadha?*" meaning, "O Glory of God! Is it to someone of my stature you say such a thing?" Bayazid replied, "Stop, stop, stop! Now you are committing the irreparable sin of association with God, *shirk*!"

He continued, "Stop now, you see how loose your tongue is. Even with thirty years [of struggle in the Way] yet you cannot control it. When you control yourself by humiliating yourself and make it known that you are truly a Sufi, then you will be accepted."

Bayazid said, "After you do this I shall let you know what is suitable for you." The man said, "I am unable to do this!"

Bayazid had sought out the defect in his disciple's character, and exposed it to him, for when he said, "*Ya subhanallah,*" it was as if he was putting himself besides God, as if to say, "I am above that as God is above His Creation."

This story illustrates the need to create a new way in your life, as mentioned to that scholar, by humbling and demeaning yourself.

Therefore justify not yourselves: He knows best who it is that guards against evil (53:32).

Do not ever uplift yourself or give excuses to yourself. For the Best of Creation, Sayyidina Muhammad ﷺ, the Master of masters, the Seal of Messengers, the perfect human being was humble. God gave him ﷺ everything: He gave him ﷺ intercession; He made him ﷺ the first in creation; He made him ﷺ the last to be sent; He made his nation the best of nations; He forgave his nation their sins large and small and vouchsafed for them Abode of Safety in the afterlife; He made him ﷺ the first to be resurrected on Judgment Day; He made him ﷺ the first to enter paradise, along with his entire nation. All this and yet the Prophet ﷺ said, *"I am the Master of the sons of Adam on Judgment Day and I say it without pride (wa la fakhr)."*[23] For God's Messenger ﷺ had no pride, therefore despite being the greatest of all, he was most pleased when His Lord called him "My servant," *abdee*.

Imminent Events

The Prophet of God ﷺ said:

After me come caliphs, and after the caliphs come princes, and after princes there will be kings and after the kings, there will be tyrants. And after the tyrants a man from My House will fill the earth with justice, and after him is al-Qahtani. By the One who sent me with the Truth! Not a word less.[24]

We see that the caliphs are spoken of in this hadith are "the Rightly-Guided Ones": Abu Bakr, Umar, Uthman and Ali, may God the Exalted be pleased with them all. The princes are the Umayyad Caliphs of Damascus and the Abbasid Caliphs of Baghdad. As for the kings, they are the Ottoman Sultans of Istanbul. Following the kings, according to the hadith, are tyrants, and that is what is commonly seen today.

God's Friends are not looking to the future, mentioned in such hadith, as far away. Rather they are communicating to those who would learn from them, that these hadith are signposts for mankind on the road to the Hereafter. If we act as the blind, ignoring what is apparent in the signs of the times, then of what benefit is such luminous guidance? The duty of the Saints, as inheritors of the Prophets, is to remind, give glad tidings (*bushra*) and to warn.

Let us heed then, the clear guidance that the Prophet ﷺ has brought us, and prepare for times of tribulation. Following these trials, we hope to be present in a Golden Age of Prophetic civilization, the like of which the world has never witnessed.

---

[23] Related by Tirmidhi, Ibn Majah and Ahmad.

[24] Naim bin Hammad in *Fitan* from Abd ar-Rahman bin Qays bin Jabir al-Sadafi. *Kanz al-ummal,* hadith #38704.

Doctrinal Foundations of the Spiritual Path

Tazkiyyat an-Nafs (Purifying the Self)

A Driving Sufi Principle

The Sufi teachers of old spread Islam across the Indian Subcontinent, throughout Central and Southeast Asia, in Africa, and even some parts of Russia—just as contemporary Sufi teachers are spreading the faith through Europe and America today. But where did the Sufis originate? When did they first appear? And what was the position of the schools of Islamic jurisprudence and the scholars of the Community regarding Sufism, or *tasawwuf*?[25]

Today, Islam is taught only with words by people who do not care to practice it purely nor to purify themselves in practice. This unfortunate devolution was foreseen in many *ahadith* that state, for example, *"They will order people and not heed their own warning, and they are the worst of people."*[26] Similarly, the Prophet ﷺ said, *"I do not fear for you only the anti-Christ." They asked, "Then who else are you afraid of?" He said, "The misguided scholars."*[27] The Prophet ﷺ also said, *"What I fear most for my nation is a hypocrite who has a scholarly tongue."*[28] Such was not the way of the Companions, including the People of the Bench (*Ahl as-Suffa*), concerning whom the following verse was revealed:

> *And restrain thyself with those who call upon their Lord at morning and evening, desiring His countenance, and let not thine eyes turn away from them, desiring the adornment of the present life; and obey not him whose heart We have made neglectful of Our remembrance so that he follows his own lust, and his affair has become all excess.* (18:28)

Nor was this the way of Abu Bakr as-Siddiq ؓ, about whom the Prophet ﷺ said, *"Abu Bakr does not precede you for praying much or fasting*

---

[25] The footnotes in the following sections are more detailed in order to assist those students of the Way that wish to conduct further research into the topics discussed in these pages.

[26] Reported on the authority of Umar, Ali, Ibn Abbas, and others. These were collected by Abu Talib al-Makki in the chapter entitled "The Difference between the scholars of the world and those of the hereafter" in his *Qut al-qulub fi muamalat al-mahbub* (Cairo: Matbaat al-maymuniyya, 1310/1893) pp. 1:140-141.

[27] Ahmad narrated it in his *Musnad*.

[28] Ahmad narrated it in his *Musnad* with a good chain.

much, but because of a secret that has taken root in his heart."[29] Nor was this the way of the Successors (*tabieen*) such as Hasan al-Basri, Sufyan al-Thawri, and others of the later generations of Sufis who looked back to them for models. Al-Qushayri relates that al-Junayd said, "*Tasawwuf* is not the profusion of prayer and fasting, but wholeness of the breast and selflessness."[30]

Nor was this the way of the Four Imams who emphasized doing-without (*zuhd*) and true god-fear (*wara*), above the mere satisfaction of obligations. Imam Ahmad ibn Hanbal composed two books with those two qualities as their respective titles. He placed the knowledge of saints above the knowledge of scholars, as is shown by the following report by his student, Abu Bakr al-Marwazi:

> I heard Fath ibn Abi al-Fath saying to Abu Abd Allah (Imam Ahmad) during his last illness, "Invoke God for us that He will give us a good successor to succeed you." He continued, "Who shall we ask for knowledge after you?" Ahmad replied, "Ask Abd al-Wahhab." Someone who was present there related to me that he said, "But he does not have much learning." Abu Abd Allah replied, "He is a saintly man, and such as he is granted success in speaking the truth."[31]

In a celebrated *fatwa* (legal ruling), the Shafii scholar al-Izz ibn Abd al-Salam gives the same priority to the gnostics, or Knowers of God (*arifin*), over the jurists. Imam Malik places the same emphasis on inner perfection in his saying, "Religion does not consist in the knowledge of many narrations, but in a light which God places in the breast." Ibn Ata Allah quoted Ibn Arabi as saying, "Certainty does not derive from the evidences of the mind but pours out from the depths of the heart."

This is why many of the imams of religion cautioned against the mere thirst for knowledge at the expense of the training of the ego. Imam Ghazali left the halls of learning in the midst of a prestigious career in

---

[29] Related by Ahmad with a sound chain in *Kitab fadail al-Sahaba*, ed. Wasi Allah ibn Muhammad Abbas (Makkah: Muassasat al-risala, 1983) 1:141 (#118).

[30] al-Qushayri, *Risalat kitab al-sama* in *al-Rasail al-qushayriyya* (Sidon and Beirut: al-maktaba al-asriyya, 1970) p. 60.

[31] Ahmad, *Kitab al-wara* (Beirut: Dar al-kitab al-arabi, 1409/ 1988) p. 10.

order to devote himself to self-purification. At its outset, he wrote his magisterial *Revival of the Religious Sciences* (*Ihya ulum al-din*), which begins with a warning to those who consider religion to consist merely of *fiqh*, or jurisprudence.

One of the early Sufis and the greatest of the *huffaz*, or *hadith* masters, of his time, Sufyan al-Thawri, sounded the same warning. He addressed those who use the narration of *hadith* for religion, when he said, "If *hadith* was a good it would have vanished just as goodness has vanished. Pursuing the study of *hadith* is not part of the preparation for death, but a disease that preoccupies people."

Dhahabi comments:

> By God he has spoken the truth. Today, in our time, the quest for knowledge and *hadith* no longer means for the *hadith* scholar the obligation of living up to it, which is the goal of *hadith*. He is right in what he said because pursuing the study of *hadith* is other than the *hadith* itself.[32]

It is for "the *hadith* itself," for the purpose of living up to the *Sunnah* of the Prophet ﷺ and the Holy Quran, that the great masters of self-purification forsook the pursuit of science as a worldly allurement, and placed above it the acquisition of *ihsan*, or perfect character. This is in accordance with the well-known *hadith* of Aisha ؓ concerning the disposition of the Prophet ﷺ.[33] An example is Abu Nasr Bishr al-Hafi, who considered the study of *hadith* a conjectural science in comparison to the certitude in belief imparted by visiting Fudayl ibn al-Iyad.[34] Both *ihsan* and the process that leads to it are known as *tasawwuf*, as illustrated in the following pages.

---

[32] Dhahabi, as cited in Sakhawi, al-*Jawahir wa al-durar fi tarjamat shaykh al-Islam Ibn Hajar* (al-Asqalani), ed. Hamid Abd al-Majid and Taha al-Zaini (Cairo: wizarat al-awqaf, al-majlis al-ala li al-shuun al-islamiyya, lajnah ihya al-turath al-islami, 1986) p. 21-22.

[33] When asked about the Prophet's ﷺ character, Aisha ؓ said, "His character was the Quran."

[34] See Ibn Sad, *Tabaqat* (ed. Sachau) 7(2):83; al-Arusi, *Nataij al-afkar al-qudsiyya* (Bulaq, 1920/1873); and Abd al-Wahhab al-Sharawi, *al-Tabaqat al-kubra* 1:57.

Sufism: Definitions, Terminology and Historical Overview

Tasawwuf among the Pious Predecessors

As is made clear in the *hadith* narrated by Sayyidina Umar ﷺ about Jibril's ﷺ meeting with the Prophet ﷺ,[35] belonging to *Ahl as-Sunnah wal-Jamaah* (the People of the Tradition and the Majority, also known as "the Saved Group") cannot stop at the rules of faith. It involves the adoption of principles that lead to *ihsan*, or the perfection of belief and practice. Hence, the Saved Group follows one of the many schools of *suluk* (personal discipline in ethics and conduct), in accordance with the guidelines of the *Shariah* and the *azaim* (strict applications) of the *Sunnah*. These practices are collectively known as the science of *tasawwuf*, or "purification of the self."

In the first century after the Hijra, renunciation of the world (*zuhd*) grew as a reaction against worldliness in the society. This reaction was inspired by God's order to His Righteous Apostle ﷺ to purify people:

> *A Messenger who shall instruct them in Scripture and Wisdom, and sanctify them.* (2:129)
>
> *We have sent among you a Messenger of your own, rehearsing Our Signs, and purifying you, and instructing you in Scripture and Wisdom.* (2:151)
>
> *A Messenger from among themselves, rehearsing unto them the Signs of God, sanctifying them, and instructing them in Scripture and Wisdom.* (3:164)
>
> *Purify and sanctify them; and pray on their behalf, verily thy prayers are a source of security for them.* (9:103)
>
> *A Messenger from among themselves, to rehearse to them His Signs, to sanctify them, and to instruct them in Scripture and Wisdom.* (62:2)

The adherents to this way held firmly to the Prophetic way of life, as it was reflected in the lives of his Companions and their Successors, in the ways they purified their hearts and character of bad manners, and in

---

[35] In Bukhari and Muslim through various chains. Nawawi included it in his collection of forty a*hadith* (#2).

the ways they impressed on themselves and those around them the manners and upright moral stature of the Prophet ﷺ. Examples of these one-man schools of purification are listed by Abu Nuaym and others as "The Eight Ascetics," and include: Amir ibn Abd Qays, Abu Muslim al-Khawlani, Uways al-Qarani, al-Rabi ibn Khuthaym, al-Aswad ibn Yazid, Masruq, Sufyan al-Thawri, and Hasan al-Basri, among many others.

The Prophet ﷺ himself attested to the power of such saints and their benefit to people, as witnessed by the many *ahadith* related about Uways al-Qarani ؓ.[36] In the following *hadith*, the Prophet ﷺ orders the people, if they meet Uways ؓ, to have him ask forgiveness on their behalf, and declares that Uways' ؓ intercession will earn entry into Paradise for large numbers of people:

> *The Prophet ﷺ said, "Uways ibn Amir will dawn upon you with the assistance (*imdad*) of the people of Yemen from the tribe of Murad and Qaran. He was a leper and was healed except in a tiny spot. He has a mother whose rights he keeps scrupulously. If he took an oath by God, God would fulfill it. If you are able to let him ask forgiveness for you, do it. More people will enter Paradise through the intercession of a certain man from my Community than there are people in the tribes of Rabia and Mudar." Al-Hasan al-Basri said, "That is Uways al-Qarani."*[37]

Through slow evolution, and as a reaction against the increasing worldliness of the social environment, Muslims flocked to saints and their followers until their regimens became schools of practical thought and moral action, each with its own structure of rules and principles. This became the basis used by Sufi scholars to direct people on the Right Path. The world soon witnessed the development of a variety of schools of purification of the ego (*tazkiyat an-nafs*). Sufi thought, as it spread everywhere, served as a dynamic force behind the growth of Islamic education. These advances occurred from the first century after the Hijra to the seventh, and paralleled the developments of the foundations of *fiqh* (Law and Jurisprudence) through the Four Imams; the development of the foundation of *Aqida* (Doctrine) through al-Ashari and others; the

---

[36] Imam Ahmad reports some of them in his book entitled *al-Zuhd*.

[37] Ahmad, *al-Zuhd* (Beirut: dar al-kutub al-ilmiyya, 1414/ 1993) p. 416, 414.

development of the sciences of *hadith* (Traditions of the Prophet ﷺ); and the arts of *nahw* and *balagha* (speaking and writing Arabic).

Tariqah: The Spiritual Path

Tariqah, or "path," is a term derived from the Quranic verse:

> *Had they kept straight on the path (tariqah), We would have made them drink of a most limpid water.* (72:16)

The meaning of "path" in this verse is elucidated by the *hadith* of the Prophet ﷺ, related by Bukhari and Muslim, ordering his followers to follow his *Sunnah* and the *Sunnah* of his successors. Like *tariqah* in the verse, the meaning of "*sunnah*" in the *hadith* is "path" or "way." *Tariqah* thus came to be a term applied to groups of individuals belonging to the school of thought led by a particular scholar, or "shaykh," as such a person was often called.

Although the shaykhs applied different methods in training their followers, the core of each one's program was identical. The situation was not unlike what happens in faculties of medicine and law today. The approaches of the various universities may be different, but the body of law and the practice of medicine remain essentially the same. When students graduate from either of these faculties, each bears the stamp of the institution he attended, but no student is considered any less a lawyer or doctor because his training was different.

In a similar way, the student of a particular shaykh will bear the stamp of that shaykh's teaching and character. Accordingly, the names given to the various schools of Sufi thought differ according to the names and perspectives of their founders. This variation manifests itself in a more concrete fashion in the different supererogatory devotions, known as *awrad, ahzab,* or *adhkar,* that are used as the practical methodology of spiritual formation. Such differences, however, have nothing to do with religious principles. In basic principle, the Sufi schools are essentially the same, just as the differences in names among *madhahib,* or schools of law, refer to methods and not to the essence of religion, which is uniform.

The Sufi regimen under which individuals undertook the path to God was a finely-honed itinerary that charted the course of inward and outward progress in religious faith and practice. Following the tradition of the Companions of the Prophet ﷺ who frequented his company, the

Ahl as-Suffa ("People of the Bench"), the practitioners of this regimen lived a communal life. Their dwelling-places were the alcove-schools (*zawiya*), border fort-schools (*ribat*), and guest-houses (*khaniqah*) where they gathered together on a regular basis and on specific occasions dedicated to the traditional festivals of the Islamic calendar. These structures often evolved into celebrated educational institutions.

Sufis also gathered in informal assemblies around the shaykh, called *suhbah*, to invoke the names of God and recite the *adhkar* (plural of *dhikr*, "remembrance") inherited from the Prophetic Tradition. Yet another reason for their gathering was to hear inspired preaching and moral exhortations (*wiaz*). The shaykhs instructed their students to actively respond to God and His Messenger ﷺ, to cleanse their hearts and purify their souls from the more base desires prompted by the ego, and to establish authentic doctrine. This was accomplished by firm adherence to the Prophetic *Sunnah*. The methods of remembering God that they instilled in their students were the very same methods passed down from the Prophet ﷺ. In this way, the shaykhs promoted upright behavior, through both word and deed, and encouraged believers to devote themselves to God wholeheartedly. The aim of their endeavor was nothing less than obtaining God's satisfaction and inspiring love for His Prophet ﷺ. In short, they aimed for a state where God was pleased with them, even as they were pleased with Him.

Sufi Leaders Who Established Thriving Communities

History books are filled with the names of wise, effective Sufis who devoted their lives to the spread of traditional, moderate Islam which enfused their communities with social justice, religious tolerance, and gender equity. Their amazing stories are too numerous to list in the span of a single book; suffice it to mention a few examples from modern history, as cited by the author of *The Reliance of the Traveller*:

> Among the Sufis whose missionary work Islamized entire regions are such men as the founder of the Sanusiyya Order, Muhammad Ali Sanusi, whose efforts from 1807 to 1859 consolidated Islam as the religion of peoples from the Libyan Desert of sub-Saharan Africa; the Shadhili shaykh Muhammad Maruf and Qadiri shaykh Uways al-Barawi, whose efforts spread Islam westward and inland from the East African Coast; and the hundreds of anonymous

> Naqshbandi shaykhs [including some of the Masters of the Golden Chain] who taught and preserved Islam among the peoples of what is now the southern Soviet Union, and who still serve the religion there despite official pressure. It is plain from the example of these and similar men that the attachment of the heart to God, which is the main emphasis of Sufism, does not hinder spiritual works of any kind, but may rather provide a real basis for them. And God alone gives success.[38]

The reader is also referred to Benningsen's *Mystics and Commissars* for the role of Sufis in preserving Islam in the Soviet Union, and *Lion of Daghestan* for their struggle against the Tsars before that. Let it also be added that it was the Naqshbandis who preserved Islam in China, both in the past and in the darkest days of Mao Tse-tung's "Cultural Revolution."

Though some opponents of *tasawwuf* have accused the Sufis of focusing on spirituality to the detriment of their societal responsibilities, the above examples provide ample evidence that *tasawwuf,* far from encouraging escapism or the sort of quietism that impedes social progress, upheld the highest values of social consciousness and action—as well as religious inquiry and spiritual science. In fact, the Sufis were unremitting protagonists in the struggles against social injustice and social inaction that took place over centuries.

Contemporary Misconceptions

It is well-known in our time that some people have misunderstood the notion of *tasawwuf.* Some people believe it is against Islam, while others say they can find no mention of it in the *Shariah,* Quran, or *Sunnah.* However, the followers of the four Imams accepted *tasawwuf,* because they knew the reality of the term's meaning was more important than its age. Even scholars such as Ibn Taymiyya and Ibn Qayyim al-Jawziyya—despite their having opposed the doctrine of *Ahl as-Sunnah* in so many respects—accepted *tasawwuf,* precisely because they knew its roots were deep in the Quran, the *Sunnah,* and the *Shariah.*

---

[38] *Reliance of the Traveller,* p. 863.

It is true that the term *tasawwuf* was not known in the time of the Prophet ﷺ. However, while its name was of later derivation, its essence is part and parcel of the religion and cannot be separated from it.

Another factor that has contributed to the misunderstanding of *tasawwuf* in the modern era is the appropriation of some of its terms and teachings by non-Muslims. Today, we find some people mixing true *tasawwuf* with pseudo-*tasawwuf*, which denies the necessity of the *Shariah* and makes up its own rules, claiming for itself an amorphous authority that is not rooted in any precedent. Such people are neither Sufis nor *mutasawwif*, but *mustaswifa* or "pseudo-Sufis," in the words of the great master Ali al-Hujwiri.[39] Enemies of *tasawwuf*, however, often blur the difference between Sufis and *mustaswifa* (those who are busy purifying themselves) in their references to *tasawwuf* in order to be rid of both, as they have known Sufis to stand against their false teachings.

An example is the Mutazila sect's aversion to Sufis, which led them to deny the *karamat* (miracles of saints), as they never saw this sign of truth among themselves. Nowadays, there are people like the Mutazila, who want to create their own definition of Islam, to decide what fits into it and what does not, mixing right with wrong. They do this so that they might rid themselves of the essence of true Islamic teaching that exposes the incompleteness and error of what they have inherited.

The purpose of *tasawwuf* is first to purify the heart of bad desires and inclinations, and of the dirtiness that accumulates due to sin and wrongdoing. The purpose of *tasawwuf* is then to remove these bad manners and sins, to clean the self, and adorn and decorate the heart with the good behavior and good manners that are demanded by the Holy Quran and the Holy *Sunnah* of the Prophet ﷺ. Its ultimate purpose is to help the believer to reach the state of *ihsan*, or perfection of character, which was the state of the Prophet ﷺ and the state that each of his Companions strove to achieve.

Development of Islamic Sciences after the Time of the Prophet ﷺ

The science of *tasawwuf* was not the only one that developed after the time of the Prophet ﷺ. For example, in the time of the Prophet ﷺ, a child in the cradle of Islam, raised in the land of Hijaz, could read a

---

[39] Al-Hujwiri, *Kashf al-mahjub*, trans. R.A. Nicholson (Karachi: *dar al-ishaat*, 1990) p. 35.

poem or Arabic text without any need for diacritical marks (*tashkil*). It came naturally, as they were raised knowing the proper pronunciation. Later, however, when many non-Arabs entered Islam and Quran was being read incorrectly, it became necessary to create disciplines to assist new Muslims in reading Quran, so grammar was developed and diacritical marks were established.

The state of perfection (*ihsan*), the state of austerity (*zuhd*), the state of great fear of God (*wara*), and the state of godwariness (*taqwa*) were naturally practiced by the Companions, because they were in company of the Prophet ﷺ and those states were a direct result of their association with him. It is for this reason that they are called Companions, because they were the associates of the Prophet ﷺ, and it was their association with him that allowed them to be purified.

Just as the entrance of converts from other regions into the fold of Islam necessitated the development of *ilm al-nahu* (science of Arabic language), development of the science of self-purification was necessitated by the passing of the Prophet ﷺ and his Companions. Without them to teach the true path of Islam by way of example, it became necessary to establish schools that would develop the spiritual disciplines to perfect belief and practice. These matters were combined under the main discipline of *ilm al-tasawwuf* (science of spiritual perfection).

Far from being an innovation, as some of its detractors contend, the science of *tasawwuf* represents the logical and necessary evolution of teachings and practices that go to the very heart of the religion of Islam. Nor are the Orientalists correct who attempt to apply the term "superstition" (*shawaza*) to the science of *tasawwuf*.

The term *tasawwuf*, which refers to the method of cleansing the heart, denotes the same thing as *tazkiyat al-nafs* in the Quran. Both have the same subject matter as the sciences of "doing-without" (*zuhd*) and perfection of character (*ihsan*). The terms *zuhd, tazkiya,* and *ihsan* were all used in the time of the Prophet ﷺ. Later, these terms were defined with extensive detail, and refined according to the guidelines of the Quran and the *hadith,* as were the other Islamic sciences.

Of course, any term may be used to name a science, and one is free to define or use any term one wishes. It is dearly hoped that no one will be prevented or forbidden from learning this important science due to prejudice against the term *tasawwuf*. If the term is problematic to someone, let him give it a different name, but let him learn the science, by whatever name he wishes to call it.

Linguistic Roots of the Term *Tasawwuf*

There are four roots given to the word *tasawwuf*. The first is from the Arabic word *safa* or *safw*, which means "purity" and "limpidity." The Prophet ﷺ compared the world to a little rain water on a mountain plateau of which the *safw* had already been drunk and from which only the *kadar*, or dregs, remained.[40] He called Sham (Damascus) God's purest of lands (*safwat Allah min biladih*).[41] Ibn al-Athir defines the word in his dictionary *al-Nihaya* as "the best of any matter, its quintessence, and purest part."[42]

Another root is derived from *Ahl as-Suffa,* (the People of the Bench), who were those who lived in the Mosque of the Prophet ﷺ during his life and who were mentioned in the Quran in the following verse:

> *(O Muhammad,) keep yourself content with those who call on their Lord" morning and evening seeking His Face; and let not your eyes pass beyond them, seeking the pomp and glitter of this life; nor obey any whose heart We have permitted to neglect the Remembrance of Us, the one who follows his own desires, whose case has gone beyond all bounds.* (18:28)

This verse emphasizes how much the believers have to keep themselves in the state of *dhikr*, or recollection of God on the tongue, in the mind, and through the heart. This root is sometimes compared to *ahl al-suff*, or "the People of the Rank," in the sense of "first rank," as the first rank is blessed and the Sufis are the elite of the Community.

The third of these roots is *al-suf* or wool, as it was the manner of the pious people of Kufa to wear it. The fourth linguistic root is from *suffat*

---

[40] In Ibn Asakir from Ibn Masud. Al-Qushayri and al-Hujwiri mention it in their chapters on *tasawwuf*, respectively in *Kashf al-mahjub* (Nicholson trans. p.) and *al-Risala*: B.R. Von Schlegell trans., Principles of Sufism (Berkeley, Mizan Press, 1990) p. 301.

[41] Tabarani related it and Haythami authenticated the chain through *Irbad ibn Sariya in Majma al-zawaid,* chapter on the merits of Syria.

[42] Ibn al-Athir, *al-Nihaya*, s.v. *s-f-w*.

al-kaffa, or soft sponge, in reference to the Sufi whose heart is very soft due to its purity.

The Primacy of the Heart over All Other Organs

The heart is the seat of sincerity in a person, without which none of his actions are accepted. The Prophet ﷺ said, as Bukhari narrated, "*Surely there is in the body a small piece of flesh; if it is good the whole body is good and if it is corrupted the whole body is corrupted and that is the heart.*" He said in two other *ahadith* narrated by Muslim, "*Surely God does not look at your bodies nor at your faces but He looks at your hearts,*" and "*No one will enter Paradise who has even an atom of pride in his heart.*"

Many other *ahadith* explicitly state the primacy of the heart. Abu Hurayra ؓ narrates:

> *I said, O Messenger of God! Who will be the foremost people in gaining your intercession on the Day of Resurrection? God's Messenger ﷺ said, "O Abu Hurayra! I knew that no one would ask me about this before you because of your longing for the knowledge of hadith. The foremost of people in gaining my intercession on the Day of Resurrection is he who said, 'There is no deity but God' purely and sincerely from his heart* (qalb) *or his soul* (nafs)*."*[43]

Ibn Hajar said in his commentary on Bukhari:

> The Prophet ﷺ mentioned the heart for emphasis, as God said of the sinner, "*Verily his heart is sinful.*" (2:283) "Foremost" alludes to their different order of entry into Paradise as distinct from their different ranks of sincerity, the latter being emphasized by his saying "from his heart" although it is clear that the seat of sincerity is the heart. However, the attribution of the action to that organ affects more emphasis.[44]

One of the Companions named Wabisa ؓ relates that all the people asked the Prophet ﷺ about the good things, but he resolved to ask him about the evil things. When he came to him, the Prophet ﷺ poked him in the chest with his fingers and said three times, "*O Wabisa, fear of God is*

---

[43] Bukhari related it (English 1:79).

[44] Ibn Hajar, *Fath al-bari* (1989 ed.) 1:258 and 11:541.

here." Then he said, *"Ask for your heart's decision, no matter the decision this one and that one gives you."*[45]

From Ibn Umar ﷺ:

The Prophet ﷺ said, "Everything has a polish, and the polish of hearts is dhikr of God. Nothing saves one from God's punishment more than dhikr of God." They said, "Not even jihad for God's sake?" He said, "Not even if you strike with your sword until it breaks."[46]

Ibn Umar ﷺ relates:

I was sitting with the Prophet ﷺ when Harmala ibn Zayd al-Ansari of the Banu Haritha tribe came to him. He sat in front of God's Messenger ﷺ and said, "O Messenger of God, belief is here"—and he pointed to his tongue—"and hypocrisy is here"—and he pointed to his heart—"and I don't make dhikr of God except little." God's Messenger remained silent. Harmala repeated his words, whereupon the Prophet ﷺ seized Harmala's tongue by its extremity and said, "O God, give him a truthful tongue and a thankful heart, and grant him to love me and to love those who love me, and turn his affairs towards good." Harmala said, "O Messenger of God, I have two brothers who are hypocrites; I was with them just now. Shall I not point them out to you (so you will pray for them)?" The Prophet ﷺ said, "(Yes,) whoever comes to us in the way you have come, we shall ask forgiveness for them as we asked forgiveness for you; and whoever keeps to this path, God becomes his protector."[47]

From Ibn Umar ﷺ also:

The Prophet ﷺ said, "Do not speak much rather than make dhikr of God; speaking much without dhikr of God hardens the heart, and no-one is farther from God than the hard-hearted."[48]

---

[45] Related in Ahmad, Tabarani, Abu Yala, and Abu Nuaym.

[46] Bayhaqi relates it in *Shuab al-iman* 1:396 #522; al-Mundhiri in *al-Targhib* 2:396; and Ibn Abi al-Dunya.

[47] Al-hafiz Abu Nuaym narrated it in *Hilyat al-awliya*. Ibn Hajar said in *al-Isaba* (2:2 #1659): "Its chain of transmission is acceptable and Ibn Mindah also extracted it. We have narrated the same through Abu al-Darda in the *Fawaid* of Hisham ibn Ammar." Al-Tabarani also narrated through Abu al-Darda. Haythami said of that chain: "It contains one unknown narrator, but the rest are trustworthy."

[48] Tirmidhi related it and said: a rare *hadith* (*gharib*); also Bayhaqi in the *Shuab* 4:245 #4951.

It is clear, therefore, that the Prophet ﷺ tied everything to the good condition of the heart. When one leaves bad manners and takes on good manners, then he will have a perfect and healthy heart. That is what God mentioned in the Quran:

> *The Day wherein neither wealth nor sons will avail, but only he will prosper who brings to God a sound heart.* (26:88-89)

God mentioned the hearts of His true knowers *(ulama)* when He said:

> *Know here are signs self-evident in the hearts of those who have been endowed with knowledge, and none but the unjust reject our signs.* (29:49)

What are the diseases of the heart? Imam Suyuti said in his book on the Shadhili Order, "The science of hearts, the knowledge of its diseases such as jealousy, arrogance, and pride, and leaving them is an obligation on every Muslim." [49] The exegetes have said that jealousy (*hasad*), ostentation (*riya*), hypocrisy (*nifaq*), and hatred (*hiqd*) are the most common bad manners, to which God referred when He said:

> *Say, the things that my Lord has indeed forbidden are: shameful deeds whether open or secret.* (7:33)

God's mentioning "whether open or secret" is the evidence for the need to not merely make the exterior actions correct, but to cleanse that which is hidden in a person's heart and is known only to his Lord.

Tasawwuf is the science and knowledge whereby one learns to purify the self of the ego's bad desires, such as jealousy, cheating, ostentation, love of praise, pride, arrogance, anger, greed, stinginess, respect for the rich, and disregard of the poor. Similarly, one must purify the external self. The science of *tasawwuf* teaches one to look at oneself, to purify oneself according to the Holy Quran and the *Sunnah* of the Prophet ﷺ, and to dress oneself with the perfect attributes (*al-sifat al-kamila*). These include repentance (*tawba*), godwariness (*taqwa*), keeping to the straight way (*istiqama*), truthfulness (*sidq*), sincerity (*ikhlas*), abstention (*zuhd*), great piety (*wara*), reliance on God (*tawakkul*), contentment with the Decree (*rida*), surrender to God (*taslim*), good

---

[49] Suyuti, *Tayid al-haqiqa al-aliyya wa-tashyid al-tariqa al-shadhiliyya,* ed. Abd Allah ibn Muhammad ibn al-Siddiq al-Ghumari al-Hasani (Cairo: *al-matbaa al-islamiyya,* 1934), p. 56.

manners (*adab*), love (*mahabba*), remembrance (*dhikr*), watchfulness (*muraqabah*), and other qualities too numerous to mention here.

Just as the science of *hadith* has dozens of classifications for *hadith*, the science of *tasawwuf* has numerous classifications for both the good characteristics (*akhlaq hasana*), which are obligatory for the believer to develop, and the bad ones (*akhlaq dhamima*), which it is necessary to eliminate to attain the state of *ihsan*. Through the science of *tasawwuf*, the heart, precious essence, and lifeblood of Islam are made manifest to us. For Islam is not only an external practice, but also has an internal life. This is as God says:

> *Leave the outwardness of sin and its inwardness.* (6:120)

> *Among the Believers are men who have been true to their Covenant with God.* (33:23)

This means that not all believers are included in the group of those who "*kept their Covenant with God*" (33:23). It means a person can be a believer, but not among those who have kept their Covenant until he has reached a state of cleanliness: the state of *ihsan*, perfection of behavior, which the Prophet ﷺ mentioned in the *hadith*. This, as has now been made clear, is what became known later as the science of *tasawwuf*.

Evidence from the Quran

GOD DESCRIBES SELF-PURIFICATION AS A DUTY OF THE PROPHET ﷺ

As mentioned previously, the evidence for *tasawwuf* from the Quran is the same as the evidence for self-purification (*tazkiyat al-nafs*), which we have established above as the definition of *tasawwuf*. God says:

> *He is the One Who raised among the people of Makkah a Messenger from among themselves who recites to them His communications and purifies them, and teaches them the Book and the Wisdom, although they were before certainly in clear error.* (62:2)

The term used here is *wa yuzakkihim* (purifies them). The various root meanings of the word *tazkiya* in Arabic are:

- *zaka:* he cleansed; he was clean
- *yuzakki*: to clean; to be purified
- *tazkiya:* purification

- *zakat:* Islamic poor-tax; charity; purity
- *azka*: the purest
- *zaki:* pure; innocent

In another verse:

By the soul and the proportion and order given to it, and its inspiration as to its wrong and its right; Truly he succeeds who purifies it, and he fails that corrupts it. (91:7-10)

This verse states the necessity of purifying and cleaning the ego (*nafs*) in order to succeed in this life and the next. This is precisely the goal of *tasawwuf.*

GOD PROMISES TO GUIDE THE BELIEVERS

In the Quran we find this command:

O Believers, be wary of God and find a means to approach Him and strive in His Way that perhaps you may be of the successful. (5:35)

This verse means that a person must strive in God's way, not in the ego's way, nor towards the ego and its desires, if he wishes to be successful. It indicates the necessity of following the footsteps of the Prophet ﷺ as the means to approaching God and of taking him and those who know him as guides. God also says:

O ye who believe, fear God and keep company with those who are truthful. (9:119)

This verse substantiates the need to accompany and associate with the best of God's servants. The *Sadiqin* are the ones who reached one of the highest stations of faith according to the verse, already mentioned:

Among the Believers are men who have been true to their Covenant with God and of them some have died and some still wait but they have never changed their determination (in the least). (33:23)

This means that in every era there are people who hold fast to the Covenant of God. These are the friends of God mentioned in other verses, including:

Nay, they are the Friends of God; no fear shall come upon them, neither shall they grieve. (10:62)

One of the Friends of God is al-Khidr عليه السلام, whom the Prophet Moses عليه السلام was ordered to accompany and learn from. God says:

> *Those who are striving in Our Way, We will guide them to Our paths, for verily God is with those who do good.* (29:69)

AL-KHIDR عليه السلام: ONE WHO LEARNED DIRECTLY FROM GOD'S PRESENCE

God describes the meeting of Moses عليه السلام with Al-Khidr عليه السلام eloquently:

> *So they found one of Our servants on whom We had bestowed mercy from Ourselves and whom We had taught knowledge from Our Own Presence. Moses said to him, "May I follow you on the condition that you teach me something of the Higher Truth which you have been taught?" The other said, "Surely you will not be able to have patience with me."* (18:65-67)

From these two verses, it is clear that even though Moses عليه السلام was a prophet, and the only prophet to speak with God directly (*kalimullah*), Khidr عليه السلام possessed knowledge that Moses عليه السلام did not have. Moses عليه السلام sought to obtain this knowledge from him, because he knew Khidr عليه السلام was receiving knowledge directly from the Presence of God (*ilm ladunni*) as one of God's Friends. God also says:

> *Follow the way of those who turn to Me.* (31:15)

Yusuf Ali correctly comments on this verse saying, "That is the way of those who love God." The state of love is related to the heart, not to the mind. Three of the many proofs that believers should follow a guide, or "teacher of upbringing" (*shaykh al-tarbiya*) in technical terms, are found in the verses of Moses' عليه السلام encounter with al-Khidr عليه السلام, and in the order to follow the path of God's true Lovers.

The Superiority of Love in Worship

Ibn Qayyim al-Jawziyya compiled some of the sayings of the great Sufis regarding love and its priority in sound worship:[50]

Junayd said:

> I heard al-Harith al-Muhasibi say, "Love is when you incline completely towards something; and then the preference of that

[50] Ibn Qayyim, *Rawdat al-muhibbin wa nuzhat al-mushtaqin* (Beirut: Dar al-kutub al-ilmiyya, 1983) p. 406-409.

thing over yourself, and your soul, and your possessions; then the compliance with that inwardly and outwardly; then your knowing of your shortcoming in your love to Him."

Abd Allah ibn al-Mubarak said:

Whoever is given a portion of love and he has not been given an equivalent amount of awe, has been cheated.

Yahya bin al-Muadh al-Razi said:

An atom's weight of love is more beloved to me than to worship seventy years without love.

Abu Bakrah al-Qattani said:

There was a discussion about love in Makkah during the Pilgrimage season and the shaykhs were speaking about it. Junayd was the youngest of them in age and they said, "Say what you have, O Iraqi." He lowered his head in deference and his eyes filled with tears then he said, "A slave taking leave of himself, connected with the remembrance of his Lord, standing with the fulfillment of his duties, looking at Him with his heart, whose heart is burned by the light of His Essence; his drink is clear from the cup of His love; and if he talks, it is by God; and if he utters, it is from God; and if he moves, it is by the order of God; and if he is silent, he is with God; and he is by God, he is for God, he is with God (*fa huwa billahi wa lillahi wa ma allahi*)." The shaykhs cried out and said, "There is nothing above that, may God strengthen you, crown of the Knowers!"

Junayd's words are related to those found in one of the foundational texts that provides evidence for the miracles of the saints, the following *hadith qudsi* (holy Tradition) related by Bukhari:

On the authority of Abu Hurayra ✿, the Messenger of God ﷺ said that God said: "Whosoever shows enmity to someone devoted to Me, I shall be at war with him. My servant draws not near to Me with anything more loved by Me than the religious duties I have enjoined upon him, and My servant continues to draw near to Me with supererogatory works so that I shall love him. When I love him I am his hearing with which he hears, his seeing with which he sees, his hand with which he strikes, and his foot with

> *which he walks. Were he to ask something of Me, I would surely give it to him, and were he to ask refuge in Me, I would surely grant him it . . . "*

Love was mentioned to Dhun Nun and he said, "Enough, do not discuss this question, as the ego (*nafs*) will hear it and take its claim in it." He continued, "For the disobedient one, fear and sorrow are better! Love is for the one who already has fear and is pure of all filth."

Dhun Nun also said:

> For everything there is punishment, and the punishment of the knower of God is the cutting from him of his remembrance of God *(dhikr Allah)*.

Junayd referred to this distinction of levels in his reply when he was told, "Over there are a people who say, they are definitely reaching the station of goodness by the leaving of deeds." He said:

> Are they talking about the cancellation of (obligatory and other) deeds? Nay, whoever commits adultery and steals is in a better condition than the one who says such a thing. For certainly God's knowers *(al arifina billah)* took the deeds from God and returned with these deeds to Him, and if I had lived a thousand years I would never decrease from the good deeds the least bit.

Junayd also said:

> The knower of God is not considered a knower until he becomes like the earth; it is the same to him whether the good person or the bad person steps on him; or like the rain, he gives without discrimination to those whom he likes and those he dislikes.

Sumnun said:

> The lovers of God have gained the honor of both the world and the hereafter. The Prophet ﷺ said, *"The human being is with the one he loves."* They are with God in the *dunya* and the next life.

Yahya ibn Muadh said:

> He is not a truthful one who pretends he loves Him and trespasses His boundaries.

He also said:

The knower of God leaves this worldly life and he does not have enough of two things: crying over his own self, and his longing for his Lord.

Another seeker of self-purification said:

The knower of God does not become a knower until, if he has been given the treasures of Sulayman ﵇, it will not busy him with other than God for the blink of an eye.

Classical Teachings on Purifying the Ego

Some of the verses referring to purification and self-purification in the Quran have already been mentioned. God says:

(A Messenger) who shall rehearse Your signs to them, instruct them in the Book and wisdom and purify them. (2:129)

A similar (favor have you already received), in that we have sent among you a Messenger of your own, rehearsing to you Our signs, and purifying you . . . (2:151)

Those will prosper who Purify themselves and glorify the Name of their Lord and pray. (87:14)

And whoever Purifies himself does so to his own soul's benefit; and to God is the Journeying. (35:18)

In all of these verses, God refers to the characteristics of the *mutassawif*, or those who are busy purifying themselves. They are always remembering their Lord, by recalling His Names and Attributes, and they are attentive to their prayers. This is the essence of *tasawwuf*, and also the essence of Islam. The reader is reminded again that this is only a technical term, and can be replaced by any synonym.

If someone claims to follow or practice Islam, this struggle to purify the self is incumbent upon him, as it is so clearly ordered in these verses. Indeed, it is meaningless to claim that there could be any surrender to God without the pursuit of self-purification. That is why some scholars, among them Imam Ghazali and Imam Suyuti, have considered *tasawwuf* a religious obligation (*wajib*).[51] Whether one is successful or not in this pursuit is in God's hands, but its necessity is incumbent on every Muslim, man or woman.

Classical Teachings on the State of Perfected Character (*Ihsan*)

Let us now turn to quote some verses that address the state of *ihsan* (excellence). God said:

> *For the Mercy of God is near to those who are good (*muhsinin*).* (7:56)
>
> *For God is with those who restrain themselves and who are good.* (16:128)
>
> *Is there any reward for Excellence (*ihsan*) other than Excellence?* (55:60)
>
> *And He rewards those who do good with what is best.* (53:31)
>
> *God commands justice, the doing of good (*ihsan*), giving to kith and kin, and He forbids all indecent deeds and evil and rebellion: He instructs you that you may receive admonition.* (16:90)
>
> *Nay, whoever submits his whole self to God and is a muhsin (in the state of ihsan), his reward is with his Lord, on those shall be no fear nor shall they grieve.* (2:112)
>
> *Whoever submits his whole self to God and is in a state of ihsan has grasped indeed the firmest handhold, and to God will all things return.* (31:21)
>
> *Who can be better in religion than one who submits his whole self to God, and does good, and follows the way of Abraham . . .* (4:125)

Verses about the state of *ihsan* are numerous, but what has been quoted is sufficient. The meaning of *ihsan*, as the Prophet ﷺ defined it, is praying with humility and submission (*khudu* and *khushu*), as if the believer is seeing God and is aware that He is seeing him. In his *Book of Definitions* (*Kitab al-tarifat*) al-Jurjani said:

> *Al-ihsan*: verbal noun denoting what one ought to do in the way of good. In *Shariah* it means to worship God as if you see Him, and if you do not see Him, He sees you. It is the attainment of true

---

[51] Ghazali's opinion is cited in *The Reliance of the Traveller*, p. 12. For Suyuti, see below, section on the sayings of the scholars.

worship-in-servanthood predicated on the sight of the Divine Lordship with the light of spiritual sight. That is: the sight of God as He is described by His Attributes and through His very Attribute, so that one will see Him with certitude, not literally (*fa huwa yarahu yaqinan wa la yarahu haqiqatan*). That is why the Prophet ﷺ said, "As if you were seeing Him." For one sees Him from behind the veil of His Attributes.[52]

The word *ihsan* and its derivatives have the following meanings in the dictionary:

- *hasuna* حَسُنَ *:* to become; to seem; to make excellent; beautiful
- Ihsanan إحساناً : to do excellently
- *Ahsana* أحسنَ*:* he did a great good
- Ihsan إحسان: kindness
- Husna حُسْنَى: reward
- *Hasan* حَسَنْ*:* excellent; beautiful
- Hisanun حِسانٌ : beautiful ones

"To become beautiful" in the first of these examples means to decorate oneself with good attributes; to beautify inwardly and outwardly. When used as an adjective, it means kindness as a trait or an internal attitude, as well as composure.

It should be clear by now that the state of *ihsan* mentioned in the Holy Quran is a very high state, one which the archangel Gabriel عليه السلام showed to be an intrinsic part of the religion, and which he placed at the same level as the states of Islam and *iman*. The religion consists of three states: Islam, *iman* and *ihsan*, each of which has its own definition. That is why it is mentioned in the Holy Quran in so many places, and why the Prophet ﷺ, when asked about it by Gabriel عليه السلام, gave it the same importance as he gave to Islam and *iman*.

The *Hadith* of Gabriel عليه السلام

Muslim narrated:

Umar رضي الله عنه *also said: "While we were sitting with God's Messenger* ﷺ *one day, all of a sudden a man came up to us. He wore exceedingly white clothes. His hair was jet-black. There was no sign of travel on his person.*

---

[52] Al-Sharif Ali ibn Muhammad al-Jurjani, *Kitab al-tarifat* (Beirut: *dar al-kutub al-ilmiyya,* 1408/1988) p. 12.

None of us knew him. He went to sit near the Prophet ﷺ leaning his knees against the knees of the Prophet and placing his hands on his thighs.

"He said, 'O Muhammad! Tell me about submission.' God's Messenger ﷺ said, 'Submission is to bear witness that There is no god but God, and that Muhammad is the Messenger of God; to perform the prayer; to pay the poor-tax; to fast during Ramadan; and to make the pilgrimage to the House if you are able to go there.'

"The man said, 'You have spoken the truth.' We wondered at him; how could he be asking the Prophet ﷺ and confirming him at the same time? Then he said, 'Tell me about belief.' The Prophet ﷺ said, 'Belief is to believe in God, His angels, His books, His messengers, and the Last Day; and to believe in what-has-been-decreed, both its good and its evil.' The man said, 'You have spoken the truth. Now tell me about excellence.' The Prophet ﷺ replied, 'Excellence is to worship God as if you see Him, for if you do not see Him, He certainly sees you.'

"The man said, 'Now tell me about the Hour.' The Prophet ﷺ replied, 'The one who is being asked knows no more about it than the questioner.' He said, 'Then tell me about its signs.' He replied, 'The slave-girl will give birth to her mistress, and you will see the barefoot, naked, destitute herdsmen outdo each other in building tall structures.' Then he left and time passed. Later he said to me, 'O Umar, do you know who that was asking questions?' I said, 'God and His Messenger know best.' He said, 'He was none other than Gabriel. He came to you to teach you your religion.'"

THE SOURCE OF ALL TRADITIONS

As said before, the term *tasawwuf* is a technical term that originated in the various meanings quoted in the first and second answers. It has deep roots in the *Sunnah* of the Prophet ﷺ, since its origin is *ihsan*, the state of Excellence that is mentioned in the *hadith* of archangel Gabriel عليه السلام which is known to all scholars as the "Source of the *Sunnah* and of all *hadith*" *(umm al-sunnah wa umm al-ahadith).*

In this *hadith*, Gabriel عليه السلام has divided religion into categories or main branches from which all religion, all *hadith*, and all *Sunnah* flow. He emphasized each branch by asking each question separate from the other. The first branch was related to his question, "What is Islam?" The second was related to the question, "What is *iman*?" The third is related to the question, "What is *ihsan*?" It cannot be said that religion is only Islam, or only *iman*, or only *ihsan*. Each of these branches is essential to the religion, and none can be left out. The Prophet ﷺ, in his answers to these questions, confirmed this and said to his Companions after Gabriel عليه السلام left, "Gabriel came to teach you your religion."

Islam, *iman*, and *ihsan* may be called three pillars of religion. The first pillar represents the practical side of the religion, including worship, deeds, and other obligations. That pillar is the external side of the self, and is related to the body and the Community. Scholars call it the first pillar of *Shariah*. Scholars learned to specialize in this, and it was called "the Science of Jurisprudence" (*ilm al-fiqh*). The second pillar represents belief in the mind and heart: belief in God, His Messengers, His Books, the Angels, the Last Day, and Destiny. This became known to the scholars as "the Science of Divine Oneness" (*ilm al-tawhid*). The third pillar represents *tasawwuf*.

THE THIRD COMPONENT OF ISLAM: IHSAN

The third aspect of the religion is known as the spiritual aspect of the heart. It is intended to make one aware when combining the first and second pillars, and to remind that one is always in the Presence of God, and that one should consider this in all thoughts and actions. If one cannot see Him—and, indeed, no one can see God in this life—then one must keep the continuous awareness of God's Presence in the heart. One must know that He is aware of every moment and detail in one's worship and one's belief. By doing these things, one will attain a state of excellence, a state of high quality, and will taste the spiritual pleasure and light of knowledge that God will direct to one's heart. That is what scholars have termed the Science of Truth or *ilm al-haqiqa,* known in the time of the Companions, as *al-siddiqiyya,* or the Path of the truthful saints. Only later did it become known by the name of *tasawwuf*.

In summary, Islam prescribes the behavior of a Muslim, *iman* relates to the beliefs and defines them, and *ihsan* refers to the state of the heart that determines whether one's Islam and *ihsan* will bear fruit in this life and the next. This is supported by the *hadith* in Bukhari mentioned earlier:

Verily there is in the body a small piece of flesh; if it is good the whole body is good and if it is corrupted the whole body is corrupted and that is the heart.

Ihsan is divided into many parts, including all the good traits of a believer, such as *taqwa* (piety), *wara* (scrupulous fear of God), *zuhd* (abstention), *khushu* (reverence), *khudu* (humility), *sabr* (patience), *sidq* (truthfulness), *tawakkul* (reliance), *adab* (good character), *tawba* (repentence), *inaba* (turning to God), *hilm* (forbearance), *rahma* (compassion), *karam* (generosity), *tawadu* (humility), *haya* (modesty), *shajaa* (courage), etc.

All of these are the qualities of the Prophet ﷺ and, "His character was the Quran," according to Aisha ﷺ.[53] The Prophet ﷺ, in turn, impressed these qualities on all his Companions, so that they became perfect and shining examples of how human beings should exist: in perfect harmony with the Creator and with each other.

In his explanation of the *hadith* of Gabriel ﷺ, Imam Nawawi refers to *ihsan* in terms of the Station of Witnessing (*maqam al-mushahada*) and the Station of the Most Truthful Saints (*maqam al-siddiqeen*), which are two of the branches of *tasawwuf.* The following is the complete text of Nawawi's commentary on the *hadith* of Gabriel ﷺ.

IMAM NAWAWI'S COMMENTARY ON THE HADITH OF GABRIEL ﷺ

[Gabriel ﷺ told the Prophet ﷺ,] "Tell me about belief (iman)."

Iman, lexically, means conviction of a general nature. Legally it is an expression for a specific conviction in the belief in God, His angels, His books, His messengers, the Last Day, and whatever is decreed, both its good and its evil. Islam is a word signifying the performance of the legal obligations. These are the external actions that one applies oneself to do.

God the Exalted has differentiated belief (*iman*) from submission (Islam) and this is also in the *hadith*. He said: "*The Arabs say: 'We believe.' Say: 'You do not believe, but say 'We submit.'*" (49:14) This is because the hypocrites prayed, fasted, and paid alms while denying everything in their hearts. When they claimed belief, God declared

[53] Muslim; Ahmad, *Musnad* 6:91, 163, and others.

their claim a lie because of the denial in their hearts, but He confirmed their claim of submission because of their performance of the duties entailed by it.

God says: *"If the hypocrites come to you and say: 'We bear witness that you truly are God's Messenger,' God knows better than they that you are indeed His Messenger, and God witnesses that the hypocrites are liars."* (63:1) They are liars in their claim of bearing witness to the Message while their hearts are denying it. The words of their mouths do not match the contents of their hearts, whereas the condition of bearing witness to the Message is that the tongue confirms the heart. When they lied in their claim, God exposed their lie.

Since belief is also a condition for the validity of submission, God the Exalted distinguishes the submitter (Muslim) from the believer (*mumin*) by saying:

We brought out the believers who dwelled in it and found none left in it but one house of submitters. (51:35-36)

This distinction links belief and submission in the way of a condition and its fulfillment. Lastly, God named prayer by the name of "belief" when He said:

It was not God's purpose that your belief should be in vain. (2:143)

You knew not what the Book was nor what the Faith. (42:52)

"And to believe in what has been decreed, both its good and its evil."

The word ("decree") is pronounced both *qadar* and *qadr*. The way of the People of Truth (i.e. *Ahl as-Sunnah wal-Jamaah*) is to firmly believe in God's Decree. The meaning of this is that God—Glorified and Exalted is He!—has decreed matters from pre-Eternity, and that He—Glorified and Exalted is He!—knows that they shall take place at times known to Him—Glorified and Exalted is He!—and at places known to Him; and they do occur exactly according to what He has decreed—Glorified and Exalted is He!

"Tell me about *ihsan*." He said: "*Ihsan* is to worship God as if you saw Him."

This is the Station of True Vision (*maqam al-mushahada*). Whoever is able to directly see the King shies away from turning to other than Him in prayer and busying his heart with other than Him.

The Station of *ihsan* is the Station of the Most Truthful Saints (*maqam al-siddiqeen*) to which we have referred in our commentary on the *hadith* of intention:[54]

"He certainly sees you."

He sees your heedlessness if you are heedless in prayer and chatting to your self.

"Tell me about the Hour." He replied: "The one who is being asked knows no more about it than the questioner."

This answer indicates that the Prophet ﷺ did not know the Hour. Knowledge of the Hour is among the matters whose knowledge God has reserved for Himself. He said:

God has with Him the knowledge of the Hour. (31:34)

It is heavy in the heavens and the earth. It comes not to you save unawares. (7:187)

What can convey its knowledge unto thee (How canst thou know)? It may be that the Hour is nigh. (34:63, 42:17)

---

[54] al-Muhasibi said, "Truthfulness (*sidq*) as an attribute of a servant of God, means evenness in the private and the public person, in visible and hidden behavior. Truthfulness is realized after the realization of all the stations (*maqamat*) and states (*ahwal*). Even sincerity (*ikhlas*) is in need of truthfulness, whereas truthfulness needs nothing, because although real sincerity is to seek God through obedience, one might seek Allah by praying and yet be heedless and absent in his heart while praying. Truthfulness, then, is to seek God Almighty by worshipping with complete presence of heart before Him. For every truthful one (*sadiq*) is sincere (*mukhlis*), while not every sincere one is truthful. That is the meaning of connection (*ittisal*) and disconnection (*infisal*): the truthful one has disconnected himself from all that is other than God (*ma siwa Allah*) and he has fastened himself to the presence before God (*al-hudur billah*). That is also the meaning of renunciation (*takhalli*) of all that is other than God and self-adornment (*tahalli*) with presence before God, the Glorified, the Exalted."

As for he who claims that the age of the world is 70,000 years and that 63,000 years remain, it is a false statement reported by al-Tawkhi in the "Causes of Revelation" from certain astrologers and mathematicians. Moreover, whoever claims that the term of the world is 7,000 years makes a bold affirmation concerning the Unknown, and it is not permitted to believe it.

"Tell me about its signs." He replied: "The slave-girl will give birth to her mistress."

Another report has: "to her master." Most commentators say that this is a sign of the multiplicity of slave-girls and their offspring. A child by the slave-girl's master is like her master, because the owner's possessions go to his children. Some say that the meaning refers to slave-girls giving birth to kings. The mother would then fall under her child's sovereignty. Another meaning is that a person may have a son from his slave-girl before selling her away; then the son grows up and buys his own mother. That is one of the conditions of the Hour.

"You will see the barefoot, naked, destitute herdsmen outdo each other in building tall structures."

It means the Bedouins who live in the desert and their like from among the needy and the poor will become experts in erecting tall structures. The world will become bountiful for them, and they will end up vying in luxury with their buildings.

"And he (the Prophet ﷺ) waited a long time."

The reports also say: "I waited (*labiththu*) a long time." Both are sound. In Abu Dawud and Tirmidhi's narrations Umar says: "After three days," and in Baghawi's *Sharh al-tanbih*: "After three days or more," which apparently means after three nights had passed. All this apparently contradicts Abu Hurayra's statement in his narration (in Bukhari): "The man turned around and left, after which God's Messenger ﷺ said, 'Bring that man back to me,' and they looked to bring him back, but they found no one. Then he ﷺ said, 'That was Gabriel.'"

It is possible to reconcile the two versions of the event by considering that Umar may not have been present at the time of the Prophet's ﷺ disclosure, but that he had already risen and left the gathering by that time. So the Prophet ﷺ spoke on the spot to those who were present, and they in turn told Umar after three days, since he had not been present at the time the rest of the Companions had been informed.

"That was Gabriel. He came to you to teach you (the prescriptions of) your religion."

There is an indication in that statement that Islam, *iman*, and *ihsan* are all named "religion" (*din*).

The *hadith* also provides a proof that belief in God's Decree is an obligation, that one should avoid probing matters, and that contentment with what comes to pass is an obligation.

A man came up to Ahmad ibn Hanbal—may God be well pleased with him—and said: "Admonish me." He answered him:

If God, the Exalted, has taken upon Himself the provision of all sustenance, why do you fret? If indeed compensation for all things belongs to God, why be stingy? If indeed there is a Paradise, why rest now? If indeed there is a Fire, why disobey? If the questioning of Munkar and Nakir is true, what good is human company?[55] If the world is bound for extinction, what peace of mind is there in it? If indeed there is a Reckoning, what good are possessions? And if all things are decreed to pass and measured out, what good is fear?

Behind the Prophet's House: The People of the Bench(*Ahl as-Suffa*)

The People of the Bench (*Ahl as-Suffa*) represent the prototype of the school of perfection and purification which the Prophet Muhammad ﷺ established in his blessed mosque in Madinah, after the Emigration. In this school, the true devotees flocked earnestly seeking nothing but God's good pleasure with them and the pleasure of the Prophet ﷺ. The

---

[55] The sufi shaykh Ibn Ata Allah said, "When God alienates you from the company of His creatures, know that He wishes to open for you the door of His own intimacy." *Kitab al-hikam* #93.

People of the Bench and the methods of training they received under the direct discipline of the Prophet ﷺ became a precedent for the later generations.

Here we will relate some of the authentic narrations regarding the People of the Bench, their asceticism, and their isolation under the training of the Prophet ﷺ. The character and devotion of this extraordinary group of believers was spoken of in the Quran and protected by heavenly decrees. Such attestations by the Lord of creation were given to make clear the rank, faith, spirituality, and true devotion of these Companions of the Prophet ﷺ.

These were men whom *"neither business nor trading can divert them from the remembrance of God."* (24:37) They rejected the material comforts of this life, in favor of the eternal one. And God helped them in this by keeping from them wealth and power, both of which have proven snares in leading people to committing injustice and tyranny. They refused to feel despondent for the portion of this worldly life they were not granted, and accepted poverty in the way of God as their lot. Instead, they considered it insignificant and passing for their utmost happiness was to be engaged in worship of their Lord.

It is said that the following verse of Quran was revealed regarding the People of the Bench:

> *And keep yourself content with those who call on their Lord in the morning and the evening, seeking His face, and let not thine eyes pass beyond them, seeking the pomp and glitter of this life. Nor obey any whose heart We have permitted to neglect the remembrance of God one who follows his own desires, and his affair has become all excess.* (18:28)

The People of the Bench, used to sit morning and evening behind the house of Prophet ﷺ reciting Quran and praising the Prophet ﷺ and making *dhikr*. Abd Allah ibn Masud related:

> *A group from among the Quraysh passed by the Messenger of God ﷺ while Suhayb, Bilal, Ammar, Khabab and other poor Muslims were with him. They said to the Prophet ﷺ, "O Messenger of God, have you chosen this class of people from among your entire followers for your closest ones? Do you want us to follow such people? Are these the ones whom God has chosen from among all of us for His utmost favors? Get rid of them and perhaps if you do that we may follow you.*

> *It is then that God revealed, "Send not away those who call on their Lord morning and evening, seeking His face. In naught art thou accountable for them, and in naught are they accountable for thee, that thou shouldst turn them away, and thus be (one) of the unjust. Thus did We try some of them by comparison with others, that they should say: 'Is it these then that God hath favoured from amongst us?' Doth not God know best those who are grateful?" (6:52-53)*

The Hafiz Abu Nuaym al-Isfahani in his commentaries about the People of the Bench said:

> God, the Lord of Majesty and Glory, moved their focus away from the world. He made the world look insignificant and small in their eyes. Furthermore, He restricted their access to it in order to protect them against its lures and to help them eschew transgression and injustices against their own souls or others. Hence, He kept them guarded under the shield of His protection, He lightened their burdens, and guarded their focus against aberrations, so that no wealth in this world could inhibit their concentration and dedication to worship Him, and nothing could lure their hearts or drive them to abandon their stations.[56]

Jafar bin Muhammad bin Amr narrated that Abi Saeed al-Khudri ؓ said:

> *We were a group of poor Muslims who lived under the canopy of the Prophet's ﷺ Mosque, and we spent our time studying the Quran at the hand of a man from among us who also regularly prayed to God on our behalf. Once, the Messenger of God ﷺ came by us, and he saw our condition. I assumed that God's Messenger ﷺ did not know any of the people present by name, and when the people saw him coming, they felt extreme reverence for him; some even tried to hide behind the others to cover up some shame they felt about their torn rags. God's Messenger ﷺ then pointed out and invited the people to form a circle around him, and when they did, he asked them, "What were you studying?" They replied, "This man was reading the Quran for us and he also prays for us." God's*

---

[56] Abu Nuaym al-Isfahani, *Hilyat al-awliya The Beauty of the Righteous and Accounts of the Elite,* translation by Shaykh Muhammad al-Akili, p 373.

Messenger ﷺ sat there for a moment, and then said, "All praise is to God, Who made among my followers a group with whom I am commanded to constrain myself and to keep my soul content in their company." (c.f. 18:28). He ﷺ then added, "Let the poor ones among the believers hearken to the glad tiding that they will enter the heavenly paradise 500 years before the rich. The poor will be enjoying its blessings while the rich will be facing their reckoning."[57]

Abu Bakr al-Talhi narrated that Khabab ibn al-Art ﷺ once spoke in reference to the Quranic verse, "*Send not away those who call on their Lord morning and evening, seeking His face . . .* " (6:52) and he spoke of two people, al-Aqra bin Habis and Uyaina bin Hisn al-Fazari, who once harbored hypocrisy and often fought and betrayed the believers, and who primarily embraced Islam for ambitious selfish reasons, but later, and by the grace of Almighty God, they were guided to true Islam after they repented to God, the Magnificent Lord, and Who in His Divine Compassion, called in another verse *al-muallafit qulubuhum* (those whose hearts have been recently reconciled to the truth).

Khabab ibn al-Art ﷺ said:

Al-Aqra bin Habis and Uyaina bin Hisn al-Fazari, once came to the mosque, and the found God's Messenger ﷺ sitting in the company of Bilal, Ammar, Suhayb, and Khabab (himself), along with other believers from among the poor and the meek who were known as the People of the Bench. When al-Aqra and Uyaina saw that, they despised the group, and they requested a private audience with God's Messenger ﷺ, and they initially spoke to him with utter disrespect regarding the class of his company, indicating, "We want you to grant us a special set of rules concerning who sits with you when we come here. Make that a rank which will become recognized by the dignitaries among the various delegations of Arab tribes, besides others, who come to see you, so that they would recognize our status in this city. In fact, delegations of various noble tribes come regularly to see you, and we feel ashamed that they should see these paupers and slaves sitting in our company! Hence, when we come to see you, ask these people to leave, and when we take off and get back to our businesses, then you may sit with them as much as you want!" The

---

[57] *Op. cit.*, p. 958.

Prophet of God ﷺ replied, "Let it be so!" the two men delighted in their condition was accepted and they hastily demanded, "Then write down your promise and make it an official decree!"

We were all sitting there observing the ramifications when the Prophet of God ﷺ asked Ali ؓ to bring a paper to write on, but suddently the archangel Gabriel descended bringing the divine revelation, "Do not segregate or evict (from God's House) those who call on their Lord morning and evening, seeking His countenance. You are not accountable for them, nor are they accountable for you, and should you turn them away, you would have committed an extreme injustice." (6:52)

In His revelation, God, Glorious and Exalted, then mentioned al-Aqra bin Habis and Uyaina bin Hisn al-Fazari, saying "And thus We put to trial (the faith and character of) some people versus others (to frustrate their vainness), so that they will come to (hear themselves) say, 'Are these the people whom God chose to favor over us?' Alas, does not God know best those who are truly grateful (from those who are not)? Therefore, when those who believe in Our signs come to see you, say 'Peace be upon you. Your Lord has decreed upon Himself to favor you with His mercy and that should any of you commit a wrongdoing out of ignorance, and then repents and amends his act, he will surely find God oft-forgiving and most compassionate.'" (6:53-54).

God's Messenger ﷺ immediately discarded the paper Ali ؓ had just brought, as he called us to himself, and he kept on looking at us, and he greeted us cheerfully, "Peace be upon you, peace be upon you." Hence we happily drew closer and nestled by him, and we blithesomely sat so tightly close to him to the point that our knees touched his.

From that day on, God's Messenger ﷺ kept us in his proximity and under his direct watch; he regularly sat with us, and whenever he needed to attend to his other duties, he simply left us. This joyous privilege went on until the day when God, the Lord of Majesty and Glory, revealed His command, "And keep thy soul content with those who call on their Lord morning and evening, seeking His Face; and let not thine eyes pass beyond them, seeking the pomp and glitter of this Life; nor obey any whose heart We have permitted to neglect the remembrance of Us, one who follows his own desires, whose case has gone beyond all bounds." (18:28)

The above verse refers to al-Aqra bin Habis and Uyaina bin Hisn al-Fazari. Almighty God then spoke of the parable of two men and their quest for the world, and He directed His blessed Messenger to reply, "Say, 'The truth comes from your Lord.' Let whosoever wants to believe in it, believe in it, and let whosoever wants to reject it, reject it . . . As to those who believe (in Our message) and who do righteous deeds, We surely do not leave unrewarded the work of someone who does good. Such ones will be rewarded with gardens beneath which rivers flow . . . " (18:29-31)[58]

Abd Allah bin Muhammad bin Jafar narrated that Abu Hurayra said:

Among the People of the Bench there were at least seventy men who were extremely poor and did not have even a single large enough robe to cover themselves.[59]

Abd Allah bin Wahab narrated that Abu Hurayra said, "I stayed with the People of the Bench for some time . . . "[60]

Abu Hurayra also said:

The People of the Bench are the guests of Islam, they had no home or family to go to, nor did they have any money or possessions. Whenever God's Messenger received a collection of charities, he never took anything for himself; instead, he immediately sent them in their entrety to the People of the Bench. However, whenever he received a gift, he took a small share of it for his family, and he sent the balance to them.[61]

The school of which these Companions partook did not die with the passing of the Prophet. On the contrary, his methods and knowledge were turned over to his Companions, and each of them, in turn, became a school from which the Community learned the Prophet's methods and knowledge. Over time, these schools developed and formalized their methods, and created the distinct science of *tasawwuf*.

---

[58] *Op. cit.*, p. 961.

[59] *Op. cit.*, p. 948.

[60] *Op. cit.*, p. 949.

[61] *Op. cit.*, p. 944.

The Relationship Between One's Deeds and Spiritual Evolution

The name "science of reality," or *ilm al-haqiqah,* is sometimes given to *tasawwuf.* Imam Ahmad said, upon hearing al-Harith al-Muhasibi speak, "I never heard on the science of realities (*ilm al-haqaiq*) such words as those uttered by that man."[62] The meaning of this expression is that the reality of the servant's worship addresses the spiritual condition of his heart, while the performance of his worship satisfies his external obligations. The second is the object of *Shariah,* and its exponents are many, while the first is the object of *haqiqah,* and its exponents are few.

An example of the fulfillment of both *Shariah* and *haqiqah* is prayer. It is obligatory to offer *salat,* or prayer, with all the required movements and details according to the *Shariah.* This is known as *jasad al-salat,* or the "body of the prayer." On the other hand, one of the essentials of prayer is to keep the heart in God's Divine Presence and know that He is looking at you throughout the *salat.* Such is the reality and essence of prayer. During the practice of *salat,* people may carry out the outward obligations of the prayer, but their hearts may not be involved. To pray from the heart is to strive for the state of *ihsan;* to keep the heart pure and clean of bad manners, and to remain immune to the distractions of the *dunya.* The Prophet ﷺ prayed this way, because he said he came to take people away from the attractions and distractions of the *dunya,* and he cursed these in many of his *ahadith.*

By analogy, the external form of *salat* is its body, and humility (*khudu*) and self-effacement (*khushu*), its soul. What is the benefit of a body without a soul? If *salat* is movement without presence, then it is to move like a robot. As the soul needs the body to sustain it, so too does the body need the soul to give it life. The relationship between the *Shariah* and the *Haqiqa* is like the relationship of body and soul. The perfect believer who has reached a state of *ihsan* is the one who can join the two.

The Prophet ﷺ also expressed this distinction, in his *hadith:*

---

[62] Related with a sound chain by al-Khatib al-Baghdadi in his *Tarikh Baghdad* 8:214, and by al-Dhahabi in *Mizan al-itidal* 1:430.

Knowledge is of two kinds: knowledge established in the heart and knowledge on the tongue.[63]

Al-Izz ibn Abd al-Salam al-Maqdisi (not shaykh al-Islam as-Sulami) explained this to refer respectively to *Haqiqa* and *Shariah*:

Knowledge is of two kinds: knowledge of the external (*ilm al-zahir*) which applies to *Shariah*, and knowledge of the internal (*ilm al-batin*) which applies to *Haqiqah*. "[64]

Imam al-Shafii alluded to the same distinction in his saying, "Knowledge is of two kinds: knowledge of beliefs and knowledge of bodies." Suyuti related it in the introduction to his book *Prophetic Medicine* (*al-Tibb al-nabawi*).[65]

Therefore, the essential understanding of *tasawwuf* is to combine *Shariah* and *Haqiqah*, soul and body, externals and internals. Due to the immense difficulty of fulfilling *tasawwuf*, its methods are sometimes called spiritual warfare or *jihad an-nafs*.

Jihad an-Nafs: The Greater Struggle Is against the Ego

God declares in the Quran that He accepts acts of worship only from those who purify themselves, *"Truly he succeeds that purifies it,"* (91:9), achieve soundness of the heart *"But only he (will prosper) that brings to God a sound heart"* (26:89), and show a humble spirit *"and truly it is hard save for the humble-minded."* (2:45) Together, these are generally called "purification of the intention." That is why the great scholars like Bukhari, Shafii, Nawawi, and others, began their books of *fiqh* (jurisprudence) with the *hadith*, "Actions are judged according to intention."

An act that is outwardly considered worship, but that is performed without pure intention, is not considered worship—even fighting and dying in defense of Muslims. The Prophet ﷺ said of one such warrior, "He is a companion of the Fire." In *Shariah*, they are called *shahid al-fasad* (corrupt martyr). Purification of intention is extremely necessary in all

---

[63] Narrated by Ibn Abd al-Barr, *Jami bayan al-ilm wa fadlih* 1:190; al-Mundhiri, al-Targhib 1:103; al-Khatib al-Baghdadi, *Tarikh Baghdad* 4:346; and others.

[64] Al-Izz ibn Abd al-Salam, *Bayn al-sharia wa al-haqiqa aw hall al-rumuz wa mafatih al-kunuz* (Cairo: *matbaat nur al-amal*, n.d.) p. 11.

[65] As mentioned by al-Ajluni in *Kashf al-khafa* 2:89 (#1765).

five pillars of Islam. It is for this reason that the term *jihad al-akbar* (the greatest jihad) is commonly understood as reference to the jihad of self-purification.

Ibn Qayyim al-Jawziyya writes in *al-Fawaid*:

> God said, "*Those who have striven for Our sake, We guide them to Our ways.*" (29:69) He has thereby made guidance dependent on jihad. Therefore, the most perfect of people are those of them who struggle the most for His sake, and the most obligatory of jihads *(afrad al-jihad)* are the jihad against the ego, the jihad against desires, the jihad against the devil, and the jihad against the lower world *(jihad al-nafs wa jihad al-hawa wa jihad al-shaytan wa jihad al-dunya).* Whoever struggles against these four, God will guide him to the ways of His good pleasure which lead to His Paradise, and whoever leaves jihad, then he leaves guidance in proportion to his leaving jihad.

Al-Junayd said:

> Those who have striven against their desires and repented for our sake, we shall guide them to the ways of sincerity, and one cannot struggle against his enemy outwardly (i.e. with the sword) except he who struggles against these enemies inwardly. Then whoever is given victory over them will be victorious over his enemy. Whoever is defeated by them, his enemy defeats him.[66]

Competition and rivalry are allowed to encourage excellence in worship. God established levels among the believers, as is written in His book, and as is clear from countless *ahadith*. The reward of the lesser, or military, jihad is immense, as attested to by the Prophet ﷺ in the *hadith* where he says, if he could, he would ask God to bring him back to life so that he could go back and die as a *shahid* (martyr) many times over. Yet, with respect to *tasawwuf*, those who remember God, including perfect scholars who truly know God, are superior to the *mujahidin* (warriors, who make jihad). For example, although Zayd ibn Haritha and Khalid ibn Walid were great generals, their demise was less serious for Islam,

---

[66] Ibn Qayyim al-Jawziyya, *al-Fawaid*, ed. Muhammad Ali Qutb (Alexandria: dar al-dawa, 1412/1992) p. 50.

than that of Abu Musa al-Ashari or Ibn Abbas ﵄. For this reason, the Prophet ﷺ explicitly declared the superiority of those who remember God, in the following authentic *hadith*:

> *The Prophet ﷺ said, "Shall I tell you something that is the best of all deeds, constitutes the best act of piety in the eyes of your Lord, elevates your rank in the hereafter, and carries more virtue than the spending of gold and silver in the service of God, or taking part in jihad and slaying or being slain in the path of God?" They said, "Yes!" He said, "Remembrance of God."*[67]

Traditions on the Jihad against the Ego

The *hadith* master Mulla Ali al-Qari relates in his book *al-Mawduat al-kubra*, also known as *al-Asrar al-marfua* that as-Suyuti said:

> Al-Khatib al-Baghdadi relates in his work *History*, on the authority of Jabir, that the Prophet ﷺ came back from one of his campaigns saying, "You have come forth in the best way of coming forth; you have come from the smaller jihad to the greater jihad." They said, "And what is the greater jihad?" He replied, "The striving *(mujahadat)* of God's servants against their idle desires." [68]

The *hafiz* Ibn Abu Jamra al-Azdi al-Andalusi says in his commentary on Bukhari, entitled *Bahjat al-nufus*:

> Umar narrated that a man came to the Prophet ﷺ asking for permission to go to jihad. The Prophet ﷺ asked, "Are your parents alive?" He said that they were. The Prophet ﷺ replied, "Then struggle to keep their rights" (*fihima fa jahid*). There is in this *hadith* evidence that the *Sunnah* for entering the path and undertaking self-discipline is to act under the expert guidance, so that he may be shown the way that is best for him to follow, and the soundest for the particular wayfarer. For when that Companion wished to go out

---

[67]Related on the authority of Abu al-Darda by Ahmad, Tirmidhi, Ibn Majah, Ibn Abi al-Dunya, al-Hakim who declared it sound, and Dhahabi confirmed him, Bayhaqi, Suyuti in *al-Jami al-saghir*, and Ahmad also related it from Muadh ibn Jabal.

[68]Ibn Hajar al-Asqalani said in *Tasdid al-qaws:*"This saying is widespread and it is a saying by Ibrahim ibn Ablah according to Nisai in *al-Kuna*. Ghazali mentions it in the *Ihya* and al-Iraqi said that Bayhaqi related it on the authority of Jabir and said: 'There is weakness in its chain of transmission.'" Ali al-Qari, *al-Asrar al-marfua* (Beirut 1985 ed.) p. 127.

to jihad, he did not content himself with his own opinion in the matter, but sought advice from one more knowledgeable than him and more expert. If this is the case in the Lesser Jihad, then what about the Greater Jihad?[69]

The Prophet ﷺ said in the Farewell Pilgrimage:

"...the mujahid is he who makes jihad against himself (jahada nafsah) *for the sake of obeying God."*[70]

Another version relates:

The strong one is not the one who overcomes people, the strong one is he who overcomes his ego (ghalaba nafsah). [71]

---

[69] Ibn Abu Jamra, *Bahjat al-nufus sharh mukhtasar sahih al-bukhari* 3:146.

[70] Ibn Hibban relates in his *Sahih* from Fadala ibn Ubayd, Tirmidhi, Ahmad, Tabarani, Ibn Majah, al-Hakim, and Qudai also relate it. The contemporary *hadith* scholar Shuayb al-Arnaut confirmed that its chain of transmission is sound in his edition of Ibn Hibban, Sahih 11:203 (#4862).

[71] Related by Al-Haythami, who declared it sound in his *Majma al-zawaid* in the chapter on *Jihad al-nafs*.

Scholarly Opinions on the Precedence of Internal Knowledge

al-Hasan al-Basri (d. 110 AH/ 732 CE)

Al-Hasan al-Basri was one of the early Sufis in both the general and the literal sense, as he wore a cloak of wool (*suf*) all his life. The son of a freedwoman (by Umm Salama ☙, the Prophet's ﷺ wife) and a freedman (by Zayd ibn Thabit ☙, the Prophet's ﷺ stepson), this great imam of Basra was a leader of saints and scholars in his day. He was widely known for his strict and encompassing embodiment of the *Sunnah* of the Prophet ﷺ. He was also famous for his vast knowledge, his austerity and asceticism, his fearless protests against the authorities, and his appeal both in discourse and appearance.

Ibn al-Jawzi wrote a 100-page book on his life and manners entitled, *Adab al-shaykh al-Hasan ibn Abi al-Hasan al-Basri*. He mentions a report that, when he died, al-Hasan left behind a white, wool cloak (*jubba*) that he had worn exclusively for twenty years, winter and summer, and that was still in a state of immaculate beauty, cleanliness, and quality.[72]

In a book he devoted to the sayings and the deeds of Sufis, Ibn Qayyim relates, "A group of women went out on the day of Eid and went about looking at people. They were asked, 'Who is the most handsome person you have seen today?' They replied, 'It is a shaykh wearing a black turban.' They meant Hasan al-Basri."[73]

The *hadith* master Abu Nuaym al-Isfahani mentions that it is al-Hasan's student, Abd al-Wahid ibn Zayd, who was the first person to build a Sufi *khaniqah*, or guest-house, and school at Abadan, on the present-day border of Iran with Iraq.[74]

It was on the basis of Hasan al-Basri and his students' fame as Sufis that Ibn Taymiyya stated, "*Tasawwuf's* place of origin is Basra."[75] This is a misleading assertion. Rather, Basra was chief among the places renowned for the formal development of the schools of purification that

---

[72] Ibn al-Jawzi, *Sifat al-safwa* 2(4):10 (#570).

[73] Ibn al-Qayyim, *Rawdat al-muhibbin wa nuzhat al-mushtaqin* (The Garden of Lovers and the Excursion of the Longing Ones) p. 225.

[74] Abu Nuaym al-Isfahani, *Hilyat al-awliya* 6:155.

[75] Ibn Taymiyya, *al-Sufiyya wa al-faqara al-Tasawwuf* in *Majmua al-fatawa al-kubra* 11:16.

became known as *tasawwuf*, and whose principles were none other than the Quran and the *Sunnah*, as already demonstrated at length.

On the topic of *jihad al-nafs*, Ghazali relates that Hasan al-Basri said:[76]

> Two thoughts roam over the soul, one from God, one from the enemy. God shows mercy on a servant who settles at the thought that comes from Him. He embraces the thought that comes from God, while he fights against the one from his enemy. To illustrate the heart's mutual attraction between these two powers the Prophet ﷺ said, "*The heart of a believer lies between two fingers of the Merciful.*"
>
> The fingers stand for upheaval and hesitation in the heart. If man follows the dictates of anger and appetite, the dominion of Satan appears in him through idle passions (*hawa*) and his heart becomes the nesting-place and container of Satan, who feeds on passions. If he does battle with his passions and does not let them dominate his *nafs*, imitating in this the character of the angels, at that time his heart becomes the resting-place of angels, and they alight upon it.

A measure of the extent of Hasan al-Basri's extreme godwariness and scrupulousness (*wara*) is offered by his following statement, also quoted by Ghazali:

> Forgetfulness and hope are two mighty blessings upon the progeny of Adam; but for them the Muslims would not walk in the streets.[77]

Imam Abu Hanifa (81-150 AH/700-767 CE)

Imam Abu Hanifa said:

> If it were not for two years, I would have perished. For two years I accompanied Jafar as-Sadiq ؓ and I acquired the spiritual knowledge that made me a knower in the Way.[78]

The book *Ad-Durr al-Mukhtar* mentions that Ibn Abidin said:

---

[76] In the section of his renowned *Ihya* entitled *Kitab riyadat al-nafs wa tahdhib al-akhlaq wa mualajat amrad al-qalb* (Book of the Training of the Ego, and the Disciplining of Manners and the Healing of the Heart's Diseases).

[77] In Ghazali, trans. T.J. Winter, *The Remembrance of Death* p. 18.

[78] *Ad-Durr al-mukhtar*, vol. 1, p. 43.

Abu Ali Dakkak, one of the Sufi saints, received his path from Abul Qasim an-Nasarabadi, who received it from Shibli, who received it from Sari as-Saqati, who received it from Maruf al-Karkhi, who received it from Dawud at-Tai, who received the knowledge, both the external and the internal, from Imam Abu Hanifa, who supported the Sufi spiritual path.[79]

Sufyan al-Thawri (d. 161 AH/ 783 CE)

Ibn Qayyim al-Jawziyya and Ibn al-Jawzi relate that Sufyan al-Thawri said:

> If it were not for Abu Hashim al-Sufi, I would have never perceived the presence of the subtlest forms of hypocrisy in the self... Among the best of people is the Sufi learned in jurisprudence. [80]

Ibn al-Jawzi also narrates the following:

> Abu Hashim al-Sufi said, "God has stamped alienation upon the world in order that the friendly company of the seekers (*muridin*) consists solely in being with Him and not with the world, and in order that those who obey Him come to Him by means of avoiding the world. The People of Knowledge of God *(ahl al-marifa billah)* are strangers in the world and long for the hereafter."[81]

Imam Malik (94-179 AH/716-795 CE)

Imam Malik said:

> Whoever studies jurisprudence and does not study Sufism will be corrupted. Whoever studies Sufism and does not study jurisprudence will become a heretic. Whoever combines both will reach the Truth.[82]

Imam Shafii (150-205 AH/767-820 CE)

Imam Shafii said:

---

[79] See Ali al-Adawi with explanation by Imam Abul Hasan, vol. 2, p. 195.

[80] Ibn Qayyim, *Madarij al-salikin;* Ibn al-Jawzi, *Sifat al-safwa* (Beirut: dar al-kutub al-ilmiyya, 1403/1989) 1 (2):203 (#254); Abu Nuaym, *Hilyat al-awliya,* s.v. "Abu Hashim al-Sufi."

[81] Ibn al-Jawzi, *Op. cit.*

[82] Imam Adjluni, *Kashf al-*khafa *wa Muzid al-albas,* vol. 1, p. 341.

> I accompanied the Sufi people, and I received from them three kinds of knowledge: they taught me how to speak; they taught me how to treat people with leniency and a soft heart; they guided me in the ways of Sufism.[83]

Imam Ahmad ibn Hanbal (164-241 AH/780-855 CE)

Imam Ahmad, advising his son, said:

> O my son, you have to sit with the Sufis, because they are like a fountain of knowledge. They recite the remembrance of God in their hearts. They are the ascetics, and they have the most spiritual power.[84]

He also said about the Sufis:

> I do not know any people better than them.[85]

Imam al-Muhasibi (d. 243 AH/857 CE)

The Prophet ﷺ said, "*My Community is going to split into seventy-three divisions. Only one of them will be in the group of salvation.*" And God knows best that the group is the people of Sufism.[86]

al-Qasim ibn Uthman al-Jui (d. 248 AH/ 870 CE)

He is one of the great saints of Damascus who took *hadith* from Sufyan ibn Uyayna. Ibn al-Jawzi relates in *Sifat al-safwa* that al-Qasim ibn Uthman al-Jui explained that he got the name al-Jui ("of the hunger") because God had strengthened him against physical hunger by means of spiritual hunger. He said:

> Even if I was left one month without food I would not care. O God, you have done this with me. Therefore complete it for me![87]

In *Siyar alam al-nubala*, adh-Dhahabi calls him: "The Imam, the exemplar, the saint, the Muhaddith, the Shaykh of the Sufis and the friend of Ahmad ibn al-Hawari."

---

[83] Shaykh Ain al-Kurdi, *Tanwir al-qulub*, p. 405.

[84] *Ghiza al-albab*, vol. 1, p. 120.

[85] *Op. cit.*

[86] Imam al-Muhasibi, *Kitab al-wasaya*, pp. 27-32.

[87] Ibn al-Jawzi, *Sifat al-safwa* 2(2):200 (#763).

Ibn al-Jawzi also relates that Ibn Abu Hatim al-Razi said:

> I entered Damascus to see the transcribers of *hadith*. I passed by Qasim al-Jui's circle and saw a large crowd sitting around him as he spoke. I approached and heard him say:
>
> > Do without others in your life in five matters:
> > 1. If you are present among people, do not be known;
> > 2. If you are absent, do not be missed;
> > 3. If you know something, your advice is unsought;
> > 4. If you say something, your words are rejected;
> > 5. If you do something, you receive no credit for it.
> >
> > I advise you five other things as well:
> > 1. If you are wronged, do not reciprocate it;
> > 2. If you are praised, do not be glad;
> > 3. If you are blamed, do not be distraught;
> > 4. If you are called a liar, do not be angry;
> > 5. If you are betrayed, do not betray in return.

Ibn Abu Hatim said, "I made these words all the benefit I got from visiting Damascus."[88]

Imam al-Junayd al-Baghdadi (d. 297 AH/ 919 CE)

The Imam of the world in his time, al-Junayd al-Baghdadi, defining a Sufi said:[89]

> The Sufi is the one who wears wool on top of purity, follows the path of the Prophet ﷺ, endures bodily strains, and leaves behind all that pertains to the world.[90]

al-Hakim al-Tirmidhi (d. 320 AH/ 942 CE)

Abu Abd Allah Muhammad ibn Ali al-Hakim al-Tirmidhi al-Hanafi, was a *faqih* and *muhaddith* of Khorasan, and one of the great early authors of *tasawwuf* who is quoted extensively by Ibn Arabi. He wrote many books, of which the following have been published:

---

[88] *Op. cit.*

[89] al-Junayd, *Kitab dawa al-arwah,* ed. & trans. A.J. Arberry in Journal of the Royal Asiatic Society (1937).

[90] A saying by Abu Ali al-Rudhabari (d. 322), narrated by Suyuti in his book on *tasawwuf* entitled *Tayid al-haqiqa al-aliyya* (Cairo: al-matbaa al-islamiyya, 1352/1934) p. 15.

- *al-Masail al-maknuna*: The Concealed Matters
- *Adab al-nafs*: The Discipline of the Ego
- *Adab al-muridin*: Ethics of the Seekers of God, or Ethics of Sufi Students
- al-amthal min al-kitab wa al-sunnah: Examples from the Quran and the Sunnah
- *Asrar mujahadat al-nafs*: The Secrets of the Struggle against the Ego
- *Ilm al-awliya*: The Knowledge of the Saints
- *Khatm al-wilaya*: The Seal of Sainthood
- *Shifa al-ilal*: The Healing of Defects
- *Kitab manazil al-ibad min al-ibadah, aw, Manazil al-qasidin ila Allah*: The Book of the Positions of Worshippers in Relation to Worship, or: The Positions of the Travelers to God
- *Kitab marifat al-asrar*: Book of the Knowledge of Secrets
- *Kitab al-Ada wa-al-nafs; wa al-aql wa al-hawa*: The Book of the Enemies, the Ego, the Mind, and Vain Desires
- *al-Manhiyyat*: The Prohibitions
- *Nawadir al-usul fi marifat ahadith al-Rasul*: The Rare Sources of the Religion Concerning the Knowledge of the Prophet's Sayings
- *Tabai al-nufus: wa-huwa al-kitab al-musamma bi al-akyas wa al-mughtarrin*: The Different Characters of Souls, or: The Book of the Clever Ones and the Deluded Ones
- *al-Kalam ala mana la ilaha illa Allah*: Discourse on the Meaning of "There is no god but God"

Imam al-Qushayri (d. 465 AH/1072 CE)

Imam al-Qushayri said about Sufism:

God made this group the best of His saints. He honored them above all of His servants after His messengers and prophets. He made their hearts the secrets of His Divine Presence. He chose them from among the Community to receive His Lights. They are the means of humanity. He purified them from all connections to this world. He lifted them to the highest states of vision. He unveiled to them the Realities of His Unique Oneness. He made them observe His Will operating in them. He made them shine in His Existence and appear as lights of His Lights.[91]

Imam Ghazali (450-505 AH/1058-1111 CE)

Imam Ghazali, the "Proof of Islam," said about Sufism:

I know to be true that the Sufis are the seekers in God's Way. Their conduct is the best conduct. Their way is the best way. Their manners are the most sanctified. They have purified their hearts from other than God and they have made them as pathways for rivers to run receiving knowledge of the Divine Presence.[92]

Imam Fakhr ad-Din Ar-Razi (544-606 AH/1149-1209 CE)

Imam Fakhr ad-Din al-Razi said:

The way the Sufis seek knowledge is to disconnect themselves from this worldly life, and keep themselves constantly busy in their mind and in their heart with *dhikr Allah* during all their actions and behaviours.[93]

Imam Nawawi (620-676 AH/1223-1278 CE)

Imam Nawawi said, in his *al-Maqasid*:

The specifications of the Way of the Sufis are five:

1. To keep the Presence of God in your heart in public and in private.
2. To follow the *Sunnah* of the Prophet ﷺ by actions and speech.
3. To keep away from dependence on people.
4. To be happy with what God gives you, even if it is little.
5. To always refer your matters to God, Almighty and Exalted.[94]

Ibn Taymiyya (661-728 AH/1263-1328 CE)

In his *Majmua fatawa*, Ibn Taymiyya says:

You have to know that the rightly guided shaykhs must be taken as

---

[91] Imam al-Qushayri, *ar-Risalat al-Qushayriyya*, p. 2.

[92] Imam Ghazali, *al-Munqidh min ad-dalal*, p. 131.

[93] Imam Fakhr ad-Din ar-Razi, *Itiqadat furaq al-muslimin*, pp. 72-73.

[94] Imam Nawawi, *Maqasid at-tawhid*, p. 20.

guides and examples in the faith, as they follow in the footsteps of the prophets and messengers. The Way of those shaykhs is to call people to God's Divine Presence and obedience to the Prophet ﷺ... The shaykhs whom we need to take as guides are our examples, and we have to follow them. As when on the prescribed pilgrimage, one needs a guide to reach the Kabah, these shaykhs are our guide to God and our Prophet ﷺ.[95]

Ibn Taymiyya quotes from Bayazid al-Bistami:

The great Sufi shaykh, Bayazid al-Bistami, and the famous story of when he saw God in a vision and said to Him, "O God, what is the way to You?" And God responded, "Leave yourself and come to Me."

I shed my self as a snake sheds its skin.[96]

Implicit in this quotation is an indication of the need for self-denial or abstention from worldly life, as that was the path followed by Bayazid al-Bistami. So we see from the above quotes that Ibn Taymiyya accepted many shaykhs by quoting them and urging people to follow guides to show the way, to obey God and to obey the Prophet ﷺ.

IBN TAYMIYYA DEFINES THE TERM "SUFISM"

What Ibn Taymiyya said about the definition of Sufism:

Praise belongs to God, the use of the word Sufism has been thoroughly discussed. This is a term that was given to those who were dealing with that branch of knowledge.[97]

Sufism is the science of realities and states of experience. The Sufi is that one who purifies himself from everything which distracts him from the remembrance of God. (The Sufi) is so filled with knowledge of the heart and knowledge of the mind that the value of gold and stones will be equal to him. Sufism safeguards the precious meanings and leaves behind the call to fame and vanity to reach the state of truthfulness. The best of humans after the

---

[95] *Majmua fatawa Ibn Taymiyya*, vol. 11 (Book of Tasawwuf), p. 497.

[96] *Op. cit.*, p. 499.

[97] *Op. cit.*, vol. 10, (Book of *Ilm as-suluk*), p. 510.

prophets are the truthful ones, as God mentioned them in the Quran, "*All who obey God and the Messenger are in the company of those on whom is the grace of God: the prophets, the sincere lovers of truth (siddiqeen), the martyrs and the righteous. Ah! What a beautiful fellowship*" (4:69) . . . (Sufis) strive to be obedient to God. Among them you will find the foremost in nearness by virtue of their striving, and some of them are among the People of the Right Hand . . .[98]

IBN TAYMIYYA ON SAINTS AND SAINTHOOD

A servant of God, Almighty and Exalted, cannot be considered a saint unless he is a true believer. God mentions in the Quran:

> *Now surely, on the friends of God there is no fear, nor shall they grieve; those who believe and guard against evil.* (10:62-63)

He then quotes the famous Tradition from Bukhari:

> *My servant draws not near to Me with anything more loved by Me than the religious duties I have enjoined upon him, and My servant continues to draw near to Me with supererogatory works so that I shall love him. When I love him I am his hearing with which he hears, his seeing with which he sees, his hand with which he strikes, and his foot with which he walks. Were he to ask (something) of Me, I would surely give it to him, and were he to ask Me for refuge, I would surely grant him it. I do not hesitate about anything as much as I hesitate about (seizing) the soul of My faithful servant: he hates death and I hate hurting him.*[99]

He explains the phrase, "*Whoever comes against one of My saints is challenging Me to fight*" thus:

> It means that God is expressing: "I will seek revenge against anyone who comes against My saints like an aggressive lion."[100]

IBN TAYMIYYA ON MIRACLES OF SAINTS

Ibn Taymiyya continues in the same book:

---

[98] *Op. cit.*, vol. 11, p. 497.

[99] *Op. cit.*, p. 190.

[100] *Op. cit.*, p. 314.

What is considered as a miracle for a saint is that sometimes the saint might hear something that others do not hear or see something that others do not see, not while asleep, but in a wakened state of vision. He can know something, through revelation or inspiration, that others cannot know.[101]

In another book, he writes:

The miracles of saints are absolutely true and correct, and acknowledged by all Muslim scholars. The Quran has pointed to it in different places, and the Traditions of the Prophet ﷺ have mentioned it. Whoever denies the miraculous power of saints are innovators or following innovators.[102]

He continues quoting the Prophet's ﷺ saying about the saints:

You are the witnesses of God on earth.

IBN TAYMIYYA ON THE UNVEILING OF APPEARANCES

God Almighty will unveil to his saints states that have never been unveiled before. He will give them support without measure. If that saint begins to speak from the things of the unseen, past or present or future, it is considered miraculous knowledge. Anything that a saint does for people or for listeners, which is from the unseen, of healing, or teaching knowledge is accepted, and we must thank God for it. [103]

IBN TAYMIYYA CITES SOME GREAT SUFI SHAYKHS

In the volume entitled *Ilm as-suluk,* he says:

The great Sufi shaykhs are well known and accepted, such as Bayazid al-Bistami, Shaykh Abd al-Qadir Gilani, Junayd ibn Muhammad, Hasan al-Basri, al-Fudayl ibn al-Ayyad, Ibrahim bin al-Adham, Abi Sulayman ad-Darani, Maruf al-Karkhi, Sari as-Saqati, Shaykh Hammad and Shaykh Abul Bayan... Those great

---

[101] *Op. cit.*

[102] *Mukhtasar al-fatawa al-masriyya,* p. 603.

[103] *Majmua fatawa Ibn Taymiyya,* vol. 11, p. 313.

> Sufis were the leaders of humanity. They call to what is right and forbid what is wrong.[104]

IBN TAYMIYYA'S QADIRI LINEAGE AS A SUFI SHAYKH

At present, we are in a position to go much further than saying that Ibn Taymiyya simply praised Sufism. We can say with definitiveness that he was an aspirant in the Sufi Way, primarily in the Qadiri Order, of Shaykh Abd al-Qadir Gilani.

In a unique manuscript of the Hanbali Yusuf ibn Abd al-Hadi (d. 909 AH/1503 CE), entitled *Bad al-ulqa bi labs al khirqa,* Ibn Taymiyya is listed in a Sufi spiritual genealogy with other well-known Hanbali scholars. The links in this genealogy are, in descending order from Abd al-Qadir Gilani:

- Shaykh Abd al-Qadir Gilani (d. 561 AH/1165 CE)
- Abu Umar ibn Qudama (d. 607 AH/1210 CE)
- Muwaffaq ad-Din ibn Qadama (d. 620 AH/1223 CE)
- Ibn Ali ibn Qudama (d. 682 AH/1283 CE)
- Ibn Taymiyya (d. 728 AH/1328 CE)
- Ibn Qayyim al-Jawziyya (d. 751 AH/1350 CE)
- Ibn Rajab (d. 795 AH/1393 CE)[105]

Furthermore, there is another unique manuscript of the work of Ibn Taymiyya himself. Here are Ibn Taymiyya's own words, as quoted from a work of his, *al-Masala at-Tabriziyya,*

> I wore the blessed Sufi cloak of my Shaykh Abd al-Qadir Gilani, there being between him and me two Sufi shaykhs.[106]

> In another manuscript he said:

> I have worn the Sufi cloak of a number of Sufi shaykhs, belonging to various Ways, among them Abd al-Qadir Gilani, whose Way is the greatest of the well-known ones, may God have mercy on him.

---

[104] *Op. cit.*, vol. 10, p. 516.

[105] *Bad al-ulqa bi labs al-khirqa,* fol. 171b-172a.

[106] Jamal al-din al-Talyani. *Targhib al-mutahabbin fi labs khirqaat al-mutamayyazin,* quoting from Ibn Taymiyya, *al-Masala at-tabriziyya,* fol. 67a.

After him the lineage continues on to his student, Ibn Qayyim al-Jawziyya and then to his student, Ibn Rajab.

THE SUFI CLOAK

Before proceeding to Imam Ibn Qayyim, it may be useful to say something about the wearing of the Sufi cloak. In the view of the trustworthy, there are three categories of shaykhs: the shaykh of the cloak; the shaykh of the *dhikr*; the shaykh of guidance.

The first two categories (the shaykh of the cloak and the shaykh of the *dhikr*) are really deputies of a shaykh, representing the reality of the shaykh of the Way through the intermediary of either the cloak or the *dhikr*. The shaykh of the cloak depends on the power of the cloak to act on the disciple. The disciple takes his support from the cloak, which a fully realized shaykh of guidance has imbued with his blessings.

The disciple of the shaykh of *dhikr* is supported by the *dhikr*, not directly by the shaykh. In these two cases, the shaykh becomes the symbol, because the real support of the disciple is the cloak or the *dhikr*.

The highest of the three categories is the shaykh of guidance. He is the one who supports the disciple without any intermediary, directly from himself to the disciple. He is the real shaykh because, without any means, he supports and directs the disciple directly through his heart. That is why Ahmad al-Faruqi said, "In our Path, the shaykh guides the disciple directly, unlike other Sufi orders which use the cloak and other means to lift up their disciples."

In the Naqshbandi Order only one shaykh, the shaykh of guidance, is therefore accepted as possessing real authority. When that shaykh passes away, the disciples must renew their initiation with his successor, to whom he has transmitted all his secrets and his inheritance from the Prophet ﷺ and all his predecessors in the Golden Chain.

Ibn Qayyim (691-751 AH/1292-1350 CE)

Ibn Qayyim stated:

> We can witness the greatness of the people of Sufism in the eyes of the earliest generations of Muslims by what has been mentioned by Sufyan al-Thawri (d. 161 AH/777 CE), one of the greatest imams in the second century and one of the foremost legal scholars. He said, "If it had not been for Abu Hisham al-Sufi (d. 115 AH/733 CE), I

would never have perceived the action of the subtlest forms of hypocrisy in the self... Among the best of people is the Sufi learned in jurisprudence."[107]

Ibn Khaldun (733-808 AH/1332-1406 CE)

Ibn Khaldun said:

> The way of the Sufis is the way of our predecessors from the scholars among the Companions, their followers, and their successors. Its basis is to worship God and to leave the ornaments of this world and its pleasures.[108]

Tajuddin As-Subki (727-771 AH/1327-1370 CE)

Tajuddin as-Subki mentioned in his book *Muid an-naam*, under the chapter entitled Sufism:

> May God praise them and greet them. May God cause us to be with them in Paradise. Too many things have been said about them and too many ignorant people have said things which have no relation to them. The truth is that they have left this world and are busy with worship... They are the people of God, whose supplications and prescribed prayers God accepts, and by means of whom, God supports human beings.[109]

Jalaluddin as-Suyuti (849-911 AH/1445-1505 CE)

He said in his book *Tayid al-haqiqat al-aliyya*:

> Sufism, in itself, is the best and most honorable knowledge. It explains how to follow the *Sunnah* of the Prophet ﷺ and to put aside innovation.[110]

Abd Allah ibn Muhammad ibn Abd al-Wahhab (1115-1201 AH/1703-1787 CE)

The following is a quotation from a book by Muhammad Mansur Numani:

---

[107] *Manazil as-sairin.*

[108] Ibn Khaldun, *Muqaddiman Ibn Khaldun*, p. 328.

[109] Tajuddin as-Subki, *Muid an-niam*, p. 190.

[110] Jalaluddin as-Suyuti, *Tayid al-haqiqat al-aliyya*, p. 57.

> Shaykh Abd Allah, the son of Shaykh Muhammad ibn Abd al-Wahhab, said about Sufism, "My father and I do not deny or criticize the science of Sufism, but on the contrary we support it because it purifies the external and the internal of the hidden sins which are related to the heart and the outward form. Even though the individual might externally be on the right way, internally he might be on the wrong way. Sufism is necessary to correct it."[111]

In the fifth volume of the collection of letters by Muhammad ibn Abd al-Wahhab, he states:

> I never accused Ibn Arabi or Ibn al-Farid of unbelief for their Sufi interpretations.[112]

Ibn Abidin (1198-1252 AH/1784-1836 CE)

The great scholar, Ibn Abidin states:

> The seekers in this Way do not hear except from the Divine Presence. They do not love any but Him. If they remember Him, they cry. If they thank Him, they are happy. If they find Him, they are awake. If they see Him, they will be relaxed. If they walk in His Divine Presence, they melt. They are drunk with His Blessings. May God bless them.[113]

Shaykh Muhammad Abduh (1265-1323 AH/1849-1905 CE)

> Sufism appeared in the first century of Islam and it received a tremendous honor. It purified the self, straightened the conduct and gave knowledge to people from the wisdom and secrets of the Divine Presence.[114]

---

[111] Muhammad Manzur Numani. *Ad-Diaat al-mukaththafa did ash-shaykh Muhammad ibn Abdul Wahhab*, p. 85.

[112] *Ar-Rasail ash-shakhsiyya* (Letters by Muhammad ibn Abdul Wahhab), pp. 12, 61, 64.

[113] Ibn Abidin, *Rasail ibn Abidin*, pp. 172-173.

[114] *Majallat al-muslim*, p. 24.

Shaykh Rashid Rida (1282-1354 AH/1865-1935 CE)

> Sufism was a unique pillar from the pillars of the religion. Its purpose was to purify the self and to take account of one's daily behavior and to raise the people to a high station of spirituality.[115]

Mawlana Abul Hasan Ali an-Nadwi (B. 1331 AH/1913 CE)

Mawlana Abul Hasan Ali an-Nadwi is a member of the Islamic-Arabic Society of India and Muslim countries. He said in his book, *Muslims in India,* written some years ago:

> These Sufis initiate people in Oneness and sincerity in following the *Sunnah* of the Prophet ﷺ, in repentance from their sins and in avoidance of every disobedience to God, Almighty and Exalted. Their guides encourage them to move in the way of perfect Love of God.[116]
>
> In Calcutta, India, everyday more than a thousand people are being initiated into Sufism. Thanks to the influence of Sufi people, thousands and hundreds of thousands in India found their Lord and reached a state of perfection through the Islamic religion.[117]

Abul Ala Mawdudi (1321-1399 AH/1903-1979 CE)

Mawdudi said in his book *Mabadi al-Islam*:

> Sufism is a reality whose signs are the love of God and the love of the Prophet ﷺ, where one absents oneself for their sake and one is annihilated from anything other than them. It instructs how to follow in the footsteps of the Prophet ﷺ.
>
> Sufism searched for sincerity of heart, purity of intention, and trustworthiness of obedience in all of an individual's actions. The Divine Law and Sufism: what is the similitude of the two? They are like the body and the soul. The body is the external knowledge, the Divine Law, and the spirit is the internal knowledge.[118]

---

[115] *Op. cit.,* p. 726.

[116] *Muslims in India,* pp. 140-146.

[117] *Op. cit.*

[118] *Mabadi al-islam,* p. 17.

Conclusion

In summary, Sufism, in the present as in the past, is the effective means for spreading the reality of Islam, extending the knowledge and understanding of spirituality, and fostering happiness and peace. With it, human beings can find themselves, and in so doing, find their Lord. With it, human beings can improve, transform, and elevate themselves and find salvation from the ignorance of this world and the misguided pursuit of some materialistic fantasy. And God knows best what He intends for His servants.

The crucible itself tells you, when you are strained,
Whether you are gold or gold-plated copper.
(Sanai)[119]

[119] Thackston, p. 156.

Dhikr: Remembrance of God

Before we speak about the Naqshbandi method of *dhikr* and specific practices, we would like to clarify the principles of *dhikr*, or remembrance of God. In this chapter, we provide clear evidence that *dhikr* is Islamic, that it provides countless benefits, and that it was observed by the Prophet ﷺ and Companions.

Dhikr is the Greatest Obligation and a Divine Command

Dhikr, or remembrance of God (*Allah*), is the most excellent act of God's servants, and is stressed over a hundred times in the Holy Quran. It is the most praiseworthy practice to earn God's pleasure, the most effective weapon to overcome the enemy, and the deed most deserving of reward. It is the flag of Islam, the polished heart, the essence of the science of faith, the immunization against hypocrisy, the foremost worship, and the key of all success.

There are no restrictions on the method, frequency, or timing of *dhikr* whatsoever. Any restrictions on method pertain to certain specific obligatory acts that are not the issue here, such as *salat*. The *Shariah* is clear and everyone is aware of these obligations. Indeed, the Prophet ﷺ said that the People of Paradise will regret only one thing, not having made enough *dhikr* in the world!

God says in His Holy Book:

O Believers, make abundant mention of God! (33:41)

He also says His servants are *"those who remember their Lord standing, sitting, and lying on their sides."* (3:191); in other words, those who remember Him at all times of the day and night.

God said:

> *The creation of heaven and earth and the changes of night and day are signs for people who have wisdom—those who remember God standing up, sitting, and lying on their sides . . .* (3:190-191)

Aisha ؓ said, as narrated by Muslim, that the Prophet ﷺ remembered God at all times of the day and night.

The Prophet ﷺ said:

If your hearts were always in the state that they are in during dhikr, the angels would come to see you to the point that they would greet you in the middle of the road.[120]

Imam Nawawi commented on this *hadith* saying, "This kind of sight is shown to someone who persists in meditation (*muraqabah*), reflection (*fikr*), and anticipation (*iqbal*) of the next world."[121]

Muadh ibn Jabal ؓ said that the Prophet ﷺ also said:

The People of Paradise will not regret except one thing alone: the hour that passed them by and in which they made no remembrance of God.[122]

God placed His remembrance above prayer in value by making prayer the means and remembrance the goal. He said:

Lo! Worship guards one from lewdness and iniquity, but verily, remembrance of God is greatest. (29:45)

He is successful who purifies himself, and remembers the name of his Lord, and so prays. (87:14-15)

So establish prayer for My remembrance. (20:14)

Qadi Abu Bakr ibn al-Arabi explains that no good deed is valid without *dhikr*, and whoever does not remember God in his heart at the time of his charity or fasting, for example, has left that deed is incomplete. Therefore, *dhikr* may be seen as the best of deeds.[123]

In fact, all creation does *dhikr*, because God said that all creation praises Him constantly, and *tasbih* is a kind of *dhikr*. God said of the Prophet Jonah (Yunus) ؑ, when the whale swallowed him:

Had he not been one of My glorifiers (musabbihin), he would have remained inside the whale's stomach until Judgment Day. (37:143-144)

---

[120] Muslim narrated it.

[121] Nawawi, *Sharh sahih muslim*

[122] Narrated by Bayhaqi in *Shuab al-iman* (1:392 #512-513) and by Tabarani. Haythami in *Majma al-zawaid* (10:74) said that its narrators are all trustworthy (*thiqat*), while Suyuti declared it *hasan* in his *Jami al-saghir* (#7701).

[123] Related by Ibn Hajar in his *Fath al-bari* (1989 ed. 11:251).

Dhikr is something of tremendous importance. Abu Hurayra 🙵 said that the Prophet 🕮 said:

> The earth and everything in it is cursed, except for dhikr and what attends dhikr, and the teacher, and the student.[124]

By the words *"the world and everything in it,"* the Prophet 🕮 refers to all that which claims status or existence apart from God. This *hadith* also stresses the importance of following a teacher of knowledge, so as not to incur curse instead of blessing. This is what Abu Yazid al-Bistami meant when he said, "Whoever has no shaykh, his shaykh is Satan." This is confirmed by two other *ahadith* of the Prophet 🕮:

> Abu Bakrah 🙵 said: I heard the Prophet 🕮 say, "Become a learned person (alim), or a student of knowledge (mutallim), or an auditor of knowledge (mustami), or an amateur of knowledge (muhibb), but do not be the fifth one for you will perish."[125]

Sakhawi said:

> Ibn Abd al-Barr said, "The fifth one is one who shows enmity towards the scholars and contempt of them, and whoever does not love them shows contempt for them or is on the brink of having contempt for them, and there lies destruction."[126]

The Prophet 🕮 said, *"Blessing is with your elders."* [127] Another narration has:

> When the young teach the old, then blessing has been lifted.[128]

---

[124] Narrated by Tirmidhi who said it is *hasan*, Ibn Majah who said the same, Bayhaqi, and others. Suyuti cites it in *al-Jami al-saghir* from al-Bazzar's similar narration from Ibn Masud and he declared it *sahih*. Tabarani also narrated it in *al-Awsat* from Abu al-Darda.

[125] Al-Haythami said in *Majma al-zawaid* (1:122): "Tabarani narrated it in *al-Mujam al-saghir* (2:9), *al-Mujam al-awsat*, and *al-Mujam al-kabir*, also al-Bazzar (in his *Musnad*), and its narrators are considered trustworthy." It is also narrated by Abu Nuaym in *Hilyat al-awliya* (7:237) and al-Khatib in *Tarikh Baghdad* (12:295).

[126] Sakhawi, *al-Maqasid al-hasana* (p. 88 #134). See Ibn Abd al-Barr's *Jami bayan al-ilm wa fadlih* (1:30).

[127] Narrated by Ibn Hibban in his *Sahih*, al-Hakim who said it is *sahih*, and Ibn Daqiq al-Eid confirmed him.

[128] See Sakhawi's *al-Maqasid al-hasana* (p. 158-159 #290).

The one who engages in *dhikr* has the highest rank of all before God. The people who call on God without distraction have been mentioned in Quran. The effect that calling has on their hearts has also been mentioned:

In houses which God has permitted to be exalted and that His name may be remembered in them; there glorify Him therein in the mornings and the evenings, Men whom neither merchandise nor selling diverts from the remembrance of God . . . (24:36-37)

Those who believe, and whose hearts find their rest in the remembrance of God—for, verily, in the remembrance of God hearts do find their rest. (13:28)

A *hadith* states:

During the Night Journey and Ascension, the Prophet ﷺ was taken up to a point where he heard the screeching of the Pens, which signifies the writing of the divine Decree. He saw a man who had disappeared into the light of the Throne. The Prophet ﷺ said, "Who is this? Is this an angel?" It was said to him, "No." He said, "Is it a Prophet?" Again the answer was no. He said, "Who is it then?" The answer was, "This is a man whose tongue was moist with God's remembrance in the world, and his heart was attached to the mosques, and he never incurred the curse of his father and mother."[129]

In another *hadith*, it is reported:

A man came to the Prophet ﷺ and said, "O Prophet of God, the laws and conditions of Islam have become too many for me. Tell me something that I can always keep." The Prophet ﷺ said, "Keep your tongue always moist with the dhikr of God."[130]

In other words, the man wanted something particular, as opposed to the many rules and conditions that must be kept in general. He wanted something that he would be sure to uphold.

---

[129] Shaykh Muhammad Alawi al-Maliki cited it in his collated text of the sound narrations on that topic entitled *al-Anwar al-bahiyya min Isra wa miraj khayr al-bariyya*.

[130] Ahmad, Tirmidhi, Ibn Majah, and Ibn Hibban declared that this *hadith* is fair *(hasan)*.

It is well-known in Islam that the best work in the path of God is jihad. Yet the Prophet ﷺ placed *dhikr* even above jihad in the following authentic *ahadith*.

Abu ad-Darda ؓ narrates:

> *The Prophet ﷺ once asked his companions, "Shall I tell you about the best of all deeds, the best act of piety in the eyes of your Lord, which will elevate your status in the Hereafter, and carries more virtue than the spending of gold and silver in the service of God or taking part in jihad and slaying or being slain in the path of God? The* dhikr *of God."*[131]

Abu Saeed narrates:

> *The Prophet ﷺ was asked, "Which of the servants of God is best in rank before God on the Day of Resurrection?" He said, "The ones who remember him much." I said, "O Messenger of God, what about the fighter in the way of God?" He answered, ". . . truly those who do* dhikr *are better than him in rank."*[132]

Abd Allah ibn Umar ؓ said that the Prophet ﷺ said:

> *Everything has a polish, and the polish of hearts is* dhikr *of God. Nothing is more calculated to rescue from God's punishment than* dhikr *of God. He was asked whether this did not apply also to jihad in God's path, and he replied, "Not even if one should ply his sword until it breaks."*[133]

Meanings of *Dhikr*

The word *dhikr* has various meanings: the Book of God and its recitation, prayer, learning, and teaching: The author of *Fiqh al-sunnah* said in his chapter on *dhikr*:

> Said ibn Jubayr said, "Anyone engaged in obeying God is in fact engaged in the remembrance of God." Some of the earlier scholars tied it to some more specified form. Aata said, "The gatherings of *dhikr* are the gatherings where the lawful and the prohibited things

---

[131] Related in Malik's *Muwatta*, the *Musnad* of Ahmad, the *Sunan* of Tirmidhi, Ibn Majah, and the *Mustadrak* of Hakim. Al-Bayhaqi, Hakim and others declared it *sahih*.

[132] Related in Ahmad, Tirmidhi, and Bayhaqi.

[133] Bayhaqi narrated it in *Kitab al-daawat al-kabir* as well as in his *Shuab al-iman* (1:396 #522), also al-Mundhiri in *al-Targhib* (2:396) and Tibrizi mentions it in *Mishkat al-masabih*, at the end of the book of Supplications.

are discussed, for instance, selling, buying, prayers, fasting, marriage, divorce, and pilgrimage."

Qurtubi said:

Gatherings of *dhikr* are the gatherings for knowledge and admonition, those in which the Word of God and the *Sunnah* of His Messenger ﷺ, accounts of our righteous predecessors, and sayings of the righteous scholars are learned and practiced without any addition or innovation, and without any ulterior motives or greed.

Dhikr can also mean: invocation of God with the tongue, according to one of the formulas taught by the Prophet ﷺ, or any other formula, and remembrance of God in the heart, or with both the heart and the tongue.

The present text is concerned with the last two meanings: that of the mentioning of God, as in the verse, "*The believers are those who, when they hear God mentioned, their hearts tremble*" (8:2); and the Prophet's ﷺ saying, "The best *dhikr* is *la ilaha illallah*."[134] The Prophet ﷺ did not say, "the best *dhikr* is giving a lecture," or "giving advice," or "raising funds."

The present text is also concerned with the meaning of remembrance through the heart, as exemplified by the verse: "*The men and women who remember God abundantly*" (33:35). The Prophet ﷺ both praised and explained the verse when he said, "The single-hearted are foremost."[135] When asked, "O Messenger of God, who are the single-hearted?" he replied, "The men and women who remember God abundantly."

The Prophet ﷺ further clarified the role of the heart in effecting such remembrance of God when he said to Abu Hurayra ؓ:

Go with these two sandals of mine and whoever you meet behind this wall that witnesses that there is no god except God with certitude in his heart, give him glad tidings that he will enter Paradise.[136]

---

[134] In Tirmidhi and Ibn Majah from Ibn Jubayr.

[135] Related in Muslim.

[136] Narrated by Muslim.

Dhikr may sometimes mean both inner remembrance and outward mention, as in the verse, *"Remember Me, and I shall remember you"* (2:152), when it is read in light of the *hadith qudsi*:

> *Those that remember Me in their heart, I remember them in My heart; and those that remember Me in a gathering (i.e. that make mention of Me), I remember them (i.e. make mention of them) in a gathering better than theirs.*

This important *hadith* will be explained in greater detail later.

Broadly speaking, there are three types of *dhikr*: that of the heart, that of the tongue, and that of the two together.

Ibn Hajar explained that, according to Abu ad-Darda's ﵁ narration of the primacy of *dhikr* over jihad, what is meant by *dhikr* is the complete *dhikr* and consciousness of God's greatness, whereby one becomes better, for example, than those who battle the disbelievers without such recollection.[137]

In another *hadith* narrated by Bukhari, the Prophet ﷺ compared those who make *dhikr* among those who do not, to those who are alive among the dead.[138]

Ibn Hajar comments:

> What is meant by *dhikr* here is the utterance of the expressions which we have been encouraged to say, and say abundantly, such as the enduring good deeds (*al-baqiyat al-salihat*), and they are: *"subhanallah," "Alhamdulillah," "la ilaha illallah," "allahu akbar,"* and all that is related to them such as the *hawqala* (*"la hawla wa la quwwata illa billah"*), the *basmala* (*"bismillah al-rahman al-rahim"*), the *hasbala* (*"hasbunallahu wa nima al-wakil"*), *istighfar*, and the like, as well as invocations for the good of this world and the next.

Dhikr also applies to diligence in obligatory or praiseworthy acts, such as the recitation of Quran, the reading of *hadith*, the study of the sciences of Islam, and supererogatory prayers.

Dhikr can take place with the tongue, for which the one who utters it receives reward—and it is not necessary for this that he understand or

---

[137] Ibn Hajar, *Fath al-Bari* (1989 ed. 11:251)

[138] Book of *daawat* ch. 66 "The merit of *dhikr Allah*."

recall its meaning, on condition that he not mean other than its meaning by its utterance. If, in addition to its utterance, there is *dhikr* in the heart, then it is more complete. If there is, added to that, the recollection of the meaning of the *dhikr* and what it entails, such as magnifying God and exalting Him above defect or need, it is even more complete. If all this takes place inside a good deed, whether an obligatory prayer or other than that, it is even more complete. If one perfects one's turning to God and purifies one's sincerity towards Him, then that is the farthest perfection.

Fakhr ad-Din al-Razi said:

> What is meant by the *dhikr* of the tongue is the expressions that stand for *tasbih* (exaltation), *tahmid* (praise), and *tamjid* (glorification). As for the *dhikr* of the heart, it consists in reflection on the proof-texts that point to God's essence and His attributes, on those of the obligations, including what is enjoined and what is forbidden, so that one may examine the rulings that pertain to them, and on the secrets of God's creation.
>
> As for *dhikr* of the limbs, it consists in their being immersed in obedience, and that is why God named prayer *"dhikr"* when He said, *"When the call is proclaimed on Friday, hasten earnestly to the remembrance of God."* (62:9)
>
> It is reported from some of the Knowers of God that *dhikr* has seven aspects:
>
> - *Dhikr* of the eyes, which consists in weeping (*buka*);
> - *Dhikr* of the ears, which consists in listening (*isgha*);
> - *Dhikr* of the tongue, which consists in praise (*thana*);
> - *Dhikr* of the hands, which consists in giving (*ata*);
> - *Dhikr* of the body, which consists in loyalty (*wafa*);
> - *Dhikr* of the heart, which consists in fear and hope (*khawf wa raja*);
> - *Dhikr* of the spirit, which consists of utter submission and acceptance (*taslim wa rida*)."[139]

[139] Ibn Hajar, *Fath al-Bari* (1989 ed. 11:250).

Loudness in *Dhikr*

The Prophet ﷺ praised a man who was *awwah* (literally: one who says, "ah, ah!"); that is, loud in his *dhikr*, even when others censured him. Ahmad narrated with a good chain from Uqba ibn Amir:

The Prophet ﷺ said of a man named Dhu al-Bijadayn, "He is a man who frequently says 'ah.'" He was a man abundant in dhikr Allah, with Quran recitation, and he raised his voice high when supplicating.[140]

God said of the Prophet Abraham ﷺ:

Verily, Abraham was most tender-hearted, forbearing. (9:114, 11:75)

That is, according to *Tafsir al-jalalayn*, "Crying out and suffering much, out of fear and dread of his Lord." The Prophet ﷺ prayed to be *awwah* in the following invocation, "O God, make me one who often cries out 'ah' to you (*rabbi ijalni ilayka awwahan*)." This is narrated by Tirmidhi,[141] Ibn Majah,[142] and Ahmad[143] with a strong chain in the following words:

The Prophet ﷺ supplicated thus:

O my Lord! help me and do not cause me to face difficulty; grant me victory and do not grant anyone victory over me; devise for me and not against me; guide me and facilitate guidance for me; make me overcome whoever rebels against me; O my Lord! make me abundantly thankful to You, abundantly mindful of You, abundantly devoted to You, perfectly obedient to You, lowly and humble before You, always crying out and turning back to You!

Gatherings of Collective, Loud *Dhikr*

The previously quoted *hadith qudsi*, beginning "*Those that remember Me in a gathering,*" presents gatherings of collective, loud *dhikr* as the gateway to realizing God's promise "*Remember Me, and I shall remember you.*" It is no wonder that such gatherings receive the highest praise and blessing from God and His Prophet ﷺ, as narrated in many authentic *ahadith*.

---

[140] Ahmad, *Musnad* (4:159).

[141] Tirmidhi, book of *daawat* #102, *hasan sahih*.

[142] Ibn Majah, *Dua* #2.

[143] Ahmad, *Musnad* 1:227.

According to Bukhari and Muslim:

The Prophet ﷺ said that God has angels roaming the roads to find the people of dhikr *[and in another version of Imam Muslim,* majalis, *or "gatherings" of* dhikr*]. When they find a group of people (*qawm*) reciting dhikr [in a version of Imam Muslim, they sit with them], and they call each other and encompass them in layers reaching up to the first heaven.*[144] *God asks His angels, and He knows already,*[145] *"What are My servants saying?"*[146] *The angels say, "They are praising You (*tasbih*) and magnifying Your Name (*takbir*), and glorifying You (*tahmid*), and giving You the best Attributes (*tamjid*). God says, "Have they seen Me?" The angels answer, "O our Lord! They did not see You . . . " He says, "What if they see Me?" The angels answer, "O our Lord, if they saw You they would be even more fervent in their worship, glorification, and praise." He says, "What are they asking?" The angels say, "They are asking Your Paradise!" He says, "Did they see Paradise?" They say, "O our Lord, no, they have not seen it." He says, "And how will they be if they see it?" They say, "If they see Paradise, they are going to be more attached and attracted to it!" He says, "What are they fearing and running away from?"*[147] *They say, "They are fearing and running away from Hellfire." He says, "And have they seen Hellfire?" They say, "O our Lord, no, they did not see Hellfire." He says, "And how will they be if they see Fire and Hell?" They say, "If they see Your Fire, they are going to be running from it and be even more afraid of it." And God says, "I am making you witness*[148] *that I have forgiven them."*[149] *One of the angels*

---

[144] This is to say, an unlimited number of angels are going to be over that group. He did not say, "when they find one person." Therefore it is a must to be in a group to get this particular reward.

[145] He asks in order to place emphasis on what His servants are doing and to facilitate our understanding.

[146] He did not say "servant," but *ibadi*, "servants" in the plural.

[147] When one says, "*Ya Ghaffar* (O Forgiver), *Ya Sattar* (O Concealer)," it means one fears Him because of his or her sins. One is asking Him to hide his or her sins and forgive him or her.

[148] God needs no witness since He said, "*God is sufficient as witness*" (4:79, 4:166, 10:29, 13:43, 29:52). "*Making you witness*" here means, "Assuring you."

[149] God has forgiven them because, as the beginning of the *hadith* states, they are a group of people reciting the Names of God and remembering Him with His *dhikr*.

says, "O my Lord, someone was there who did not belong to that group, but came for some other need."[150] *God says, "Those are such a group that anyone who sits with them that person will also have his sins forgiven."*

The late Imam Ahmad Mashhur al-Haddad (d. 1416/1995) said in his book *Miftah al-jannah*:

> This *hadith* indicates what merit lies in gathering for *dhikr*, and in everyone present doing it aloud and in unison, because of the phrases, "They are invoking You" in the plural, and "They are the people who sit," meaning those who assemble for remembrance and do it in unison, something which can only be done aloud, since someone whose *dhikr* is silent has no need to seek out a session in someone else's company.
>
> This is further indicated by the *hadith qudsi*:
>
> *God says, I am to My servant as he expects of Me, I am with him when he remembers Me. If he remembers Me in his heart, I remember him to Myself, and if he remembers Me in an assembly, I mention him in an assembly better than his...*[151]

Thus, silent *dhikr* is differentiated from *dhikr* said out loud by His saying: *"remembers Me within himself,"* meaning silently, and *"in an assembly,"* meaning aloud.

Dhikr in a gathering can only be done aloud and in unison. The above *hadith* thus constitutes proof that *dhikr* done out loud in a gathering is an exalted kind of *dhikr*, which is mentioned in the Highest Assembly by our Majestic Lord and the angels who are near to Him, who extol Him night and day, and never tire. (21:20)

The affinity is clearly evident between those who do *dhikr* in the transcendent world, who have been created with an inherently obedient and remembering nature—namely, the angels—and those who do *dhikr* in the dense world, whose natures contain lassitude and distraction—namely, human beings. The reward of the latter for their *dhikr* is that they

---

[150] That person came for some other purpose than *dhikr*, to ask someone for something.

[151] Narrated by both Bukhari and Muslim.

be elevated to a rank similar to that of the Highest Assembly, which is a sufficient honor and favor for anyone.[152]

God has bestowed a special distinction upon those who remember Him. Abu Hurayra ﷺ said:

> *While on the road to Makkah the Prophet ﷺ passed on top of a mountain called Jumdan (frozen in its place), at which time he said, "Move on! Here is Jumdan Mountain, and the single-minded* (al-mufarridun) *are foremost." They said, "Who are the single-minded, O Messenger of God?" He said, "The men and women who remember God."*[153]

In other words, the mountain has overtaken the people because the mountain is reciting *dhikr* also. Ibn Qayyim al-Jawziyya explains that the term *mufarridun* has two meanings here: either the *muwahhidun,* the people engaged in *tawhid* who declare God's Oneness as a group (i.e., not necessarily alone), or those whom he calls *ahad furada,* those engaged in *tawhid* individually, while sitting alone.[154]

From this example it is evident that in Ibn al-Qayyim al-Jawziyya's explanation, sittings of *dhikr* can be in a group or alone. In another explanation of *mufarridun,* also cited by Ibn Qayyim, the reference is to "those that tremble from reciting *dhikr Allah,* entranced with it perpetually, not caring what people say or do about them." This is because the Prophet ﷺ said:

Remember and mention God as much as you want, until people say that you are crazy and foolish.[155]

The *mufarridun* are the people who are really alive. Abu Musa ﷺ reported, "The likeness of the one who remembers his Lord and the one who does not remember Him is like comparing a living to a dead person."[156]

Ibn Umar ﷺ reported:

---

[152] Imam Ahmad Mashhur al-Haddad, *Miftah al-janna,* translated by Mostafa Badawi in *Key to the Garden,* Quilliam Press p. 107-108.

[153] Narrated by Tirmidhi and Muslim, in his *Sahih,* beginning of the book of *Dhikr.*

[154] Ibn Qayyim al-Jawziyya, *Madarij al-salikin.*

[155] Narrated by Ahmad in his *Musnad,* Ibn Hibban in his *Sahih,* and al-Hakim who declared it *sahih.*

[156] Bukhari.

The Prophet ﷺ said, "When you pass by the gardens of Paradise, avail yourselves of them." The Companions asked, "What are the gardens of Paradise, O Messenger of God?" He replied, "The circles of dhikr. There are roaming angels of God who go about looking for the circles of dhikr, and when they find them they surround them closely."[157]

Abu Saeed al-Khudri and Abu Hurayra ؓ reported that the Prophet ﷺ said:

When any group of men remembers God, angels surround them and mercy covers them, tranquility descends upon them, and God mentions them to those who are with Him.[158]

Muslim, Ahmad, and Tirmidhi narrate from Muawiya ؓ:

*The Prophet ﷺ went out to a circle of his Companions and asked, "What made you sit here?" They said, "We are sitting here in order to remember and mention God (*nadhkurullaha*) and to glorify Him (*nahmaduhu*) because He guided us to the path of Islam, and he conferred favors upon us." Thereupon he adjured them by God and asked if that was the only purpose of their sitting there. They said, "By God, we are sitting here for this purpose only." At this the Prophet ﷺ said, "I am not asking you to take an oath because of any misapprehension against you, but only because Gabriel came to me and informed me that God, the Exalted and Glorious, was telling the angels that He is proud of you!*

Note that the *hadith* used the term *jalasna*, or "we sat," in the plural, not singular. It referred to an association of people in a group, not one person.

Shahr ibn Hawshab relates:

One day Abu ad-Darda ؓ entered the Masjid of Bayt al-Maqdis (Jerusalem) and saw people gathered around their admonisher (*mudhakkir*) who was reminding them, and they were raising their voices, weeping, and making invocations. Abu ad-Darda said, "My father's life and my mother's be sacrificed for those who moan over their state before the Day of Moaning!" Then he said, "O Ibn Hawshab, let us hurry and sit with those people. I heard the

[157] Tirmidhi narrated it *(hasan gharib)* and Ahmad.

[158] Narrated by Muslim, Tirmidhi, Ahmad, Ibn Majah, and Bayhaqi.

Prophet say, 'If you see the groves of Paradise, graze in them.' And we said, 'O Messenger of God, what are the groves of Paradise?' He said, 'The circles of remembrance, by the One in Whose hand is my soul, no people gather for the remembrance of God Almighty except the angels surround them closely, and mercy covers them, and God mentions them in His presence, and when they desire to get up and leave, a herald calls them saying, Rise forgiven, your evil deeds have been changed into good deeds!'" Then Abu ad-Darda made towards them and sat with them eagerly.[159]

The above shows evidence for the permissibility of loud *dhikr*, group *dhikr*, and the understanding of *dhikr* as including admonishment and the recounting of stories that benefit the soul.

Types and Frequency of *Dhikr*

Because *dhikr* is the life of the heart, Ibn Taymiyya is quoted by his student, Ibn Qayyim, as saying that *dhikr* is as necessary for the heart as water for the fish. Ibn Qayyim himself wrote a book, *al-Wabil al-sayyib*, on the virtues of *dhikr*, where he lists more than one hundred such virtues, among them: [160]

- It induces love for God. He who seeks access to the love of Almighty God should make *dhikr* profusely. Just as reading and repetition is the door of knowledge, so *dhikr* of God is the gateway to His love.
- *Dhikr* involves *muraqabah* (watchfulness, meditation), through which one reaches the state of *ihsan* (excellence), wherein a person worships God as if he is actually seeing Him.
- The gatherings for *dhikr* are gatherings of angels, and gatherings without *dhikr* are gatherings of Satan.

---

[159] The *hafiz* Ibn al-Jawzi relates it with his chain of transmission in the chapter entitled: "Mention of those of the elite who used to attend the gatherings of story-tellers" of his book *al-Qussas wa al-mudhakkirin* (The Storytellers and the Admonishers) ed. Muhammad Basyuni Zaghlul (Beirut: dar al-kutub al-ilmiyya, 1406/1986) p. 31.

[160] Quoted in Maulana M. Zakariyya Kandhalvi, *Virtues of Dhikr* (Lahore: Kutub Khana Faizi, n.d.) p. 74-76

- By virtue of *dhikr,* the person doing *dhikr* is blessed, as also the person sitting next to him.
- In spite of the fact that *dhikr* is the easiest form of worship (the movement of the tongue being easier than the movement of any other part of the body), it is the most virtuous form.

Dhikr is also a form of *sadaqah* (charity).

Abu Dharr al-Ghifari ﷺ said:

*The Messenger of God ﷺ said, "Charity is for every person every day the sun rises." I said, "O Messenger of God, from what do we give charity if we do not possess property?" He said, "The doors of charity (*sadaqah*) are takbir (i.e. to say, "*Allahu Akbar,*" or God is Greatest);* Subhanallah *(God is exalted high);* alhamdulillah *(all praise is for God);* La ilaha illallah *(there is no god other than God);* Astaghfirullah *(I seek forgiveness from God); enjoining good; forbidding evil. These are all the doors of charity (*sadaqah*) from you which is prescribed for you, and there is a reward for you even in havng intercourse with your wife."*[161]

All words of praise and glory to God, extolling His Perfect Attributes of Power and Majesty, Beauty and Sublimity, whether one utters them by tongue or says them silently in one's heart, are known as *dhikr,* or remembrance of God. He has commanded us to remember Him at all times. God says:

O you who believe! Celebrate the praises of God, and do so often; and glorify Him morning and evening. (33:41-42)

Remember me, I shall remember you. (2:152)

Remembrance of God is the foundation of good deeds. Whoever succeeds in it is blessed with the close friendship of God. That is why the Prophet ﷺ was in a state of remembrance of God at all times. When a man complained, "The laws of Islam are too heavy for me, so tell me something that I can easily follow," the Prophet ﷺ told him, "Let your tongue be always busy with the remembrance of God."[162]

---

[161] Narrated by Ahmad and Ibn Hibban, and there is something of similar effect in Muslim.

[162] Narrated by Ahmad with two sound chains, also by Tirmidhi and Ibn Majah through other chains, and Ibn Hibban who declared it *sahih* as well as al-Hakim.

Remembrance of God is also a means of deliverance from Hellfire. Muadh 🕮 reported:

> The Prophet 🕮 said, "No other act of man is a more effective means for his deliverance from the chastisement of God than the remembrance of God."[163]

Ahmad also reports that the Prophet 🕮 said:

> All that you say in celebration of God's Glory, Majesty, and Oneness, and all your words of Praise for Him gather around the Throne of God. These words resound like the buzzing of bees, and call attention to the person who uttered them to God. Do you not wish to have someone there in the presence of God who would call attention to you?

Meditate as Often as Possible

God ordered that He should be remembered abundantly. Describing the wise men and women who reflect on His signs, the Quran mentions:

> Those who remember God standing, sitting, and lying on their sides. (3:191)

> Those men and women who engage much in God's praise, for them has God prepared forgiveness and a great reward. (33:35)

The author of *Fiqh al-sunnah* says that Mujahid explained, "A person cannot be one of '*those men and women who engage much in God's praise,*' as mentioned in the above verse of the Quran, unless he or she remembers God at all times, standing, sitting, or lying in bed." He also says that when asked how much *dhikr* one should do to be considered one of "*those who remember God much,*" that Ibn as-Salah said that "much" is "when one is constant in supplicating, in the morning, and evening, and in other parts of the day and the night as reported from the Prophet 🕮."

Concerning the above Quranic verses, Ibn Abbas 🕮 said:

All obligations imposed on man by God are clearly marked (by conditions of fulfillment) and one is exempted from them only when one completes them. The only thing that is never considered to have been completed is *dhikr*, for God has set no specific limits for it, and under no circumstances is one allowed to be negligent of it.

---

[163] Narrated by Ahmad.

> God imposed obligations on mankind, and whoever fulfils their conditions does his duty. Whoever prayed at the specified times fulfilling its conditions, completed the obligation of prayer; whoever fasted Ramadan did his duty and completed it; and whoever made the pilgrimage fulfilled that obligation. The exception to this condition is *dhikr*: God did not want to limit it, rather He said in Quran, *"O you who believe! Remember God with much remembrance"* (33:41) and, thus, He did not assign it a limit nor a condition of completion.

It is clear through the above evidence that there is no such thing as too much *dhikr*. The Prophet ﷺ said, "He who loves something mentions it much."[164] Those who love God and His Prophet ﷺ mention God and His Prophet ﷺ. No one will limit this practice except those who do not feel such love.

Imam Ghazali said:[165]

> It is man's soul and spirit that constitute his real nature. Upon death, his state changes in two ways. First, he is now deprived of his eyes, ears and tongue, his hand, his feet, and all his parts, just as he is deprived of family, children, relatives, and all the people he knew, and of his horses and other riding-beasts, his servant-boys, his houses and property, and all that he once owned. There is no distinction to be drawn between his being taken from these things and these things being taken from him, for it is the separation itself that causes pain.

If there was anything in the world in which he had found consolation and peace, then he will greatly lament for it after he dies, and feel the greatest sorrow over losing it. His heart will turn to thoughts of everything he owned, of his power and estates, even, for example, to a shirt he wore and took pleasure from.

However, had he taken pleasure only in the remembrance of God, and consoled himself with Him alone, then his will be great bliss and

---

[164] Narrated by Abu Nuaym in the *Hilya* and Daylami in *Musnad al-firdaws*. Sakhawi cites it in *al-Maqasid al-hasana* p. 393 #1050 and does not comment upon it.

[165] Imam Ghazali, in the fortieth book of his *Ihya* entitled *The Remembrance of Death and The Afterlife* (p. 124 in the translation of T.J. Winter).

perfect happiness. For the barriers that lay between him and his Beloved will now be removed, and he will be free of the obstacles and cares of the world, all of which had distracted him from the remembrance of God. This is one of the aspects of the difference between the states of life and death.

On the same topic Imam Habib al-Haddad said:[166]

> Time and days are a man's capital, while his inclinations, desires, and various ambitions are the highway robbers. The way in which one profits on this journey lies in succeeding in coming to God and in attaining everlasting happiness, while one loses by being veiled from God, and being consigned to the painful torment of the Fire.

For this reason the intelligent believer transforms his breathing into acts of obedience, and interrupts them only with the *dhikr* of God.

The Importance of Silent Remembrance

The author of *Fiqh al-sunnah* writes: The purpose of *dhikr* is to purify hearts and souls and awaken the human conscience. The Quran says:

> *And establish regular prayer, for prayer restrains from shameful and unjust deeds, and remembrance of God is the greatest thing in life, without doubt.* (29:45)

In other words, the remembrance of God has a greater impact in restraining one from shameful and unjust deeds than just the regular, formal prayer. This is so because when a servant opens up his soul to his Lord, extolling His praise, God strengthens him with His light, increasing thereby his faith and conviction, and reassuring his mind and heart. This refers to:

> *Those who believe, and whose hearts find their rest in the remembrance of God—for, verily, in the remembrance of God hearts do find their rest.* (13:28)

And when hearts are satisfied with the Truth, they turn to the highest ideals without being deflected by impulses of desire or lust. This underscores the importance of *dhikr* in man's life. Obviously it would be unreasonable to expect these results just by uttering certain words, for

---

[166] Imam Habib al-Haddad, *Key to the Garden* p. 104.

words of the tongue unsupported by a willing heart are of no consequence. God Himself has taught us the manner in which a person should remember Him, saying:

> *And do bring your Lord to remembrance in your very soul, with humility and in reverence, without loudness in words, in the mornings and evening, and be not of those who are unheedful.* (7:205)

This verse indicates that doing *dhikr* in silence and without raising one's voice is better. Once during a journey the Prophet heard a group of Muslims supplicating aloud. Thereupon the Prophet ﷺ said:

> *Give yourselves a respite, you are not calling upon someone deaf or absent. Surely He Whom you are calling upon is near you and He listens to all. He is nearer to you than the neck of your mount.*[167]

This *hadith* underlines the love and awe a person should feel while engaged in *dhikr*. It is related from Saad ؓ that the Prophet ﷺ said,

> *The best dhikr is the hidden dhikr, and the best money is what suffices.*[168]

Ibn Hajar said, in response to an inquiry regarding Nawawi's saying, "*Dhikr* of the tongue with presence of the heart is preferable to *dhikr* of the heart (without):"[169]

> It is not because *dhikr* of the heart is an established worship in the lexical sense (i.e. consisting in specific formulae) that it is preferable, but because, through it, one intently means in his heart to exalt and magnify God above all else. That is the meaning both of the aforementioned saying of Nawawi and of the saying of some that "There is no reward in *dhikr* of the heart." By denying there is a reward in it, one means "There is no reward in the words, which are not uttered"; and by establishing that there is reward in it, one means "in the fact that the heart is present," as we have just said. Consider this, for it is important. And God knows best. [170]

---

[167] Muslim.

[168] Ahmad narrates it in his *Musnad*, Ibn Hibban in his *Sahih*, and Bayhaqi in *Shuab al-iman*. Nawawi said the *hadith* was not firmly established.

[169] Nawawi, at the end of the chapter entitled "*Dhikr* Gatherings" in his Commentary on *Sahih Muslim*.

[170] Ibn Hajar al-Asqalani, quoted in the *Fatawa hadithiyya* of al-Haytami (p. 48).

Shaykh Muhammad Bahauddin Shah Naqshband, from whom this Order takes its name, said, "There are two methods of *dhikr*; one is silent and one is loud. I chose the silent one because it is stronger and, therefore, more preferable."

Shaykh Amin al-Kurdi said:[171]

> Know that there are two kinds of *dhikr*: "by heart" (*qalbi*) and "by tongue" (*lisani*). Each has its legal proofs in the Quran and the *Sunnah*. The *dhikr* by tongue, which combines sounds and letters, is not easy to perform at all times, because buying, and selling, and other such activities altogether divert one's attention from such *dhikr*. The contrary is true of the *dhikr* by heart, which is named that way in order to signify its freedom from letters and sounds. In that way, nothing distracts one from his *dhikr*: with the heart remember God, secretly from creation, wordlessly, and speechlessly. That remembrance is best of all: out of it flowed the sayings of the saints.

That is why many scholars following the way of Shah Naqshband have chosen the *dhikr* of the heart. Moreover, the heart is the place where the Forgiver casts his gaze, the seat of belief, the receptacle of secrets, and the source of lights. If it is sound, the whole body is sound, and if it is unsound, the whole body is unsound, as was made clear for us by the Chosen Prophet ﷺ.

Something confirming this was narrated on the authority of Aisha ﵂:

> *God favors dhikr above dhikr seventy-fold (meaning, silent dhikr over loud dhikr). On the Day of Resurrection, God will bring back human beings to His account, and the Recording Angels will bring what they have recorded and written, and God the Almighty, will say, "See if something that belongs to My servant was left out." The angels will say, "We left nothing out concerning what we have learnt and recorded, except that we have assessed it and written it." God will say, "O my servant, I have something good of yours for which I alone will reward you, it is your hidden remembrance of Me."*[172]

Also on the authority of Aisha ﵂ it is said:

---

[171] Shaykh Amin al-Kurdi, *Tanwir al-qulub* (Enlightenment of Hearts) p. 522.

[172] Bayhaqi narrated it.

The dhikr not heard by the Recording Angels equals seventy times the one they hear.[173]

Spiritual Retreat, or Seclusion (*khalwah, uzla*)

Silent *dhikr* is the *dhikr* of the servant who secludes himself away from people. Abu Saeed al-Khudri ﷺ narrated:

A Bedouin came to the Prophet ﷺ and said, "O God's Apostle! Who is the best of mankind?" The Prophet said, "A man who strives for God's Cause with his life and property, and also a man who lives (all alone) in a mountain path among the mountain paths to worship his Lord and save the people from his evil."[174]

Abu Saeed al-Khudri ﷺ said:

I heard the Prophet ﷺ say, "There will come a time upon the people when the best property of a Muslim man will be his sheep which he will take to the tops of mountains and to the places of rainfall to run away with his Religion far from trials.[175]

Muslim and Tirmidhi narrate:

Abu Hurayra said, "While on the road to Makkah the Prophet ﷺ passed on top of a mountain called Jumdan (frozen in its place), at which time he said: 'Move on! Here is Jumdan Mountain, and the single-minded (al-mufarridun) are foremost.' They said, 'Who are the single-minded, O Messenger of God?' He said, 'The men and women who remember God unceasingly.'"[176]

The version in Tirmidhi reads:

The Prophet ﷺ said, "The single-minded (al-mufarridun) are foremost." They said, "Who are the single-minded?" He said, "Those who dote on the remembrance of God and are ridiculed because of it, and whose burdens the dhikr removes from them, so that they come to God fluttering."

Imam Nawawi writes:

---

173 Bayhaqi narrated it.

174 Bukhari (English translation), Volume 8, Book 76, Number 501.

175 Bukhari (English translation), Volume 8, Book 76, Number 502.

176 Muslim related it in his *Sahih*, beginning of the book of *Dhikr*.

Some pronounced it *mufridun* (those who isolate themselves). Ibn Qutayba and others said, "The original meaning of this is those whose relatives have died and they have become single (in the world) with regard to their passing from them, so they have remained remembering God the Glorious and Exalted." Another narration has, *"They are those who are moved at the mention or remembrance of God,"* that is, they have become fervently devoted and attached to His remembrance. Ibn Arabi said, "It is said that a man becomes single *(farada al-rajul)* when he becomes learned, isolates himself, and concerns himself exclusively with the observance of God's orders and prohibitions."[177]

Al-Mundhiri said:

These are the ones who are fired up with the remembrance of God.[178]

Dhikr in isolation or seclusion (*khalwah*) is corroborated by the *hadith* in Bukhari, beginning, *"Seven people will be shaded by God . . . "* The seventh person mentioned is, "A person who remembers God in seclusion, and his eyes get flooded with tears."

According to Tirmidhi:

Aisha ﵂ relates: "In the beginnings of the Messenger of God's Prophethood ﷺ, at the time God desired to bestow honor upon him and mercy upon His servants through him, he would not have any vision except it came to pass as surely as the sun rises. He continued like this for as long as God wished. Most beloved to him was seclusion (al-khalwa), and there was nothing he loved more than to be alone in seclusion."[179]

Ibn Hajar said in his commentary on Bukhari:[180]

Ibn al-Mubarak relates in *Kitab al-raqaiq* from Shuba, from Khubayb ibn Abd al-Rahman, from Hafs ibn Asim, that Umar ﵁ said, "Take

---

[177] Nawawi, *Sharh Sahih Muslim*, Bk. 48, Ch. 1, *Hadith* 4.

[178] Al-Mundhiri, *al-Targhib wa al-tarhib* (The Encouragement to Good and the Discouragement from Evil).

[179] Tirmidhi narrates it and said: *hasan sahih gharib*. Bukhari and Muslim narrate something very similar through different chains and the word *khala* is used instead of *khalwa*.

[180] Ibn Hajar, *Fath al-Bari* in the commentary on Bukhari's chapter on seclusion.

your part of fortune from seclusion." And what a good saying is al-Junayd's (may God grant us the benefit of his blessings) saying: "Undergoing the difficulty of seclusion is easier than mixing with society unscathed." Al-Khattabi said in his *Book of Seclusion* (*Kitab al-uzla*), "If there were not in seclusion other than safety from backbiting and the sight of what is forbidden but cannot be eliminated, it would have been enough of an immense good." Bukhari's title ("Chapter on Seclusion As Rest From Keeping Company Towards Evil") refers to the *hadith* cited by al-Hakim from Abu Dharr from the Prophet ﷺ with a fair *(hasan)* chain, "Isolation is better than to be sociable in committing evil." However, what is usually retained is that it is a saying of Abu Dharr ﷺ or Abu ad-Darda ﷺ. Ibn Abi Asim cited it.

Al-Qushayri said in his *Risalah:*

The method of the one who enters seclusion is that he must have the belief that he is keeping people from his evil, not the reverse, for the former presupposes belittlement of himself, which is the attribute of the humble, while the latter indicates that he considers himself better than others, which is the attribute of the arrogant.

Abu Bakr ibn al-Arabi writes:

If it is said that the times have become so corrupt that there is nothing better than isolating oneself, we say one isolates oneself from people in one's actions, while he keeps mixing with them with his physical body; however, if he cannot succeed, then at that time he isolates himself from them physically, but without entering into monasticism *(yataziluhum bi badanihi wa la yadkhulu fi al-rahbaniyya)* which is condemned and rejected by the *Sunnah.*[181]

Empowering *Dhikr* with the Divine Name "Allah"

God said in the Quran:

And mention the name of your Lord and devote yourself to Him with a complete devotion. (73:8)

---

[181] Abu Bakr ibn al-Arabi, *Aridat al-ahwadhi sharh sahih al-Tirmidhi,* Book 45 *(daawat),* Ch. 4.

Qadi Thanaullah Panipati said, "Know that this verse points to the repetition of the name of the Essence (*ism al-dhat*); that is, 'Allah.'"[182] The same meaning is intimated also by the following verse:

. . . *Say, "Allah." Then leave them to their play and vain wrangling.* (6:91)

According to one *hadith*, the Prophet ﷺ said:

The Hour will not rise before "Allah, Allah" is no longer said on earth.

According to another chain he said:

The Hour will not rise on anyone saying, "Allah, Allah."[183]

Imam Nawawi said, in his commentary on this chapter, "Know that the narrations of this *hadith* are unanimous in the repetition of the name of God, the Exalted, for both versions, and that is the way it is found in all the authoritative books."[184]

Imam Muslim placed the *hadith* under the chapter-heading, "Disappearance of Belief (*iman*) at the End of Times," although there is no mention of belief in the *hadith*. This shows that saying "*Allah, Allah*" indicates belief. Those who say it show belief, while those who do not say it, do not show belief. Therefore, those who fight those who say it are actually worse than those who merely lack belief and do not say "*Allah, Allah*."

Nawawi highlights the authenticity of the form's repetition to establish that the repetition of the words "*Allah, Allah*" is a *sunnah mathura*, or practice inherited from the Prophet ﷺ and the Companions. Ibn Taymiyya's insistence that the words must not be used alone, but only with a vocative form (i.e., "*Ya Allah*"), therefore contradicts the *Sunnah*.

It is noteworthy that the Siddiqi translation of *Sahih Muslim* mistranslates the first narration cited above as, "The Hour (Resurrection) would not come so long as God is supplicated in the world," and the second as "The Hour (Resurrection) would not come upon anyone so long as he supplicates God." This is wrong as a translation, but accepted as a commentary, since saying "*Allah, Allah*" is supplicating Him. This is

---

182 Qadi Thanullah Panipati, *Tafsir Mazhari* (10:111).

183 Muslim narrated both in his *Sahih,* Book of Iman (Belief), chapter 66 entitled: *dhahab al-iman akhir al-zaman* "The Disappearance of Belief at the End of Times."

184 Nawawi, *Sharh Sahih Muslim,* Dar al-Qalam, Beirut ed. vol. 1/2 p. 537.

true of all worship, according to the *hadith* of the Prophet ﷺ, "*Supplication; that is what worship is.*"[185] However, for the translation to be accurate, the word form highlighted by Nawawi must be retained in any explanation of this *hadith*. It is not merely "supplicating God;" it is saying, "*Allah, Allah*" according to the Prophet's ﷺ own words.

One who knows that the *dhikr* "*Allah, Allah*" has been mentioned by the Prophet ﷺ himself is not at liberty to debate whether or not it was used by the Companions in order to establish its validity. Its validity is sufficiently established in confirming that the Prophet ﷺ said it. Yet, it is established that, while undergoing torture, Bilal often recited the *dhikr* "*Ahad, Ahad.*" Ibn Hisham says in his *Sira*:

Ibn Ishaq narrates (with his chain of transmission) saying:

Bilal was a faithful Muslim, pure of heart. Umayya ibn Khalaf often brought him out in the hottest part of the day and would throw him on his back in the open valley and have a great rock put on his chest; then he would say to him, "You will stay here until you die or deny Muhammad and worship al-Lat and al-Uzza." He said while he was enduring this, "*Ahad, Ahad*"—"One, One!"[186]

Dhikr with "*Hu,*" "*Hayy,*" and "*Haqq*"

One who knows that "*Allah, Allah*" is a *dhikr* used by the Prophet ﷺ is also not at liberty to object to similar forms of *dhikr*, such as "*Hu,*" or "*Hayy,*" or "*Haqq.*"

"*Hu*" is a pronoun of God Almighty, and "*Hayy*" is His Name, according to the Verse of the Throne (*ayat al-Kursi*):

> *Allah! There is no god except He (Hu) the Living (al-Hayy), the Self-Subsistent (*Allahu la ilaha illa Hu al-Hayy al-Qayyum*).* (2:255)

"*Haqq*" is one of the names listed in the *hadith* that enumerates the ninety-nine Names of God, in Bukhari and Muslim.[187] Furthermore, the Prophet ﷺ prayed to God with the following invocations:

"*At your command, O God of Truth (Labbayka ilah al-Haqq).*"[188]

---

[185] Tirmidhi and others narrate it.

[186] Ibn Hajar cites it in *al-Isaba* (1:171 #732).

[187] see below

[188] It is narrated in the book of *Hajj* in al-Nasai's *Sunan*, and in the book of *Manasik* in Ibn Majah's.

*"You are Truth (*Anta al-Haqq*)."*[189]

God said:

To God belong the Most beautiful Names, so call Him with them. (7:180)

These names are not confined to ninety-nine, as Nawawi explicitly stated in his commentary on the *hadith* whereby the Prophet ﷺ said:

There are ninety-nine names which belong to God, one hundred less one; whoever memorizes (or recites) them enters Paradise.[190]

Nawawi and others showed that the meaning of this *hadith* is not, "There are only ninety-nine names," but "There are ninety-nine well-known names," or "There are ninety-nine names that suffice to enter Paradise if memorized."

The Prophet ﷺ called God by *all* His Names, as is clear from the following *hadith*:

O God, I invoke You with all of Your beautiful Names.[191]

***Dhikr* in Dimly lit Surroundings**

God said to the Prophet ﷺ:

And some part of the night awake for it, a largess for thee. (17:79)

Lo! the vigil of the night is a time when impression is more keen and speech more certain. (73:6)

The superiority of prayer at night is known in all books of *hadith* and *fiqh* because of the elimination of worldly distractions at that time. That is why Imam Ghazali wrote on that topic:

> The root of thought is the eye. He whose *niyyat* (intention) is fine and who aims high cannot be diverted by what occurs in front of him, but he who is weak falls prey to it. The medicine is to cut off the roots of these distractions and to shut up the eyes, to pray in a dark room, not to keep anything in front which may attract

[189] Bukhari and Muslim.

[190] Bukhari and Muslim

[191] Arabic: *Allahumma inni aduka bi asmaika al-husna kulliha.* Narrated by Ibn Majah, book of *Dua*; and by Imam Malik in his *Muwatta, Kitab al-Shir.*

attention and not to pray in a decorated place. For this reason, the saints worshipped in dark, narrow and unspacious rooms.[192]

Movement During *Dhikr*

In reference to the *hadith* of Muslim whereby the Prophet ﷺ praised the *mufarridun*, or those who are single-minded in their remembrance of God, Nawawi said:

> They are those who shake or are moved at the mention or remembrance of God, that is, they have become fervently devoted and attached to His remembrance.

Imam Habib al-Haddad said:

> *Dhikr* returns from the outward feature, which is the tongue, to the inward, which is the heart, where it becomes solidly rooted, so that it takes firm hold of its members. The sweetness of this is tasted by the one who has taken to *dhikr* with the whole of himself, so that his skin and heart are softened. As God said, *"Then their skins and their hearts soften to the remembrance of God."* (39:23)[193]

The "softening of the heart" consists in the sensitivity and timidity that occur as a result of nearness and *tajalli* (manifestation of one or more Divine Attributes). Sufficient is it to have God as one's Intimate Companion!

As for the "softening of the skin" this is the ecstasy and swaying from side to side which result from intimacy and manifestation, or from fear and awe. No blame is attached to someone who has reached this rank if he sways and chants, for in the painful throes of love and passion, he finds something which arouses the highest yearning.

The exhortation provided by fear and awe brings forth tears and forces one to tremble and be humble. These are the states of the righteous believers (*abrar*) when they hear the Speech and *dhikr* of God, the Exalted. *"Their skins shiver,"* and then soften with their hearts and incline to *dhikr* of Him, as they are covered in serenity and dignity, so that they are neither frivolous, pretentious, noisy, or ostentatious. God,

---

[192] Imam Ghazali, *Ihya Ulum al-Din*, Book of *Salat*.

[193] Imam Habib al-Haddad, in *Key to the Garden* (p. 116).

the Exalted, has not described them as people whose sense of reason has departed, who faint, dance, or jump about.

More Traditions on the Virtues of *Dhikr*

Abu Hurayra ⬥ reported that the Prophet ⬥ said:

When a servant of God utters the words "la ilaha illallah" (there is no god except God) sincerely, the doors of heaven open up for these words until they reach the Throne of God, so long as its utterer keeps away from the major sins.[194]

Abu Hurayra ⬥ also reported:

The Prophet ⬥ said, "Renew your faith." "How can we renew our faith?" they asked. The Prophet ⬥ replied, "Say always, 'la ilaha illallah.'"[195]

Jabir reported that the Prophet ⬥ said:

The best remembrance of God is to repeat "la ilaha illallah" and the best invocation (dua) is alhamdulillah (all praise belongs to God).[196]

Abu Hurayra ⬥ reported that the Prophet ⬥ said:

There are two phrases that are light on the tongue, but heavy on the scale of rewards and are dear to the Gracious One. These are: "Glorified is God with all praise to Him," and, "Glorified is God, the Great."[197]

Abu Hurayra ⬥ also reported that the Prophet ⬥ said:

I love repeating, "Glorified is God, and Praise be to God, and There is no God but God, and God is most Great," more than all that the sun shines upon.[198]

---

[194] Narrated by Tirmidhi, who says it is *hasan gharib*. Al-Mundhiri included in *al-Targhib* 2:414.

[195] Narrated by Ahmad with a fair chain of authorities.

[196] Narrated by Nasai, Ibn Majah, and Hakim who declared its chain sound.

[197] Arabic: *"Subhanallah wa bi hamdihi,"* and *"Subhanallah al-azim."* Narrated by Bukhari, Muslim, and Tirmidhi.

[198] Arabic: *"Subhanallah, wa alhamdulillah, wa la ilaha illallah, wallahu akbar."* Narrated by Muslim and Tirmidhi.

Abu Dharr ⬥ reported:

The Prophet ⬥ said, "Shall I tell you the words that God loves the most?" I said, "Yes, tell me, O Messenger of God." He said, "The words dearest to God are, "Glorified is God with all praise to Him."[199]

In Tirmidhi's version, the following is also found:

The words most dear to God which He has chosen for His angels are, "Glorified is my Lord with all praise to Him, Glorified is my Lord with all praise to Him!"[200]

Jabir ⬥ reported that the Prophet ⬥ said:

Whoever says, "Glorified is God, the Great, with all praise to Him," will have a palm tree planted for him in Paradise.[201]

Abu Saeed ⬥ reported:

The Prophet ⬥ said, "Perform the enduring goods deeds (al-baqiyat al-salihat) more frequently." They asked, "What are these enduring good deeds?" The Prophet ⬥ replied: Takbir ("allahu akbar"), Tahlil ("la ilaha illallah"), Tasbih ("subhanallah"), "alhamdulillah," and "la hawla wa la quwwata illa billah."[202]

Abd Allah ibn Masud ⬥ reported that the Prophet ⬥ said:

During the Night Journey I met Abraham who said to me, O Muhammad, convey my greetings to your Community, and tell them that the Paradise is of pure land, its water is sweet, and its expanse is vast, spacious, and even. And its seedlings are:

Glory to God (subhanallah)

Praise to God (walhamdulillah)

There is no god but God (wa la ilaha illallah)

---

[199] Arabic: *"Subhanallah wa bi hamdihi."* Narrated by Muslim and Tirmidhi.

[200] Arabic: *"Subhana rabbi wa bi hamdihi subhana rabbi wa bi hamdihi."*

[201] Narrated by Tirmidhi, who said it is *hasan*.

[202] Narrated by Nasai and Hakim, who said its chain is authentic.

God is greatest (wallahu akbar)[203]

Samura ibn Jundub 🌸 reported:

The Prophet 🌺 said: "The dearest phrases to God are four: 'Glorified is God, and Praise be to God, and There is no God but God, and God is most Great,'[204] There is no harm in beginning them in any order you choose while remembering God."[205]

Ibn Masud 🌸 reported that the Prophet 🌺 said:

If anyone recites the last two verses of Surat al-Baqara at night (2:285-286), they will suffice for him.[206]

That is, these two verses will bring him a reward equivalent to that of a night prayer, and will safeguard him from any hurt during that night.

Abu Saeed al-Khudri 🌸 narrated:

The Prophet 🌺 asked, "Can anyone of you recite a third of the Quran during the night?" The Companions considered this difficult and they said: "Who among us can do so, O Prophet of God?" Thereupon the Prophet 🌺 said: "God, the One, the Eternally-Besought (i.e., Surat al-Ikhlas) is a third of the Quran."[207]

Abu Hurayra 🌸 reported that the Prophet 🌺 said:

Whoever says, "There is no god but God, alone, without partner. His is the sovereignty, and His the praise, and He has power over everything,"[208] a hundred times a day will have a reward equivalent to the reward for freeing ten slaves. In addition, a hundred good deeds will be recorded for him and a hundred bad deeds of his will be wiped off, and it will be a

---

[203] Narrated by Tirmidhi and Tabarani whose version adds, "There is no power nor strength save through God."

[204] Arabic: *subhanallah, wa al-hamdulillah, wa la ilaha illallah, wallahu akbar.*

[205] Narrated by Muslim.

[206] Narrated by Bukhari and Muslim, Ibn Khuzayma in his *Sahih* mentioned it under the chapter "The Recitation of the Quran Equivalent in Reward to a Night Prayer."

[207] Narrated by Bukhari and Muslim.

[208] Arabic: *la ilaha illallahu wahdahu la sharika lah, lahul-mulku wa lahul-hamd, wa huwa ala kulli shayin qadir.*

safeguard for him from Satan that day until evening, and no one will be better in deeds than such a person except he who does more than that.[209]

In the version of Muslim, Tirmidhi, and Nasai, it is added:

Whoever says, "Glorified is God with all praise to Him,"[210] *a hundred times during a day, will have all his sins wiped off even if they were as numerous as the foam on the surface of the sea.*

Istighfar—Asking God's Forgiveness

Anas ﷺ reported that he heard the Prophet ﷺ saying that God says:

O son of Adam, whatever you asked Me and expect from Me I forgave—respecting that which you owed to Me—and I do not care (how great this was). O Son of Adam, even if your sins pile up to the sky and then you seek My forgiveness I will forgive you, and O son of Adam, even if you have an earthful of sins, but you meet Me without associating any other thing with Me, I will forgive you.[211]

Abd Allah ibn Abbas ﷺ said:

If one supplicates without fail for forgiveness from God, He finds a way out for him to get out of every distress and difficulty, and gives him sustenance through ways utterly not thought of.[212]

Juwayriyya bint al-Harith ﷺ, one of the wives of the Prophet ﷺ, reported that one day the Prophet ﷺ left her apartment in the morning as she was busy observing her dawn prayer in her place of worship. He came back in the forenoon and she was still sitting there. The Prophet ﷺ said to her, "You have been in the same place since I left you?" She said: "Yes." Thereupon the Prophet ﷺ said:

I recited some words three times after I left you and if these are to be weighed against what you have recited since morning these would outweigh them, and these words are: "Glory to God and praise to Him to the number of His creation, and to the extent of His pleasure, and to the

---

[209] Narrated by Bukhari, Muslim, Tirmidhi, Nasai and Ibn Majah.

[210] Arabic: *subhanallah wa bi hamdihi.*

[211] Narrated by Tirmidhi who said it is *hasan sahih.*

[212] Narrated by Abu Dawud, Nasai, Ibn Majah, and Hakim, who said its chain of authorities is sound.

extent of the weight of His Throne, and to the extent of ink used in recording words for His Praise."[213]

Ibn Umar ﵁ reported that the Prophet ﷺ told them:

A servant of God said, "My Lord! All praise belongs to You as much as befits Your Glory and Sublime Majesty."[214] *This was too much for the two angels to record. They did not know how to record it. So they soared to the heaven and said, "Our Lord! Your servant has said something which we do not know how to record." God asked them—and, of course, He knew what the servant had said—"What did My servant say?" They said, "He said, 'My Lord! All praise belongs to You as much as befits Your Glory and Sublime Majesty.'" God said to them, "Write it down as My servant has said until he should meet Me and I reward him for it."*[215]

Abd Allah ibn Amr ibn al-As ﵁ said:

I saw the Prophet counting the glorifications of God on his right hand's fingers.[216]

Yusayra bint Yasir ﵁ reported that the Prophet ﷺ commanded them (the Emigrant women) to be regular in remembering God by saying *tahlil ("la ilaha illallah")* and *tasbih ("subhanallah")* and *takbir ("allahu akbar")*, and never to be forgetful of God and His Mercy, and to count them on their fingers, for the fingers will be questioned and will speak.[217]

Use of *Dhikr* Beads (*Masbaha, Sibha, Tasbih*)

Saad ibn Abi Waqqas ﵁ reported:

Once the Prophet ﷺ saw a woman who had some date-stones or pebbles which she was using as beads to glorify God. The Prophet ﷺ said to her, "Let me tell you something that would be easier or more excellent for you than that." So he told her to say instead:

---

[213] Arabic: *Subhanallahi wa bi hamdihi adada khalqihi wa rida nafsihi wa zinata arshihi wa midada kalimatihi.* Narrated by Muslim and Abu Dawud.

[214] Arabic: *Ya rabbi laka al-hamdu kama yanbaghi li jalali wajhika wa li azimi sultanik.*

[215] Narrated by Ibn Majah.

[216] Narrated by Tirmidhi who said *hasan gharib,* Nasai, Abu Dawud, and Ahmad.

[217] Narrated by Ahmad, Tirmidhi who said it is *gharib,* Abu Dawud, and al-Hakim. Shawkani in *Nayl al-awtar* 2:316 said that Suyuti declared sound *(sahih)* its chain of transmission.

"Glory be to God as many times as the number of what He has created in Heaven,

"Glory be to God as many times as the number of what He has created on Earth,

"Glory be to God as many times as the number of what He has created between them,

"Glory be to God as many times as the number of that which He is creating."

And then repeat all of the above four times but substituting "Glory be to God" with:

"God is the most great" in the first repetition,

"Praise be to God" in the second repetition,

"There is no god but God" in the third repetition, and

"There is no change and no power except with God" in the fourth repetition.

Safiyya bint Huyayy ⚯ the Prophet's ﷺ wife said:

The Prophet ﷺ came in to see me and in front of me there were 4,000 date-stones with which I was making tasbih (counting "subhanallah"). He said, "You make tasbih with so many! Shall I teach you what surpasses your number of tasbih?" She said, "Teach me!" He said, "Say: Glory to God the number of His creation."[218]

God says in His Holy Book, addressing His Holy Prophet ﷺ:
Remind people, for reminding benefits them. (51:55)

Reminder has various forms, public and private. A public form of reminder is the *adhan*. The *masbaha*—or *sibha, tasbih,* or *dhikr* beads—has had, since the earliest Companions, the function of private reminder. It is for that reason that the *tasbih* was called by them *mudhakkir* or *mudhakkira*

---

[218] Arabic: *Subhanallah adada khalqihi.* Narrated by Tirmidhi who said it is *gharib,* and both al-Hakim and Suyuti declared it *sahih.*

(reminder). There is a narration traced to the Prophet ﷺ whereby he said, "*What a good reminder are the* dhikr *beads!*"[219]

The statement that counting *dhikr* on beads is an innovation is undoubtedly false. The use of beads for counting *dhikr* was definitely allowed by the Prophet ﷺ and was a *Sunnah* of the Companions. This is proven by the *sahih hadith* of Saad ibn Abi Waqqas ؓ, who related that the Prophet ﷺ once saw a woman using some date-stones or pebbles to count *dhikr*, and did not prohibit her use of them.[220] Another *sahih hadith* to that effect was related by Safiyya ؓ, who was seen by her husband the Prophet ﷺ counting "*Subhanallah*" with four thousand date stones.[221]

Shawkani said:

> The Prophet ﷺ justified the counting of *dhikr* on the fingers by the fact that the fingers will be questioned and will speak; that is, they will witness to that effect. It follows that counting *tasbih* on them, because of this, is better than using *dhikr* beads or pebbles. However, the two other *ahadith* (of Saad ibn Abi Waqqas ؓ and Safiyya bint Huyayy ؓ) indicate the permissibility of counting *tasbih* with date-stones and pebbles, and with *dhikr* beads, because there is no distinguishing factor among them in the Prophet's stipulation to the two women, and no disapproval of it. As for directing to what is better, this does not negate permissibility. There are reports to that effect.
>
> It is related in Hilal al-Haffar's monograph, through Mutamar ibn Sulayman, from Abu Safiyya ؓ, the Prophet's freedman, that a mat would be spread for him (Abu Safiyya) and a basket made of palm leaves brought which was filled with pebbles with which he would make *tasbih* until mid-day. Then it would be taken away, and then brought back after he had prayed, and he would make *tasbih* again

---

[219] Arabic: *nima al-mudhakkir al-sibha.* Shawkani narrates it from Ali ibn Abi Talib as evidence for the usefulness of *dhikr*-beads in *Nayl al-awtar* (2:317) from Daylami's narration in *Musnad al-firdaws* with his chain, and Suyuti cites it in his *fatwa* on *dhikr*-beads in *al-Hawi li al-fatawi* (2:38).

[220] This *hadith* is found in Abu Dawud, Tirmidhi, Nisai, Ibn Maja, Ibn Hibban, and Hakim. Dhahabi declared it *sahih*.

[221] This *hadith* is found in Tirmidhi, Hakim, and Tabarani, and was confirmed as *sahih* by Suyuti.

until evening. Imam Ahmad narrates it in *Kitab al-zuhd* (with his chain).

Ahmad also narrates from al-Qasim ibn Abd al-Rahman ❀ that Abu ad-Darda ❀ had a bag filled with date-stones and that whenever he prayed the noon prayer he would bring them out one by one and make *tasbih* on them until they were finished.

Ibn Saad in his *Tabaqat* narrates (with his chains) that Saad ibn Abi Waqqas ❀ counted *tasbih* on pebbles, and that Fatimah bint al-Husayn ibn Ali ibn Abi Talib ❀ said *tasbih* with a thread stringed with knots, and that Abu Hurayra ❀ made *tasbih* with a string of pebbles (*al-nawa al-majmu*).

Abd Allah, the son of Imam Ahmad, narrated in *Zawaid al-zuhd* that Abu Hurayra ❀ had a thread stringed with one thousand knots and that he would not sleep until he had counted *tasbih* on them.

Ad-Daylami narrates, in *Musnad al-firdaws* through Zainab bint Sulayman ibn Ali, and from Umm al-Hasan bint Jafar, from her father, from her grandfather, from Ali ❀, and it is traced back to the Prophet ❀, "*What a good reminder are the* dhikr *beads!*"

Suyuti related reports with their chains in his monograph on the subject entitled *al-Minha fi al-sibha*, and it is part of his collected *fatwas*. He says towards the end of it, "It is not related from any one of the Predecessors (*salaf*) nor the later scholars (*khalaf*) that it is forbidden to count *tasbih* on the *sibha* (*dhikr* beads). On the contrary, most of them counted *tasbih* on it, and they did not consider it disliked."[222]

The Indian *hadith* scholar, Zakariyya al-Khandlawi, relates that Abu Hurayra ❀ said, "I recite *istighfar* (the formula for asking forgiveness) 12,000 times daily." He also relates that, according to Abu Hurayra's grandson, he had a piece of thread with 1,000 knots and would not go to sleep until he had said "Glory to God" (*subhanallah*) on all of these

---

[222] Shawkani, *Nayl al-awtar* (2:316-317).

knots.[223] According to her grand-daughter, through Imam al-Husayn ﷺ, Fatimah ﷺ also counted her *dhikr* on a thread with knots.

Mawlana Zakariyya continues:

> It is well-known that many other Companions of the Prophet ﷺ used beads in their private devotions, such as Saad ibn Abi Waqqas ﷺ himself; Abu Safiyya, the slave of the Prophet ﷺ; Abu Saad ﷺ; Abu ad-Darda ﷺ; and Fatima ﷺ. Stringing, or not stringing, the beads together does not make any difference.

It is well established that counting *dhikr* is a *Sunnah* of the Prophet ﷺ. He himself advised his wives, Ali ﷺ, and Fatimah ﷺ to count *tasbih, tahmid,* and *takbir* thirty-three times each before going to bed at night. Ibn Amr ﷺ relates that he saw the Prophet ﷺ count the times he said *"subhanallah"* on his right hand. This does not mean that it is not allowed to use the left also, as the Prophet ﷺ simply said, "Count (the *dhikr*) on your fingers."

Imam Suyuti recounted, in one of his *fatwas*, the story of Ikrima, who asked his teacher, Umar al-Maliki, about *dhikr* beads.[224] Umar answered that he had also asked his teacher, Hasan al-Basri, about it and was told, "Something we have used at the beginning of the road we are not desirous to leave at the end. I love to remember God with my heart, my hand, and my tongue." Suyuti comments, "And how should it be otherwise, when the *dhikr* beads remind one of God, the Exalted, and a person seldom sees *dhikr* beads except he remembers God, which is among the greatest of its benefits."

As for Albani's statements against *dhikr* beads, his rejection of the *hadith "What a good reminder are the* dhikr *beads!"*[225] and his astounding claim that whoever carries *dhikr* beads in his hand to remember God is misguided and innovating, let the reader be directed to their refutation in Mahmud Said's *Wusul al-tahani bi ithbat sunniyyat al-sibha wa al-radd ala al-albani* (The Alighting of Mutual Benefit, and the Confirmation That the *Dhikr* Beads Are a *Sunnah*, and the Refutation of Albani).

---

[223] Zakariyya al-Khandlawi, *Hayat al-sahaba.*

[224] Suyuti, *al-Minha fi al-sibha* (The profit derived from using *dhikr*-beads).

[225] See Albani's *Silsila daifa* #83.

The spurious claim that *dhikr* beads come from Buddhism or Christianity is not supported by the scholars but may simply be dismissed as just one more of the scholar Ignaz Goldziher's dubious legacies to orientalist literature.

Weak Report on Collective *Dhikr* in Darimi's *Sunan*

The following weak narration is sometimes used by the uninformed in their attacks against collective *dhikr*:

Al-Darimi narrates the following from from al-Hakam ibn al-Mubarak, who narrates from Amr ibn Salima al-Hamadani:[226]

We sat by the door of Abd Allah ibn Masud ﵁ before the morning prayer, so that when he came out we would walk with him to the mosque. (One day) Abu Musa al-Ashari ﵁ came to us and said, "Has Abu Abd al-Rahman come out yet?" We replied, "No." So he sat down with us until he came out. When he came out, we all stood along with him, so Abu Musa said to him, "O Abu Abd al-Rahman! I have just seen something in the mosque which I considered wrong, but all praise is for God, I did not see anything except good in it." He inquired, "What is it?"

Abu Musa replied, "If you live, you will see it. I saw in the mosque people sitting in circles awaiting the Prayer. In each circle they had pebbles in their hands and a man would say, 'Repeat allahu akbar a hundred times.' So they would repeat it a hundred times. Then he would say, 'Say la ilaha ill-Allah a hundred times.' So they would say it a hundred times. Then he would say, 'Say subhanallah a hundred times.' So they would say it a hundred times." Ibn Masud asked, "What did you say to them?" Abu Musa said, "I did not say anything to them. Instead I waited to hear your view on it." Ibn Masud replied, "Would that you had ordered them to count their evil deeds and assured them that their good deeds would not be lost!" Then we went along with him until he came to one of these circles whereby he stood and said, "What is this I see you doing?"

They replied, "O Abu Abd al-Rahman! These are pebbles upon which we are counting takbir, tahlil and tasbih." He said, "Count your evil deeds instead. I assure you that none of your good deeds will be lost. Woe to you, O Ummah of Muhammad ﷺ, how quickly you go to

---

226 Al-Darimi, *Muqaddima* of his *Sunan.*

destruction! Here are your Prophet's Companions available in abundance (mutawafirun). And there are his clothes which have not yet decayed and his bowl which is unbroken. By Him in Whose Hand is my soul! Either you are following a Religion that is better guided than the Religion of Muhammad ﷺ or you are opening a door of misguidance."

They said, "O Abu Abd al-Rahman! By God, we only intend good!" He said, "How many are there who intend good but do not achieve it. Indeed, God's Messenger said to us, 'A people will recite the Quran but it will not pass beyond their throats.' By God! I do not know, but perhaps most of them are from among you." Then he left them. Amr ibn Salima said, "We saw most of those people fighting against us on the day of Nahrawan, on the side of the Khawarij."

The chain of the above report is unacceptable because it includes the name of Amr ibn Yahya al-Hamadani, Amr ibn Salima's grandson, and he is considered *daif*, or "weak."[227] A single weak report can never overrule something that is established by many sound reports, as cited in relation to each of the issues discussed above.

Even if the report were not weak, it would not be enough to support the stance against collective gatherings of *dhikr*, against gathering for *dhikr* in a circle, against counting *dhikr* by the hundreds, or against using pebbles for counting *dhikr*. All the above shows that the report narrated by Darimi can never be used to contest the lawfulness of gathering for *dhikr*, sitting in a *dhikr* circle, counting *dhikr*, or using pebbles to count *dhikr*; whoever says it does is clearly unaware of the *Sunnah* on this issue. If the *hadith* is authentic, then the key to Darimi's report lies in the context of the following passages:

- Abu Musa al-Ashari's ﷺ words: "I have just seen something in the mosque which I considered wrong, but I did not see anything except good in it."
- Ibn Masud's ﷺ words: "Here are your Prophet's Companions available in abundance."

---

[227] Ibn Main saw him and said, "his narrations are worth nothing." Ibn Kharrash said, "he is not accepted." Dhahabi listed him among those who are weak and whose *hadith* is not retained in *al-Duafa wa al-matrukin* (p. 212 #3229), *Mizan al-itidal* (3:293), and *al-Mughni fi al-duafa* (2:491). and al-Haythami declared him weak (*daif*) in *Majma al-zawaid*, chapter entitled *Bab al-ummal ala al-sadaqa*

- Ibn Masud's ﷺ words: "God's Messenger said to us, 'A people will recite the Quran but it will not pass beyond their throats.' By God! I do not know, but perhaps most of them are from among you."
- Amr ibn Salima's words, "We saw most of those people fighting against us on the day of Nahrawan, on the side of the Khawarij."

It is clear that Abu Musa's ﷺ reaction was mixed because, on the one hand, he disapproved of the people themselves, but not of their *dhikr*. The reason for the disapproval is left unsaid, while Ibn Masud alludes to it by blaming the people in question for their isolationist stance away from the Companions. This is confirmed by Ibn Masud's citing of one of the most famous *ahadith* concerning the Khawarij, or Separatists, about whom it is known that they considered themselves more pious than all other Muslims, and better than even the Companions. This is again confirmed, beyond the shadow of a doubt, by Amr ibn Salima's explicit identification of the people in question as allies of the Khawarij on the day of Nahrawan.

This demonstrates that Abu Musa's view and Ibn Masud's condemnation are directed against the fact that the people in question were Separatists, not that they were making *dhikr*. The shamefulness of separating oneself from the Companions is underlined by Ibn Masud's exclamation, "Here are your Prophet's Companions available in abundance." The *hadith* master Abu Zura al-Razi said, "At the time the Prophet's ﷺ soul was taken back, the Companions who had narrated from and/or heard him directly (including his tacit presence) numbered 114,000."[228]

The Khawarij are from among the tribes of Banu Hanifa, Banu Tamim, and Wail in the Najd area of Eastern Arabia. They committed *baghi* (or rebellion) against Prince of the Believers, Sayydina Ali ﷺ, and opposed the larger group of Muslims. They declared both Ali ﷺ and Muawiya ﷺ disbelievers, and declared licit their blood and property as

---

228 This is related by the *hadith* master Ibn Jamaa in his book *al-Manhal al-rawi fi mukhtasar ulum al-hadith al-nabawi* (The quenching spring: Abridged manual of the sciences of the prophetic *hadith*), 3rd ed., ed. Muhyiddin Abd al-Rahman *Ramadan* (Damascus: Dar al-fikr, 1406/1986) p. 113.

well as the blood and property of those who accompanied them. The Khawarij made their land a land of war and declared their own land an abode of faith.

They accepted from the Prophet's *Sunnah* only what agreed with their own doctrine, and drew evidence for their beliefs from seemingly ambiguous verses in the Quran. They were known to apply Quranic verses meant to refer to unbelievers to the believers, as predicted by the Prophet.[229] Ibn Abbas 🕮 debated them until four thousand returned to the truth. They were the first to separate from the Congregation of Muslims. The Prophet 🕮 referred to them as "The dogs of the people in Hell,"[230] and he gave the order to fight and kill them by saying, "They will pass through Islam like an arrow passes through its quarry. Wherever you meet them, kill them!"[231]

As a final note on the descendents of the Khawarij of our time, Imam Muhammad ibn Abidin (d. 1252/1836) said:

> The name of *Khawarij* is applied to those who part ways with Muslims and declare them disbelievers, as took place in our time with the followers of Ibn Abd al-Wahhab, who came out of Najd and attacked the Two Noble Sanctuaries (Makkah and Madina). They (Wahhabis) claimed to follow the Hanbali school, but their belief was such that, in their view, they alone are Muslims and everyone else is a *mushrik* (polytheist). Under this guise, they said that killing *Ahl al-Sunnah* and their scholars was permissible, until God, the Exalted, destroyed them in the year 1233/1818 at the hands of the Muslim army.[232]

Benefits of Invoking Blessings on the Prophet 🕮

Sakhawi says Abd Allah ibn Amr ibn al-As 🕮 said that he heard the Prophet 🕮 say:

> *When you hear the* muadhdhin, *repeat his words after him, then invoke blessings upon me. Whoever invokes blessings upon me once, God bestows*

---

[229] See *Sahih Bukhari*, English ed. 9:50.

[230] A sound narration related through various chains by Ibn Majah, and Ahmad.

[231] *Sahih Bukhari* and *Sahih Muslim*.

[232] Imam Muhummad ibn Abidin, *Hashiyat radd al-muhtar ala al-durr al-mukhtar* (3:309), Chapter entitled *Bab al-Bughat* (Chapter on Rebels).

blessings upon him ten times. Then ask God for the wasila *to be granted to me. It is a position in Paradise that may not be granted to any but one of God's servants, and I dearly hope that I will be that servant. Whoever asks God the* wasila *for me, my intercession is guaranteed for him.*[233]

It has already been expounded that there is no such thing as invoking too much *salawat* on the Prophet ﷺ. Further evidence on this topic is mentioned here only by way of a reminder.

Abu Hurayra ◈ narrated that the Prophet ﷺ said:

Dust for the face of the one before whom I am mentioned, and he does not invoke blessings upon me.[234]

Abu Hurayra ◈ also reported that the Prophet ﷺ said:

If people sit in an assembly in which they do not remember God nor invoke a blessing on the Prophet, it will be a cause of grief for them on the Day of Judgment.[235]

The author of *Fath al-allam* said:

This *hadith* proves that it is incumbent on one to remember God and invoke blessings on the Prophet ﷺ while sitting in an assembly, for whether we take the words "cause of grief" to mean torment of fire or any other chastisement, obviously a punishment is incurred only when an obligatory act is neglected, or a forbidden act is committed. Here it is both the remembrance of God and the invoking of blessings on His Prophet ﷺ that are apparently incumbent.

Ibn Rajab al-Hanbali said in his book on love of God and love of the Prophet ﷺ:

Love for the Prophet ﷺ is on two levels: The first level is obligatory. This is the love that requires one to accept whatever the Prophet ﷺ brought from God and to receive it with love, pleasure, esteem, and submission, without seeking guidance from any other source whatsoever.

---

[233] Sakhawi, *al-Qawl al-badi* (p. 179), chapter on the *salawat* after *adhan*. He continues: "It is narrated by Muslim and the Four (Tirmidhi, Abu Dawud, Ibn Majah, Nasai) except Ibn Majah, and also by Bayhaqi, Ibn Zanjawayh, and others."

[234] A sound *hadith* narrated by Tirmidhi (*hasan gharib*) and al-Hakim.

[235] Narrated by Tirmidhi, who graded it *hasan*.

The second level is superior. This type of love requires following his example in an excellent way and fulfilling the following of his *Sunnah* with respect to his behavior, manners, voluntary deeds, superogatory actions, eating, drinking, dressing, excellent behavior with his wives, and other aspects of his perfect manners and pure behavior. It also includes learning about his life and days. It also includes the heart trembling when mentioning him, saying prayers and blessings upon him often out of what resides in the heart of love for him, esteem for him, and respect for him. It also includes loving to listen to his words and preferring them over the words of the rest of creation. And one of the greatest aspects of this love is to follow him in his abstinence of this world, to suffice with little, and to desire and pine after the everlasting Hereafter.[236]

Abi Talhah al-Ansari ﵁ said:

The Messenger of God ﷺ arose one morning and in a very pleasant mood with signs of good tidings apparent on his face. They said, "O Prophet of God, you are in a very pleasant mood with signs of good tidings showing on your face." He said, "Verily, the angel (Gabriel) came to me, and said, Are you not pleased, O Muhammad, that your Lord says that no one of your nation asks God to bless you except that God will bless him tenfold and that no one from your nation asks God to send you greetings of peace except that God will to send him greetings peace tenfold.' The Prophet ﷺ responded, Yes, indeed.'"[237]

Anas ﵁ reported God's Messenger ﷺ as saying:

If anyone invokes a blessing on me once, God will grant him ten blessings, ten sins will be remitted from him, and he will be raised ten degrees.[238]

---

[236] Ibn Rajab al-Hanbali, *Istinshaq nasim al-uns min nafahat riyad al-quds* (Inhaling the Breeze of Intimacy from the Whiffs of the Gardens of Sanctity).

[237] Narrated by Ibn Abi Shaybah, Ahmad, 'Abd bin Hamid and at-Tirmidhi. Cited with slightly different wording in Imam Abu Sulayman al-Jazuli's *Dalail al-Khayrat* (The Index of Good Things).

[238] Related by Bukhari and Muslim (with two narrators) from Abu Hurayra. Also from Ahmad in his *Musnad*, Abu Dawud in his *Sunan*, at-Tirmidhi and an-Nasai all from Abu Hurayra. Another extended version to this is related from Anas by al-Bukhari in his *Adab al-mufrad*, Ahmad in his *Musnad*, Nasai and by al-Hakim in his *Mustadrak*, in which the

Abd ar-Rahman ibn Auf ﷺ related:

God's Messenger ﷺ went out and entering among some palm trees prostrated himself so long that I was afraid God had taken his soul. I went and looked, and he raised his head and said, "What is the matter with you?" I mentioned that to him, and he told me that Gabriel had come and given him the good tidings that God said, "If anyone invokes one blessing on you I will bless him, and if anyone greets you I will greet him."[239]

Al-Abbas ﷺ said:

When God says, "Send prayers (on the Prophet)," *(33:56) it means to seek blessings.*[240]

Abu al-Aliyyah ﷺ said:

Allah's praising of him is His Tribute to him ﷺ in the presence of the angels. And the praising of the angels is the supplication for him ﷺ.[241]

Ibn Abbas ﷺ said:
The Children of Israel said to Musa, "Does your Lord invoke blessings on anyone?" And His Lord called to him, 'O Musa, did they ask you if your Lord invoke blessings? Say to them, 'Yes, I and the angels invoke blessings on My Prophets and Messengers.'" Then God revealed: *Verily! Allah and His angels shower blessings on the Prophet...* (33:51)[242]

Malik ibn Aws ﷺ reported:

---

narrator added: "...and ten faults will be erased from him and God will raise him ten levels." Al-Hafiz as-Suyuti graded both hadiths as authentic.

[239] Ahmad transmitted it from Abd ar-Rahman bin Auf, al-Hakim in his *Mustadrak* with an authentic *isnad*, Ibn Najar. Again Ahmad and al-Haythami in his *Majma al-zawaid* recorded it with a different wording. All hadiths on this subject are authentic based on the criteria of the two Shaykhs, Imams al-Bukhari and Muslim.

[240] Ibn Jarir, Ibn Mundhir, Ibn Abi Hatim reported it.

[241] Abd bin Hamid and Ibn Abi Hatim reported it.

[242] Reported by Ibn Abi Hatim (from Abu Hurayrah), Abd ar-Razzaq and Abu ash-Shaykh in his Azhamah, Ibn Mardawayah from Ibn Abbas. Abd ar-Razzaq also recorded it from al-Hasan.

Surely the Prophet ﷺ said: Gabriel came to me and said, "He who invokes blessings on you once, God blesses him ten times and raises him ten levels."[243]

Abu Said al-Khudri ؓ related that the Prophet ﷺ said:

If a man is without anything to give in charity (sadaqa) let him say in his supplication, 'O God pray on Muhammad, your servant and Messenger and pray on the believers and the Muslims.' Then it will be for him poor-due (zakah).[244]

Abu Hurayra ؓ related that the Prophet ﷺ said:

Whoever says, "O God send prayers on Muhammad and the Family of Muhammad. And Bless Muhammad and the Family of Muhammad just as You have sent prayers upon and blessed Abraham and the Family of Abraham and bless Muhammad and the Family of Muhammad just as You have blessed Abraham and the Family of Abraham," it will bear witness for him on the Day of Judgment and will intercede for him.[245]

Ibn Masud ؓ said that the Messenger of God ﷺ said

The closest to me on the Day of Judgment are those who invoke blessings upon me the most.[246]

The Prophet ﷺ said:

Verily God has an angel standing at my grave until the Day of Judgment. There are none who invoke blessings on me except the angel names him and his father and he says, "O Muhammad, invoke blessings on so-and-so the son of so-and-so." For my Lord hath commissioned me to return the blessings invoked on me tenfold.[247]

The Prophet ﷺ said:

---

243 Imam al-Bukhari relates it in his *Adab al-mufrad* with a chain up to Anas.

244 Bukhari related it in *Adab al-mufrad*.

245 Bukhari narrated it.

246 Ahmad, at-Tirmidhi and Ibn Hibban said it had a good chain (*hasan*).

247 Reported in al-Muttaqi al-Hindi's *Kanz al-Ummal* by Ammar bin Yasir.

I asked my Lord that no servant invokes blessings on me except that God blesses him ten the like thereof.[248]

Abd Allah bin Amir bin Rabiah ❀ related from his father that the Messenger of God ❀ said:

One does not invokes blessings on me except that the angels invokes blessings on him as long as he is invoking blessings on me. So you do as little or as much as you like.[249]

It is reported from Jabir ❀ that the Prophet ❀ said:

Sufficient for one to be considered a miser is that when I am mentioned in his presence he does not invoke blessings on me.[250]

Abu Hurayra ❀ related that the Messenger of God ❀ said:

Increase your invoking of blessings on me on Friday, for surely it will be presented to me.[251]

In a different version from Anas ❀ the Prophet ❀ said:

Increase your invoking of blessings on me on Friday and on the night before Friday. Whoever invokes blessings on me, God will bless him tenfold.[252]

It is also related from Abu ad-Darda ❀ that the Prophet ❀ said:

Increase prayers upon me on Friday, it is witnessed by the angels.[253]

Imam al-Ghazali recorded in his *Ihya* that the Prophet ❀ said:

Whoever from my nation invokes blessings upon me, ten good deeds are written for him and ten sins are effaced.[254]

---

[248] Reported in al-Muttaqi Hindi's *Kanz al-Ummal.*

[249] Imam Ahmad reported it in his *Musnad.*

[250] Reported in *Kanz al-Ummal.*

[251] Al-Bukhari and At-Tabarani recorded it as did ash-Shafi in his *Musnad,* Ibn Abi Shaybah and ibn Mardawayh.

[252] Related in al-Hafiz as-Suyuti's *Saghir.*

[253] Recorded in the *Sunan* of Ibn Majah in which al-Haythami in his *Majma al-zawaid* said it is authentic.

[254] Al-Haythami reported it in his *Majma al-zawaid,* as did al-Bazzar. Al-Hindi also recorded it in his *Kanz al-Ummal* with slightly different wording.

Specific Benefits of *Salawat*

Here again are the principal benefits obtained by invoking blessings on the Prophet ﷺ (*salawat*) as compiled by Hafiz as-Sakhawi in his book devoted to the topic:

> Among the rewards of one who performs *salawat* upon God's Messenger ﷺ are the following:
>
> - The *salawat*—blessing—of God, His angels, and His Prophet ﷺ on that person;
> - The expiation of his faults;
> - The purification of his works;
> - The exaltation of his rank;
> - The forgiveness of his sins;
> - The asking of forgiveness for him by his own *salat*;
> - The recording of rewards, the like of Mount Uhud, for him and his repayment in superabundant measure;
> - The comfort of his world and his hereafter if he devotes his entire *salat* to invoking blessings upon him;
> - The obliteration of more faults than that effected by the manumission of a slave;
> - His deliverance from affliction because of it;
> - The witnessing of the Prophet ﷺ himself to it;
> - The guarantee of the Prophet's ﷺ intercession for him;
> - God's pleasure, mercy, and safety from His anger;
> - Admission under the shade of the Throne for him;
> - Preponderance of his good deeds in the Balance;
> - His admission to drink from the Prophet's ﷺ Pond;
> - His safety from thirst and deliverance from the Fire;
> - His ability to cross the Bridge swiftly;
> - The sight of his seat in Paradise before he dies;
> - The preponderance of his prayers over more than twenty military conquests;
> - Its equivalency to giving alms to the needy;
> - Its being *zakat* and purification for him;
> - His wealth will increase because of its blessing;
> - More than one hundred of his needs will be fulfilled through it;

- It constitutes worship;
- It is the most beloved of all deeds to God;
- It beautifies meetings;
- It cancels out poverty and material duress;
- It lets him expect and find goodness everywhere;
- It makes him the most deserving of goodness;
- He benefits from it as well as his children and theirs, as well as those to whom its reward is gifted in the register of his good deeds;
- It brings him near to God and to His Prophet ﷺ;
- It is a light that helps him against his enemies;
- It cleans his heart of hypocrisy and rust;
- It commands the love of people and the sight of the Prophet ﷺ in dreams;
- It forbids slander (*ghiba*) against him.

In summary, it is among the most blessed, most meritorious, most useful of deeds in religion and in the life of the world, and carries desirable rewards other than all this for those who are clever and eager to acquire the deeds that constitute treasures for them, and harvest the most flourishing and glowing of hopes. They do this by focusing on the deed that includes all these tremendous merits, noble qualities, manifold and all-encompassing benefits which are not found together in any other.[255]

Excerpts on the Remembrance of God

Abd al-Rahman al-Sufuri wrote in his book *Nuzhat al-majalis wa muntakhab al-nafais* (The Pleasant Gatherings and the Select Precious Matters):

God, the Exalted, said, *"Verily in the remembrance of God do hearts find rest!"* (13:28) If it is asked, how is the meaning of this verse reconciled with that of His saying, *"They only are the true believers whose hearts feel fear ("wajilat,"* to tremble or shake*) when God is mentioned"* (8:2); it is answered that in the latter, the purpose of God's mention is to bring to mind His greatness and the intensity of

[255] Al-Sakhawi, *al-Qawl al-badi fi al-salat ala al-habib al-shafi* (The Radiant Discourse Concerning the Invocation of Blessings on the Beloved Iintercessor). p. 98.

His vengeance against those who disobey Him. This verse was revealed at a time when the Companions had a disagreement concerning the spoils of the Battle of Badr. Therefore, the mention or the remembrance of what is fearsome became appropriate. As for the former verse, it concerns whoever God guided and who has turned to God with love. Therefore, the mention of God's mercy became appropriate.

The two meanings of fearsomeness and mercy are reunited in *Surat al-Zumar*:

> *God hath now revealed the fairest of statements, a Scripture consistent, wherein promises of reward are paired with threats of punishment, whereat doth creep the flesh of those who fear their Lord, so that ("thumma,"* and then*) their flesh and their hearts soften to God's reminder (or, to the celebration of God's praises; or, to God's remembrance; meaning, to God's mercy and generosity).* (39:23)

The Prophet ﷺ said:

> *He who remembers God much, God loves him. The night that I was enraptured to my Lord I passed by a man extinguished within the light of God's Throne. I asked, "Who is this, and is he an angel?" I was told "No," and I asked again, "Is it a Prophet?" I was told "No," and I said, "Who then?" It was said, "This is a man who, while he was in the world, his tongue was constantly moist with the mention of God, and his heart was attached to the mosques."*

On the authority of Muadh ibn Jabal ؓ, the Prophet ﷺ said that God said:

> *No servant of Mine mentions Me in himself, except I mention him in an assembly of My angels, and he does not mention Me in an assembly, except I mention him in the Highest Company.*

On the authority of Abu Hurayra ؓ, who said that, while on the road to Makkah, the Prophet ﷺ passed on top of a mountain called Jumdan, at which time he said, *"Move on, for here is Jumdan which has overtaken the single-minded."* They said, "What are the single-minded (*mufarridun*)?" He said, *"The men and women who remember God abundantly"* (33:35).[256]

Tirmidhi stated:

It was said, "And what are the single-minded?" He replied, "Those who dote on the remembrance of God and are ridiculed because of it, whose burden the dhikr *removes from them, so that they come to God fluttering!"*

Al-Mundhiri said:

The single-minded and those who dote on the dhikr *and are ridiculed for it; these are the ones set afire with the remembrance of God.*[257]

The Prophet ﷺ said:

The one who mentions or remembers God among those who forget Him is like a green tree in the midst of dry ones.

The one who mentions or remembers God among those who forget Him, God shows him his seat in Paradise during his life.

The one who mentions or remembers God among those who forget Him is like the fighter behind those who run away.

The one who mentions or remembers God among those who forget Him, God looks at him with a look after which He will never punish him.

The one who mentions or remembers God among those who forget Him is like a light inside a dark house.

The one who mentions or remembers God among those who forget Him, God forgives him his sins to the amount of every eloquent and dumb speaker (that is, animals and human beings).

The one who mentions or remembers God in the marketplace will have light in every hair of his on the Day of Resurrection.

The Sufis say *dhikr* has a beginning, which is a truthful application;[258] it has a middle, which is a light that strikes; it has an end,

---

[256] Muslim related it.

[257] Al-Mundhiri, in *al-Targhib wa al-tarhib*

which is a piercing difficulty; it has a principle, which is purity; it has a branch, which is loyalty; it has a condition, which is presence; it has a carpet, which is righteous action; it has a peculiar characteristic, which is the Manifest Opening (cf. Quran 48:1).

Abu Saeed al-Kharraz said:

> When God desires to befriend a servant of His, He opens the door of *dhikr* for that servant. After the latter takes pleasure in *dhikr*, He opens the door of proximity for him. After that, He raises him to the meetings of intimacy, and after that, He makes him sit on a throne of Oneness.
>
> Then He removes the veils from him, and He makes him enter the abode of Singleness, and unveils Majesty and Sublimity to him. When the servant beholds Majesty and Sublimity, he remains without "he." He becomes extinguished, immune to the claims and pretensions of his ego, and protected for God's sake.[259]

Another seeker of Divine Truth said:

> *Dhikr* is the medicine (*"tiryaq,"* literally treacle; antidote for poison) of the sinners, the familiarity of the estranged, the treasure of those who practice reliance, the repast of those who possess certitude, the adornment of those who are connected, the starting-point of knowers, the carpet of those brought near Him, and the intoxicant of lovers.

The Prophet ﷺ also said:

---

[258]Truthfulness should not be confused with sincerity, since it is possible to act with sincerity but not to reach truthfulness, as Nawawi explained in his commentary to the second of his "forty *ahadith*" (*ahadith* about *islam, iman,* and *ihsan*) entitled *Sharh al-arbain hadith.* Ibn al-Jawzi relates in *Sifat al-Safwa* (4:98) that Mansur said he heard Musa ibn Isa say he heard his uncle say: "I heard Aba Yazid (al-Bistami) say: 'If once I could utter purely *"la ilaha illallah"* (there is no god except God alone), I would not care about anything after that.'"

[259] T.J. Winter: Ahmad ibn Isa Abu Said al-Kharraz (d. 277/890-1) was an important Sufi who, according to Huwjiri, was "the first to explain the doctrine of annihilation (*fana*) and subsistence (*baqa*)." He was the close companion of Dhul-Nun, Bishr al-Hafi, and al-Sari al-Saqati, and was renowned for the emphasis he placed on *ishq,* the passionate love of Allah, and upon the scrupulous observance of the Law. Sources: Sulami, *Tabaqat al-Sufiyya* 223-228; Qushayri, *al-Risala* 1:161-162; Brockelmann, 1:646.

Remembrance of God is firm knowledge of one's belief, immunity from hypocrisy, a fortress against Satan, and a guarded refuge from the Fire. [260]

Ibn al-Salah was asked about the measure by which the servant is estimated to be among *"those who remember God much."* (33:35) He said, "If he perseveres in the forms of *dhikr* inherited in the *Sunnah* morning and evening and in the various times and occasions, then he is of those who remember God much."

Moses 🌿 said, "O my Lord! Are You near, so that I may speak to You intimately, or are You far, so that I may call out to You?" God inspired to him, "I am sitting next to the one who remembers Me." He said, "O my Lord, we are sometimes in a state of major impurity, and we hold You in too high regard to dare remember You at that time." He replied, "Remember me in every state."[261]

Abd al-Rahim ibn al-Hasan al-Isnawi (al-Shafii) said in his *Alghaz* (Riddles):

A man in a state of minor impurity is forbidden from certain forms of *dhikr*, as illustrated by the nullification of the act of worship incurred when entering such a state during the Friday sermon, because ritual purity is a condition for its validity.

On the *Dhikr* of Inanimate Objects

The seven heavens and the earth and all that is therein praise Him, and there is not a thing but sings His praise; but ye understand not their praise. Lo! He is ever Clement, Forgiving. *(17:44)*

Ibrahim al-Nakhai said concerning God's saying, *"There is not a thing but sings His praise"* (17:44): "Everything praises Him, including the door when it squeaks."[262] It has also been said, "The verse is general, and it applies particularly to the one endowed with speech, as in God's

---

[260] Mentioned by al-Layth al-Samarqandi.

[261] Ghazali mentioned it in the *Ihya.*

[262] T.J. Winter: I. ibn Yazid al-Nakhai was a devout and learned scholar of Kufa who opposed the writing of *ahadith* as an unjustified innovation. He studied under al-Hasan al-Basri and Anas ibn Malik, and taught Abu Hanifa, who may have been influenced by his extensive use of personal judgment (*ray*) in matters of jurisprudence. Sources: Ibn Hibban, *Mashahir ulama al-amsar* 101; M.M. Azami, *Studies in Early Hadith Literature* 65-66; Ibn al-Jazari, *Ghayat al-nihaya* 1:29.

saying, 'Everything was destroyed,'[263] whereas the houses of Ad were not destroyed, and in His saying concerning Sheba (Balqis), '*And she has been given from all things*' (27:23) whereas she had not been given anything from Solomon's (Sulayman's) ﷺ kingdom."

It was also said that the verse has a universal meaning, whereby the one endowed with speech glorifies God by word, while the silent one glorifies through his state. This is by virtue of his being in existence; he testifies to His Maker through having been made.

In Taj al-Din ibn al-Subki's *Tabaqat al-Shafiiyya al-kubra,* the interpretation favored by the Shafii *madhdhab* is that all things make glorification through actual utterance, because such a thing is not impossible and is indicated by many proof-texts. God, the Exalted, said:

> *We have placed the mountains under His dominion; they praise God at nightfall and at sunrise.* (38:18)

The mountains' glorification through actual utterance does not necessitate that we hear it. In *al-Wujuh al-musfira an ittisa al-maghfira* (The Faces Made Radiant by the Vastness of Mercy) is related the following commentary:

> It is more likely that they literally glorify, except that this phenomenon is hidden from the people and is not perceived except through the rupture of natural laws. The Companions heard the glorification of food and other objects placed before the Prophet ﷺ.

Concerning God's saying at the end of the verse, "*Lo! He is ever Clement, Forgiving*" (17:44), it applies to the state of those addressed by the verse in three ways. First, in the vast majority of cases, people are distracted from glorifying God, the Exalted—unlike the heavens, and the earth, and all that is therein. These distracted ones become in need of clemency and forgiveness. Second, they do not understand the praise of all these objects, and this may be because they do not sufficiently contemplate and reflect upon them; they then become in need of clemency and forgiveness. Third, the fact that they do not hear the praises may cause them to feel contempt towards these objects and drive

---

[263] "*Destroying all things by commandment of its Lord. And morning found them so that naught could be seen save their dwellings. Thus do we reward the guilty folk.*" (46:25)

them to deny the rights of creation; they again become in need of clemency and forgiveness.

Without doubt he who beholds with full understanding the glorification of things in existence honors and magnifies them in respect to this glorification, even if the Lawgiver ordered him to disdain them in another respect.

The author of *al-Wujuh al-musfira* cited the following story:

> One of God's servants sought to perform the purification from defecation by using stones to clean himself. He took one stone, and God removed the veil from his hearing so that he was now able to hear the stone's praise. Out of shame he left it and took another one, but he heard that one praising God also. And every time he took another stone he heard it glorifying God. Seeing this, at last he turned to God so that He would veil from him their praise to enable him to purify himself. God then veiled him from hearing them. He proceeded to purify himself despite his knowledge that the stones were making *tasbih*, because the one who reported about their *tasbih* is the same Law-giver who ordered to use them for purification. Therefore, in the concealment of *tasbih* there is a far-reaching wisdom.

This is true, and in Fakhr ad-Din al-Razi's *Tafsir* it is said that what the scholars have agreed upon is that whoever is not alive is not empowered with speech, and it has been firmly established that inanimate objects praise God through the medium of their state. And God knows best.

Six Benefits of Remembrance of God

1. THE RANKS OF *DHIKR*

One of the commentators of Quran said concerning God's saying, *"But among them are some who wrong themselves and among them are some who are lukewarm, and among them are some who outstrip others through good deeds, by God's leave"* (35:32), that they are respectively the rememberer by tongue, the rememberer by heart, and the one who never forgets his Lord.

Ibn Ata Allah said:

> The one who utters the Word of Oneness needs three lights: the light of guidance, the light of sufficiency, and the light of Divine help. Whoever God graces with the first light, he is immune (*masum*) from associating a partner to God. Whoever God graces with the second light, he is immune from committing great sins and indecencies; and whoever God graces with the third light, he is protected (*mahfuz*) from the corrupt thoughts and motions that typify those given to heedless actions. The first light belongs to "the ones who wrong themselves," the second to "those that are lukewarm," and the third to "the ones who outstrip others through good deeds."[264]
>
> Al-Wasiti was asked about the remembrance of God.[265] He said:
>
> It is the exiting from the battlefield of heedlessness into the outer space of direct vision (*mushahada*) on the mount of victory over fear and intensity of love.

One of the special attributes of the remembrance of God is that it has been placed in direct correspondence with God's own remembrance of us. God Mighty and Exalted said, "*Remember Me, and I shall remember you*" (2:152). Musa said, peace be upon him, "O my Lord, where do you

---

[264] Nuh Keller, Victor Danner: Abu al-Fadl Ibn Ata Allah (d. 709/1309) of Alexandria, Egypt: One of the great Sufi imams and a Maliki jurist, author of the *Hikam* (Aphorisms), *Miftah al-falah* (The Key to Success), *al-Qasd al-mujarrad fi marifat al-ism al-mufrad* (The Pure Goal Concerning Knowledge of the Unique Name), *Taj al-arus al-hawi li tadhhib al-nufus* (The Bride's Crown Containing the Discipline of Souls), *Unwan al-tawfiq fi adab al-tariq* (The Sign of Success Concerning the Discipline of the Path), the biographical *al-Lataif fi manaqib Abi al-Abbas al-Mursi wa shaykhihi Abi al-Hassan* (The Subtle Blessings in the Saintly Lives of Abu al-Abbas al-Mursi and His Master Abu al-Hasan), and others, five of which were transmitted with their chains by the *hadith* master and historian al-Sakhawi (d. 902/1497) to the Shadhili commentator Ahmad Zarruq (d. 899/1493). Ibn Ata Allah was the student of Abu al-Abbas al-Mursi (d. 686/1288), the second successor of Imam Abu al-Hasan al-Shadhili, and the shaykh of the Shafii imam Taqi al-Din al-Subki. He related from al-Shadhili the following saying: "This path is not monasticism, eating barley and bran, or the garrulousness of affectation, but rather perseverance in the divine commands and certainty in the divine guidance." Some sources: al-Zirikly, *al-Alam* 1:221; Asqalani, *al-Durar al-kamina* 1:273; Subki, *Tabaqat al-shafiiyya* 9:23.

[265] T.J. Winter: Muhammad ibn Musa al-Wasiti (d. 320/932): A Sufi who associated with al-Junayd and al-Nuri in Baghdad and who later moved to Merv where he died. He was also an authority on *fiqh*. Sources: Qushayri, *Risala* 1:174; Sulami, *Tabaqat* 302-307.

dwell?" He replied, "In the heart of my believing servant."[266] The meaning of this is the heart's rest brought about by His remembrance.

Muhammad ibn al-Hanafiyya ﷺ said:

> Verily the angels lower their gaze in the presence of the rememberer of God, just as the people lower their gaze before lightning.[267]

2. REMITTANCE OF SINS THROUGH *DHIKR*

It is related that a servant of God will join the gatherings of *dhikr* with sins the like of mountains and then rise and leave one such gathering with nothing left of them to his name. This is why the Prophet ﷺ called it one of the groves of Paradise when he said, "If you pass by the groves of Paradise, be sure to graze in them," and someone said, "What are the groves of Paradise?" to which he replied, "The circles of *dhikr*."

Aata ﷺ said:

> Whoever sits in a gathering in which God is remembered, God will remit for him ten evil gatherings of his.

Abu Yazid al-Bistami, "I have entrusted you with a secret for which you shall render Me an account under the Tree of Bliss (*shajarat tuba*)." He said, "We are under that tree as long as we remain in the remembrance of God."

---

[266] Ibn Majah narrates from Abu Anbasa, and Tabarani from Abu Utba that the Prophet ﷺ said: "God has vessels from among the people of the earth *(lillahi aniyatun min ahli al-ard),* and the vessels of your Lord are the hearts of His righteous servants, and the most beloved of those to Him are the softest and the most sensitive." Al-Jarrahi said in *Kashf al-khafa* that this was the basis of the saying attributed to the Prophet ﷺ: "The heart of the believer is the house of God" al-Qari said that the latter, though not a saying of the Prophet ﷺ, was correct in meaning. Imam Ahmad narrates in his *Kitab al-zuhd* from Wahb ibn Munabbih: God opened the heavens to Ezekiel ﷺ until he beheld the very Throne, whereupon he said: "Glory to Thee, what greatness is Thine, O my Lord!" God said: "Verily the heavens and the earth are unable to encompass Me, and the devoted, soft heart of My faithful servant is able to encompass Me." Imam Ghazali mentioned it in his *Ihya Ulum al-din.*

[267] Abu al-Qasim Muhammad ibn Ali ibn Abi Talib ﷺ, named ibn al-Hanafiyya: A saintly son of Sayyidina Ali ﷺ. He took *hadith* from him and from several other Companions including Jabir ibn Abd Allah ﷺ, the last of the Companions who died in Madina. Sources: Ibn Adi, *al-Kamil* 2:113b; Ibn Hajar, *Tahdhib al-tahdhib* 9:354 (M.M. Azami). The Prophet ﷺ gave Ali ﷺ special permission to name him both Abu al-Qasim and Muhammad, which he otherwise forbade: Tirmidhi (#2846) and Abu Dawud (*Adab* #4967).

It is related on Ali's ﷺ authority that God manifests Himself (*yatajalla*) to the rememberers during *dhikr* and the recitation of Quran.

The Prophet ﷺ said:

No group gathers and remembers God seeking nothing other than Him except a caller from Heaven calls out to them: Arise forgiven, for your bad deeds have been turned into good ones!

Abu ad-Darda ﷺ said:

The Prophet ﷺ said, "God verily will raise on the Day of Resurrection people bearing light in their faces, carried aloft on pulpits of pearl, whom the people will envy. They are neither prophets nor martyrs." Upon hearing this a Bedouin Arab fell to his knees and said, "Show them to us (ajlihim), O Prophet of God!" that is, "describe them for us." He replied, "They are those who love one another for God's sake alone. They come from many different tribes, countries, and cities. They gather together for the remembrance of God the Exalted, remembering Him."

Someone said concerning God's saying with reference to Solomon ﷺ, *"Verily, I will punish him with hard punishment"* (27:21) that it means, "Verily I shall drive him far from the gatherings of *dhikr*." Al-Junayd concerning God's saying, *"And (He is the One) Who causeth me to die, then giveth me life again"* (26:81), said that this means, "He causes me to die with heedlessness (of Him), then He causes me to live with remembrance (of Him)." Al-Hasan al-Basri said, "No people sit remembering God, the Exalted, with one of the people of Paradise in their midst except God grants him to intercede for all of them."

3. *DHIKR* OF THE FROGS

The Prophet David (Dawud) ﷺ said, "I shall praise God with a kind of praise that none among his creatures ever used before." Thereupon a frog called out to him, "Do you pride yourself before God for your praise, while for seventy years my tongue has been moist from remembering Him, and I have eaten nothing in the past ten nights because I kept busy uttering two words?" David ﷺ said, "What are these two words?" The frog replied, "O Praiser of Thyself with every tongue, O Remembered One in every place!"

It is related in *Nuzhat al-nufus wa al-afkar* (The Recreation of Minds and Thoughts) that an angel once said to David ﷺ, "O David, understand what the frog is saying!" whereupon he heard it saying, "Glory and praise to You to the farthest boundary of Your knowledge!" David ﷺ said, "By the One Who made me a prophet, verily I shall sing my Lord's praise in this way." The commentators have said that the frogs' words were: "Glory to the King, the Holy One!" *(subhan al-malik al-quddus)* while al-Baghawi has, "Glory to my Lord Most Holy!" *(subhana rabbi al-quddus),* and Ali ﷺ uses the words, "Glory to the One Who is worshipped in the abysses of the sea!"

4. *DHIKR* OF THE PROPHET JONAH

Ali ﷺ said:

In the time of Jonah (Yunus) ﷺ, there was a frog which had lived past the age of 4,000 years. It never rested from glorifying God. One day it said, "O my Lord, no one glorifies You like I do!" Jonah ﷺ said, "O my Lord, I say what it says!" and he said, "Glory to You by the number of times each of your creatures says 'Glory to You,' and glory to You by the number of times each of Your creatures does not say 'Glory to You,' and glory to You according to the expanse of Your knowledge, and the light of Your countenance, and the adornment of Your throne, and the reach of Your words!"

5. LENGTHENING THE PRONUNCIATION OF *LA ILAHA ILL-ALLAH*

Ibn Abbas and his father ﷺ, narrated the Prophet ﷺ said:

*The day God created the heavens and the earth He created an angel and ordered him to say, "There is no god except God alone" (*la ilaha ill-Allah*). The angel lengthens his delivery as he utters it and will not rest from this until the Trumpet is blown.*

One of the Companions said that whoever says, "No god except God" and lengthens his pronunciation intending thereby to magnify God, God will remit 4,000 grave sins for him, and if he did not commit 4,000, God will remit the difference for his family and neighbors. It is related in the *hadith,* "Whoever says 'No god except God' and lengthens his pronunciation intending thereby to magnify God, 4,000 of his sins are struck thereby from the register of his sins." Hence it is praiseworthy to lengthen one's pronunciation upon uttering it, as Nawawi said.

The Prophet ﷺ also said:

Whoever lengthens his pronunciation upon saying "No god except God," God will make him dwell in Paradise in the Abode of Majesty by which he has named Himself when He said: "There remaineth but the countenance of thy Lord of Might and Glory" (55:27), and God will grant him to behold His Gracious Countenance.

Anas ibn Malik ؓ narrated from the Prophet ﷺ:

O human beings! Whoever says "No god except God" in astonishment at something, God creates from each letter of his utterance a tree with as many leaves as the days of this world, each leaf asking forgiveness for him and praising God on his behalf until the Day of Judgment . . .

It has been related that this phrase has on the side of Iblis (Satan) the effect that a gangrenous sore would have on the side of a human being. Qadi Iyad relates in the *Shifa* from Ibn Abbas ؓ that written on the door of Paradise is the inscription, "There is no god but God alone, Muhammad is the Messenger of God; Whoever says this, I shall not punish him." [268]

The following account is part of the explanation of God's saying, "*And speak (O Moses and Aaron) unto him (Pharaoh) a gentle word*" (20:44). Moses ؑ said, "O Lord, how can a word be gentle?" God replied, "Say to him, 'Would you like a good compromise? You have followed your own self for four hundred and fifty years; follow our intent but for one year, and God will forgive you all your sins. If not one year, then one month; if not, one week; if not, one single day; if not, one single hour. If

---

[268] Abu al-Fadl Iyad ibn Musa al-Yahsubi al-Maliki of Andalusia and Fes, Morocco. The imam of his time in the sciences of *hadith*, and a scholar of *tafsir*, *fiqh*, Arabic grammar and language, and Arab genealogy. He wrote many books including a commentary on the *Sahih* of Muslim which Nawawi used in his own great commentary. Ibn Farhun in *Dibaj al-dhahab* says of his book *al-Shifa*: "No one disputes the fact that it is totally unique nor denies him the honor of being the first to compose such a book. Everyone relies on it and writes about its usefulness and encourages others to read and study it. Copies of it have spread East and West." (Qadi Iyad, *Muhammad Messenger of Allah: Al-shifa of Qadi Iyad,* trans. Aisha Abdarrahman Bewley (Granada, Spain: Madinah Press, 1991) p. 511.

you do not (wish to humor us) for all of an hour, then say in a single breath, "There is no god but God" so that I may bring peace to you.'"

After Moses ﷺ conveyed the message, Pharaoh gathered his armies and said to them, *"I am your Most High Lord!"* (79:24) At this the heavens and the earth shook and pleaded before God the Glorious and Exalted that Pharaoh be put to death. God said, *"He is like the dog: only the stick is good for him. O Moses, cast your staff."* (cf., 7:117, 27:10, 28:31) Moses ﷺ cast his staff (which became a huge snake or dragon) and the magicians of Pharaoh's court immediately submitted. Pharaoh fled to his bedchamber. Moses ﷺ said, "If you do not come out, I shall order it to enter where you are." Pharaoh said, "Give me a little respite." Moses ﷺ answered, "I have no permission to respite you." But God, the Exalted, inspired to him, "Respite him, for verily I am the Clement, I do not hasten to punish."

Pharaoh began to relieve himself forty times a day while previously he would relieve himself only once every forty days. Moses ﷺ gave him a respite. When the day came, Pharaoh exceeded his bounds and rebelled. God therefore *"seized him and made him an example for the afterlife and the former"* (79:25); that is, He punished him with drowning because of his former word ("I am your Most High Lord"), and He punished him with Hell because he said, *"I know not that ye have a god other than me."* (28:38) Ibn Abbas ؓ said, "This is the former word, while the other came later, and between them lay forty years."

It is mentioned in the book *Zumrat al-ulum wa zuhrat al-nujum* (The Array of the Sciences and the Brightness of Stars) that the Prophet ﷺ said:

> *Gabriel told me, "I stood in wait before God at the time Pharaoh said: 'And what is the Lord of the Worlds?' (26:23) whereupon I outstretched two of my wings to smite him with punishment, but God, the Exalted, said, 'Wait, O Gabriel! He hastens to punish who fears the lapse of time.'"*

It was also mentioned in that book that when Pharaoh said, *"I am your Lord the Most High"* (79:24) Gabriel wanted to shake the earth from under his feet, but when he sought permission from his Lord, the Exalted, He did not give it to him and ordered him to ignore Pharaoh instead.

Al-Alai said in his explanation of the *surah* of the Story (*al-qasas*) that Iblis entered Pharaoh's presence as the latter was in the bath and said,

"O Pharaoh, I enticed you with every transgression, but I never told you to claim absolute Lordship!" Then he gave him forty lashes and left him in anger. Pharaoh said to him, "O Iblis, should I take back this claim?" He replied, "It would not be right for you to take it back after making it." [269]

A group of the disbelievers of Quraysh gathered among the Pharaoh of their community, Abu Jahl, at Abu Talib's house during the latter's last illness. Abu Jahl said to him, "You know what has taken place between us and your brother's son. Therefore obtain what is rightfully ours from him and what is rightfully his from us before you die." Abu Talib called the Prophet ﷺ and said, "O my nephew, these are the nobility of your people, so leave them be, and they shall leave you be." He replied, "Do they agree to obey me if I ask them to say but one word?" Abu Jahl said, "Nay, we shall obey you if you ask us to say ten!" The Prophet ﷺ then said, "Say, *La ilaha ill-Allah,*" whereupon they said, "Are you asking us to reduce all our gods to only one? Truly you are asking us for the strangest thing!" and they dispersed. Abu Talib said, "O Muhammad, you have asked them for nothing excessive." That is, "You have not asked them for anything difficult."

Concerning God's saying, *"Judge aright between us and be not unjust (lit. do not exceed the proper bounds)"* (38:22); that is, "Do not swerve in your judgment," the Prophet ﷺ hoped that his uncle would profess Islam, so he said to him, "Say it (the phrase: There is no god but God alone), so that I will be permitted to intercede for you on the Day of the Rising." Abu Talib replied, "Were it not that people—that is, the Quraysh—might think that I said it out of fear (of death), indeed I would say it."

> Al-Razi said in his explanation of the *surah* of the Cattle (al-Anam): Abu Talib said, "Ask me to say other than this because your people hate it." The Prophet ﷺ replied, "I will never say other than this even if they were to dislodge the sun from its place and put it in my hand." They said, "Then stop cursing our gods, otherwise we will curse you and Him Who orders you to do this," whereupon God's saying was revealed, *"Revile not those unto whom they pray beside God lest they wrongfully revile God through ignorance."* (6:108)

[269] Author of a massive commentary on Bukhari's *Sahih* entitled *Umdat al-Qari.*

If it is said, "To curse the idols is among the most meritorious acts of obedience to God; why then did God forbid it?" The answer is, God forbade it because cursing them might lead to the gravest of transgressions—exalted is God far above the saying of wrong-doers—namely cursing God and His Messenger ﷺ, and it is an obligation to take precautions against it.

6. GOD'S SIMILES FOR THE "PHRASE OF ONENESS"

God compared the Phrase of Declaring Oneness *(kalimat al-tawhid)* to the following:

- Water, because water cleanses; similarly, this phrase cleanses from sins;
- Soil, because the soil gives forth much in exchange for a single seed; similarly, this phrase multiplies its return;
- Fire, because fire burns, and this phrase burns sins;
- The Sun, because the latter sheds light on the worlds, and this phrase illumines even the grave;
- The Moon, because it dispels the darkness of night, and this phrase sheds light with the same certainty;
- Stars, because they are guides for travelers, and this phrase is a guide for the people of misguidance to follow the right way;
- Date palms, when He said, "*A goodly tree, its root set firm, its branches reaching into heaven, giving its fruit at every season by permission of its Lord*" (14:24-25);
- The date palm does not grow in every land; similarly, this phrase does not grow in every heart;
- The date palm is the tallest fruit tree; similarly, the root of this phrase is in the heart and the top of its branches are under the Throne;
- The value of the fruit does not diminish because of the pit; similarly, the value of the believer does not diminish despite the disobedience lodged between himself and God the Exalted; and,
- The bottom of the date palm is thorns while its top is moist dates; similarly, the initial stages of this phrase are duties,

> and whoever fulfills them reaches the fruit which is to behold God the Exalted.

The Phrase of Oneness is the key to the Garden of Paradise: "Every key must have teeth,"[270] and its teeth are to forsake all that is forbidden and do what is ordained. God, the Exalted, says, *"Therefore know that there is no god but God alone"* (47:19) and the Prophet ﷺ said, *"Whoever said, 'There is no god but God alone,' taking care that it is unalloyed* (mukhlisan bihi*) and from the heart, enters Paradise."* It was asked in what being-unalloyed (*ikhlas*) consisted. He said, *"In barring one from what God, the Exalted, has declared forbidden."*

The Prophet ﷺ also said:

> *O Abu Hurayra! Every good deed on your part shall be weighed on the Day of Rising except the Witnessing that there is no god but God alone, for verily it can never be placed in the Balance.* ۞

---

[270] A saying by Wahb ibn Munabbih, reported by *Bukhari* in the title of the first chapter of the Book of Funeral Prayers (*Janaiz*).

Guidebook of the Saints of the Golden Chain

The Naqshbandi Way of *Dhikr*

Among the readers of this book may be some Sufi aspirants who have been practicing one or several of the other Sufi paths or their branches other than the Naqshbandi Path. If you are one of these people you may be wondering what difference there is between the Naqshbandi and the other Sufi ways.

It is axiomatic that all Sufi paths lead to the Divine Presence. The Prophet ﷺ said, *"The ways to God are as numerous as the breaths of human beings."* The differences lie mostly in the realm of style and taste, and reflect the need to accommodate the variety of types among the aspirants. Differences also stem from the unique individualities of the great luminaries who imprinted each of the Sufi orders—may God be pleased with all of them!

There are also some differences of approach. Most Sufi paths offer aspirants a gradual unveiling of the heart's eye, accomplished through the practice of *dhikr,* the remembrance of God. This spiritual exercise may contain repetition of various of God's Holy Names. Some forms of *dhikr* involve practices designed to break the spell of mundane consciousness and propel the practitioner into a state of altered awareness. Such practices may include repetition of many thousands of holy phrases, sometimes connecting with breathing exercises and often with physical movements. Without a doubt, through the steadfast and dedicated practice of these methods, the aspirant may experience spiritual states and attain stations unimaginable in a normal state of consciousness. The aspirant may feel himself to be flying towards the heavenly goals, beholding the wonders of the mysterious and hidden aspects of creation.

If your eyes have been thus opened, and if you are greatly enamored of the wide vistas you have beheld, then be warned. Should you embark upon the Naqshbandi Path, your colorful plumage will be clipped and replaced with the humble cloak of obscurity. For the main difference between the Naqshbandi Way and others is that, while they are giving, we are taking away. Everything must go, even your separate existence. First you will be without anything, then you will be nothing. Only those who are prepared to take such a step can be real Naqshbandi disciples. As long as a drop is falling from the heavens, it may be called a drop. When it falls into the ocean, it is no longer a drop; it is the ocean.

If anyone is interested in spiritual stations and powers, he may attain them through following any of the forty Sufi paths, as these ways are quite efficacious. Through the recitation of the most beautiful Names of God everyone receives bountifully in accordance with his intention. In the end, however, the sincere seeker will be struck with remorse if he becomes fixated at the stage of stations and states. One day, he will perceive how he has fallen victim to distraction and say: "O my Lord, I have been wasting myself and my efforts on something other than You."

Should a seeker's life end while he is in those states, he will regret that they distracted him from seeking the Divine Countenance of his Lord. Therefore, grandshaykhs have been ordered to strip their followers of their spiritual adornments, so that they may be presented to their Lord in perfect lowliness: "This is your servant, oh our Lord; accept him. He is lost to himself and exists only for You." This is their top priority, and helping their followers attain such a reality is their duty.

It is understood by all orders that strange and enchanting experiences are the scenery of the journey, not the goal. The goal is to reach the Divine Presence by the attraction of the Beloved Himself. The Holy Prophet Muhammad ﷺ is the guide and example. On His miraculous Night Journey, in which he was conducted by the angel Gabriel عليه السلام first from Makkah to Jerusalem and then up to the seven heavens and into the Divine Presence, he passed through the whole universe. God Almighty informs us in the Holy Quran that the Prophet's ﷺ vision *"neither swerved nor wavered"* (53:2). In other words, he looked and beheld but never let those sights distract him from ascending towards his most exalted destination. The Holy Prophet ﷺ was able to behold those sights without being distracted because his heart was only for his Lord. He is the Beloved of God. As for ourselves, we are vulnerable and weak-willed. Those experiences and attainments may accord with our ego's desires, whereas annihilation is never an attractive proposition for the ego.

Therefore, in order to provide maximum protection, the Naqshbandi masters take a different approach to the unveiling of the heart's eye. There are 70,000 veils between us and the station of the

Prophet ﷺ. A Naqshbandi master rends these veils in descending order, starting with those closest to the Divine Presence and then successively downwards towards the level of the disciple. This process continues throughout the training of the disciple until there is but one veil, the veil of humanity, restraining the disciple's vision from contemplation of the Divine Reality. In order to protect the disciple from attraction to something other than his Lord, however, the shaykh does not rend that last veil until the disciple reaches the highest state of perfection or until his final seven breaths on his deathbed.

If the veils are removed from the bottom up by means of mystical practices, the disciple beholds a succession of new panoramas. That very vision may keep him from progressing. Those who attain such stations during this life may discover that they have become powerful and famous among people. This is also a danger. Power and recognition are conditions conducive to worldliness. The ego will never neglect such an opportunity to demand its share of the excitement and admiration, and by doing so taint the whole process of spiritual endeavor.

The Sufi aspirant must seek his Lord, not fame. Look at history's most renowned holy woman, the Virgin Mary عليها السلام, who once prayed, *"Would that I had been a thing forgotten and out of sight!"* (19:23). She has taught all humanity to seek only obscurity in the sight of the world and not to look for recognition. The striving for power and fame is a heavy burden. The Sufi seeks rather to be forgotten in the ocean of Unity of God Almighty.

The Naqshbandi Sufi shaykhs say that whoever works according to the following series of recommendations, and acts on it, will attain the exalted stations, especially the station of nearness to God, Who is Powerful and Sublime, on the Day of Resurrection. The faithful and diligent application of these practices is certain to temper the influence of the lower elements which exist in every human being: the ego, worldliness, vain desires, and Satan. A person who manages to keep these principles of the Naqshbandi Order will achieve the light of his shaykh, who will lift him to the Presence of the supreme teacher, the Prophet ﷺ, who in his turn, will lift him up to the station of annihilation in God.

God, Almighty and Exalted, taught Prophet Muhammad ﷺ good manners, for which reason the Holy Prophet ﷺ said, *"My Lord taught me good manners and perfected His teaching."* The best of manners is to keep the orders of God, and the seeker must follow the example of the Prophet ﷺ in keeping the obligations of His Lord and in following the spiritual path. He must be persistent in keeping to the conduct of the Order, until he attains the knowledge of the Divine Law and the Way.

The beginner must always begin at the beginning. He should recognize the difference between the Divine Law and the Way. The Divine Law is a reality that is obligatory for every believing man and woman. Concretely speaking, the Divine Law consists of practicing that which God has ordered and avoiding that which He has forbidden. The believer relies on guides to indicate clearly to him what to discard and what to follow. The Quran and *Sunnah* are the foundation of all guidance. The schools of the Divine Law, the writing of the scholars, and their living inheritors relay and explain the guidance. Whoever keeps to this guidance will be on the Straight Path.

The Way is the firm intention of the Divine Law. It does not exist outside the Divine Law. It is the resolution to follow the *Sunnah* of the Prophet ﷺ as completely as possible in every aspect, both external and internal, exposed and hidden, exoteric and esoteric, physical and spiritual. To follow the Way, the disciple puts his trust in the judgment of the shaykh for the correct understanding and application of the guidance of the Quran and the *Sunnah.* The disciple places his hand in the hand of an authorized, living shaykh and must proceed as indicated by him. He must be ready at all times to receive the orders of his shaykh, just as the Prophet ﷺ awaited the coming of Gabriel عليه السلام with revelation from God, Almighty and Exalted. In the same way, he must follow the shaykh's orders, carrying them out to the letter. He must have the "conduct of anticipation," which means that he must constantly await the orders of his guide. He must adopt the attitude of a hunter to its prey, being oblivious to all other directions. His sight, hearing, existence, and thoughts should be ready to receive orders, and he should always be ready to carry out some new order. Such a person will be a master of the proper conduct of the Exalted Naqshbandi Order, and this manifestation will become apparent in him.

The disciple should keep to his daily *dhikr* and should obey the order of his shaykh without veering to the right or to the left. Grandshaykh, Shaykh Abd Allah ad-Daghestani, said, "My tongue is the tongue of the secret of the Divine Law and of the secret of the Quran." Then he asked a question saying, "Who are the bearers and protectors of the Quran?" and answered himself: "The bearers and protectors of the Quran are the ones who set foot in all the exalted stations and know them with true understanding. And is it not right, my children, that I should indicate to you that you should follow this path so that you may reach and discover these stations?"

Shaykh Abd Allah ad-Daghestani continued saying, "Whoever receives the keys to the five stations: heart, secret, secret of the secret, hidden, and most hidden is the one who takes care to conduct himself properly and perform the spiritual practices in their correct manner. This enables him to reach the station of Bayazid al-Bistami, in which he said, "I am also the Real (*al-Haqq*)." Whoever wishes to enter the station of the two Attributes of the Real, Almighty and Exalted, the Attribute of Beauty and that of Majesty, must follow this Way.

The Spiritual Practices

The spiritual practices of seekers are of three kinds: for Initiates, for the Prepared, and for the People of Determination.[271]

Daily Spiritual Practices for Initiates

ADAB		ادب		
Practice	Dhikr	Arabic	Meaning	Repeat
Bear witness - shahāda	ash-hadu an lā ilāha ill-Allāh wa ash-hadu anna Muḥammadan ʻabduhū wa rasūluh	أَشْهَدُ أَنْ لا إله إلا الله وَأَشْهَدُ أَنَّ مُحَمَّدًا عَبْدُهُ وَرَسُولُهُ	I testify that there is no god but God, and I testify that Muhammad is the Servant and Messenger of God.	3
Seek forgiveness – istighfār	Astaghfirullāh	أَسْتَغْفِرُ الله	God forgive me.	70
Seek blessings	Sūratu 'l-Fātiḥah	الفَاتِحَة الشريفة		1
	Āman ar-rasūlu (Quran 2:285-6)	See Page 169		1
	Sūratu 'l-Ikhlāṣ	سورة الإخلاص		11
	Sūratu 'l-Inshirāḥ	سورة الانشراح		7
	Sūratu 'l-Falaq	سورة الفلق		1
	Sūratu 'n-Nās	سورة الناس		1
kalimah	Lā ilāha illa-llāh	لا إله إلا الله		9

---

[271] To facilitate proper pronunciation for non-Arab speakers, text in the following sections are rendered in a special diacritical font using the system of Arabic transliteration adopted by the Library of Congress in the United States.

	Lā ilāha illa-llāh Muḥammadun Rasūl Allāh	لا إله إلا الله مُحَمَّدًا رَسُولُ الله	There is no god but God, and Muhammad is the Servant and Messenger of God.	1
Prayers on the Prophet - ṣalawāt	Allāhumma ṣalli ʿalā Muḥammadin wa ʿalā āli Muḥammadin wa sallim	اللَّهُمَّ صلّ على مُحَمَّد وعلى آل مُحَمَّد وسلِّم	O God send blessings and peace upon Muhammad and the family of Muhammad.	10
Gift the reward - Ihdā	See page 172	إهداء		1
Recitation	Sūratu 'l-Fātiḥah	الفاتحة الشريفة		1

WIRD		ورد		
Practice	Dhikr	Arabic	Meaning	Repeat
Remember God- dhikr	Allāh, Allāh	ذِكْرُ الجَلالة: الله الله الله حق	God, God.	1500
Prayers on the Prophet- ṣalawāt	Allāhumma ṣalli ʿalā Muḥammadin wa ʿalā āli Muḥammadin wa sallim	اللَّهُمَّ صلّ على مُحَمَّد وعلى آل مُحَمَّد وسلِّم	O God send blessings and peace upon Muhammad and the family of Muhammad.	100
Recitation of Qur'ān	One juz' (1/30) of the Qur'ān -or- Sūratu 'l-Ikhlāṣ	جزء من القرآن او اخلاص الشريفة		1 -or- 100
Prayers on the Prophet- Ṣalawāt	One chapter of Dalā'il al-Khayrāt	دلائل الخيرات	O God send blessings and peace upon	1 -or-

	-or- Allāhumma ṣalli ʻalā Muḥammadin wa ʻalā āli Muḥammadin wa sallim	او اللّٰهُمَّ صلِّ على مُحَمَّد وعلى آل مُحَمَّد وسلّم	Muhammad and the family of Muhammad	100

Spiritual Practices for the Prepared

The *adab* and *wird* for the Prepared (*musta'id*) seeker is identical to that of the Initiate (*muḥib*), with the following additions:

- *Increase* the number of repetitions of God's name from 1,500 to 2,500 by tongue and add another 2,500 by heart, meditating upon it.
- *Increase* the number of *ṣalawāt* from 100 to 300 on all days except Monday, Thursday, and Friday when it is done 500 times.

Spiritual Practices for People of Determination

The *adab* and *wird* for the People of Determination are similar to that of the Prepared (*musta'id*), with the following additions:

- *Sayyid aṣ-ṣalawāt* (chief of the Prayers on the Prophet) is recited before the *Ihdā* (see page 172).
- After the *Sūratu 'l-Fātiḥah* of the *Ihdā,* the seeker repeats *Allāh Hū Allāh Hū Allāh Hū Ḥaqq* three times, imagining himself between the Hands of his Lord.
- There is an increase in the number of repetitions of God's name from 2,500 to 5,000 each by tongue and by heart, and an increase in the number of *ṣalawāt* from 300 to 1,000 on all days except Monday, Thursday, and Friday, when it is done 2,000 times.

Notes to the Spiritual Practices

Prayers

The essence of the practices of the Naqshbandī shaykhs is built on the pillar (*rukn*) of prayer (*ṣalāḥ*) and on remembrance of God (*dhikrullāh*). For those desiring high stations and distinguished ranks, the observance of prayer is the key. The seekers must strive to imitate their shaykhs in the observance of not only the obligatory prayers, but the supererogatory *sunan* and *nawāfil* prayers that the shaykhs maintain as a constant daily practices. You will find the following practices are based around the five obligatory prayers, in addition to the night vigil, which consists of *ṣalātu 'n-najāt, Ṣalātu 'sh-shukr, Ṣalātu 't-tasbīh,* and *ṣalātu 't-tahajjud.*

Thus, it is incumbent on the seeker—before attempting the large number of voluntary forms of prayer described in this book—to learn and practice the fundamental principles of the prescribed prayers (*Ṣalāt*) correctly, based on the prescription of a recognized school (*madhhab*) of Islamic jurisprudence (*fiqh*). These include purification from greater or lesser impurities (*ṭahārah*) consisting of the greater ablution (*ghusl*) or the lesser (*wuḍu*); proper intention (*nīyyat*); facing the *qiblah* determined according to the principles of the madhhab; and, where possible, praying in congregation. Additionally, the integrals of the prayers should be observed correctly, including the proper movements, for the Prophet ﷺ said, "*There is no* ṣalāh *for one who does not straighten his back in bowing* (ruku') *and prostration* (sujūd)*.*" Thus the new seeker in this Way, if not already acquainted and familiar with these fundamentals, must seek out an authorized teacher and learn them.

Testification of Faith

The Testification of Faith (*shahādah*) is pronounced three times. The first testification is for one's self, bringing to mind the Presence of the Prophet ﷺ and saying in one's heart, "O my master; O Prophet of God! You are my witness; God is my witness; all angels are my witness; all the Companions are my witness; all the prophets are my witness; everyone in creation is my witness; and my shaykh is my witness," then pronounce the testification, for you are renewing your Islam. Then pronounce the second testification on behalf of yourself, your parents, your children, your family, your brothers and sisters, your relations, your friends and neighbors, and all Muslim people. The third testification is said on behalf of unbelievers with the intention that they become believers.

Allahu Allahu Allahu Haqq

Sit on the knees, meditating on the connection (*rābiṭah*) to your shaykh, from your shaykh to the Prophet ﷺ, and from the Prophet ﷺ to the Divine Presence.

The Verse "*The Messenger believeth...*" (2:285-286)

<table>
<tr><td>ĀYAT ĀMAN AR-RASŪLU (2:285-286)</td><td></td><td>آمَنَ الرَّسُولُ</td></tr>
<tr><td>Āmana ar-rasūlu bimā unzila ilayhi min rabbihi wa 'l-mu'minūn. kullun āmana billāhi wa malā'ikatihi wa kutubihi wa rusulihi lā nufarriqu bayna āhadin min rusulihi wa qālū sam'inā wa aṭanā ghufrānaka rabbanā wa ilaykal maṣīr. Lā yukallif-ullāhu nafsan illa wus'ahā. lahā mā kasabat wa 'alayhā māktasabat. Rabbanā lā tū'ākhidhnā in nasīnā aw akhṭānā. Rabbanā wa lā taḥmil 'alaynā iṣran kamā ḥamaltahu 'alā alladhīnā min qablinā. Rabbanā wa lā tuḥamilnā mā lā ṭāqata lanā bihi w'afu 'anā waghfir lanā warḥamnā Anta mawlānā f'anṣurnā 'alā l-qawmi 'l-kāfirīn.</td><td></td><td>آمَنَ الرَّسُولُ بِمَا أُنزِلَ إِلَيْهِ مِن رَّبِّهِ وَالْمُؤْمِنُونَ كُلٌّ آمَنَ بِاللَّهِ
وَمَلَائِكَتِهِ وَكُتُبِهِ وَرُسُلِهِ لَا نُفَرِّقُ بَيْنَ أَحَدٍ مِّن رُّسُلِهِ
وَقَالُوا سَمِعْنَا وَأَطَعْنَا غُفْرَانَكَ رَبَّنَا وَإِلَيْكَ الْمَصِيرُ لَا
يُكَلِّفُ اللَّهُ نَفْسًا إِلَّا وُسْعَهَا لَهَا مَا كَسَبَتْ وَعَلَيْهَا مَا
اكْتَسَبَتْ رَبَّنَا لَا تُؤَاخِذْنَا إِن نَّسِينَا أَوْ أَخْطَأْنَا رَبَّنَا وَلَا
تَحْمِلْ عَلَيْنَا إِصْرًا كَمَا حَمَلْتَهُ عَلَى الَّذِينَ مِن قَبْلِنَا رَبَّنَا
وَلَا تُحَمِّلْنَا مَا لَا طَاقَةَ لَنَا بِهِ وَاعْفُ عَنَّا وَاغْفِرْ لَنَا
وَارْحَمْنَا أَنتَ مَوْلَانَا فَانصُرْنَا عَلَى الْقَوْمِ الْكَافِرِينَ</td></tr>
<tr><td colspan="3">The Messenger believeth in what hath been revealed to him from his Lord, as do the men of faith. Each one (of them) believeth in God, His angels, His books, and His apostles. "We make no distinction (they say) between one and another of His apostles." And they say: "We hear, and we obey: (We seek) Thy forgiveness, our Lord, and to Thee is the end of all journeys." On no soul doth God place a burden greater than it can bear. It gets every good that it earns, and it suffers every ill that it earns. (Pray:) "Our Lord! Condemn us not if we forget or fall into error; our Lord! Lay not on us a burden Like that which Thou didst lay on those before us; Our Lord! Lay not on us a burden greater than we have strength to bear. Blot out our sins, and grant us forgiveness. Have mercy on us. Thou art our Protector; Help us against those who stand against faith."</td></tr>
</table>

Whoever recites this verse will attain a high rank and a great position. He will receive the station of safety in this world and the next. He will enter the circle of security in the Presence of God, Almighty and Exalted. He will reach all the stations of the most distinguished Naqshbandi Order. He will be an inheritor of the secret of the Prophet ﷺ and of the saints, and will arrive at the stage of Bāyazīd al-Bisṭāmī, the Īmām of the Order, who said, "I am also the Real (al-Ḥaqq)." This is the magnificent manifestation which belongs to this verse, and to other verses also. Grandshaykh Khālid al-Baghdādī received the vision and the secret of this verse, through which God made him special for his time.

Suratu-l-Fatiha (1)

The first time Sūratu 'l-Fātiḥah is recited, it is with the intention of participating in the blessings sent down with it when it was revealed in Makkah. The second time it is recited should be with the intention of sharing in the Divine Grace which was sent down when it was revealed the second time in Madinah. Grandshaykh said, "If someone recites Sūratu 'l-Fātiḥah, he will not leave this world without attaining those Divine Blessings that are hidden behind the meaning of Sūratu 'l-Fātiḥah which enable him to reach a state of submission to God, Almighty and Exalted."

The blessings that God has sent down with Sūratu 'l-Fātiḥah when it was revealed to the Prophet ﷺ will never cease, and will last forever with the one who recites Sūratu 'l-Fātiḥah. No one is able to know how much blessings there are except God and His Messenger ﷺ. Whoever recites it without this intention receives general Divine Favors, while whoever recites Sūratu 'l-Fātiḥah, with the intention of sharing in the Divine Grace, will attain a high position and a great rank. This Sūrah possesses innumerable and limitless stations in the Sight of God, Who is Powerful and Sublime.

Chief of prayers on the Prophet

SAYYID AṢ-ṢALAWĀT	سَيِّدالصلاة الشريفة المأثورة
'Alā ashrafi 'l-'ālamīna Sayyidinā Muḥammadini 'ṣ-ṣalawāt ṣalla-llāhū 'alayhi wa sallam. 'Alā afḍali 'l-'ālamīna Sayyidinā Muḥammadini 'ṣ-ṣalawāt ṣalla-llāhū 'alayhi wa sallam. 'Alā akmali 'l-'ālamīna Sayyidinā Muḥammadini 'ṣ-ṣalawāt ṣalla-llāhū 'alayhi wa sallam.	على أَشْرَفِ العالمينَ سَيِّدنا مُحَمَّد الصَّلوات. على أَفْضَلِ العالمينَ سَيِّدنا مُحَمَّد الصَّلوات. على أَكْمَلِ العالمينَ سَيِّدنا مُحَمَّد الصَّلوات.

Upon the Noblest of all Creation, our Master Muhammad, blessings.

Upon the most Preferred of all Creation, our Master Muhammad, blessings.

Upon the most Perfect of all Creation, our Master Muhammad, blessings.

Ṣalawātullāhi ta'alā wa malā'ikatihi wa anbiyā'ihi wa rusulihi wa jamī'i khalqihi 'alā Muḥammadin wa 'alā āli Muḥammad, 'alayhi wa 'alayhimu 's-salām wa raḥmatullāhi ta'alā wa barakātuhu, wa raḍī-Allāhū tabāraka wa ta'alā 'an sādātinā aṣḥābi Rasūlillāhi ajma'īn, wa 'ani 't-tabi'īna bihim bi iḥsān, wa 'ani 'l-a'immati 'l-mujtahidīni 'l-māḍīn, wa 'ani 'l-'ulamā il-muttaqqīn, wa 'ani 'l-awlīyā 'iṣ-ṣāliḥīn, wa 'ām-mashayikhinā fi 'ṭ-ṭarīqati 'n-Naqshbandiyyati 'l-'alīyyah, qaddas-Allāhū ta'alā arwāḥahumu 'z-zakīyya, wa nawwar Allāhū ta'alā aḍrihatahumu 'l-mubāraka, wa a'ād-Allāhū ta'alā 'alaynā min barakātihim wa fuyūḍātihim dā'iman wa 'l-ḥamdulillāhi Rabb il-'ālamīn, al-Fātiḥā.	صَلَوَاتُ الله تعالى ومَلائكتِه وأنبيائه ورُسُله وجميع خَلْقِه على مُحَمَّد وعلى آل مُحَمَّد، عليه وعليهم السَّلام ورَحْمَةُ الله تعالى وبَرَكاتُه ورَضِى الله تَبَارَك وتعالى عَنْ سادَاتنا أصْحاب رَسُول الله أَجْمَعين وعَنْ التَّابعين بهم بإحْسان وعَنْ الأَئِمَّة المُجْتَهدين الماضين وعَنْ العُلماء المُتَّقين وعَنْ الأَوْلياء الصالحين وعَنْ مَشايخنا في الطَّريقة النَّقْشْبَنْدِيَة العَلِيَّة، قدَّسَ الله تعالى أَرْواحَهُم الزَّكِيَّة ونوَّر الله تعالى أَضْرِحَتَهُم المباركة وأعادَ الله تعالى علينا من بَرَكاتِهم وفيُوضاتهم دائمًا والحَمْدُ لله رَبِّ العالمين – الفاتحة

Blessings of God (Exalted is He!), of His angels, of His prophets, of His Emissaries, and of all creation be upon Muhammad and the family of Muhammad; may the peace and mercy of God (Exalted is He!) and His blessings be upon him and upon them. May God, the Blessed and Most High, be pleased with every one of our Masters, the Companions of the Emissary of God, and with those who followed them in excellence, and with the early masters of juristic reasoning, and with the pious scholars, and the righteous saints and with our Shaykhs in the exalted Naqshbandi Order. May God (Exalted is He!) sanctify their pure souls, and illuminate their blessed graves. May God (Exalted is He!) return to us of their blessings and overflowing bounty, always. Praise belongs to God, the Lord of the worlds, al-Fātiḥah.

Dedication

IHDĀ	إهداء
Allāhumma balligh thawāba mā qarā'nāhū wa nūra mā talawnāhū hadīyyatan wāṣilatan minnā ila rūḥi Nabīyyīnā Sayyidinā wa Mawlānā Muḥammadin ṣalla-llāhū 'alayhi wa sallam. Wa ilā arwāḥi ikhwānihi min al-anbiyā'i wa 'l-mursalīn wa khudamā'i sharā'ihim wa ila arwāḥi 'l-a'immati 'l-arba'ah wa ila arwāḥi mashāyikhinā fi 'ṭ-ṭarīqati 'n-naqshbandīyyati 'l-'aliyyah khāṣṣatan ila rūḥi Imāmi 'ṭ-ṭarīqati wa ghawthi 'l-khalīqati Khwājā Baḥā'uddīn an-Naqshband Muḥammad al-Uwaisī 'l-Bukhārī wa ḥaḍarati Mawlanā Sulṭānu 'l-awlīyā ash-Shaykh 'Abd Allāh al-Fā'iz ad-Dāghestanī wa sayyidunā ash-Shaykh Muḥammad Nāẓim al-Ḥaqqānī Mu'ayyad ad-dīn wa sa'iri sādātinā waṣ-ṣiddiqīna al-Fātiḥā.	اللهمَّ بَلِّغ ثوابَ ما قرأناهُ ونورَ ما تلوناهُ هديّةً واصلةً منّا إلى روحِ نبيّنا محمَّد (صلّى الله عليه وسلّم) وإلى أرواحِ إخوانه من الأنبياءِ والمرسَلينَ وخُدَماءِ شَرائعِهم وإلى أرواحِ الأئمّة الأربعة وإلى أرواحِ مَشايخنا في الطريقة النقشبنديّة العَليّة، خاصةً إلى روحِ إمامِ الطَّريقة وغوثِ الخَليقة خَواجه بَهاءُ الدينِ النقشبند مُحَمَّد الأويسي البخاري وإلى حضرة مَولانا سُلطان الأولياءِ الشيخ عَبْدُ الله الفائزِ الداغستاني وإلى مولانا سيدنا الشيخ محمّد ناظم الحقّاني مؤيد الدين وإلى سائرِ ساداتنا والصدّيقِين الفاتحة

O God! Grant that the merit of what we have read, and the light of what we have recited, are (considered) an offering and gift from us to the soul of our Prophet Muhammad, and to the souls of the prophets, and the saints; in particular the soul of the Imām of the ṭarīqat and arch-Intercessor of the created world, Khwaja Bahauddin an-Naqshband Muhammad al-Uwaisi al-Bukhari, and our venerable teacher and master, the Sultan of Saints, our Shaykh Abd Allah ad-Daghestani, and our master Shaykh Muhammad Nazim al-Haqqani Mu'ayyad ad-din, and to all our masters and to the righteous ... al-Fātiḥah.

This presents the reward of the preceding recitations to the Prophet ﷺ and to the shaykhs of the Naqshbandi Order.

Suratu-l-Ikhlas (112)

Whoever recites this Sūrah should obtain the Divine Grace of the two Names of Glory, al-Aḥad (the One), and as-Ṣamad (the Eternal). Anyone who reads it must receive a portion of this.

Suratu-l-Inshirah (94)

On each letter and on each verse of the Quran there is a Divine manifestation, which is different from that on any other. Whoever recites a verse or letter of the Quran, will attain the Divine Grace that is particular to that verse or letter. If anyone recites this Sūrah of the Quran, he will receive that Divine Grace and those virtues. Whoever wishes to obtain these virtues, must keep these spiritual practices daily along with his obligations. Then he will gain true and eternal life.

Suratu-l-Falaq (113) and Suratu-n-Nas (114)

The reality of the secret and the perfect wholeness of God's Greatest Name are connected with these two chapters. Since they mark the end of the Quran, they are linked with the completion of the Divine Grace. By means of these spiritual practices, the masters of the most distinguished Naqshbandi Order became oceans of knowledge and gnosis. Grandshaykh Abd Allah ad-Daghestani said:

> You have now reached the beginning, where each verse, letter and Surah of the Quran has its own special manifestation which does not resemble any other. For that reason the Messenger of God ﷺ said, *"I left three things with my Community—death which makes them afraid, true dreams which give them good tidings, and the Quran which speaks to them."* By means of the Quran, God will open up the gates of Divine Grace in the Last Times, as it came down in the time of the Holy Prophet ﷺ and the Companions, and in the times of the caliphs, and in the time of the saints.

These stations and continuous Divine Graces are closely bound together and they cannot be separated, so any deficiency in the spiritual practices will automatically create a deficiency in the Divine Grace being sent down. As an example, if we want to wash our hands, we may wait in front of the tap for water to come out. If the pipes are disconnected so that the water escapes before reaching the tap, then no matter how long we wait, the water will not flow out. So we must not let any deficiency enter our *dhikr* until we obtain the Divine Grace.

These spiritual practices for the three different levels of followers must be performed once every twenty-four hours, together with all other obligations, according to the Divine Law. Everything which the Prophet ﷺ brought was founded on these spiritual practices. It is the way that the servant reaches the key of Nearness to God, the All-Powerful, the Sublime. It was by means of it that the prophets, messengers, and saints reached their Creator, and it is by means of these spiritual practices that we reach all these stations of the most distinguished Order.

The masters of the most distinguished Naqshbandi Order say that whoever claims that he is affiliated with one of the other orders or with the most distinguished Naqshbandi Order, but nevertheless has not entered seclusion even once in his life, then such a person should be ashamed of connecting himself with the people of the path.

In our time, Grandshaykh Abd Allah ad-Daghestani said:

> Whoever of the people of the end of time wishes to attain a high rank and an exalted state and receive what a disciple normally receives by means of seclusion and spiritual exercises must continuously perform these spiritual practices and remembrances of God. With these as the foundation, we have set the way for the higher stations which are built on this foundation. The disciple ought to know that if he fails to attain an exalted station and high grade in this world because of his lack of effort, then he shall not be separated from this world, but that the shaykhs make him reach it, and reveal for him his station, either during his lifetime, or at the time of the seven last breaths during the agonies of death.

If anyone performs these spiritual practices and then performs an action which is forbidden, he will be like the one who builds his house on the side of a cliff, and then his house collapses down the side of the cliff. So we should always be aware of our actions, gauging them to see if they are permitted or forbidden, if God is going to be angry with our actions or not. And we need to think about every action so much that ultimately we do not do any unlawful thing which might weaken our foundation. As the Prophet ﷺ said in his Tradition, *"One hour's contemplation is better than seventy years of worship."* We should perform our actions in the perfectly correct way, that is to say without any prohibited deeds intervening.

On this basis, God has divided the day into three parts: eight hours for worship, eight hours for earning a living, and eight hours for sleeping. Anyone who does not accept and follow this division of energies will exemplify the Tradition, *"He who is erratic will be erratic in the Hellfire."* He who goes according to his own will and reasoning does not progress, and he who wishes to obtain exalted stations, levels, and stages which previous generations earned by means of retreats and other spiritual exercises must remember God throughout the course of the day.

He who makes a regular practice of these spiritual exercises shall attain the Water of True Life, with which he will perform ablution. He will bathe in it, and drink it, and by means of it he shall reach his goal. There may be a person who claims that he has been in the Order for thirty years and as yet has not seen anything and not attained anything. That person should look at his actions over the past years. How many deficient actions has he performed? When he sees the deficiency he should quickly avoid it, then he will reach God, Who is Powerful and Sublime. When the disciple forsakes the daily duties which the shaykhs have told him to perform, then he will be absolutely incapable of making further progress, and he will be unable to keep any state he had previously attained. No prophet ever attained prophethood, nor did any saint ever attain sainthood, nor did any believer ever attain the stage of faith without utilizing his time for his daily *dhikr*.

Accounting: *Muhasabah*

Al-Hasan ibn Ali ibn Abi Talib ﷺ said:

> A believer polices his own self; he criticises and appraises it for the sake of God. The Final Accounting (*hisab*) may turn out to be mild on some people simply because they were wont to appraise themselves in this life; and the Final Accounting on the Day of Judgment may turn out to be rigorous on a people who took this life with levity, and thought they would not be called to account.

In our way, in order to eliminate the darkness of the heart, it is necessary for the seeker to take a notebook and write down the bad characteristics of one's ego. Everyone is able to document at least 200 bad manners; to write them down is the key to dissolving them. Whoever has not done it must do it. Among these bad characteristics are stealing, lying and anger. One of the worst of bad characters is anger. If you are angry with someone restrain yourself for forty days.

Shaykh Nazim wrote for himself over one hundred bad manners so we are not above blame. When you observe the bad characteristics of your ego you will be disgusted: This process will demolish the inciteful ego (*an-nafs al-ammara*). If you write what is coming to your heart with the spiritual support of your Shaykh your ego will become afraid. If anyone finds your notebook, let them look for it is better to feel ashamed in this life than on Judgment Day.

In addition the seeker must pause at the end of each day to take account of himself: what has he done and why has he done it? What has he omitted and why? Who has he harmed and whom has he helped? Then take one's *tasbih* and seek God's forgiveness (*istighfar*) for each wrong act of commission or omission.

Meditation: *Muraqabah* and *Rabitah*

> *O ye who believe! Persevere in patience and constancy; vie in such perseverance; strengthen each other (*rabitu*) and fear God that ye may prosper*. (3:200)

The meaning of *rābiṭah,* is for the seeker to look by means of the inner eye of the heart with unqualified love and longing to the spiritual presence of his or her Shaykh.

There are two kinds of *rābiṭah*:

- In the presence of the Shaykh. The method for this is that the seeker turn with love towards the heart of the Shaykh, by means of submitting to him, and becoming consumed in him, until his own attributes become annihilated in the attributes of (*ṣifāt*) of the Shaykh.
- In the absence of the Shaykh. The method for this is that the seeker imagines the appearance of the Shaykh before him, and then directs himself towards the spiritual presence (*ruḥānīyah*) of the Shaykh contained in that image, and to maintain directing himself towards it, until he experiences annihilation in his presence, or the effects of spiritual attraction (*jazbah*).

After achieving either one of these two states, the seeker's own personality, self and characteristics become effaced in the appearance of his shaykh's image (*fanā fi 'sh-shaykh*), at which time he will witness with the Shaykh's perfection.

After that the spiritual reality of the Shaykh will train him until it delivers him to the presence of the Prophet ﷺ, when he becomes among the perfected ones who have arrived at the second stage.

Rābiṭah brings the seeker closer to the Shaykh, such that even if one is in the east and the other is in the west, by means of that connection the Shaykh transmits to the perfect seekers. The living receive the transmission from those passed on beyond the veil of this worldly life, for they have the power of dispensation (*al-mutaṣarifīn*). *Rābiṭah* brings the one receiving the transmission under the dispensation of the governance of the spirituality of the one who is transmitting, and with that dispensation of his affairs, the Divine Perfections and the lordly Manifestations will overflow within him, causing him to approach the Divine Presence, whether the one who is transmitting is living or passed on, or whether he knew about it or he did not know.

The *rābiṭah* is the shortest way to reach to Divine Presence, for after achieving it the seeker is not in need of anything else; for through it the stations of annihilation(*fanā*) and presence (*ḥudūr*) are rapidly ascended and the realities (*ḥaqā'iq*) are granted. *Rābitah* is the foundation of all attainment, because all other practices are in need of *rābiṭah* in order to manifest their specialties, particularly in the most distinguished Naqshbandi Tradition. Because all practices are in need of the support derived from *rābiṭah*, their benefit depends on the strength of *rābiṭah* and its intensity. That is why this way was called the Way of *Rābiṭah*.

Know that *rābiṭah* is a type of love (*maḥḥabah*), therefore, without great love towards the shaykh one cannot achieve *rābiṭah*. Similarly, the spiritual outpourings (*fayd*) are dependent upon the strength of the connection. The one who has connection with the Shaykh, has the possibility of being trained, and is also able to receive these outpourings; while whoever has no connection is deprived. For this the Naqshbandi masters say:

> The one who doesn't have *rābiṭah* is unable receive these outpourings, even if he has accompanied Khidr ﵇.

You must know that *rābiṭah* is accepted when it is with the Perfect Human Being who has been granted the dispensation from God through the power of governance. This is because the Perfect Human Being (*al-Insān al-Kāmil*) is the mirror of the Truth (*al-Haqq*) so that the one who looks at the spiritual presence of Sayyidina Muhammad ﷺ with the eye of inner vision, witnesses in it themanifestation of the Truth (*al-Haqq*).

The levels of orbit around the presence of the Shaykh depends on the strength of *rābiṭah*. Whoever is consistent in keeping it, will obtain all the states of the *ṭariqah* and the perfection of Divine Realities. And whoever has a faulty *rābiṭah*, will be cut off from spiritual emanations, and will not obtain the states of wayfaring in the path of God, and the secrets of attainment will never be revealed to him.

Dhikr in Congregation: Khatmu-l-Khwajagan

In the Naqshbandi Order, the daily spiritual exercises and the weekly congregational *dhikr*, known as *Khatmu 'l-Khwājagān*, are important practices which the disciple must not leave. The *Khatmu 'l-Khwājagān* is done sitting with the shaykh in congregation. This is held once a week, preferably on Thursday night or Friday, two hours before sunset. The *Khatmu 'l-Khwājagān* is of two categories: the long *khatm* and the short *khatm*.

The Long Khatm		خَتْمُ الخَواجَكان الكبير
1. Distribute 79 of the smaller pebbles among the attendees and the shaykh, dividing them as evenly as possible based on the number of those present. The Imam retains 21 of the pebbles, along with the 7 larger stones and one big stone. *2. The shaykh begins the Khatm, which is performed silently:*		
Intention: Niyyatu ādā' al-khatm ibtighā' riḍwān Allāhi ta'la		نِيةُ أداءِ الخَتْم اٖبتِغاء رِضْوان اللهِ تعالى
Intention to perform the Khatm seeking the pleasure of God the most High.		
Shahāda (3 times): Ash-hadu an lā ilāha ill-Allāh wa ash-hadu anna Muḥammadan 'abduhu wa rasūluh I testify that there is no god but God, and I testify that Muhammad is the Servant and Messenger of God.		كَلمةُ الشَّهادتِين (٣ مرات) أشْهَدُ أنْ لا إله إلا الله وأشْهَدُ أنَّ مُحَمَّدًا عَبْدُهُ ورَسُولُهُ
Istighfār (70 times): Astaghfirullāh God forgive me.		إستغفار: ٧٠ مرة أستغفر الله
Astaghfirullāhi 'l-'Aẓīm alladhī lā ilāha illa Hū al-Ḥayyu 'l-Qayyūm wa atūbu ilayh innahu hūwa 't-tawābu 'r-raḥīm min kulli dhanbin wa ma'ṣīyatin wa min kulli mā yukhālifu dīn al-Islām, yā arḥam ar-Rāḥimīn, min kulli mā yukhālifu 'sh-sharī'at, min kulli mā yukhālifu 'ṭ-ṭarīqata, min kulli mā yukhālifu 'l-ma'rifata, min-		يتلو الإمام: اسْتَغْفِرُ اللهَ العَظيم الذي لا إله إلا هُوَ الحيُّ القَيُّوم وأتوبُ إليه إنَّهُ هو التَّوابُ الرَحيم. من كُلِّ ذَنْبٍ ومَعْصيّةٍ ومن كُلِّ ما يُخالِفُ دينَ الإسْلام ومن كُلِّ ما يُخالِفُ الشَريعة ومن كُلِّ ما يُخالِفُ الطَريقة ومن كُلِّ ما

<table>
<tr><td>kulli mā yukhālifu ’l-ḥaqīqata, min kulli mā yukhālifu ’l-‘azīmata, yā arḥam ar-rāḥīmin.</td><td></td><td>يُخالفُ المَعْرفةَ ومن كُلِّ ما يُخالفُ الحَقيقةَ ومن كُلِّ ما
يُخالفُ العَزيمةَ يا أرْحَمَ الراحمين</td></tr>
<tr><td colspan="3">I ask forgiveness from God Almighty, there is no god but He, the Living, the Self-Subsisting, and I turn in repentance to Him, verily He is the Forgiver, the Merciful, from every sin and disobedience and from all that opposes the religion of Islam, from all that opposes the Divine Law, from all that opposes the Path, from all that opposes Spiritual Realization, from all that opposes Reality, from all that opposes firm Intention, O most Merciful of the Merciful.</td></tr>
<tr><td>The shaykh recites the following supplication:
Allāhumma yā Musabbib al-asbāb, yā Mufattiḥ al-abwāb, yā Muqallib al-qulūbi wa ’l-abṣār, yā Dalīl al-mutaḥayyirīn, yā Ghiyāth al-mustaghīthīn, yā Ḥayyu, yā Qayyūm, yā Dhal-Jalāli wa ’l-Ikrām! Wa ufawwiḍu amrī ilā-Allāh, inna-llāha baṣīrun bil-‘ibād.</td><td></td><td>يَتلو الإمامُ:
اللّهمَّ يا مُسَبِّبَ الأسباب ويا مُفَتِّحَ الأبواب. يا مُقَلِّبَ
القُلوبِ والأبصار. يا دَليلَ المُتَحَيِّرين يا غياثَ المُسْتَغيثين
يا حيُّ يا قَيُّوم. يا ذا الجلالِ والإكرام. وأُفَوِّضُ أمْري إلى
الله. إنَّ اللهَ بَصيرٌ بالعباد</td></tr>
<tr><td colspan="3">O Bestower! O Bestower! O Bestower! O Originator of causes! O Opener of doors! O Tuner (Changer) of hearts and eyes! O Guide of the perplexed! O Succor for those who seek Your aid! O Living! O Self-Subsisting One! O (You who are) possessed of Majesty and Bounty! I entrust my affair unto God. Truly, God is aware of His servants.</td></tr>
<tr><td>Rābiṭat ash-sharīfā.</td><td></td><td>الرابِطةُ الشَّريفة</td></tr>
<tr><td colspan="3">Connect your heart to the heart of the shaykh, from him to the heart of the Prophet, from the Prophet to the Divine Presence;
3. The shaykh then distributes 7 of the larger stones, keeping 1 for himself and passing the other 6 among the attendees to his right. Those who receive a large stone recite the Fātiḥā. The larger stones are then returned to the shaykh.</td></tr>
<tr><td>Sūratu ’l-Fātiḥah (7 times)</td><td></td><td>سورة الفاتحة (٧ مَرات)</td></tr>
<tr><td colspan="3">4. The shaykh then asks the group to recite As-Ṣalawātu ’sh-Sharīfah. Each person recites it one time for each pebble that he holds in his hand. The Imam completes the recitation by counting on the 21 pebbles he reserved.</td></tr>
<tr><td>Ṣalawāt (100 times):
Allāhumma ṣalli ‘alā Muḥammadin wa ‘alā āli Muḥammadin wa sallim.</td><td></td><td>صلوات: ١٠٠ مرة
اللّهمَّ صلِّ على مُحَمَّد وعلى آلِ مُحَمَّد وسلِّم</td></tr>
</table>

5. The shaykh then asks the group to recite Sūratu 'l-Inshirāḥ, following the same methodology.		
Sūratu 'l-Inshirāḥ (79 times)		سُورةُ الانشراح (٧٩ مَرة)
6. The shaykh then distributes the remaining 21 pebbles among the attendees as evenly as possible. *7. Then the shaykh asks the group to recite Sūratu 'l-Ikhlāṣ, with the Basmalah. Each one recites according to the number of pebbles in his hand. This is repeated 10 times. After completing the tenth round of recitation, the shaykh takes the big stone and reads Ikhlāṣ on it, making for 1,001 recitations of this surah.*		
Sūratu 'l-Ikhlāṣ (1,001 times)		سُورةُ الإخلاص (١٠٠١ مَرّة)
8. The shaykh again distributes 7 of the larger stones, keeping one for himself and passing the other 6 to the attendees to his left. Once again, those who receive a large stone recite the Fātiḥā and the stones are then returned to the shaykh.		
Sūratu 'l-Fātiḥā (7 times)		سُورةُ الفاتحة (٧ مَرّات)
9. The shaykh again asks the group to recite aṣ-Ṣalawātu 'sh-Sharīfah, each according to the number of pebbles in his hand.		
Ṣalawāt (100 times): Allāhumma ṣalli 'alā Muḥammadin wa 'alā āli Muḥammadin wa sallim.		صَلوات ١٠٠ مرة اللّهمّ صلِّ على مُحَمّد وعلى آل مُحَمّد وسلّم
O God send blessings and peace upon Muhammad and the family of Muhammad.		
10. The shaykh, or a person designated by him, then recites Chapter 12, Verse 101 (12:101) of the Holy Quran.		
Rabbi qad ātaytanī min al-mulki wa 'allamtanī min ta'wīlil aḥādīth fāṭira as-samāwāti wa 'l-arḍi anta waliyyī fī ad-dunyā wa 'l-ākhirati tawaffanī musliman wa alḥiqnī biṣ-ṣāliḥīn; Āmantu billāhi sadaq-Allāhul 'Aẓīm. Subḥāna rabbika rabbi 'l-'izzati 'amā yaṣifūn wa salāmun 'alā 'l-mursalīn wa 'lḥamdulillāhi rabbi l-'alamīn.		يتلو الإمام: أعوذُ بالله من الشّيطان الرّجيم. بِسْمِ الله الرّحمن الرّحيم. ربِّ قدْ آتيْتني من المُلك وعَلّمْتني من تأويل الأحاديث فاطر السّماوات والأرْض أنتَ وليّ في الدّنيا والآخرة. توَفّني مُسْلمًا وألحقْني بالصالحين.
O my Lord! You have indeed bestowed on me some power, and taught me something of the interpretation of dreams and events. Creator of the Heavens and the Earth! You are my Protector in this world and in the Hereafter. Take my soul (at		

death) as one submitting to Your Will (as a Muslim), and unite me with the righteous.		
11. The shaykh reads the dedication.		
Ihdā: (see page 172)		إهْداء
12. The shaykh then proceeds with the loud portion of the dhikr.		

Loud Part		
F'alam annahū: Lā ilāhā ill-Allāh (100 times) There is no god but God.		فَاعْلَمْ أَنَّهُ: لا إله إلا الله (١٠٠ مَرَّة)
Ila sharaf in-Nabī ṣalla-llāhū 'alayhi wa sallam wa ālihi wa ṣaḥbih, wa ila arwāḥi sā'iri sādātinā waṣ-ṣiddiqīn, al-Fātiḥah.		إلى شَرَفِ النَّبِي صلى الله عليه وسلم وإلى آله وصَحْبِه وإلى أَرْواح مشائخنا وسائر ساداتنا والصدِّيقين الفاتحة
For the honor of the Prophet ﷺ and to the souls of the prophets and the veracious ones ... al-Fātiḥah. Present the reward of the preceding recitations to the Prophet ﷺ and to the shaykhs of the Naqshbandi Order.		
Dhikr al-Jālāla: Allāh, Allāh (100 times) God, God		ذِكْرُ الجَلالة الله الله الله (حَوالي ١٠٠ مَرَّة)
Ḥasbun-Allāh wa ni'm al-wakīl, ni'm al-Mawlā wa ni'm an-Naṣīr, lā ḥawla wa lā quwwata illa billāh il-'Alīyy il-'Aẓīm.		الإمام: حَسبنا الله ونِعمَ الوكيل نِعْمَ المولى ونعم المصير ولا حَوْل ولا قُوَّة إلا بالله العَليّ العَظيم
God is sufficient for us and the Best of Protectors, the Best Patron, and the Best of Helpers; there is no power and no might except in God, the High, the Exalted.		
Hū, Hū (33 times) He, the Absolute Unknown One.		هُو. هُو. هُو. (حَوالي ٣٣ مَرَّة)
Ḥasbun-Allāh wa ni'm al-wakīl, ni'm al-Mawlā wa ni'm an-Naṣīr, lā ḥawla wa lā quwwata illa billāh il-'Alīyy il-'Aẓīm.		الإمام: حَسبنا الله ونِعْمَ الوكيل نِعْمَ المولى ونعم المصير ولا حَوْل ولا قُوَّة إلا بالله العَليّ العَظيم
God is sufficient for us and the Best of Protectors, the Best Patron, and the Best of Helpers; there is no power and no might except in God, the High, the Exalted.		
Ḥaqq, Ḥaqq (33 times) The Ultimate Reality.		حَق. حَق. حَق. (حَوالي ٣٣ مَرَّة)

Ḥasbun-Allāh wa ni'm al-wakīl, ni'm al-Mawlā wa ni'm an-Naṣīr, lā ḥawla wa Lā quwwata illa billāh il-'Alīyy il-'Aẓīm.		الإمام: حَسبنا الله ونِعْمَ الوكيل نِعْمَ المولى ونعم المصير ولا حَوْل ولا قوَّة إلا بِالله العَليّ العَظيم
God is sufficient for us and the Best of Protectors, the Best Patron, and the Best of Helpers; there is no power and no might except in God, the High, the Exalted.		
Ḥayy, Ḥayy (33 times) Ever-living One.		حَيّ. حَيّ. حَيّ. (حَوالي ٣٣ مرّة)
Ḥasbun-Allāh wa ni'm al-wakīl, ni'm al-Mawlā wa ni'm an-Naṣīr, lā ḥawla wa lā quwwata illa billāh il-'Alīyy il-'Aẓīm.		الإمام: حَسبنا الله ونِعْمَ الوكيل ولا حَوْل ولا قوَّة إلا بِالله العَليّ العَظيم
God is sufficient for us and the Best of Protectors, the Best Patron, and the Best of Helpers; there is no power and no might except in God, the High, the Exalted.		
Allāh Hū, Allāh Ḥaqq (10-12 times) God is He the Absolute Unknown One, God is the Ultimate Reality.		الله هُو الله حَقّ الله هُو لله حَقّ (١٠ أو ١٢ مَرّة)
Allāh Hū, Allāh Ḥayy (10-12 times) God is He the Absolute Unknown One, God is Ever-living		الله هُو الله حَيّ . الله هُو الله حَيّ (١٠ أو ١٢ مَرّة)
Allāh Ḥayy Yā Qayyūm (10-12 times) God Ever-living, O Self-sufficient One		الله حَيّ يا قيُّوم الله حَيّ يا قيُّوم (١٠ أو ١٢ مَرّة)
Ḥasbun-Allāh wa ni'm al-wakīl, ni'm al-Mawlā wa ni'm an-Naṣīr, lā ḥawla wa lā quwwata illa billāh il-'Alīyy il-'Aẓīm.		الإمام: حَسبنا الله ونِعْمَ الوكيل ولا حَوْل ولا قوَّة إلا بِالله العَليّ العَظيم
God is sufficient for us and the Best of Protectors, the Best Patron, and the Best of Helpers; there is no power and no might except in God, the High, the Exalted.		
Yā Hū, Yā Hū, Yā Dā'im (3 times); Allāh Yā Hū, Yā Dā'im (1 time) O Absolute Unknown One, O Eternal One, God is He the Absolute Unknown One, O Eternal One.		الإمام: يا هُو يا هُو يا دائِم (٣ مَرّة), الله يا هو يا دائم
Yā Dā'im x3, Yā Allāh (2 times) O Eternal One x3, O God		يا دائِم. يا دائِم. يا دائِم يا الله (مَرّتانِ)
Yā Ḥalīm x3, Yā Allāh (2 times) O Clement One, x3, O God		يا حَليم. يا حَليم. يا حَليم يا الله (مَرّتانِ)

Yā Ḥafī· x3 Yā Allāh (2 times) O Preserver x3, O God		يا حَفِيظ . يا حَفِيظ . يا حَفِيظ يا الله (مَرَّتان)
Yā Laṭīf x3, Yā Allāh (2 times) O Subtle One x3, O God		يا لَطِيف . يا لَطِيف . يا لَطِيف يا الله (مَرَّتان)
Yā Ghaffār x3, Yā Allāh (2 times) O Forgiver x3, O God		يا غَفَّار . يا غَفَّار . يا غَفَّار يا الله (مَرَّتان)
Yā Sattār x3 Yā Allāh (2 times) O Concealer x3, O God		يا سَتَّار . يا سَتَّار . يا سَتَّار يا الله (مَرَّتان)
Yā Fattāḥ x3, Yā Allāh (2 times) O Opener x3, O God		يا فَتَّاح. يا فَتَّاح. يا فَتَّاح يا الله (مَرَّتان)
Yā Mujīb x3, Yā Allāh (2 times) O Answerer of Prayers x3, O God		يا مُجِيب . يا مُجِيب . يا مُجِيب يا الله (مَرَّتان)
Yā Mu'iz x3, Yā Allāh (2 times) O Honorer x 3, O God		يا مُعِز . يا مُعِز . يا مُعِز يا الله (مَرَّتان)
Yā Mu'īn x3, Yā Allāh (2 times) O Giver of Aid, x 3, O God		يا مُعِين . يا مُعِين . يا مُعِين يا الله (مَرَّتان)
Yā Wadūd x3, Yā Allāh (2 times) O Most Loving x3, O God		يا وَدود . يا وَدود . يا وَدود يا الله (مَرَّتان)
Yā Raḥmān x3, Yā Allāh (2 times) O Most Compassionate x3, O God		يا رَحْمن. يا رَحْمن. يا رَحْمن يا الله (مَرَّتان)
Yā Raḥīm x3, Yā Allāh (2 times) O Most Merciful x3, O God		يا رَحِيم. يا رَحِيم. يا رَحِيم يا الله (مَرَّتان)
Yā Ḥannān x3, Yā Allāh (2 times) O Most Caring x3, O God		يا حَنَّان. يا حَنَّان. يا حَنَّان. يا الله (مَرَّتان)
Yā Mannān x3, Yā Allāh (2 times) O Beneficent x3, O God		يا مَنَّان. يا مَنَّان. يا مَنَّان. يا الله (مَرَّتان)
Yā Dayyān x3, Yā Allāh (2 times) O Most Just x3, O God		يا دَيَّان. يا دَيَّان. يا دَيَّان. يا الله (مَرَّتان)
Yā Subḥān x3 , Yā Allāh (2 times) O Most Glorious One x3, O God		يا سُبْحان. يا سُبْحان. يا سُبْحان. يا الله (مَرَّتان)
Yā Sulṭān x3, Yā Allāh (2 times) O Supreme Ruler x3, O God		يا سُلْطان. يا سُلْطان. يا سُلْطان. يا الله (مَرَّتان)
Yā Amān x3, Yā Allāh (2 times)		يا أمان. يا أمان. يا أمان. يا الله (مَرَّتان)

O Giver of Safety x3, O God		
Yā Allāh x3, Yā Allāh (2 times) O God x 4		يا الله. يا الله. يا الله. يا الله. . . .(مَرّتان)
The Shaykh may add more of God's Beautiful Names as he is inspired.		
Ḥasbun-Allāh wa ni'm al-wakīl, ni'm al-Mawlā wa ni'm an-Naṣīr, lā ḥawla wa lā quwwata illa billāh il-'Alīyy il-'Aẓīm.		الإمام: حَسبنا الله ونِعْمَ الوكيل ولا حَوْل ولا قُوَّة إلا بالله العَليّ العَظيم
God is sufficient for us and the Best of Protectors, the Best Patron, and the Best of Helpers; there is no power and no might except in God, the High, the Exalted.		
Inna-Allāha wa malā'ikatahū yuṣalluna 'alā an-Nabī, yā ayyuh-alladhīnā āmanū, ṣallū 'alayhi wa sallimū taslīmā. (Ṣadaq-Allāhu 'l-'Aẓīm)		إنَّ الله ومَلائكَتَهُ يُصلّونَ على النّبي يا أيّها الذينَ آمَنُوا صَلُّوا عليه وسَلِّمُوا تَسْليمًا
God and His angels send blessings on the Prophet: O you who believe! Send blessings on him and greet him with all respect. (God speaks the Truth).		
Ṣalawāt (10 times): Allāhumma ṣalli 'alā Muḥammadin wa 'alā āli Muḥammadin wa sallim		صلوات: ١٠ مرات – اللَّهُمَّ صلِّ على مُحَمَّد وعلى آل مُحَمَّد وسلِّم
O God send blessings and peace upon Muhammad and the family of Muhammad.		
The shaykh then makes invocation as he is inspired.		
The shaykh then recites the Chief of Prayers (see page 171)		الصلاة الشريفة المأثورة
The shaykh then recites the Ihdā (see page 172).		إهداء

Short Khatm (Aloud)		خَتْمُ الخَواجَكانِ الصغير – جهر
The Short Khatm is identical to the Long Khatm except that it is recited aloud in its entirety, and has the following differences in number of repetitions in the Adab.		
Sūratu 'l-Fātiḥah (7 times)		الفاتحة (٧ مَرات)
Prayers on the Prophet ﷺ (ṣalawāt) (10 times): Allāhumma ṣalli 'alā Muḥammadin wa 'alā āli Muḥammadin wa sallim		صَلَوات (١٠ مَرات) اَللّٰهُمَّ صلِّ على مُحَمَّدٍ وعلى آل مُحَمَّدٍ وسلِّم
O God send blessings and peace upon Muhammad and the family of Muhammad.		
Sūratu 'l-Inshirāḥ (7 times)		سُورةُ الانْشراح (٧ مَرات)
Sūratu 'l-Ikhlāṣ (11 times)		سُورةُ الإِخْلاص (١١ مَرّة)
Sūratu 'l-Fātiḥah (7 times)		سُورةُ الفَاتحة (٧ مَرّات)
Prayers on the Prophet ﷺ (ṣalawāt) (10 times): Allāhumma ṣalli 'alā Muḥammadin wa 'alā āli Muḥammadin wa sallim		صَلَوات (١٠ مَرات) اَللّٰهُمَّ صلِّ على مُحَمَّدٍ وعلى آل مُحَمَّدٍ وسلِّم
O God send blessings and peace upon Muhammad and the family of Muhammad.		

The remainder of the Khatm is identical to the Long Khatm (section 10) from the point the shaykh assigns someone to recite from the Qur'ān (12:101) (see page 181).

Invoking the Masters

Our Grandshaykh, Shaykh Abd Allah ad-Daghestani, called on the Prophet ﷺ through the shaykhs of the Order in the manner described below when asking for their intercession. This formulation was transmitted to him by his shaykh who received it through the Golden Chain, each shaykh passing it from one to another. It begins with a prayer and then each of the saints of the Golden Chain is invoked.

Yā sayyid as-sādāt wa nūr al-mawjudāt, yā man hū al-malja'u liman massahu ḍaymun wa ghammun wa alam. Yā aqrab al-wasā'ili ilā-Allāhi ta'alā wa yā aqwā'l-mustanad, attawasalu ila janābīk al-'a·am bi-hādhihi's-sādāti, wa āhlillāh, wa āhli baitika al-kirām, li-daf'i ḍurrin lā yudfa'u illā bi wāsiṭatik, wa raf'i ḍaymin lā yurfa'u illā bi-dalālatika bi Sayyidī wa Mawlāy, yā Rasūl Allāh, yā Raḥmatan lil-'ālamīn:		يا سَيِّدَ السّادات ويا نُورَ المَوْجُودات، يا من هُوَ المَلْجأ لمنْ مَسَّهُ ضَيْمٌ وغَمٌّ وأَلَمٌ، يا أَقْرَبَ الوَسائِلِ إلى اللهِ تَعالى ويا أقْوى المُسْتَنَد، أتَوَسَّلُ إلى جنابِكَ الأعْظمِ بِهؤلاء السّادات وأَهْلِ الله وأهْلِ بيْتِكَ الكِرامِ لِدَفْعِ ضُرٍّ لا يُدْفَعُ إلا بِواسِطَتِكَ ورَفْعِ ضَيْمٍ لا يُرْفَعُ إلا بِدَلالَتِكَ بِسَيِّدي ومَوْلاي يا سَيِّدي يا رَسُولَ الله يا من أرسله الله رَحْمَةً لِّلعالمين
Nabī		نَبِيٌّ
Ṣiddīq		الصدّيق
Salmān		سلمان
Qāsim		قاسمُ
J'afar		جعفر
Ṭayfūr		طيفور
Abu 'l-Ḥasan		ابو الحسن
Abū 'Alī		ابو علي
Yūsuf		يُوسف
Abu 'l-'Abbās		أبو العباس

ʻAbd al-Khāliq		عبد الخالق
ʻArif		عارفُ
Maḥmūd		محمود
ʻAlī		علي
Muḥammad Bābā as-Samāsī		محمد بابا السماسي
Sayyid Amīr Kulālī		سيد أمير كلالي
Khwājā Bahā'uddīn Naqshband		خواجه بهاء الدين النقشبند
ʻAlā'uddīn		علاء الدين
Yaʻqūb		يعقوب
ʻUbayd Allāh		عبيد الله
Muḥammad Zāhid		مُحَمَّد زاهد
Darwīsh Muḥammad		درويش مُحَمَّد
Khwājā Amkanākī		خَواجه الامكناكي
Muḥammad al-Bāqī		مُحَمَّد الباقي
Aḥmad al-Fārūqī		أحمد الفاروقي
Muḥammad Maʻṣūm		مُحَمَّد معصوم
Sayfuddīn		سيف الدين
Nūr Muḥammad		نور مُحَمَّد
Ḥabībullāh		حبيب الله
ʻAbd Allāh		عبد الله
Shaykh Khālid		الشيخ خالد

Shaykh Ismā'īl		الشيخ إسماعيل
Khāṣ Muḥammad		خاص مُحَمَّد
Shaykh Muḥammad Effendi al-Yarāghī		الشيخ محمد أفندي اليراغي
Sayyid Jamāluddīn al-Ghumūqī al-Ḥusaynī		سيد جمال الدين الغموقي الحسيني
Abū Aḥmad aṣ-Ṣughūrī		ابو أحمد الصغوري
Abū Muḥammad al-Madanī		ابو مُحَمَّد المدني
Shaykh Sharafuddīn ad-Dāghestānī		الشيخ شرف الدين الداغستاني
Shaykh 'Abd Allāh al-Fā'iz ad-Dāghestānī		الشيخ عبد الله الفائز الداغستاني
Shaykh Muḥammad Nāẓim 'Adil al-Ḥaqqānī		الشيخ مُحَمَّد ناظم الحقاني

Invocation of Imam al-Mahdi and His Deputies

Today, many no longer believe in the coming of the al-Mahdi al-Muntadhar عليه السلام (the Awaited Savior). In their ignorance, some claim that the concept of al-Mahdi عليه السلام is a Shiite one. However, belief in al-Mahdi عليه السلام is part of both the Sunni and Shiite doctrines, and his reality is firmly established by many authentic Traditions. For example, the Prophet ﷺ said:

> *If this world has just one day remaining, God will extend that day until a man comes. He is from me (or "from my family"). His name is like my name (i.e., Muhammad) and his father's name is like my father's name (i.e., Abd Allah). He fills the earth with equality and justice, as it has been filled with injustice and oppression.*[272]

The advent of al-Mahdi عليه السلام has long been awaited by the saints, for it heralds the return of the Prophet Jesus (Isa) عليه السلام and the restoration of justice and peace in the world. The Prophetic Traditions also make it clear that al-Mahdi عليه السلام will be accompanied by seven ministers. Their names were sought by the saints of the Golden Chain, including Shaykh Abd Allah ad-Daghestani, through their visions, leading to the formulation of this invocation:

Sāḥib az-Zamān Imāmu 'l-Mahdī		صاحبُ الزَمانِ الإمام مُحَمَّد المَهْدي عليه السلام
Shahāmatu 'l-Fardānī		شهامة الفرداني
Yūsuf as-Ṣiddīq		يُوسف الصدّيق
'Abdur-Ra'uf al-Yamānī		عَبْدُ الرؤوف اليماني
Imāmu 'l-'Ārifīn Amānu 'l-Ḥaqq		إمامُ العارفين أمان الحَقّ

---

[272] It is related from Ibn Masud, Abu Dawud recorded it in his ***Sunan***. Al-Hafiz as-Suyuti recorded it both in his *Jami* and his *Tafsir*, Ibn Abi Shaybah and Ahmad in his *Musnad*, some with different wording.

Lisānu 'l-Mutakallimīn 'Awnullāh as-Sakhāwī		لسانُ المُتَكلّمين عَوْن الله السَخاوي
'Ārifu 't-ṭayyār al-Mā'rūf bi Mulḥān		عارفُ الطيّار المَعْرُوف بِمُلْحان
Burhānu 'l-Kuramā' Ghawth il-Anām		بُرْهان الكُرَماء غَوْثُ الأنام
Yā Ṣāḥib z-Zamān, yā Ṣāḥib al-'Unṣur.		يا صاحِبُ الزَمان، يا صاحِبُ العُنْصر
Yā rijāl-Allāh āa'lā Allāhu ta'alā darajātihim dā'iman wa amadnā bi-maddadihim wa-nafa'anā bi-barakātihim wa anfāsihim al-qudsīyya, bi-ḥurmati man lā Nabīyya ba'dah, bi sirri Sūratu 'l-Fātiḥah.		يا رِجالَ الله أعلى الله تَعالى دَرَجاتهم دائماً وأمدنا بِمددهم ونَفعنا بِبَرَكات أنْفاسِهِم القُدُسيَّة بِحُرْمة من لا نَبِي بَعْدَه وبِسرّ سُورة الفاتحة

O Master of the Period, O one of high pedigree, O men of God. May God (Exalted is He!) raise their stations always, support us with their support and benefit us through the blessings of their holy breath. By the sanctity of the one after whom there is no other prophet, and by the secret of ... al-Fātiḥah.

صَلاةُ المغربِ

Salatu-l-Maghrib

Adhan (call to prayer)		الآذان
Allāhu akbar (4 times) God is Greatest		الله أكْبر، الله أكْبر، الله أكْبر، الله أكْبر
Ash-hadu an lā ilāha ill-Allāh (2 times) I bear witness that there is no god but God		اشْهَدُ أنْ لا إلهَ إلاّ الله اشْهَدُ أنْ لا إلهَ إلاّ الله
Ash-hadu anna Muḥammadan Rasūlullāh (2 times) I bear witness that Muhammad is the Messenger of God.		اشْهَدُ أنَّ محمداً رسول الله – اشْهَدُ أنَّ محمداً رسول الله
Ḥayya ʻalā ʼṣ-ṣalāh (2 times) Hasten to the prayer		حيَّ عَلى الصَلاة حيَّ عَلى الصَلاة
Ḥayyā ʻāla ʼl-falāḥ (2 times) Hasten to salvation		حيَّ عَلى الفَلاح حيَّ عَلى الفَلاح
Allāhu akbar (2 times) God is Greatest		الله أكْبرُ الله أكْبر
Lā ilāha illa-Allāh There is no god but God		لا إله إلاّ الله

<table>
<tr>
<td>AṢ-ṢALĀTU WAS-SALĀM
(to be made aloud by the muadhdhin):
Aṣ-ṣalātu was-salāmu ‘alayk, yā man arsalahullāhu ta‘alā raḥmatan lil-‘ālamīn.
Aṣ-ṣalātu was-salāmu ‘alayk, wa ‘alā ālika wa aṣḥābika ajma‘īn.
Aṣ-ṣalātu was-salāmu ‘alaykum, yā anbiyā’Allāḥ.</td>
<td>الصلاة والسلام
الصلاة والسلام عليك يا من أرسله الله تعالى رحمة للعالمين
الصلاة والسلام عليك وعلى آلك وأصحابك أجمعين
الصلاة والسلام عليكم، يا أنبياء الله</td>
</tr>
<tr>
<td colspan="2">Blessings and peace be upon you, whom God Most High sent as mercy to the Worlds.
Blessings and peace be upon you, and upon all your family and your Companions.
Blessings and peace be upon you, O Prophet of God.</td>
</tr>
<tr>
<td>INVOCATION (DU‘A):
(to be made silently by all who hear the adhān):
Allāhumma rabba hādhihī ’d-da‘wat it-tāmma waṣ-ṣalāt il-qā’ima, āti Sayyidinā Muḥammadan al-wasīlata wa ’l-fadīlata wa ’d-darajati ’r-raf‘īati ’l-‘alīyya wab‘athhu Rabbī al-maqām al-maḥmūd alladhī w‘adtahu, warzuqnā shaf‘atahu yawm al-qīyāma. Innaka lā tukhlifu ’l-mī‘ad.</td>
<td>دُعاءُ:
اللَّهمَّ رَبَّ هَذه الدعْوة التّامّة والصَلاة القائمة آت مُحَمَّداً الوَسيلة والفَضيلة والدَرَجة الرَفيعة العالية وأبعَثْه ربّي المقام المَحْمُودَ الذي وَعَدْته وارْزقْنا شَفاعَتَهُ يوْمَ القيامةإنكَ لا تُخْلفُ الميعاد (وزوّجْنا من الحُور العين)</td>
</tr>
<tr>
<td colspan="2">O God! Lord of this perfect supplication and of this established prayer, grant Muhammad the Means (of nearness to You) and the excellence of the sublime and supreme rank. Raise him, O my Lord, to the Praiseworthy Station, which You promised him, and grant us his intercession on the Day of Judgment, for You do not fail Your promise.</td>
</tr>
</table>

2 RAK'ATS SUNNAH performed After Adhān.		رَكعَتَيْنِ سُنَّة
IQAMATU 'Ṣ-ṢALĀT		إقامةُ الصَلاة
Identical to Adhān with the insertion after Ḥayyā 'āla 'l-falāḥ of: Qad qāmati 'ṣ-Ṣalāt (2 times) The prayer is beginning		مثل الآذان ولكن مع إدخال قد قامت الصلاة قد قامت الصلاة – بعد حي على الفلاح
3 RAK'ATS FARḌ		ثلاثُ ركْعات فَرْض
After the final salām:		
Recite: lā ilāha ill-Allāh Muḥammadur Rasūlullāh (3 times)		بعد التّسليم لا إلَهَ إلاَّ الله (ثلاثُ مرّات) مُحمّد رَسُولُ الله
Astaghfirullāh 3 times I ask God's forgiveness		إسْتِغفار (ثَلاثُ مَرّات)
Astaghfirullāh al-'Aẓīm alladhī lā ilāha illa Hū al-Ḥayyu 'l-Qayyūm wa atūbu ilayḥ I ask forgiveness from God Almighty, there is no god but He, the Living, the Self-Subsisting, and I turn in repentance to Him.		أَسْتَغْفِرُ اللهَ العَظيم الذي لا إله إلا هُوَ الحيُّ القيُّوم وأتوبُ إلَيْه أوْ أَسْتَغْفِرُ الله. أَسْتَغْفِرُ الله. أَسْتَغْفِرُ الله
INVOCATION (DU'A): Allāhumma anta 's-Salām wa minka 's-salām tabārakta wa ta'ālayta yā Dhal-jalāli wa 'l-ikrām. Lā ilāha ill-Allāhu wāḥdahu lā sharīka lah, lahu 'l-mulku wa lahu 'l-ḥamd, wa Hūwa 'alā kulli shay'in qadīr. Sami'nā wa aṭa'nā, ghufrānaka, Rabbanā, wa ilayk al-maṣīr.		دُعاء: اللّهمَّ أنتَ السَّلامُ ومنكَ السَّلام تبارَكْتَ وتعاليت يا ذا الجلال والإكْرامِ. لا إلَهَ إلاَّ الله وَحْدَهُ لا شَريكَ لَهُ، لَهُ المُلْكُ ولَهُ الحَمْدُ يحي ويميت وهُوَ على كُلِّ شَيْءٍ قَدير. سَمِعْنا وأطَعْنا غُفْرانَكَ رَبّنا وإلَيْكَ المَصير
O God! You are Peace and from You comes Peace. Blessed and lofty are You, O Lord of Majesty and Bounty. There is no god but God, He is One, no partner has		

<table>
<tr><td colspan="2">He. His is the Kingdom and His is all praise, and He is over all things Powerful. We have heard and obeyed. Your forgiveness, O our Lord! And to Thee is the end of all journeys.</td></tr>
<tr><td>2 RAK'ATS SUNNAH</td><td>ركعتين سنّة</td></tr>
<tr><td>'Alā Rasūlinā 'ṣ-ṣalawāt. Astaghfirullāh, subḥānallāh wa 'l-ḥamdulillāh, wa lā ilāha ill-Allāh w-Allāhū akbar, wa lā ḥawla wa lā quwwata illa billāhi 'l-'Alīyy il-'Āẓīm.</td><td>على رَسُولنا الصَّلَوات. أَسْتَغْفِرُ الله. أَسْتَغْفِرُ الله.
أَسْتَغْفِرُ الله سُبْحانَ الله والحَمْدُ لله ولا إلهَ إلاّ الله
والله أُكْبَر ولا حَوْلَ ولا قُوَّةَ إلا بالله العَليِّ العَظيم</td></tr>
<tr><td colspan="2">Blessings upon our Prophet. I ask God's forgiveness. Glory be to God! Praise be to God! There is no god but God and God is Greatest. There is no power and no strength save in God, All-High and Almighty.</td></tr>
<tr><td>CHAPTER 2: VERSE 163
A'udhū billāhi min ash-shayṭān ir-rajīm. Bismillāhi 'r-Raḥmāni 'r-Raḥīm.
Wa ilāhukum ilāhun wāḥidun, lā ilāha illa Hū ar-Raḥmānu 'r-Raḥīm.</td><td>البقرة ١٦٣
أَعُوذُ بالله من الشَّيْطانِ الرَّجيم
بِسْمِ الله الرَّحْمنِ الرَّحيم
وإلهُكُم إلهٌ واحِدٌ لا إلهَ إلاّ هُوَ الرَّحْمنِ الرَّحيم</td></tr>
<tr><td colspan="2">I seek refuge with God from Satan, the Cursed. In the name of God, the All-Beneficent, the All-Merciful. Your God is One God; there is no god but He, the All-Merciful, the All-Compassionate.</td></tr>
<tr><td>ĀYATU 'L-KURSĪ (THRONE VERSE)</td><td>آية الكُرْسي</td></tr>
<tr><td>Allāhū lā ilāha illa Hūwa 'l-Ḥayyu 'l-Qayyūm, lā tākhudhuhū 's-sinatun wa lā nawm, lahū mā fis-samāwāti wa mā fil-arḍ. Man dhā-ladhī yashfa'u 'indahū illā bi idhniḥ ya'lamu mā bayna aydīhim wa mā khalfahum wa lā yuḥīṭunā bi-shay'im min 'ilmihi illā bimā shā'. Wasi'a kursīyyuhu 's-samāwāti wa 'l-arḍa, wa lā ya'uduhū ḥifẓuhuma, wa Hūwa al-'Alīyyu 'l-'Aẓīm.
Ṣadaq-Allāhu 'l-'Aẓīm.</td><td>الله لا إلهَ إلا هُوَ الحيُّ القَيُّوم لا تَأْخُذُهُ سِنَةٌ ولا نَوْمٌ لَهُ
ما في السماوات وما في والأَرْضِ من ذا الذي يَشْفَعُ
عِنْدَهُ إلا بِإذْنِه يَعْلَمُ ما بَيْنَ أيديهم وما خَلْفَهُم ولا
يُحيطُونَ بِشَيْءٍ من عِلْمِه إلا بِما شاء وَسِعُ كُرْسِيُّه
السماوات والأَرْضَ ولا يَؤُدُهُ حِفْظُهُما وهُوَ العَلِيُّ
العَظيمُ – صَدَقَ الله العَظيم</td></tr>
<tr><td colspan="2">God, there is no god but He, the Living, the Everlasting. Slumber seizes Him not, neither sleep; to Him belongs all that is in the heavens and the earth. Who is</td></tr>
</table>

there that shall intercede with Him save by His leave? He knows what lies before them, and they comprehend not anything of His knowledge save such as He wills. His Throne comprises the heavens and the earth; the preserving of them oppresses Him not; He is the All-High, the Almighty.

God spoke the Truth.

TASBĪḤ	تسبيح
Subḥānak yā ʿAẓīm subḥānallāh, subḥānallāh (33 times)	سُبْحانَكَ يا عَظيم: سُبْحانُ الله (٣٣ مَرَّة)
Glory be to You, O Almighty! Glory be to God.	
ʿAlā nʾimat il-Islām wa sharaf al-īmān dāʾiman alḥamdulillāh, alḥamdulillāh (33 times)	على نِعْمة الإسْلام وشَرَف الإيمان دائماً: الحَمْدُ لله (٣٣ مَرَّة)
For the gift of Islam, the nobility of faith, always, praise be to God.	
Taʿalā shāʾnuhū wa lā ilāha ghayruhū, Allāhū akbar, Allāhū akbar (33 times)	تَعالى شأْنُهُ ولا إله غَيْرُهُ: الله أَكْبَر (٣٣ مَرَّة)
Exalted is His Affair, and there is no god but He, God is Greatest.	
Allāhū akbaru kabīran wa ʾlḥamdulillāhi kathīran wa subḥānallāhi bukratan wa aṣīla. Lā ilāha illa-llāh wāḥdahū lā sharīka lah, lahul-mulku wa lahul-ḥamd yuḥīy wa yumīt wa Hūwa ʿalā kulli shayʾin qadīr. Subḥāna Rabbīu ʾl-ʿAlīyyu ʾl-ʿāla ʾl-Wahhāb.	الله أَكْبَرُ كَبيراً والحَمْدُ لله كَثيراً وسُبْحانَكَ اللهم بُكْرَةً وأَصيلاً لا إله إلا الله وَحْدَهُ لا شَريكَ له، له الملُكُ وله الحَمْدُ يُحي ويُميت وهُوَ على كل شيء قَدير سُبْحانَ رَبِّي العَليِّ الأَعْلى الوهاب

God is most Great in His Greatness and much praise be to God. Glory be to God, early and late. There is no god but God. He is One, no partner has He. His is the Kingdom and all praise. He brings to life and makes to die, and He is over all things Powerful. Glory be to my Lord, All-High, Supreme, Most Munificent.

SUPPLICATION (DUʿA)	دُعاء شخصي
Recite a personal invocation as one is inspired.	
AL-FĀTIHA	الفاتحة
Allāhumma ṣalli ʿalā Muḥammadin wa ʿalā āli Muḥammadin wa sallim.	اللَّهُمَّ صَلِّ على مُحَمَّد وعلى آل مُحَمَّد وسلِّم

Then pray (the funeral prayer)		
Salatu-l-Janazah		
ṢALĀT AL-JANĀZATU ʻALĀ AL-GHĀʼIB Funeral Prayer in Absentia		صلاةُ الغائب
F'ātabiru yā ulil-abṣār la'allakum tufliḥun. Inna lillāhi wa inna īlayhi rāji'un. Ṣalātu 'l-janāza 'an il-ghā'ibīn alladhīna antaqalu ilā raḥmatillāhi min ummati Muḥammad ṣalla-llāhū 'alayhi wa sallam.		فَاعْتَبِرُوا يا أُولي الأبصار لعلكم تفلحون. إنَّا لله وإنَّا إليه راجعُون. صَلاةُ الجَنازة عَن الغائبِينَ الذينَ أنتقلوا إلى رَحْمة الله من أمَّةِ مُحَمَّد (صلَّى اللهُ عليه وسلَّم)
Therefore, take heed, you who can see. Surely we belong to God and to Him we return. This is the funeral prayer for the deceased who have parted to the mercy of God of the nation of Muhammad ﷺ.		
AT-TAKBĪRATU 'L-ŪLĀ (FIRST TAKBĪR) Allāhū akbar. God is Greatest!		التَّكْبيرة الأولى: اللهُ أكْبر
Subḥānaka Allāhumma wa bi ḥamdika, wa tabāraka ismuka wa ta'alā jadduka, wa jalla thāna'uka, wa lā ilāha ghayruka. (In Shāfi'ī madhab: Recite al-Fātiḥah)		سُبْحانَكَ اللَّهمَّ وبِحَمْدِك، وتَبارَكَ اسْمُكَ وتَعالى جَدُّكَ وجَلَّ ثناؤكَ ولا إله غَيْرُكَ
Glory and praise be to You, O my God. Great is Your Praise, and there is not god but You. (In the Shāfi'ī Madhhab: Recite al-Fātiḥah).		
AT-TAKBĪRATU 'TH-THĀNĪYA (SECOND TAKBĪR) Allāhū akbar. God is Greatest!		التَّكْبيرة الثانية : اللهُ أكْبر
Allāhumma ṣalli 'alā Muḥammadin wa 'alā āli Muḥammadin, kama ṣallayta 'alā Ibrāḥīma wa 'alā āli Ibrāḥīma innaka ḥamīdun majīdun. Allāhumma bārik 'alā Muḥammadin wa 'alā āli Muḥammadin,		اللَّهمَّ صَلِّ على مُحَمَّد وعلى آل مُحَمَّد كما صَلَّيْتَ على إبراهيم وعلى آل إبراهيم إنكَ حَميدٌ مَجيدٌ. اللَّهمَّ بارِكْ على مُحَمَّد وعلى آل مُحَمَّد كما بارَكْتَ

<table>
<tr><td>kamā bārakta ʻalā Ibrāhīm wa ʻalā āli Ibrāhīma, innaka ḥamīdun majīdun.</td><td></td><td>على إبراهيم وعلى آلِ إبراهيم إنكَ حَميدٌ مَجيدٌ.</td></tr>
<tr><td colspan="3">O God! Exalt Muhammad and the family of Muhammad, as You have exalted Abraham and the family of Abraham. Truly, You are All-Laudable, All-Glorious. O God! Bless Muhammad and the family of Muhammad, as You have blessed Abraham and the family of Abraham. Truly, You are All-Laudable, All-Glorious.</td></tr>
<tr><td>AT-TAKBĪRATU TH-THĀLITHA (THIRD TAKBĪR)
Allāhū akbar.
God is Greatest!</td><td></td><td>التَّكْبيرة الثالثة:
الله أكبر</td></tr>
<tr><td>Allāhumma ʼghfir li ḥayyinā wa mayyitinā wa shāhidinā wa ghā'ibinā wa ṣaghīrinā wa kabīrinā wa dhakarinā wa unthānā. Allāhumma man aḥyaytahū minna fa aḥyihi ʻalā al-Islām wa man tawaffaytahū minnā fa tawaffahū ʻalā al-īmān. Allāhumma ʼghfir lahum wa ʼrḥamhum. Allāhumma lā taḥrimnā ajrahum wa lā taftinā bʻādahum.</td><td></td><td>اللَّهُمَّ اغْفِرْ لحَيّنا ومَيّتنا وشاهدنا وغائبنا وصَغيرنَا وكَبيرنَا ذَكَرنا وأنثانا . اللَّهُمَّ من أحْيَيْتَهُ منّا فَأَحْيِه على الإسْلامِ ومن توَفَّيْتَهُ منّا فتَوَفّهُ على الإيمان. اللَّهُمَّ اغْفِرْ لَهم وارْحَمْهُم اللَّهُمَّ لا تحْرِمْنا أجْرَهُم ولا تَفْتِنّا بَعْدهُم</td></tr>
<tr><td colspan="3">O God! Forgive our living and our dead, those present and absent, our young and our old, male and female. O God! To those of us whom You have given life, make them live according to the religion of Islam, and whosoever dies, make him die in faith. O God! Forgive them and have mercy on them. O God! Do not deny us their reward (and) do not lead us astray after them (i.e. after their death).</td></tr>
<tr><td>AT-TAKBĪRATU R-RĀBIʻA (FOURTH TAKBĪR)
Allāhū akbar.
God is Greatest!</td><td></td><td>التَّكْبيرة الرَّابعةُ:
اللهُ أكْبَرُ
اللهم لا تحرمنا أجرهم ولا تفتنا بعدهم واغفر لنا ولهم</td></tr>
<tr><td>TASLĪM
(To the right) as-salāmu ʻalaykum wa raḥmatullāḥ
Peace be upon you and the mercy of God.</td><td></td><td>تسليم
إلى اليمين: السَلامُ عَلَيْكم ورَحْمَةُ الله</td></tr>
<tr><td>(To the left) as-salāmu ʻalaykum wa raḥmatullāḥ
Peace be upon you and the mercy of God.</td><td></td><td>إلى اليَسار: السَلامُ عَلَيْكم ورَحْمَةُ الله</td></tr>
</table>

DU'A (SUPPLICATION)		دُعاء
Allāhumma 'ghfir li aḥyā'inā wa 'rḥam mawtānā washf'i marḍānā bi ḥurmat il-Fātiḥā.		اللَّهُمَّ اغْفِرْ لأَحْيائنا وارْحَمْ مَوْتانا واشْفِ مَرْضانا وانصر سلطاننا بِحُرْمَة من أرسلته رحمة للعالمين وبسر سورة الفاتحة
O God! Forgive the living and have mercy on our dead, and cure our sick, by the sanctity of al-Fātiḥā.		
Ṣalātu 'l-Janaza is then followed by six rak 'ats of Ṣalātu 'l-Awwābīn.		
Salatu-l-Awwabin 6 rak 'ats (3 sets of 2 Rak'āts).		صلاة الأوابين (ست ركعات)
KALIMATU SH-SHAHĀDA (3 TIMES) Ash-hadu an lā ilāha ill-Allāh wa ash-hadu anna Muḥammadan 'abduhu wa rasūluh.		كَلمةُ الشّهادة (٣ مرّات): أشْهَدُ أن لا إله إلا الله وأشْهَدُ أنّ مُحَمّدً عَبْدَهُ ورَسُولُهُ
I bear witness that there is no god but God, and Muhammad is His Servant and Messenger.		
ISTIGHFĀR (100 TIMES)		استغفار (١٠٠ مرّة)
Astaghfirullāh I ask God's forgiveness.		أَسْتَغْفِرُ الله
DU'A (SUPPLICATION)		دعاء
Astaghfirullāh min kulli dhanbin wa ma'ṣīyatin wa min kulli mā yukhālifu dīn al-Islām, yā arḥam ar-Rāḥimīn.		أَسْتَغْفِرُ اللهَ من كُلّ ذنب ومَعْصِيّة ومن كُلّ ما يُخالِفُ دينَ الإسْلامِ يا أَرْحَمَ الراحمين
I ask God's forgiveness for every sin and desobedience and from all that opposes the religion of Islam, O most Merciful of Merciful.		
SŪRATU S-SAJDA (PROSTRATION)		سُورةُ السَّجْدة
A'udhūbillāhi min ash-shayṭān ir-rajīm. Bismillāhi 'r-Raḥmāni 'r-Raḥīm.		أَعُوذُ بِالله من الشَّيْطانِ الرَّجيم. بِسْمِ اللهِ الرَّحْمن

		الرَّحيمِ
I seek refuge with God from Satan, the Cursed. In the Name of God, the Most Merciful, the Most Compassionate (This will be omitted hereafter, but must be read before any Quran reading). Then, read Sūratu 'l-Fātiḥah, followed by Sūratu 's-Sajda.		
SŪRATU 'L-IKHLĀṢ (SINCERITY) (3 TIMES)		سُورةُ الإخْلاص (٣ مرات)
SŪRATU 'L-FALAQ (DAYBREAK) ONCE		سُورةُ الفَلَق
SŪRATU 'N-NĀS (MANKIND) ONCE		سُورةُ الناس
TAHLĪL (10 TIMES) Lā ilāha ill-Allāh There is no god but God. (After the tenth) Muḥammadur Rasūlullāh ﷺ. Muhammad is the Messenger of God ﷺ.		تهليل: لا إله إلا الله (١٠ مرات) (بَعْدَ العاشرة) مُحَمَّدٌ رَسُولُ الله صلّى الله عليه وسلّم
ṢALAWĀT (10 TIMES) Allāhumma ṣalli 'alā Muḥammadin wa 'alā āli Muḥammadin wa sallim.		صلوات: اللّهُمَّ صَلِّ على مُحَمَّدٍ وعلى آلِ مُحَمَّد وسلّم (١٠ مرّة)
Blessings and peace be upon Muhammad and the family of Muhammad.		
DU'A (INVOCATION)		دعاء
Ṣalli, yā Rabbī, wa sallim 'alā jamī'i il-anbīyā'i wa 'l-mursalīn, wa ālin kullin ajma'īn wa 'l-ḥamdulillāhi Rabb il-'ālamīn.		صلِّ يا ربّي وسلّم على جَميعِ الأنْبياء والمُرْسَلينَ وآلِ كُلٍّ أجْمَعينَ والحَمْدُ لله رَبِّ العالَمينَ
Blessings, O my Lord, and peace be upon all the prophets and messegers, and on the family of every one of them. Praise belongs to God, the Lord of the worlds.		

CHIEF OF THE PRAYERS ON PROPHET (see page 171)		الصلاة الشريفة المأثورة
DEDICATION Recite the Ihdā (see page 172)		إهْداء

صلاةُالعِشاء

Salatu-l-Isha

Performed in the same manner as Ṣalātu 'l-Maghrib with the following changes:	
4 RAK'ATS SUNNAH	٤ رَكْعات سُنّة: رَكْعَتَيْن سُنّة وركْعَتَيْن نافِلة بِتَسْليمٍ واحِد أو بِتَسْليمَيْنَ
4 RAK'ATS FARḌ	٤ رَكْعات فَرْض
4 RAK'ATS SUNNAH	٤ رَكْعات سنة: رَكْعَتَيْن سُنّة وركْعَتَيْن نافِلة بِتَسْليمٍ واحِد أو بِتَسْليمين
ṢALATUL-WITR (3 RAK'ATS)	صَلاة الوِتْر (ثَلاثُ رَكْعات)
Before the ruku', or bowing, in the third rak'at, recite:	

<table>
<tr>
<td>

QUNŪT PRAYER (SEE NOTES)

Allāhu akbar. Allāhumma innā nasta'īnuka wa nastahdīka; wa nastaghfiruka wa natūbu ilayk wa nu'minu bika, wa natawakkalu 'alayk, wa nuthnī 'alayk al-khayr kullahā wa nashkuruka, wa lā nakfuruka, wa nakhla'u wa natruku man yafjuruka.

Allāhumma iyyāka na'budu wa laka nuṣalli wa nasjudu wa ilayka nas'ā wa naḥfiḍu wa narju raḥmataka, wa nakhshā 'adhābak, inna 'adhābak al-jidda bil-kuffāri mulḥaq, wa ṣalla-llāhū 'alā an-Nabī wa 'alā ālihi wa sallam. Allāhu akbar!

</td>
<td>

دعاء القُنوت

(فِي الرَكْعةِ الثالِثة قبل الركوع على مذهب الامام ابو حنيفة)

اللهُ أكْبَر. اللَّهمَّ إنَّ نَسْتَعينُكَ ونَسْتَهْدِيكِ ونَسْتَغْفِرُكَ ونَتُوبُ إليك ونُؤْمنُ بِكَ ونَتَوَكَّلُ عليك ونُثني عليكَ الخَيْر كلّه نَشْكُرُكَ ولا نَكْفُرُ ونَخْلَعُ ونَتْرُكُ من يَفْجُرُكَ. اللَّهمَّ إيّاكَ نَعْبُدُ ولك نُصَلّي ونَسْجُدُ إليك نَسْعى ونَحْفِدُ ونَرْجو رَحْمَتَكَ ونَخْشَى عَذابَكَ إنَّ عَذابَكَ الجِدّ بالكُفَّارِ مُلْحَقْ وصلّى اللهُ على النَبِي وآله وسلّم

</td>
</tr>
<tr>
<td colspan="2">

God is Greatest! O God! To You alone we pray for succour, for guidance, and for forgiveness. And to You we return in repentance; We believe in You, and trust in You, and praise You by all that is good. We thank You and are not ungrateful. We remove and leave those who sin against You. O God! We serve only You, and to You we pray and prostrate, and towards You we strive. We hope for your mercy and fear Your chastisement, for truly, Your severe punishment will befall the disbelievers. God's blessings and peace be upon the Prophet and upon his family. God is Greatest!

Go into ruk'ū

</td>
</tr>
<tr>
<td colspan="2">

Ṣalātu 'l-Witr is followed by the customary tasbīḥ and waẓīfā (see Ṣalātu 'l-Maghrib) reciting Sūratu 'l-Mulk in place of Sūratu 's-Sajda, followed by the customary adhkār.

</td>
</tr>
</table>

صَلاةُ الفَجرِ

Salatu-l-Fajr

The adab of Ṣalātu 'l-Fajr is presented in its entirety because it differs greatly from the other prayers.		
Adhan (call to prayer)		الآذان
Allāhu akbar (4 times) God is Greatest		اللهُ أكْبر، اللهُ أكْبر، اللهُ أكْبر، اللهُ أكْبر
Ash-hadu an lā ilāha ill-Allāh (2 times) I bear witness that there is no god but God		اشْهَدُ أنْ لا إلَهَ إلاَّ الله اشْهَدُ أنْ لا إلَهَ إلاَّ الله
Ash-hadu anna Muḥammadan Rasūlullāh (2 times) I bear witness that Muhammad is the Messenger of God.		اشْهَدُ أنَّ محمداً رسول الله – اشْهَدُ أنَّ محمداً رسول الله
Ḥayya 'alā 'ṣ-ṣalāh (2 times) Hasten to the prayer		حيَّ عَلى الصَّلاة حيَّ عَلى الصَّلاة
Ḥayyā 'āla 'l-falāḥ (2 times) Hasten to salvation		حيَّ عَلى الفَلاح حيَّ عَلى الفَلاح
Aṣ-ṣalātu khayrun min an-nawm (2 times, only before Fajr) Prayer is better than sleep		الصلاة خير من النوم الصلاة خير من النوم
Allāhu akbar (2 times) God is Greatest		اللهُ أكْبر اللهُ أكْبر
Lā ilāha illa-Allāh There is no god but God		لا إلَهَ إلاَّ الله

<table>
<tr>
<td>AṢ-ṢALĀTU WAS-SALĀM
(to be made aloud by the muadhdhin):
Aṣ-ṣalātu was-salāmu ʻalayk, yā man arsalahullāhu taʻalā raḥmatan lil-ʻālamīn.
Aṣ-ṣalātu was-salāmu ʻalayk, wa ʻalā ālika wa aṣḥābika ajmaʻīn.
Aṣ-ṣalātu was-salāmu ʻalaykum, yā anbiyāʼAllāḥ.</td>
<td></td>
<td>الصلاة والسلام
الصلاة والسلام عليك يا من أرسله الله تعالى رحمة للعالمين
الصلاة والسلام عليك وعلى آلك وأصحابك أجمعين الصلاة والسلام عليكم، يا أنبياء الله</td>
</tr>
<tr>
<td colspan="3">Blessings and peace be upon you, whom God Most High sent as mercy to the Worlds.
Blessings and peace be upon you, and upon all your family and your Companions.
Blessings and peace be upon you, O Prophet of God.</td>
</tr>
<tr>
<td>INVOCATION (DUʻA):
(to be made silently by all who hear the adhān):
Allāhumma rabba hādhihī 'd-daʻwat it-tāmma waṣ-ṣalāt il-qāʼima, āti Sayyidinā Muḥammadan al-wasīlata wa 'l-fadīlata wa 'd-darajati 'r-rafʻīati 'l-ʻalīyya wabʻathhu Rabbī al-maqām al-maḥmūd alladhī wʻadtahu, warzuqnā shafʻatahu yawm al-qīyāma. Innaka lā tukhlifu 'l-mīʻad.</td>
<td></td>
<td>دُعاءُ:
اللَّهُمَّ رَبَّ هَذه الدعْوة التّامّة والصَلاة القائمة آتِ مُحَمَّداً الوَسيلةَ والفَضيلةَ والدَرَجة الرَفيعةَ العالية وابْعَثْه رَبّي المقام المَحْمُودَ الذي وَعَدْته وارْزُقْنا شَفاعَتَهُ يَوْمَ القِيامةِ إنكَ لا تُخْلِفُ الميعاد (وزَوّجْنا من الحُورِ العين)</td>
</tr>
<tr>
<td colspan="3">O God! Lord of this perfect supplication and of this established prayer, grant Muhammad the Means (of nearness to You) and the excellence of the sublime and supreme rank. Raise him, O my Lord, to the Praiseworthy Station, which You promised him, and grant us his intercession on the Day of Judgment, for You do not fail Your promise.</td>
</tr>
<tr>
<td>٢ رَكْعتان سنة</td>
<td></td>
<td>2 RAKʻATS SUNNAH</td>
</tr>
</table>

<table>
<tr><td>KALIMATU SH-SHAHĀDA (3 TIMES)
Ash-hadu an lā ilāha ill-Allāh, wa ash-hadu anna Muḥammadan ʻabduhū wa rasūluḥ.</td><td>كلمة الشَهادة:
أشْهدُ أنْ لا إله إلا الله وأشْهدُ أنَّ مُحَمَّدًا عَبْدُهُ ورَسُولُهُ (3 مَرّات)</td></tr>
<tr><td colspan="2">I bear witness that there is no god but God, and Muhammad is His servant and Messenger.</td></tr>
<tr><td>Iqāmat ʻuṣ-ṣalāt wa ītāu ʼz-zakāt wa ṣawmu ramaḍān, wa Ḥajju ʼl-bayti Ḥaqq. Āmantu billāhi wa malāʼikatihi wa kutubihi wa rusulihi wa ʼl-yawm il-āhkiri wa bil-qadari khayrihi wa sharrihi min Allāhi taʻalā. Awdaʻnā hātayni ʼl-kalimatayni ʼsh-shahādatayn ʻindaka yā Rasūlullāh wa hīya lanā wadīʻatun yawma ʼl-qiyāmati ya man arsalahullāhū taʻalā raḥmatan li ʼl-ʻālamīn.</td><td>إقامةُ الصَلاةِ وإيتاءُ الزَكاةِ وصَوْمُ رَمَضانَ وحَجُّ البيْتِ حَقٌّ آمَنْتُ باللهِ ومَلائكته وكُتُبه ورُسُله وباليَوْمِ الآخرِ وبِالقَدَرِ خَيْره وشَرّه. أوْدَعْنا هاتَيْن الشَهادَتَيْن عِنْدَكَ يا سيدي يا رَسُول الله وهي لنا وَديعَة يَوْمَ القِيامة يا من أرْسَلَهُ اللهُ رَحْمَةً للعالمينَ.</td></tr>
<tr><td colspan="2">The performance of prayer, the payment of alms, the fast in Ramadān, and the Pilgrimage to the House, are true. I declare my belief in God, His Angels, His Books, His messengers, the Day of Judgment, and in Destiny—both its good and evil being from God (Exalted is He!). May the truth of what I say be accepted, O Lord.

We have commended these two testimonials to your safekeeping, O Messenger of God. They are for us a trust on the Day of Judgment, O you who were sent by God (Exalted is He!) as a mercy to the worlds.</td></tr>
<tr><td>Subḥānallāh wa bi ḥamdhihi subḥānallāh il-ʻAzīm Astaghfirullāh (100 times)</td><td>سُبحانَ الله وبِحَمْده. سُبْحانَ اللهِ العَظيمِ أسْتَغفِرُ الله – 100 مرة</td></tr>
<tr><td colspan="2">Glory be to God, and to Him be praise. Glory be to God Almighty. I ask God's forgiveness.[275]</td></tr>
<tr><td>(after the 100th time)
Astaghfirullāh al-ʻAẓīm alladhī lā ilāha illa Hū al-Ḥayyu ʼl-Qayyūm wa atūbu</td><td>بَعْدَ المئة:
اسْتَغْفِرُ اللهَ العَظيم الذي لا إله إلا هُوَ الحيُّ القيُّوم</td></tr>
</table>

[275] The Prophet said, "Whoever says: "Glorified is God, the Great, and to Him be praise," will have a palm tree planted for him in Paradise." (Narrated by Tirmidhi, who said it is *hasan*).

<table>
<tr><td>ilayḥ innahu hū at-tawābu 'r-raḥīm min kulli dhanbin wa ma'ṣīyatin wa min kulli mā yukhālifu dīn al-Islām, yā arḥam ar-Rāḥimīn, min kulli mā yukhālif ush-sharī'at, min kulli mā yukhālif uṭ-ṭarīqata, min kulli mā yukhālifu 'l-ma'rifata, min-kulli mā yukhālifu 'l-ḥaqīqata, min kulli mā yukhālifu 'l-'azīmata, yā arḥam ar-rāḥīmin.</td><td></td><td>وأتوبُ إليه إنَّهُ هو التّوّابُ الرَّحيم، من كُلِّ ذنْبٍ ومَعْصيّةٍ ومن كُلِّ ما يُخالفُ دينَ الإسْلام ومن كُلِّ ما يُخالفُ الشَرِيعة ومن كُلِّ ما يُخالفُ الطَرِيقَةَ ومن كُلِّ ما يُخالفُ المَعْرِفَةَ ومن كُلِّ ما يُخالفُ الحَقيقَةَ ومن كُلِّ ما يُخالفُ العَزِيمة يا أرْحَمَ الراحمين.</td></tr>
<tr><td colspan="3">I ask forgiveness from God Almighty, there is no god but He, the Living, the Self-Subsisting, and I turn in repentance to Him, verily He is the Forgiver, the Merciful, from every sin and disobedience and from all that opposes the religion of Islam, from all that opposes the Divine Law, from all that opposes the Path, from all that opposes Spiritual Realization, from all that opposes Reality, from all that opposes firm Intention, O most Merciful of the Merciful.</td></tr>
<tr><td>Astaghfirullāhu 'l-'Aẓīm, wa atūbu ilayh (100 times)</td><td></td><td>أسْتَغْفِرُ اللهَ العَظيم وأتوبُ إليه — ١٠٠ مرة</td></tr>
<tr><td colspan="3">I ask forgiveness from God Almighty and I turn to Him in repentance.[274]</td></tr>
<tr><td>(after the 100th time)
Tawbatan 'abdin ẓālimin li nafsihi, lā yamliku li nafsihi mawtan wa lā ḥayātan wa lā nushūrā.
Allāhumma anta Rabbī, lā ilāha illa Ant. Khalaqtanī wa anā 'abduka wa anā 'alā 'ahdika wa wa'dika ma 'staṭa't. A'udhū bika min sharri mā ṣan'āt, abū'u laka bi ni'matika 'alayya, wa abū'u bi dhanbī faghfir lī fa innahū lā yaghfir udh-dhunūba illa Anta Yā Allāḥ.</td><td></td><td>تَوْبة عَبْدٍ ظالمٍ لنَفْسه لا يَمْلكُ لنفْسه مَوْتًا ولا حَياةً ولا نُشُورًا اللَّهُمَّ رَبِّي لا إله إلا أنتَ خَلَقْتَني وأنا عَبْدُكَ وأنا على عَهْدِكَ ووَعْدِكَ ما اسْتَطَعْتُ أعُوذُ بِكَ من شَرِّ ما صَنَعْتُ وأبوء لَكَ بنِعْمَتكَ عليّ وأبوء بِذَنْبي فاغفر لي فإنَّهُ لا يَغْفِرُ الذنوبَ إلا أنتَ يا اللهُ.</td></tr>
<tr><td colspan="3">The repentance of a slave who has oppressed himself, who neither has power over his death, nor his life, nor his resurrection.
O God! You are my Lord. There is no god but You. You have created me. I am Your slave, and I hold fast to Your convenant and Your promise (as much as I am able). I take refuge in You from the evil I have done, and testify that Your Grace</td></tr>
</table>

274 The Prophet said: "If one supplicates without fail for forgiveness from God, He finds a way out for him to escape every distress and difficulty, and gives him sustenance through ways utterly unthought of."
Narrated by Abu Dawud, Nasa'i, Ibn Majah, and Hakim, who said its chain of authorities is sound.

<table>
<tr><td colspan="2">is upon me, and profess my sin. Forgive me, for there is none who forgives sins except You, O God!</td></tr>
<tr><td>CHAPTER 3, VERSE 8
Rabbanā lā tuzigh qulūbanā ba'da idh hadaytanā wa hab lanā min ladunka raḥmatan innaka Anta' l-Wahhāb.</td><td>سُورَةُ آل عمْران آية ٨
رَبَّنا لا تُزِغْ قلوبَنا بَعْدَ إذْ هَدَيْتَنا وهَبْ لنا من لَدُنْكَ
رَحْمةً إنكَ أنتَ الوَهّاب.</td></tr>
<tr><td colspan="2">Our Lord, make not our hearts to swerve after You have guided us, and give us Your Mercy; You are the Bestower.</td></tr>
<tr><td>Yā Wahhāb. Yā Wahhāb. Yā Wahhāb. Yā Musabbib al-asbāb, yā Mufattiḥu 'l-abwāb, yā Muqallibu 'l-qulūbi wa 'l-abṣār, yā Dalīl al-mutaḥayyirīn, yā Ghiyāth al-mustaghīthīn, yā Ḥayyu, yā Qayyūm, yā Dhal-Jalāli wa 'l-Ikrām! Wa ufawwiḍu amrī ila-Allāh, inna-llāha baṣīrun bi 'l-'ibād.</td><td>يا وَهّاب يا وَهّاب يا وَهّاب،
يا مُسَبِّبَ الأسباب. ويا مُفَتِّحُ الأبواب. يا مُقَلِّبُ
القُلُوب والأبصار. يا دَليل المُتَحَيِّرين يا غياثَ
المُسْتَغيثين يا حيُّ يا قَيُّوم. يا ذا الجلالِ والإكْرام.
وأُفَوِّضُ أمْري إلى الله. إنَّ اللهَ بَصيرٌ بالعباد.</td></tr>
<tr><td colspan="2">O Bestower! O Bestower! O Bestower! O Originator of causes! O Opener of doors! O Tuner (Changer) of hearts and eyes! O Guide of the perplexed! O Succour for those who seek Your aid! O Living! O Self-Subsisting One! O (You who are) possessed of Majesty and Bounty! I entrust my affair unto God. Truly, God is aware of His servants.</td></tr>
<tr><td>DU'Ā</td><td>دُعاء</td></tr>
<tr><td>Yā man lā maljā'a minhu illa ilayhi fa lā tukhayyib rajā'anā, yā Qadīm al-iḥsān. lā taqnaṭu min raḥmati-llāh, inna-llāha yaghfir udh-dhūnuba jamī'an, innahū Hū al-Ghafūru 'r-Raḥīm.
Allāhumma innā nas'aluka 'l-'afwa wal 'āfīyata fi 'd-dīni wad-dunyā wa 'l-ākhira.
Allahumma 'sturnā bi satrik al-jamīl.
Allāhumm 'ustur 'awratī, wa āmin raw'atī, waqḍi lī daynī. Allāhumma inna nā'ūdhū bika min jahdil-balā'i, wa darki 'sh-shaqā'i, wa sūi 'l-qaḍā'i, wa shamātati</td><td>يا من لا ملجأَ منه إلا إليه فلا تُخَيِّبْ رَجاءَنَا يا قَديمَ
الإحْسان لا تَقْنَطُوا من رَحْمةِ الله إنَّ اللهَ يَغْفِرُ
الذنُوبَ جَميعًا إنَّهُ هو الغَفُور الرَحيم
اللَّهُمَّ إنَّا نَسْأَلُكَ العَفْوَ والعافيةَ في الدينِ والدُنْيا
والآخرَةِ اللَّهُمَّ اسْتُرْنا بِسَتْرِكَ الجميل. اللَّهُمَّ اسْتُرْ
عَوْرَتي وآمِنْ رَوْعَتي واقْضِ دَيْني. اللَّهُمَّ إنّا نَعُوذُ بِكَ
من جَهْدِ البَلاء ودَركِ الشَقاءِ وسُوءِ القَضاء</td></tr>
</table>

<table>
<tr><td>'l-a'dā'i, bi ḥurmati man arsaltahū raḥmatan li 'l-'ālamīn.</td><td></td><td dir="rtl">وشَماتةِ الأَعْداءِ بِحُرْمةِ من أَرْسَلتَهُ رَحْمةً للعالَمينَ.</td></tr>
<tr><td colspan="3">O From whom there is no refuge except in Him, do not disappoint our hopes, O Eternally Beneficent. Do not despair of the mercy of God, for God forgives every sin. Truly, He is the All-Forgiving, All-Merciful. O God! We ask Your pardon, and ask for strength in religion, in this life and the Hereafter.
O God! Veil us with Your Beautiful Veil.
O God! Veil my imperfection and set me rest when I fear, and settle my debts.
O God! We take refuge in You from the pangs of tribulations, from being overtaken by misfortune, and from an evil destiny, and from the gloating of mine enemies. By the sanctity of the one whom you sent as a mercy to the worlds (Sayyidinā Muhammad ﷺ).</td></tr>
<tr><td>Salatu munajiyyah</td><td></td><td dir="rtl">صلاة المنجية</td></tr>
<tr><td>Allāhumma ṣalli 'alā Muḥammadin ṣalātan tunjīnā bihā min jamī'i 'l-ahwāli wa 'l-āfāt, wa taqḍī lanā bihā min jamī'i 'l-ḥājāt, wa tuṭahhirunā bihā min jamī'i 's-sayyi'āt, wa tarfa'unā bihā 'indaka 'alā 'd-darajāt, wa tuballighunā bihā aqṣā 'l-ghāyāt min jamī'i 'l-khayrāti fi 'l-ḥayāt wa ba'd al-mamāt.</td><td></td><td dir="rtl">اللَّهُمَّ صلِّ على سَيِّدنا مُحَمَّدٍ صَلاةً تُنجينا بِها من جَميعِ الأَهْوالِ والآفاتِ وتَقْضي لَنا بِها جَميعَ الحاجاتِ وتُطَهِّرُنا بِها من جَميعِ السَيِّئاتِ وتَرْفَعُنا بِها عِنْدَكَ أَعْلى الدَرجاتِ وتُبَلِّغُنا بِها أَقصى الغاياتِ من جَميعِ الخَيْراتِ في الحَياةِ وبَعْدَ المَماتِ</td></tr>
<tr><td colspan="3">O God! Blessings upon Muhammad. May they be blessings that delivers us from every fear. And appoint for us the fulfillment of every need. May we be cleansed by them (the blessings) from every sin, and by them may we be raised to the highest stations. And by them make us attain the furthest degrees in all that is good in this life and the life and after death.</td></tr>
<tr><td>Allāhumma 'sliḥ ummata Muḥammad.</td><td></td><td dir="rtl">اللَّهُمَّ أَصْلِحْ أُمَّةَ مُحَمَّد</td></tr>
<tr><td colspan="3">O God! Reconcile the nation of Muhammad.</td></tr>
<tr><td>Allāhumma 'rḥam ummata Muḥammad.</td><td></td><td dir="rtl">اللَّهُمَّ ارْحمْ أُمَّةَ مُحَمَّد</td></tr>
<tr><td colspan="3">O God! Have mercy on the nation of Muhammad.</td></tr>
<tr><td>Allāhūmma 'stur ummata Muḥammad.</td><td></td><td dir="rtl">اللَّهُمَّ استُرْ أُمَّةَ مُحَمَّد</td></tr>
<tr><td colspan="3">O God! Veil the imperfection of the nation of Muhammad.</td></tr>
<tr><td>Allāhūmm 'ghfir li ummati Muḥammad.</td><td></td><td dir="rtl">اللَّهُمَّ اغفِرْ لأُمَّةِ مُحَمَّد</td></tr>
</table>

O God! Forgive the nation of Muhammad.		
Allāhūmm 'aḥfaẓ ummata Muḥammad.		اللَّهُمَّ احْفَظْ أمّةَ مُحَمَّد
O God! Preserve the nation of Muhammad.		
Allāhūmma 'nṣur ummata Muḥammad.		اللَّهُمَّ أنصُرْ أمّةَ مُحَمَّد
O God! Succour the nation of Muhammad.		
Yā arḥam ar-Rāḥīmīn arḥamnā. Yā arḥam ar-Rāḥīmīn fa'fu 'annā. Yā arḥam ar-Raḥīmīn, yā Ghaffār adh-dhūnub, Yā Sattār al-'uyūb, Yā Fattāḥ al-qulūb.		يا أرْحَمَ الراحمين ارْحَمْنا . يا أرْحَمَ الراحمين اعفُ عَنّا . يا أرْحَمَ الراحمين يا غفّارَ الذنوبَ يا ستّارَ العُيوبَ يا فتّاحَ القلوب
O Most Merciful of the Merciful! Have mercy on us. O Most Merciful of the Merciful! Forgive us. O Most Merciful of the Merciful! O Pardoner of sins! O Veiler of our shortcomings! O Opener of hearts!		
Allāhumma 'sqināl-ghaytha suqyā raḥmatin wa lā taj'alnā min al-qāniṭīn. Āmīn. Āmīn. Āmīn.		اللَّهُمَّ اسْقِنا الغيثَ سُقْيَةَ رَحْمَةٍ ولا تَجْعَلنا من القانطينَ رب اغفر وارحم وأنتَ خيرُ الرّاحمين. آمين آمين آمين
My Lord, pardon and forgive, for You are the best of those who forgive. Āmīn. Āmīn. Āmīn.		
Wa salāmun 'alā l-mursalīn, wa 'lḥamdu-lillāhi Rabb il-'alamīn.		وسَلامٌ على المُرْسَلينَ والحَمْدُ لله رَبّ العالمين.
Peace be upon the messengers and praise be to God, the Lord of the worlds.		
SŪRATU 'L-IKHLĀṢ (CHAPTER 112) (3 TIMES)		سُورةُ الإخْلاص — ٣ مرات
CHAPTER 37: VERSE 180 Subḥāna Rabbika Rabbi 'l-'izzati 'ammā yaṣifūn wa salāmun 'ala 'l-mursalīn wa 'l-ḥamdulillāhi Rabbi 'l-'ālamīn.		سورة الصافات ١٨٠ سُبْحانَ رَبّكَ رَبّ العزّة عَمّا يَصفُونَ وسَلامٌ على المُرْسَلينَ والحَمْدُ لله رَبّ العالمينَ
Glory be to Your Lord, the Lord of Power, above what they describe! And peace be upon the Emissaries. Praise belongs to God, the Lord of the Worlds.		
Lā ilāhā ill-Allāh, wāḥdahū lā sharīka lah, lahu 'l-mulku wa lahu 'l-ḥamd, yuḥī		لا إله إلا اللهُ وَحْدَهُ لا شَريكَ لَه، له المُلكُ وله الحَمْدُ

wa yumīt, wa Hūwa Ḥāyyun dā'imun, lā yamūt, bi yadihi 'l-khayr, wa Hūwa 'alā kulli shay'in qadīr.	يُحيِي ويُميت وهُوَ حيٌّ دائمٌ لا يَموتُ بِيَده الخَيرُ وهُوَ على كُلِّ شَيْءٍ قَدير.

There is no god but God. He is One, no partner has He. His is the Kingdom, and His is all praise, He brings to life and causes to die. He is forever Living, never dying. In His Hands is (all) good, and He is over all things Powerful.

DEDICATION Ila sharaf in-Nabī ṣall-Allāhū 'alayhi wa sallama wa ālihi wa ṣaḥbih, wa ilā arwāḥi ikhwānihi min al-anbiyā'i wa 'l-mursalīn wa khudamā'i sharā'ihim wa ila arwāḥi 'l-a'immati 'l-arba'ah wa ila arwāḥi mashāyikhinā fi 'ṭ-ṭarīqati 'n-naqshbandīyyati 'l-'aliyyah khāṣṣatan ila rūḥi Imāmi 'ṭ-ṭarīqati wa ghawthi 'l-khalīqati Khwājā Baḥā'uddīn an-Naqshband Muḥammad al-Uwaisī 'l-Bukhārī wa ḥaḍarati Mawlanā Sulṭānu 'l-awlīyā ash-Shaykh 'Abd Allāh al-Fā'iz ad-Dāghestanī wa sayyidunā ash-Shaykh Muḥammad Nāẓim al-Ḥaqqānī wa sa'iri sādātinā waṣ-ṣiddiqīna al-Fātiḥā	إهْداء إلى شَرَفِ النبي وآله وصحْبه، وإلى أرْواحِ إخْوانه من الأُنبياء والمُرسَلين وخُدَماء شَرائعهم وإلى أرْواحِ الأئمّة الأرْبَعة، وإلى أرْواحِ مَشايِخنا في الطَرِيقة النَقْشْبَنْدِيّة العَلِيّة خاصّة إلى رُوحِ إمامِ الطّريقة وغوْث الخَلِيقَة خَواجَه بَهاءُ الدّينِ النَقْشْبَنْد مُحَمَّدُ الأُوَيْسي البُخاري وإلى حَضْرَة مولانا سلطان الأولياء الشيخ عبد الله الدغستاني ومولانا الشيخ محمد ناظم الحقاني وإلى سائر ساداتنا والصدّيقين. الفاتحة

Honor be to the Prophet ﷺ, and his family, and his distinguished Companions, and to our honored Shaykhs and to our Master, Sulṭānu 'l-awlīyā Shaykh 'Abd Allāh al-Fā'izi 'd-Daghestanī and our Master ash-Shaykh Muḥammad Nāẓim al-Ḥaqqānī and to all our masters, and (those who are) the righteous ... al-Fātiḥah.

(LIE DOWN ON RIGHT SIDE RECITING CHAPTER 20: VERSE 55) Minhā khalaqnākum, wa fīhā nu'īdukum, wa minhā nukhrijukum tāratan ukhrā.	اسْتَرِحْ على جَنْبِكَ الأيمن: سورة طه ٥٥ منها خلقْناكم وفيها نُعيدُكم ومنها نُخْرِجُكم تارةً أخرى

Thereof (earth) We created you, and we shall return you unto it, and bring you forth from it a second time.

<table>
<tr><td>CHAPTER 2: 156
Wa innā lillāhi wa innā ilayhi rāji‘ūn.</td><td></td><td>سورة البقرة ١٥٦
إِنَّا لله وإِنَّا إليه راجِعُونَ</td></tr>
<tr><td colspan="3">And truly we belong to God and to Him we return.</td></tr>
<tr><td>CHAPTER 40: 12
Fal-ḥukmu lillāh il-‘Alīyyi il-Kabīr. Allāhumma thabbitnā ‘alā al-īmān.</td><td></td><td>سورة غافر ١٢
فَالحُكْمُ للهِ العَلِيِّ الكَبِيرِ
اللَّهُمَّ ثَبِّتْنا على الإيمان</td></tr>
<tr><td colspan="3">And the decree belongs to God, Most High, Most Great. O God! Keep us steadfast in faith.</td></tr>
<tr><td>IQĀMATU ṢALĀT (AS IN ṢALĀTUL-MAGHRIB)</td><td></td><td>إقامة الصلاة</td></tr>
<tr><td>2 RAK‘ATS FARḌ</td><td></td><td>رَكْعتان فَرْض</td></tr>
<tr><td>QUNŪT PRAYER (SEE NOTES)
Allāhumma ’hdinā bi-faḍlika fī-man hadayt, wa ‘āfinā fī-man ‘āfayt, wa tawallanā fī-man tawallayt, wa bārik lanā fī-mā a‘ṭayt, wa qinā w’aṣrif ‘annā sharra mā qaḍayt [palms turned down from wa qinā to qaḍayt]. Fa innaka taqḍī wa lā yuqḍā ‘alayk, wa innahū lā yadhillu man wālayt, wa lā ya‘izzu man ‘ādayt. Tabārakta Rabbanā wa ta‘ālayt, wa laka ’l-ḥamdu ‘alā mā qaḍayt. Nastaghfiruk ’allāhumma wa natūbu ilayk, wa ṣalla-llāhu ‘alā ’n-Nabī il-ummīyy wa ‘alā ālihi wa ṣaḥbihi wa sallam.</td><td></td><td>دعاء القُنوت
بعد سمع الله لمن حمده:
اللَّهمَّ اهْدنا بفضلك فيمَنْ هَديتَ، وَعافنا فيمَنْ عَافَيْتَ، وَتَوَلَّنا فيمَنْ تَوَلَّيتَ، وَبَارِك لنا فيما أَعْطيْتَ، وَقنا وَاصرف عنّا شَرَّ مَا قَضَيْتَ، فَإِنَّكَ تَقْضي بالحقّ، ولاَ يُقضَى عَلَيْك، وإنّه لا يَذِلُّ مَنْ وَالَيتَ، ولاَ يعِزُّ من عَادَيْتَ تَبارَكْتَ رَبَّنا وتعاليت فَلَكَ الحَمْدُ على ما قَضَيْتَ نَسْتَغْفِرُكَ اللَّهُمَّ من كل الذنوب ونتوبُ إليكَ وصَلّى الله على النَّبِي الأمّي وعلى آله وصَحْبه وسَلّم</td></tr>
<tr><td colspan="3">O God! Guide us, by Your favor, to those whom You guided, and pardon us with those whom You have pardoned. Bring us close to those whom You have brought nigh (befriended), and bless us in all that You gave us. Protect us and</td></tr>
</table>

<table>
<tr><td colspan="3">turn away from us the evil of what You have decreed. For it is You that decrees and there is no decree upon You. You do not humiliate the one whom You have befriended and do not increase (empower) the one whom You have taken as an enemy. Blessed and Exalted are You, our Lord. To You is all praise for what You have decreed. We ask Your forgiveness, O God, and turn in repentance to You; God's blessings and peace be upon the unlettered Prophet and on his family and his Companions.</td></tr>
<tr><td>Allāhumma 'kshif 'anā minal-balāya mā lā yakshifuhu ghayruk</td><td></td><td>اللَّهُمَّ اكْشِفْ عنّا من البَلايا ما لا يَكْشِفُهُ غيْرُكَ</td></tr>
<tr><td colspan="3">O God! Lift from us trials which no one but You can lift.</td></tr>
<tr><td>Allāhumma 'sqina 'l-ghaytha suqyā raḥmatin wa lā taj'alna min al-qāniṭīn. Rabbi 'ghfir warḥam wa Anta khayru 'r-rāḥimīn.</td><td></td><td>اللَّهُمَّ اسْقِنا الغيثَ سُقْيا رَحْمة ولا تجْعَلنا من
القانطِينَ ربِّ اغفرْ وارْحَمْ وأنتَ خيْرُ الراحمين</td></tr>
<tr><td colspan="3">O God! Give us to drink from the rain of Your Mercy and let us not be of the despondent; Lord, forgive and have mercy, for You are (Most) Merciful.</td></tr>
<tr><td>Allāhumma 'ftaḥ lanā fatḥan mubīnan wa Anta khayru 'l-fātiḥīn</td><td></td><td>اللَّهُمَّ افْتَحْ لنا فتحاً مُبينًا وأنتَ خيْرُ الفاتحين</td></tr>
<tr><td colspan="3">O God! Open for us a manifest opening for You are the best of Openers.</td></tr>
<tr><td>CHAPTER 6: VERSE 45
Fa-quṭi'a dābiru 'l-qawm illadhīna ẓalamū wa 'l-ḥamdulillāhi Rabbi 'l-'ālamīn. (Then go to prostration without wiping face nor chest with hands.)</td><td></td><td>سورة الأنعام ٤٥
فقطع دابرُ القوم الذين ظلموا والحمد لله رب العالمين</td></tr>
<tr><td colspan="3">So the last remnant of the people who did evil was cut off. Praise be to God, Lord of the Worlds. God is Greatest.</td></tr>
<tr><td>(AFTER THE SALUTATIONS)
Lā ilāhā ill-Allāh (3 times)
Muḥammadur-Rasūlullāḥ</td><td></td><td>بعد التّسليم من الصلاة
لا إِلَهَ إِلَّا الله محمد رسول الله – ٣ مرات</td></tr>
<tr><td colspan="3">There is no god except God, Muhammad is the Prophet of God.</td></tr>
<tr><td>ISTIGHFĀR
Astaghfirullāh (3 times)
I ask God's forgiveness.</td><td></td><td>اسْتغفار (٣ مرّة)</td></tr>
</table>

<table>
<tr><td>DU'A (INVOCATION)
Allāhumma Anta 's-Salām wa minka 's-salām wa ilayka ya'ūdu 's-salām, fa ḥayyinā Rabbanā bis-salām, wa 'dkhiln'al-Jannata bi luṭfika wa karamika wa jūdika dāraka, dār as-salām. Tabārakta Rabbanā wa tā'alayta, yā Dhal-Jalāli wa 'l-Jamāli wa 'l-Baqā'i wa 'l-'Aẓamati wa 'l-Ikrām. Yā Rabbanā, Yā Rabbi 'ghfir warḥam wa Anta Khayru 'r-Raḥīmīn.</td><td>دُعاء
اللهم أنتَ السلام ومنك السلام وإليك يعود السلام فحينا ربنا بالسلام وادخلنا الجنة بلطفك وكرمك وجودك دارك دار السلام. تباركت ربنا وتعاليت يا ذا الجلال والجمال والبقاء والعظمة الإكرام. يا ربنا يا رب اغفر وارحم وأنتَ خير الراحمين.</td></tr>
<tr><td colspan="2">O God! You are Peace and from You comes Peace and to You returns Peace; Make us live in peace, our Lord. Enter us into the Garden by Your Grace and Generosity and Presence. And Your Abode is the Abode of Peace. Blessed and lofty are You, O Lord of Majesty, and Beauty, and Everlastingness, and Greatness, and Bounty. O our Lord! O Lord forgive and have mercy, for Yours is the best of Mercy.</td></tr>
<tr><td>Lā ilāhā ill-Allāh, wāḥdahū lā sharīka lah, lahul-mulku wa lahul-ḥamd, yuḥī wa yūmīt, wa Hūwa 'alā kulli shay'in qadīr. (9 times).</td><td>لا إلهَ إلاّ الله وَحْدَهُ لا شَرِيكَ لَه، لَهُ المُلكُ ولَه الحَمْدُ ويُحْيِ ويُميتُ وهُوَ على كلِّ شَيْءٍ قدير (٩ مرّات).</td></tr>
<tr><td colspan="2">There is no god but God. He is One, no partner has He. His is the Kingdom and His is all praise, He gives life and gives death, and He is over all things Powerful.</td></tr>
<tr><td>Lā ilāhā ill-Allāh, wāḥdahū lā sharīka lah, lahu 'l-mulku wa lahu 'l-ḥamd, yuḥī wa yumīt, wa Hūwa Ḥāyyun dā'imun, lā yamūt, bi yadihi 'l-khayr, wa Hūwa 'alā kulli shay'in qadīr.</td><td>لا إله إلا الله وَحْدَهُ لا شَرِيكَ له، له المُلكُ وله الحَمْدُ يُحيِ ويُميت وهُوَ حيٌّ دائمٌ لا يَموتُ بيده الخَيْرُ وهُوَ على كُلِّ شَيْءٍ قدير.</td></tr>
<tr><td colspan="2">There is no god but God. He is One, no partner has He. His is the Kingdom, and His is all praise, He brings to life and causes to die. He is forever Living, never dying. In His Hands is (all) good, and He is over all things Powerful.</td></tr>
<tr><td>Sam'inā wa ata'nā, ghufrānaka Rabbanā wa ilayk al-maṣīr</td><td>سَمِعْنا وأطَعْنا غُفْرانَكَ ربّنا وإليكَ المصير</td></tr>
<tr><td colspan="2">We have heard and obeyed, O our Lord! Yours is our destiny.</td></tr>
<tr><td>'Alā Rasūlinā 'ṣ-ṣalawāt (in a low voice): Allāhūma ṣalli 'alā sayyidinā Muḥammad</td><td>على رَسُولنا الصَّلَوات</td></tr>
</table>

<table>
<tr><td colspan="2">On the Prophet of God, prayers. O God, bless our master Muhammad.</td></tr>
<tr><td>Astaghfirullāh, subḥānallāh wa 'l-ḥamdulillāh, wa lā ilāha ill-Allāh w'Allāhū akbar, wa lā ḥawla wa lā quwwata illa billāhi 'l-'Alīyy il-'Āẓīm.</td><td>أَسْتَغْفِرُ اللهَ. أَسْتَغْفِرُ اللهَ. أَسْتَغْفِرُ اللهَ سُبْحانَ اللهِ والحَمْدُ للهِ ولا إلهَ إلاَّ اللهُ واللهُ أَكْبَر ولا حَوْلَ ولا قُوَّةَ إلا باللهِ العَلِيِّ العَظيم</td></tr>
<tr><td colspan="2">I ask God's forgiveness. Glory be to God! Praise be to God! There is no god but God and God is Greatest. There is no power and no strengh save in God, All-High and Almighty.</td></tr>
<tr><td>CHAPTER 2, VERSE 163
A'udhū billāhi min ash-shayṭān ir-rajīm. Bismillāhi 'r-Raḥmāni 'r-Raḥīm. Wa ilāhukum ilāhun wāḥidun, lā ilāha illa Hūwa 'r-Raḥmānu 'r-Raḥīm.</td><td>البقرة ١٦٣
أَعُوذُ بِاللهِ من الشَّيْطانِ الرَّجيمِ. بِسْمِ اللهِ الرَّحْمنِ الرَّحيمِ. وإلٰهكُم إلٰهٌ واحدٌ لا إلَهَ إلاَّ هُوَ الرَّحْمنُ الرَّحيمُ.</td></tr>
<tr><td colspan="2">I seek refuge with God from Satan, the Cursed. In the name of God, the All-Beneficent, the All-Merciful. Your God is One God; there is no god but He, the All-Merciful, the All-Compassionate.</td></tr>
<tr><td>ĀYATU 'L-KURSĪ (THE VERSE OF THE THRONE)
Allāhū lā ilāha illa Hūwa 'l-Ḥayyu 'l-Qayyūm, lā tākhudhuhū 's-sinatun wa lā nawm, lahū mā fis-samāwāti wa mā fil-arḍ. Man dhā-ladhī yashfa'u 'indahū illā bi idhniḥ ya'lamu mā bayna aydīhim wa mā khalfahum wa lā yuḥīṭunā bi-shay'im min 'ilmihi illā bimā shā'. Wasi'a kursīyyuhu 's-samāwāti wa 'l-arḍa, wa lā ya'uduhū ḥifẓuhuma, wa Hūwa al-'Alīyyu 'l-'Aẓīm.
Ṣadaq-Allāhu 'l-'Aẓīm.</td><td>آيةُ الكُرْسي
اللهُ لا إلهَ إلا هُوَ الحيُّ القَيّوم لا تَأْخُذُهُ سِنَةٌ ولا نَوْمٌ لَهُ ما في السماوات وما في الأَرْض من ذا الذي يَشْفَعُ عِنْدَهُ إلا بِإذْنِه يَعْلَمُ ما في بَيْنَ أَيديهم وما خَلْفَهُم ولا يُحيطونَ بِشَيْءٍ من عِلْمِه إلا بما شاء وَسِعَ كُرْسِيُّهُ السَماوات والأَرْضَ ولا يَؤُدُهُ حِفْظُهُما وهُوَ العَلِيُّ العَظيمُ. صَدَقَ اللهُ العَظيم</td></tr>
<tr><td colspan="2">God, there is no god but He, the Living, the Everlasting. Slumber seizes Him not, neither sleep; to Him belongs all that is in the heavens and the earth. Who is there that shall intercede with Him save by His leave? He knows what lies before them, and they comprehend not anything of His knowledge save such as He wills. His Throne comprises the heavens and the earth; the preserving of them oppresses Him not; He is the All-High, the Almighty.</td></tr>
</table>

CHAPTER 3, VERSE 18-19 Shahid-Allāhu annahū lā ilāha illa Hū. Wa 'l-malā'ikatu wa ūlu 'l-'ilmi qā'iman bi 'l-qisṭ. Lā ilāha illa Hūwa 'l-'Azīzu 'l-Ḥakīm. Inna 'd-dīna 'ind Allāhi 'l-islām.	سورة آل عمران ١٨–١٩ شَهِدَ اللهُ أَنَّهُ لا إله إلا هُوَ والمَلائِكَةُ وأُولُو العِلْمِ قائمًا بالقِسْطِ لا إله إلا هُوَ العَزِيزُ الحَكِيمُ إِنَّ الدين عِنْدَ الله الإِسْلام

God bears witness that there is no god but He—and the angels and men of knowledge—upholding justice; there is no god but He, the All-Mighty, the All-Wise. The religion with God is Islam.

CHAPTER 3, VERSE 26-27 Qul 'illāhumma Mālik al-mulki. Tu'tī 'l-mulka man tasha'u wa tanzi'u 'l-mulka mimman tashā'u wa tu'izzu man tashā'u wa tudhillu man tashā'u, bi yadik al-khayr, innaka 'alā kulli shay'in qadīr. Tūliju 'l-layla fi 'n-nahāri wa tūliju 'n-nahāra fi 'l-layl, wa tukhriju 'l-ḥāyya min al-mayyiti, wa tukhriju 'l-mayyita min al-ḥāyy, wa tarzuqu man tashā'u bi ghayri ḥisāb.	سورة آل عمران ٢٦–٢٧ قل اللَّهُمَّ مالِكَ المُلْكِ تُؤْتِي المُلْكَ من تشاء وتَنْزِعُ المُلْكَ ممَّن تشاء وتُعِزُّ من تشاء وتُذِلُّ من تشاءُ بِيَدِكَ الخَيْرُ إنكَ على كُلِّ شيءٍ قدير تولجُ الليلَ في النهار وتولجُ النهارَ في الليل وتُخْرِجُ الحيَّ من المَيِّت وتُخْرِجُ المَيِّتَ من الحيِّ وتَرْزُقُ من تشاءُ بِغَيْرِ حساب

Say: O God, Master of the Kingdom, Thou givest the Kingdom to whom Thou wilt, and seizest the Kingdom from whom Thou wilt, Thou exaltest whom Thou wilt, and Thou abasest whom Thou wilt; in Thy hand is the good; Thou art over all things Powerful. Thou makest the night to enter into the day, and Thou makest the day to enter into the night, Thou bringest forth the living from the dead, and Thou bringest forth the dead from the living, and Thou providest for whomsoever Thou wilt without reckoning.

Allāhumma lā māni'a limā āa'ṭaytu, wa lā mu'ṭīya limā man'ata wa lā rādda limā qaḍayta, wa lā yanfa'u dhāl-jaddi minka 'l-jadd. Rabbī wa lā ḥawla wa lā quwwata illa billāhi 'l-'Alīyy il-'Aẓīm.	اللَّهُمَّ لا مانع لما أَعْطَيْتَ ولا مُعْطِي لما مَنَعْتَ ولا رادَّ لما قَضَيْتَ ولا يَنْفَعُ ذا الجدِّ منك الجَدُّ رَبِّي لا حَوْلَ ولا قُوَّةَ إلا بالله العَلِيِّ العَظِيم

O God! No one can disallow the one to whom You are giving, and there is no giver to the one whom You have denied. And there is no refusing Your decree. Riches and good fortune will not profit the possessor thereof with You (for nothing will profit him but acting in obedience to You). My Lord, there is no power and no strengh save in God, All-High and Almighty.

CHAPTER 57, VERSE 3 Hūwa 'l-Awwalu wa 'l-Ākhiru, waẓ-Ẓāhiru wa 'l-Bāṭin, wa Hūwa bi kulli shay'in 'alīm.		سورة الحديد ٣ هو الأول والآخر والظاهر والباطن وهو بكل شيء عليم
He is the First and the Last, the Outward and the Inward; He has knowledge of everything.		
SŪRATU 'L-FĀTIḤĀ		سورة الفاتحة
SŪRATU 'L-IKHLĀṢ		سورة الإخلاص
SŪRATU 'L-FALAQ		سورةُ الفلق
SŪRATU 'N-NĀS		سُورةُ الناس
TASBĪḤ Yā rabbi dhul-Jalāli wa 'l-Ikrām, Subḥānaka yā 'Aẓīm subḥānallāh, subḥānallāh (33 times)		تَسْبيح يا رَبيَّ ذا الجلال والكَمال سُبحانَكَ يا عَظيم: سُبْحان الله (٣٣ مَرّة)
O my Lord, Possessor of Glory and Perfection, Glory be to You, O Almighty One! Glory be to God.		
'alā n'imat il-Islām wa sharaf al-īmān dā'iman alḥamdulillāh, alḥamdulillāh (33 times)		على نِعْمةِ الإسْلامِ وشَرَفِ الإيمانِ دائمًا: الحَمْدُ لله (٣٣ مَرّة)
For the gift of Islam, the nobility of faith, always, praise be to God.		
Ta'alā shā'nuhū wa lā ilāha ghayruhū, Allāhū akbar, Allāhū akbar (33 times)		تَعَالَى شانُهُ ولا إله غيرُهُ: الله أُكْبَر (٣٣ مَرّة)
Exalted is His Affair, and there is no god but He, God is Greatest.		
Allāhū akbaru kabīran wa 'lḥamdulillāhi kathīran wa subḥānallāhi bukratan wa aṣīla. Lā ilāha illa-Allāh wāḥdahū lā sharīka lah, lahu 'l-mulku wa lahu 'l-ḥamd yuḥīy wa yumīt wa Hūwa 'alā kulli shay'in qadīr. Subḥāna Rabbīu 'l-'Alīyyu 'l-'āla 'l-Wahhāb.		الله أُكْبَرُ كَبيرًا والحَمْدُ لله كَثيرًا وسُبْحانَ الله وبِحمده بُكْرةً وأصيلاً لا إله إلا الله وَحْدَهُ لا شَريكَ له، له المُلْكُ وله الحَمْدُ يُحيِي ويُميت وهُوَ على كُلِّ

<table>
<tr><td></td><td></td><td>شيءٍ قدير. سُبْحانَ رَبّي العَليّ الأعلى الوهّاب</td></tr>
<tr><td colspan="3">God is most Great in His Greatness and much praise be to God. Glory be to God, early and late. There is no god but God. He is One, no partner has He. His is the Kingdom and all praise. He brings to life and makes to die, and He is over all things Powerful. Glory be to my Lord, All-High, Supreme, Most Munificent.</td></tr>
<tr><td>CHAPTER 33, VERSE 56
Inna-Allāha wa malā'ikatahū yuṣallūna 'alā an-Nabī, yā ayyuh-alladhīnā āmanū, ṣallū 'alayhi wa sallimū taslīmā. (Ṣadaq-Allāhu 'l-'Aẓīm)</td><td></td><td>سورة الأحزاب ٥٦
إنّ اللهَ ومَلائكتَهُ يُصَلّونَ على النّبيِ، يا أيُها الذينَ آمَنُوا
صَلّوا عليه وسَلِّموا تَسْليمًا</td></tr>
<tr><td colspan="3">God and His angels send blessings on the Prophet: O you who believe! Send blessings on him and greet him with all respect. (God speaks the Truth).</td></tr>
<tr><td>ṢALAWĀT (3 TIMES)
Allāhumma ṣalli 'alā Sayyidinā Muḥammadin wa 'alā āli Sayyidinā Muḥammad. Bi 'adadi kulli dā'in wa dawā'in wa bārik wa sallim 'alayhi wa 'alayhim kathīrā.

(AFTER THE 3RD TIME)
kathīran kathīra, wa 'l-ḥamdulillāhi Rabbi 'l-'ālamīn.</td><td></td><td>صَلوات
اللّهمّ صَلِّ على سَيِّدنا مُحَمَّدٍ وعلى آلِ سَيِّدنا
مُحَمَّدٍ بِعَدَدِ كُلِّ داءٍ ودَواءٍ وبارِكْ وسَلِّمْ عليه
وعليهم كَثيرًا
في المَرّة الثالثة كَثيرًا كَثيرًا</td></tr>
<tr><td colspan="3">O God! Upon Muhammad and the family of Muhammad be blessings, according to the number of every illness and cure. Bless and grant peace to him and them, many times, endlessly. And praise belongs to God, the Lord of the worlds.</td></tr>
<tr><td>TAHLĪL
F'ālam annahū: lā ilāha illa-llāh, lā ilāha illa-llāh (100 times).
Know that: There is no god but God.</td><td></td><td>تهليل:
فاعْلَمْ أنَّهُ
لا إله إلا الله (١٠٠ مَرّة)</td></tr>
<tr><td>ṢALAWĀT (10 TIMES)
Allāhumma ṣalli 'alā Muḥammadin wa 'alā āli Muḥammadin wa sallim.</td><td></td><td>صَلوات (١٠ مرات)
اللّهمّ صَلِّ على مُحَمَّدٍ وعلى آلِ مُحَمَّدٍ وسلّم</td></tr>
<tr><td colspan="3">O God send blessings and peace upon Muhammad and the family of</td></tr>
</table>

Muhammad.		
DU'A (INVOCATION) Ṣalli, yā Rabbī, wa sallim 'alā jamī'i il-anbīyā'i wa 'l-mursalīn, wa ālin kullin ajma'īn wa 'l-ḥamdulillāhi Rabb il-'ālamīn		دُعاء صلِّ يا ربِّي وسلِّم على جميعِ الأنبياء والمُرْسَلينَ وآلِ كُلٍّ أجْمَعينَ والحَمْدُ لله ربِّ العالمينَ
Blessings, O my Lord, and peace be upon all the prophets and Emissaries, and on the family of every one of them. Praise belongs to God, the Lord of the worlds.		
CHIEF OF PRAYERS ON THE PROPHET (SEE PAGE 171)		الصلاة الشريفة المأثورة
Subḥāna Rabbīu 'l-'Alīyyu 'l-'Ala 'l-Wahhāb.		سُبْحانَ رَبِّيَ العَلِيِّ الأعْلى الوَهّاب
Glory be to my Lord, All-High, Supreme, Most Munificent.		
PERSONAL DU'A (INVOCATION) followed by:		دعاء شخصي ثم تقرأ:
CHAPTER 59, VERSE 22-24		سورة الحشر ٢٢–٢٤
A'udhūbillāhi min ash-shayṭān ir-rajīm. Bismillāhi 'r-Raḥmāni 'r-Raḥīm. Hūwa Allāhu 'lladhī lā ilāha illa Hū. 'Ālimu 'l-ghaybi wa 'sh-shahādati, Hūwa 'r-Raḥmānu 'r-Raḥīm. Hūwa Allāh 'ulladhī lā ilāha illa Hūw al-Maliku 'l-Quddusu 's-Salāmu 'l-Mu'minu 'l-Muhayminu 'l-'Azīzu 'l-Jabbāru 'l-Mutakabbir. Subḥānallāhi 'ammā yushrikūn. Hūw 'Allāh 'ul-Khāliqu 'l-Barī'u 'l-Musawwiru lahu 'l-asmā'u 'l-ḥusnā. Yusabbiḥu lahū mā fi 's-samāwāti wa 'l-arḍ, wa Hūwa 'l-'Azīzu 'l-Ḥakīm.		أعوذُ بالله من الشَّيْطانِ الرَّجيم. بِسْمِ الله الرَّحْمنِ الرَّحيم. هُوَ اللهُ الذي لا إله إلا هُوَ عالِمُ الغَيْبِ والشَّهادة هُوَ الرَّحْمنُ الرَّحيمُ هُوَ اللهُ الذي لا إله إلا هُوَ المَلِكُ القُدُّوسُ السَّلامُ المُؤْمِنُ المُهَيْمِنُ العَزيزُ الجَبّارُ المُتَكَبِّرُ، سُبْحانَ الله عَمّا يُشْرِكون. هُوَ اللهُ الخالِقُ البارِئُ المُصَوِّرُ له الأسْماءُ الحُسْنى يُسَبِّحُ له ما في السَّماواتِ والأرْضِ وهُوَ العَزيزُ الحَكيمُ
He is God; there is no god but He. He is the Knower of the Unseen and Visible; He is the All-Merciful, the All-Compassionate. He is God; there is no god but He. He is the King, the All-Holy, the All-Peacable, the All-Faithful, the All-Preserver, the All-Mighty, the All-Compeller, the All-Sublime. Glory be to God, above what they associate! He is God, the Creator, the Maker, the Shaper. To Him belong the		

Names Most Beautiful. All that is in the heavens and the earth magnifies Him; He is the All-Mighty, the All-Wise.

| CHAPTER 57, VERSE 3

Hūwa 'l-Āwwalu wa 'l-ākhiru waẓ-Ẓāhiru wa 'l-Bāṭin, wa Hūwa bi kulli shay'in 'Alīm. Ṣadaq-Allāhu 'l-'Aẓīm. | سورة الحديد ٣

هُوَ الأَوَّلُ الآخِرُ والظَّاهِرُ والباطِنُ وهُوَ على كُلِّ شَيْءٍ عليم. صَدَقَ اللهُ العظيم |

He is the First and the Last, the Outward and the Inward; He has knowledge of everything. (God speaks the Truth).

| DU'A (INVOCATION) | دُعاءٌ : |
| Rabbanā taqabbal minna, wa'fu 'annā, waghfir lanā, warḥamnā, wa tub 'ālaynā, wasqinā, wasliḥ shā'nanā wa shā'n al-Muslimīn, fanṣurna 'alā al-qawm il-mufsidīn, bi ḥurmati man anzalta 'alayhi Sūratu 'l-Fātiḥah. | رَبَّنا تَقَبَّل مِنّا واعْفُ عَنّا واغْفُر لَنا وارْحَمْنا وتُبْ علينا واهدِنا واسْقِنا واصْلِحْ شَأْنَنا وشَأْنَ المُسْلِمينَ وانْصُرْنا على القَومِ الكافِرينَ بِحُرْمَةِ مَن أنْزَلْتَ عليه سُورةُ الفاتِحة |

O our Lord! Accept (this) from us and absolve us. Forgive us and have mercy on us. Accept our repentance and guide us. Quench (our thirst), and improve our condition and the condition of the Muslims. Give us success over those who falsify the Truth, by the sanctity of the one to whom You revealed Sūrat al-Fātiḥah.

| KALIMATU 'SH-SHAHĀDA (3 TIMES)

Ash-hadu an lā ilāha ill-Allāh, wa ash-hadu anna Muḥammadan 'abduhū wa rasūluḥ. | كلمة الشَّهَادة

أَشْهَدُ أَنْ لا إله إلا الله وأَشْهَدُ أَنَّ مُحَمَّدًا رَسُولُ الله
(٣ مَرّات) (بِصَوْت خفي) صلّى اللهُ عليه وسلم |

I bear witness that there is no god but God, and Muhammad is His servant and Messenger.

| ISTIGHFĀR

Astaghfirullāh (100 times)
I ask God's forgiveness. | اسْتِغْفار:

أَسْتَغْفِرُ اللهَ (١٠٠ مَرّة) |
| Astaghfirullāh min kulli dhanbin wa ma'ṣīyatin wa min kulli mā yukhālifu dīn | أَسْتَغْفِرُ اللهَ مِن كُلِّ ذَنْبٍ ومَعْصِيَة ومِن كُلِّ ما يُخالِفُ |

al-Islām, yā arḥama 'r-Rāḥimīn.	دينَ الإِسْلام يا أَرْحَمَ الراحمين

I ask God's forgiveness for every sin and disobedience and from all that opposes the religion of Islam. O Merciful of the Merciful.

SŪRATU 'L-FĀTIḤĀ	الفاتحة
SŪRAT YĀ SĪN (CHAPTER 36)	سُورة يس
CHAPTER 28, VERSE 88 Kullu shay'in hālikun illa Wajhah, lahu 'l-ḥukmu wa ilayhi turja'ūn.	سورة القصص ٨٨ ثم تنتهي: كُلُّ شَيْءٍ هَالكٌ إلا وَجْهه له الحُكْمُ وإليه تُرْجَعُونَ

All things perish except His Face. His is the Judgment, and unto Him you shall be returned.

99 Beautiful Names of God

أَسْماءُ اللهِ الحُسنى

(Asmā'ullah)

A'udhūbillāhi min ash-shayṭān ir-rajīm. Bismillāhi 'r-Raḥmāni 'r-Raḥīm. Hūwa Allāhu 'lladhī lā ilāha illa Hū. 'Ālimu 'l-ghaybi wa 'sh-shahādati, Hūwa 'r-Raḥmānu 'r-Raḥīm (Jalla Jallāluhū). Hūwa Allāh 'ulladhī lā ilāha illa Hūw al-Maliku 'l-Quddusu 's-Salāmu 'l-Mu'minu 'l-Muhayminu 'l-'Azīzu 'l-Jabbāru 'l-Mutakabbir (Jalla Jallāluhū). Al-Khāliqu 'l-Bāri'u 'l-Musawwiru 'l-Ghaffāru 'l-Qahhāru 'l-Wahhābu 'r-Razzāqu 'l-Fattāḥu 'l-'Alīm (Jalla Jallāluhū), al-Qābiḍu 'l-Bāsiṭu 'l-Khāfiḍu 'r-Rāf'iu 'l-Mu'izzu 'l-Mudhillu 's-Samī'u 'l-Baṣīr, (Jalla Jallāluhū), al-Ḥakamu 'l-'Adlu 'l-Laṭīfu 'l-Khabīru 'l-Ḥalīmu 'l-'Aẓīmu 'l-Ghafūr ush-Shakūru 'l-'Aliyyu 'l-Kabīr, (Jalla Jallāluhū), al-Ḥafīẓu 'l-Muqītu 'l-Ḥasību 'l-Jalīlu 'l-Karīmu 'r-Raqību 'l-Mujību 'l-Wās'iu 'l-Ḥakīmu 'l-

أَعُوذُ بِاللهِ من الشَّيْطانِ الرَّجِيمِ. بِسْمِ اللهِ الرَّحْمنِ الرَّحِيمِ.

هُوَ اللهُ الذي لا إلهَ إلا هُوَ، الرَّحْمَنُ، الرَّحِيمُ، الملِكُ،

القُدُّوسُ، السَّلامُ، المُؤْمِنُ، المُهَيْمِنُ، العَزِيزُ، الجَبَّارُ،

المُتَكَبِّرُ، الخَالِقُ، البَارِىءُ، المُصَوِّرُ، الغَفَّارُ، القَهَّارُ،

الوَهَّابُ، الرَّزَّاقُ، الفَتَّاحُ، العَلِيمُ، البَاسِطُ، الخَافِضُ،

الرَّافِعُ، المُعِزُّ، المُذِلُّ، السَّمِيعُ، البَصِيرُ، الحَكَمُ، العَدْلُ،

اللَّطِيفُ، الخَبِيرُ، الحَلِيمُ، العَظِيمُ، الغَفُورُ، الشَّكُورُ،

العَلِيُّ، الكَبِيرُ، المُغِيثُ، الحَسِيبُ، الجَلِيلُ، الكَرِيمُ،

الرَّقِيبُ، المُجِيبُ، الوَاسِعُ، الحَكِيمُ، الوَدُودُ، المَجِيدُ،

البَاعِثُ، الشَّهِيدُ، الحَقُّ، الوَكِيلُ، القَوِيُّ، المَتِينُ، الوَلِيُّ،

Wadūdu 'l-Majīd, (Jalla Jallāluhū), al-Bā'ith ush-Shahīdu 'l-Ḥaqqu 'l-Wakīlu 'l-Qawīyyu 'l-Matīnu 'l-Walīyyu 'l-Ḥamīdu 'l-Muḥsīyu 'l-Mubd'īu 'l-Mu'īdu 'l-Muḥīyyu 'l-Mumītu 'l-Ḥāyyu 'l-Qayyūm (Jalla Jallāluhū), al-Wājidu 'l-Mājidu 'l-Wāḥidu 'l-Āḥad uṣ-Ṣamadu 'l-Qādiru 'l-Muqtadir (Jalla Jallāluhū), al-Muqaddimu 'l-Mu'akhkhiru 'l-Awwalu 'l-Ākhir uẓ-Ẓāhiru 'l-Bāṭinu 'l-Wālīyu 'l-Muta'ālu 'l-Barru 't-Tawwāb (Jalla Jallāluhū), al-Muntaqimu 'l-'Afuwwu 'r-Ra'uf Māliku 'l-mulki dhul-Jalāli wa 'l-Ikrām (Jalla Jallāluhū), al-Muqsiṭu 'l-Jāmi'u 'l-Ghanīyyu 'l-Mughnīyyu 'l-Mu'ṭīu 'l-Māni'u 'd-Ḍārr un-Nāfi' un-Nūr (Jalla Jallāluhū), al-Hādīyu 'l-Bad'īu 'l-Bāqīyu 'l-Wārithu 'r-Rashīd uṣ-Ṣabur.

Jalla Jallāluhū wa jallat 'āẓamatahū wa lā ilāha ghayruhu 'lladhī lam yalid wa lam yūlad wa lam yakun lahū kufuwan āḥad

الحَميدُ، المُحْصِي، المُبْدِئ، المُعِيدُ، المُحْيِي، المُمِيتُ، الحَيُّ، القَيُّومُ، الوَاجِدُ، المَاجِدُ، الوَاحِدُ، الصَّمَدُ، القَادِرُ، المُقْتَدِرُ، المُقَدِّمُ، المُؤَخِّرُ، الأَوَّلُ، الآخِرُ، الظَّاهِرُ، البَاطِنُ، الوَالِي، المُتَعَالِ، البَرُّ، التَّوَّابُ، المُنْتَقِمُ، العَفُوُّ، الرَّؤُوفُ، مَالِكُ المُلْكِ، ذُو الجَلَالِ وَالإِكْرَامِ، المُقْسِطُ، الجَامِعُ، الغَنِيُّ، المُغْنِي، المَانِعُ، الضَّارُ، النَّافِعُ، النُّورُ، الهَادِي، البَدِيعُ، البَاقِي، الوَارِثُ، الرَّشِيدُ، الصَّبُورُ

جلَّ جلاله وجلَّت عظمته ولا إلهَ غيره الذي لَمْ يَلِدْ وَلَمْ يُولَدْ وَلَمْ يَكُن لَهُ كُفُواً أَحَدٌ

In the Name of God, the Most Merciful, the Most Compassionate. May He be Glorified and Exalted! He is God; there is no god but He. He is the Knower of the Unseen and Visible; He is the All-Merciful, the All-Compassionate, (His Greatness has become manifest). The King, the All-Holy, the Source of Peace, the All-Faithful, the the Guardian, the Mighty, the Compeller, the Greatest, (His Greatness has become manifest). The Creator, the Maker, the Fashioner, the All-Forgiver, the Irrestible, the All-Bounteous, the Provider, the Opener, the Omniscient, (His Greatness has become manifest). The Contracter, the Expander, the Abaser, the Exalter, the Bestower of Honor, the Humiliator, the All-Hearing, the All-Seeing, (His Greatness has become manifest). The Supreme Arbiter, the Just, the Subtle, the All-Cognizant, the Forbearing, the Magnificent, the Most Forgiving, the Appreciative, the Most High, the Grand, (His Greatness has become manifest). The Preserver, the Nourisher, the Reckoner, the Sublime, the Generous, the Ever-Watchful, the Responsive, the Limitless, the All-Wise, the Loving, the Glorious, (His Greatness has become manifest). The Resurrector, the Witness, the Ultimate Truth, the Trustee, the Most Strong, the Firm, the Protecting Friend, the Praiseworthy, the Reckoner, the Originator, the Restorer, the Granter of Life, the Bringer of Death, the Ever-Living, the Self-Subsisting, (His Greatness has become manifest). The Founder Who has no needs, the Glorified, the Unique, the Eternally Besought, the All-Powerful, the Bestower of Power, (His Greatness has become manifest). The Advancer, the Delayer, the

<table>
<tr><td colspan="3">First, the Last, the Manifest, the Hidden, the Governor, the Highly Exalted, the Beneficent, the Accepter of Repentance, (His Greatness has become manifest). The Avenger, the Eraser of Sin, the Most Compassionate, the Lord of All Dominion, the Possessor of Majesty and Bounty, (His Greatness has become manifest). The Upholder of Equity, the Gatherer, the All-Wealthy, the Enricher, the Giver, the Preventer, the Distresser, the Creator of Good, the Light, (His Greatness has become manifest). The Guider, the Originator, the Everlasting, the Inheritor, the Guide, the Patient, (His Greatness has become manifest).
His Greatness has become manifest, and there is no god but He, Who has not begotten and has not been begotten, and equal to Him is not any one.</td></tr>
<tr><td>Yā Āḥad, Yā Ṣamad, ṣalli ʻalā Muḥammad (3 times).</td><td></td><td>يا أحَد . يا صَمَد صل على محمد (٣ مرات)</td></tr>
<tr><td colspan="3">O Unique One! O Eternally Besought! Bless Muhammad.</td></tr>
<tr><td>SŪRATU ʼL-IKHLĀṢ (CHAPTER 112)
(11 TIMES)</td><td></td><td>سُورَةُ الإخْلاصِ (١١ مرة)</td></tr>
<tr><td>SŪRATU ʼL-FALAQ (CHAPTER 113)
(ONCE)</td><td></td><td>سُورَةُ الفَلَق</td></tr>
<tr><td>SŪRATU ʼN-NĀS (CHAPTER 114)
(ONCE)</td><td></td><td>سُورَةُ الناس</td></tr>
<tr><td>TAHLĪL WITH ṢALAWĀT (10 TIMES)
Lā ilāhā ill-Allāh Muḥammadur Rasūlullāh, Ṣalla-llāhū taʻalā ʻalayhi wa ʻalā ālihi wa ṣaḥbihi wa sallam.</td><td></td><td>تهليل:
لا إله إلا الله مُحَمَّدٌ رَسُولُ الله صلّى الله تعالى عليه
وعلى آله وصحبه وسلّم (١٠ مرات)</td></tr>
<tr><td colspan="3">There is no god but God. Muhammad is the Messenger of God, blessings and peace of God (Exalted is He!) be upon him, his family, and his Companions.</td></tr>
<tr><td>ṢALAWĀT (10 TIMES)
Allāhumma ṣalli ʻalā Muḥammadin wa ʻalā āli Muḥammadin wa sallim.</td><td></td><td>الصَلَوات الشريفة (١٠مرّات)
اللَّهُمَّ صلّ على مُحَمَّد وعلى آل مُحَمَّد وسلّم</td></tr>
<tr><td colspan="3">Blessings and peace be upon Muhammad and the family of Muhammad.</td></tr>
</table>

DU'A (INVOCATION) Ṣalli, yā Rabbī, wa sallim 'alā jamī'i il-anbīyā'i wa 'l-mursalīn, wa ālin kullin ajma'īn wa 'l-ḥamdulillāhi Rabb il-'ālamīn		دُعاء صَلِّ يا رَبِّي وسَلِّم على جَميعِ الأُنْبياءِ والمُرْسَلينَ وآلِ كُلٍّ أَجْمَعينَ والحَمْدُ لله رَبِّ العالَمينَ
Blessings, O my Lord, and peace be upon all the prophets and emissaries, and on the family of every one of them. Praise belongs to God, the Lord of the worlds.		
CHIEF OF PRAYERS ON PROPHET (PAGE 171)		الصلوات الشريفة المأثورة
IHDĀ (SEE PAGE 172)		إهْداء

صَلاةُ الظُهرِ

Salatu-z-Zuhr

Ṣalātu 'ẓ-Ẓuhr is performed in the same sequence as Ṣalātu 'l-'Ishā, from the Adhān to the end, with the exception of Ṣalātu 'l-Witr, which is omitted.		
4 RAK'ATS SUNNAH		4 ركْعات: ركْعَتَيْنِ سُنّة وركْعَتَيْن نافلة بِتَسْلِيمٍ واحد أو بتسليمين
4 RAK'ATS FARḌ		أرْبَعُ ركْعات فَرْض
4 RAK'ATS SUNNAH		أرْبَعُ ركْعات سُنّة
SŪRATU 'L-MULK (CHAPTER 67)		سُورةُ المُلك
At the end of Sūratu 'l-Mulk add: Allāhu ta'alā Rabbunā wa Rabbu 'alamīn. Then continue with the same practices as in Ṣalātul-'Ishā with the exception of Ṣalātu 'l-Witr.		

صَلاةُ العصر

Salatu-l-Asr

Ṣalātu 'l-'Asr is performed exactly in the same way a Ṣalātu 'l-'Ishā, with the exception of the final 4 rak'āts Sunnah prayer and Ṣalātu 'l-Witr.		
4 RAK'ATS SUNNAH		٤ رَكْعات سُنّة رَكْعَتَيْنِ سُنّة ورَكْعَتَيْنِ نافلة بِتَسْليمٍ واحدٍ أو بتسليمين
4 RAK'ATS FARḌ		٤ رَكْعات فَرْض
SŪRATU 'N-NABĀ(CHAPTER 78)		ثم تقرأ سُورةُ النبأ
Continue reading with Chapter 89, Verses 24-30 Fa yawmaydhin lā yu'adhibu 'adhābahu āḥadun wa lā yuthiqu wathāqahu āḥad. Yā ayyatuhā 'n-nafsu 'l-muṭma'innatu 'rji'ī ilā rabbika rāḍīyyatan marḍīyyah. f'adkhulī fī 'ibādī w'adkhulī jannatī. Then add: Razzaqanā Allāhu, yā Allāḥ, Āmannā billāhi. Ṣadaqa-Allāhu 'l-'Aẓīm.		فَيَوْمَئِذٍ لا يُعَذِّبُ عَذَابَهُ أَحَدٌ . وَلا يُوثِقُ وَثَاقَهُ أَحَدٌ يَا أَيَّتُهَا النَّفْسُ الْمُطْمَئِنَّةُ ارْجِعِي إِلَى رَبِّكِ رَاضِيَةً مَرْضِيَّةً فَادْخُلِي فِي عِبَادِي وَادْخُلِي جَنَّتِي رزقنا الله يا الله. آمَنَّا بالله. صدق الله العظيم
Then continue the recitation to the end as in Ṣalātu 'l-'Ishā.		

Practices During Rajab, Shaban and Ramadan

Practice of the Month of Rajab		ادب شهر رجب
This Adab is performed on the day before Rajab begins between Ṣalātu 'l-'Asr and Ṣalātu 'l-Maghrib and is repeated as the daily practice of the seeker every day, beginning before Ṣalātu 'l-Fajr by an hour and a half but without the Grand Transmitted Invocation of Grandshaykh (Ad-du'āu 'l-māthūr li Sulṭān al-Awliyā on page 242) which is done only the first night.		
BATHING OF PURIFICATION When the month of Rajab is entered, the murīd begins its night between Ṣalātu 'l-'Asr and Ṣalātu 'l-Maghrib receiving the month of Rajab. One performs the major ritual purification (ghusl, or shower).		غُسل إذا دخل شهر رجب بادر المريد في ليلة ابتدائه للغسل ما بين العصر والمغرب.
One dresses in the best clothes and (for a man) puts on a nice scent, then prays 2 rak'ats sunnat al-wuḍū'.		ثم يلبس أفضل الثياب واطهرها يتطيب ويستقبل القبلة ثم يصلي ركعتين سنة الوضوء ثم يقرأ:
Recite: Yā Rabb al-'izzati wa 'l-'aẓamati wa 'l-jabbarūt		يا رب العزة والعظيمة الجبروت
O Lord of Honor and Greatness, Imposer of Thy Will.		
The murīd takes three steps in the direction of the Qiblah in his place of worship.		و يتقرب في محرابه ثلاثة اقدام نحو القبلة
NĪYYAT		النية:
Nawaytu 'l-arbā'īn, nawaytu 'l-'itikāf, nawaytu 'l-khalwa, nawaytu 'l-'uzla, nawaytu 'r-riyāda, nawaytu 's-sulūk, lillāhi ta'ala fī hādhā 'l-masjid (or fī hādha al-jāmi')		نَوَيتُ الأربَعين، نَوَيتُ الاعتكاف نَوَيتُ الخَلوَة نَوَيتُ العُزْلة، نَوَيتُ الرِياضَة نَوَيتُ السُلوك، لله تعالى في هَذا المسجد

<table>
<tr><td colspan="3">INTENTION:
I intend the forty (days of seclusion); I intend seclusion in the mosque; I intend seclusion; I intend isolation; I intend discipline (of the ego); I intend to travel in God's Path; I intend to fast for the sake of God in this mosque.</td></tr>
<tr><td>100 times Yā Ḥalīm (for removing anger).
O Clement One!</td><td></td><td>يا حَليم. يا حَليم. يا حَليم (١٠٠مرّة)</td></tr>
<tr><td>100 times Yā Ḥafīz (for removing affliction).
O Guardian!</td><td></td><td>يا حَفيظ. يا حَفيظ. يا حَفيظ (١٠٠ مرّة)</td></tr>
<tr><td colspan="3">Imagine yourself in the blessed Garden (al-Rawḍah) in front of the maqām of the Prophet ﷺ facing God's Messenger ﷺ and saying:</td></tr>
<tr><td>ṢALAWĀT
100 times Allāhummā ṣalli 'alā Sayyidina Muḥammadin wa 'alā āli Muḥammadin wa sallim.</td><td></td><td>صَلَوات —١٠٠ مرة
اللَّهمَّ صلِّ على مُحَمَّدٍ وعلى آلِ مُحَمَّدٍ وسلِّم</td></tr>
<tr><td colspan="3">O God, pray on our master Muhammad and on his family and greet them with peace. Make the intention that God makes you to be in the spiritual Presence of God's Messenger ﷺ, Imām al-Mahdī عليه السلام, and our shaykhs.</td></tr>
<tr><td>NĪYYAT:
Yā Rabbī innanī nawaytu an ataqaddama nahwa baḥri waḥdanīyyatika ilā maqāmi 'l-fanā'i fīka. Falā tarudanī yā Rabbi, yā Allāh khā'ibān ḥatta tuwaṣṣilanī ila dhāk al-maqām al-maqāmu 'l-fardānī.</td><td></td><td>النية:
يا ربي إنِي نويت ان أتقدم نحو بحر واحدانيتك إلى مقام الفناء فيك فلا تردني يا ربي يا الله خائبا حتى توصلني إلى ذاك المقام — المقام الفرداني.</td></tr>
<tr><td colspan="3">INTENTION:
O my Lord, I am moving and stepping forward for the Station of Annihilation in the Divine Presence. O God—glory be to You, the Most High—I am asking you to cause me to vanish before Your Existence and, O my Lord, I am moving toward your Ocean of Unity. O my Lord, do not reject me until I reach the Unique Station.</td></tr>
<tr><td>Yā Rabbī, yā Allāh ḥaithu hādha ash-shahru hūwa shahruka, ji'tuka ḍa'ifan wa nāwī'an an 'amala 'amalan bidūn 'iwaḍun aw an yakūna fīhi ṭālaban lil-faḍīlati qāsidan iyyāka Ilāhī anta maqsūdī wa riḍāka maṭlūbi.</td><td></td><td>يا ربي يا الله حيث هذا الشهر هو شهرك جئتك ضيفا وناويا ان أعمل عملا بدون عوض أو ان يكون فيه طلبا للفضيلة. قاصدا اياك الهي أنتَ مقصودي</td></tr>
</table>

<table>
<tr><td></td><td></td><td>ورضاك مطلوبي</td></tr>
<tr><td colspan="3">O my Lord, O God, since this month is your month, I came to you as a weak guest and intending to worship You without asking anything in return. My God, You are my aim, and Your good pleasure is what I seek, and that is why I am coming. Please do not reject me.</td></tr>
<tr><td>Yā Rabbī, kullu ‘umrī qad amḍaytuhu fī ’l-ma‘āsī wash-shirkil-khafī. Wa innanī uqirru bi-annanī lam ā’ti ilā bābika bi-‘amalin maqbūlin ‘indaka anta-Allāhu ’lladhī lā yā‘tī āḥad ilā bābika bi ‘amalihi bal bi-faḍlika wa jūdika wa karamika wa iḥsānika. Anta-Allāhu ’lladhī la taruddu ‘abdan jā’a ilā bābika falā taruddanī yā Allāh.</td><td></td><td>يا ربي كل عمري قد امضيته في المعاصي والشرك
الخفي وانني اقر بأنني لم أئت إلى بابك بعمل مقبول
عندك أنتَ الله الذي لا يأتي احد إلى بابك بعمله بل
بفضلك وجودك وكرمك واحسانك أنتَ الله الذي لا
ترد عبدا جاء إلى بابك فلا تردني يا الله</td></tr>
<tr><td colspan="3">O my Lord, I say out of abject humility that it as if I spent all my life in unbelief, polytheism, and bad behavior, and I am declaring wholeheartedly that I did not do any deed that is accepted by You. You are God, Who never threw away anyone that came to Your door. You are God, and no one came to Your door by his deeds, but (only) by Your grant and reward.</td></tr>
<tr><td>Yā Rabbī, kullu umūrī fawwaḍtuhā ilayka, ḥayātī wa mamātī wa b‘ada mamāti, wa yawmu ’l-ḥashr. Kullu umūri ḥawwaltuhā ‘indaka. Wa fawwaḍtu amrī ilayka, lā amliku min amri nafsī shay-an. Lā naf‘an, wa lā ḍarran, wa lā mawtan, wa lā ḥayātan, wa lā nushūran. Kullu umūri wa ḥisābī wa su’ālī wa jawābī ḥawwaltuhu ‘indaka yā Rabbī yā Allāḥ. Nāṣīyatī bi-yadika wa anā ‘ājizun ‘an il-jawābi wa law mithqāla dharratin.</td><td></td><td>يا ربي كل اموري فوضتها إليك حياتي ومماتي وبعد
مماتي ويوم الحشر كل اموري حولتها عندك وفوضت
أمري إليك لا املك من امر نفسي شيئًا لا نفعا ولا
ضرا ولا موتا ولا حياة ولا نشورا . كل اموري
وحسابي وسؤالي وجوابي حولته عندك يا ربي يا
الله، ناصيتي بيدك وانا عاجز عن الجواب ولو مثقال
ذرة</td></tr>
<tr><td colspan="3">O my Lord, I have given everything into Your hands—my life, my death, my afterlife, and Judgment Day. All my things I have transferred to You, and You are the One Who controls me. O my Lord, I do not possess anything with my ego and my soul. I cannot give good to myself, or bad to myself, or life to myself, or death to myself, but I have transferred all my accounts, and all Your judgment on me, and all your questions to me, and all my answers I have transferred to You. Whatever You want to do with me, You do. My neck is in Your hand. I am helpless in answering Your</td></tr>
</table>

<table>
<tr><td colspan="3">questions; even the smallest answer I cannot give. With all this weakness, and helplessness, and hopelessness, I am coming to Your door.</td></tr>
<tr><td>law kāna laka yā Rabbī bābayni āḥadahumā mukhaṣaṣṣun lit-tā'ibīna min 'ibādika al-mu'minīn wa 'l-ākharu lit-tā'ibīna min 'ibādika al-'aṣīn. Ji'tuka yā Allāh naḥwu bābik alladhī yaḥtāju an yadkhula minhu 'ibāduka al-'aāṣīn. Wa innanī uqirru wa āa'tarif annahu yajibu an ujaddida islāmī wa īmānī min hādhal-bāb li-iẓhāri 'l-'ajzi.</td><td></td><td>لو كان لك ياربي بابين احدهما مخصص للتائبين من عبادك المؤمنين والأخر للتائبين من عبادك العاصين ، جئتك يا الله نحو بابك الذي يحتاج ان يدخل منه عبادك العاصين وانني اقر واعترف انه يجب ان اجدد إسلامي وإيماني من هذا الباب لاظهار العجز.</td></tr>
<tr><td colspan="3">O my Lord, if you had two doors for Your servant to enter through—one for the believers from Your servants and one for the unbelievers from Your servants—I am coming to You from the door that the unbeliever needs to come through, and I am declaring my belief that this is the only door for me to come through. I am saying to you that I have to renew my faith and my testimony of faith from this door to show humility and helplessness.</td></tr>
<tr><td>Wa hādhā al-'amalu hūwa āwwalu 'amalin lī b'ada mā shahidtu bi 'l-islāmi ḥaqqan. Yā Rabbī wa Anta wakīlī yā Wakīl ḥaithu naqūlu Allāha 'alā mā naqūlu Wakīl wa Shahīd.</td><td></td><td>و هذا العمل هو اول عمل لي بعد ما شهدت بالإسلام حقا يا ربي وأنتَ وكيلي يا وكيل حيث نقول الله على ما نقول وكيل وشهيد .</td></tr>
<tr><td colspan="3">This deed and this Shahāda is the first deed for me after I am pronouncing the Shahāda and entering Islam, and You are my Protector from whence we say: God is the Protector and Witness over what we say.</td></tr>
<tr><td>3 times Shahādah.</td><td></td><td>ثم تبدأ بكلمتي الشهادة (٣ مرات)</td></tr>
<tr><td>Iqāmu 'ṣ-ṣalāti wa ītāu 'z-zakāt wa ṣawmu ramaḍāna, wa Ḥajju 'l-bayt.</td><td></td><td>تجديد اركان الإسلام: اقام الصلاة وايتاء الزكاة وصوم رمضان وحج البيت</td></tr>
<tr><td colspan="3">Re-affirmation of Islam's five pillars:
I believe in the establishment of prayer, paying the poor-due, fasting Ramadan, and the Pilgrimage to the House of God.</td></tr>
<tr><td>Āmantu billāhi wa malā'ikatihi wa kutubihi wa rusulihi wa 'l-yawmi 'l-ākhiri wa bi 'l-qadari khayrihi wa sharrihi min Allāhi ta'alā.</td><td></td><td>تجديد الإيمان: آمنت بالله وملائكه وكتبه ورسله وباليوم الاخر وبالقدر خيره وشره .</td></tr>
</table>

<table>
<tr><td colspan="3">Re-affirmation of the pillars of faith:
I believe in God, His Angels, His books, His Messengers, the Last Day, and that the Destiny—its good and its bad—is from God, the Most High.</td></tr>
<tr><td>Yā Rabbī, yā Allāhu, kam ẓahara minnī min adh-dhunūbi wa 'l-ma'āṣīyy ẓāhiran wa bāṭinan wa sirran min 'ahdi ījādi dharratī wa rūḥī, wa dukhūli rūḥī ilā jismī wa ẓuhūrī min al-'adami ilā 'l-wujūdi wa ẓuhūrī fī 'ālami 'd-dunyā ilā yawminā hādha, raj'atu 'ani 'l-jamī'i ilayka bi 't-tawbati wa 'l-istighfār.</td><td></td><td>يا ربي يا الله كم ظهر مني من الذنوب والمعاصي ظاهرا وباطنا وسرا من عهد ايجاد ذرتي وروحي ودخول روحي إلى جسمي وظهوري من العدم إلى الوجود وظهوري في عالم الدنيا إلى يومنا هذا، رجعت عن الجميع اليك بالتوبة والإستغفار</td></tr>
<tr><td colspan="3">O my Lord, from the Day of Promises, whatever there was of promise from Me to You, I accept and promise to do it all. O my Lord, O God, from the day You created my atom, my essence, and from the day You brought up my soul, and from the day my soul came from the absolute abstract to existence, until our day, how much of disobedience has appeared from me and my essence, and from my soul and my body, spiritually and physically! I am regretting it all, and regretting what I did, and coming back to You asking forgiveness and repentance.</td></tr>
<tr><td>Wa innanī qad dakhaltu wa salaktu fī raḥmāti shahrika hādha 'l-mubārak falā taruddnī yā Rabbī, 'an bābika wa lā tatruknī li-aḥwāli nafsī wa law li-laḥzah wa anā astaghfiruka.</td><td></td><td>و انني قد دخلت وسلكت في رحمات شهرك هذا المبارك فلا تردني يا ربي عن بابك ولا تتركني لاحوال نفسي ولو لحظة، وانا استغفرك</td></tr>
<tr><td colspan="3">O my Lord, I entered and I moved into the ocean of blessings of Your praised month. O my Lord, do not reject me from Your door, and do not leave me to my ego for the blink of an eye, and I am asking forgiveness of You.</td></tr>
<tr><td>ISTIGHFĀR
100 times Astaghfirullāh
I ask God's forgiveness</td><td></td><td>أستغفار
أستغفر الله (١٠٠ مرات)</td></tr>
<tr><td>Continue with the remainder of the Naqshbandi Adab from the verse Āmanar-Rasūl until its end.</td><td></td><td>اية آمن الرسول. . . . .إلى الأخر</td></tr>
<tr><td colspan="3">In the case of the daily practice of Rajab, continue to the Adhkār al-yawmi, the daily recitation of the wird, including "Allah, Allah" and ṣalawāt, at the level of the People of Determination (see page 167)</td></tr>
</table>

500 TIMES YĀ ṢAMAD		يا صمد .(٥٠٠ مرة)
With the intention to eliminate the bad aspects of the ego.		
500 TIMES ASTAGHFIRULLĀH		أستغفر الله (٥٠٠ مرة)
Recite with the intention of asking God to forgive your sins, from the day of creation of your soul to the present day.		
500 TIMES ASTAGHFIRULLĀH		أستغفر الله (٥٠٠ مرة)
Recite with the intention that, from the present day to the last day on earth, God will protect you against sins.		
500 TIMES ALḤAMDULILLĀH		الحمدُ لله (٥٠٠ مرَة) .
Out of gratitude that God did not create you from the nation of other prophets.		
500 TIMES ALḤAMDULILLĀH		الحمدُ لله (٥٠٠ مرَة) .
Out of gratitude that God has created you from the nation of the Prophet Muḥammad ﷺ and honored you by Sayyidina Abū Bakr aṣ-Ṣiddīq ؓ, 'Abd al-Khāliq al-Ghujdawānī, Shaykh Sayyid Sharafuddīn ad-Daghestānī, and honored you by Grandshaykh Shaykh 'Abd Allāh al-Fā'iz ad-Daghestānī, and honored you by making you a follower of Mawlana Shaykh Muhammad Nā·im al-Ḥaqqānī.		
THE GRAND TRANSMITTED INVOCATION (AD-DU'AU 'L-MĀTHŪR) OF SULṬĀN AL-AWLĪYĀ (see page 242)		الدعاء المأثور عن سلطان الأولياء

Daily Practices Between Maghrib and Isha in Rajab		ادب اليومي بين المغرب والعشا في شهر رجب
1. Avoid the company of people and perform the Naqshbandi Adab in the last third of the night until sunrise, and/or between Ṣalātu 'l-'Asr and Ṣalātu 'l-Maghrib and/or between Ṣalātu 'l-Maghrib and Ṣalātu 'l-'Ishā.		
NĪYYAT:		
Nawaytu 'l-arbā'īn, nawaytu 'l-'itikāf, nawaytu 'l-khalwa, nawaytu 'l-'uzla, nawaytu 'r-riyāda, nawaytu 's-sulūk, lillāhi ta'ala fī hādhā 'l-masjid (or fī hādha al-jāmi').		نَوَيْتُ الأَرْبَعِين، نَوَيْتُ الاعتِكاف، نَوَيتُ الخَلْوَة، نَوَيتُ العُزْلَة، نَوَيْتُ الرِياضَة، نَوَيْتُ السُلوك لله تعالى في هَذا المسجد
INTENTION: I intend the forty (days of seclusion); I intend seclusion in the mosque; I intend seclusion; I intend isolation; I intend discipline (of the ego); I intend to travel in God's Path; I intend to fast for the sake of God in this mosque.		
SŪRATU 'L-AN'AM Recite each day if possible.		سورة الأنعام كل يوم (إذا امكن)
One juz' of Quran everyday (as part of daily wird)		جزء من القرآن كل يوم
DALĀ'ILU 'L-KHAYRĀT (as part of daily wird)		دلائل الخيرات
DAILY WIRD		الأوراد اليومية
FASTING		الصيام
Increase in fasting, particularly on Monday and Thursday, as well as on Raghā'ib the 7th, the middle of Rajab, and the 27th.		الإكثار من الصيام ، وخاصة صيام يوم الإثنين والخميس ونهار ليلة الرغائب. اي السابع من رجب ونصف شهر رجب ويوم السابع العشرين

<table>
<tr><td>Invocation of Rajab</td><td></td><td>دعاء رجب</td></tr>
<tr><td>Bismillāhi ’r-Raḥmāni ’r-Raḥīm
Allāhuma innī istāghfiruka min kulli mā tubtu ‘anhu ilayka thumma ‘udtu fīh. Wa istāghfiruka min kulli mā ‘aradtu bihi wajhika fa-khālatanī fīhi mā laysa fīhi riḍā’uk. Wa istāghfiruka li ’n-ni‘am allatī taqawwaytu bihā ‘alā ma‘sīyatik. Wa istāghfiruka min adh-dhunūb allatī lā ya‘lamuhā ghayruka wa lā yaṭṭali‘u ‘alayhā āḥadun siwāk wa lā yas‘uha illa raḥmatika wa lā tunjī minhā illa maghfiratuka wa ḥilmuka. Lā ilāha illa-Anta, subhānak! Innī kuntu min aẓ-ẓālimīn.</td><td></td><td>اللهم اني استغفرك من كل ما تبت عنه اليك ثم عدت فيه، استغفرك من كل ما اردت به وجهك فخالطني فيه ما ليس فيه رضائك. واستغفرك للنعم التي تقويت بها على معصيتك، واستغفرك من الذنوب التي لا يعلمها غيرك ولا يطلع عليها احد سواك ولا تسعها الا رحمتك ولا تنجي منها الا مغفرتك وحلمك لا اله الا أنتَ سبحانك اني كنت من الظالمين</td></tr>
<tr><td colspan="3">In the name of Allah, the All-Beneficent, the All-Merciful
O Allah, I ask forgiveness of You for everything for which I repented to You then returned to. And I ask forgiveness of You for everything I displeased You with and all that concerns me with which You are displeased. And I ask forgiveness of You for the favors which I used for increasing my disobedience towards You. And I ask forgiveness of You for the sins which no one knows except You and no one sees except You and nothing encompasses except Your Mercy and nothing delivers from except Your forgiveness and clemency. There is no god except You alone. Glory be to You! Indeed I was an oppressor to myself.</td></tr>
<tr><td>Allāhuma innī istaghfiruka min kulli ẓulmin ẓalamtu bihi ‘ibādak. Fa ayyumā ‘abdin min ‘ibādika aw ’amatin min ’imā’ika ẓalamtu fī badanihi aw ‘irdihi aw mālihi fa-ā‘atihi min khazā’iniki ’llatī lā tanquṣ. Wa as’aluka an tukrimanī bi-raḥmatiki ’llatī wasi‘at kulla shay’in wa lā tuhīnanī bi-‘adhābika wa tu‘ṭīyyanī mā as’aluka fa-innī ḥaqīqun bi-raḥmatika ya arḥamu ’r-Rāhimīn. Wa ṣalla-Allāhu ‘alā Sayyidinā Muḥammadin wa ‘alā ālihi wa ṣāḥbihi ajm‘aīn. Wa lā ḥawla wa lā quwatta illa billāh il-‘Alīyyi ’l-‘Āẓīm.</td><td></td><td>اللهم اني استغفرك من كل ظلم ظلمت به عبادك فايما عبد من عبادك أو امة من امائك ظلمت في بدنه أو عرضه أو ماله فأعطه من خزائنك التي لا تنقص وأسألك ان تكرمني برحمتك التي وسعت كل شيء ولا تهينني بعذابك وتعطيني ما أسألك فاني حقيق برحمتك يا ارحم الراحمين. وصلى الله على سيدنا محمد وآله وصحبه أجمعين، ولا حول ولا قوة الا بالله العلي العظيم</td></tr>
</table>

O Allah, I ask forgiveness of You for the injustice I committed against Your servants. Whatever of Your male or female servants whom I have hurt, physically or in their dignity or in their property give them of Your bounty which lacks nothing. And I ask You to honor me with Your mercy which encompasses all things. Do not humble me with Your punishment but give me what I ask of You, for I am in great need of Your mercy, O Most Merciful of the merciful. May Allah send blessings upon Muhammad and upon all his companions. There is no power and no might except in Allah the High, the Exalted.

Practices on the Blessed Night of Desires		ادب ليلة الرغائب
To be done after Ṣalātu 'l-'Ishā on the night of the first Thursday of the month of Rajab, considered by scholars to be the night in which the light of the Prophet ﷺ passed from his father 'Abd Allah ibn 'Abd al-Muṭṭalib ؓ to the womb of his mother Āmina bint Wahb ؓ.		بعد صلاة العشاء
NĪYYAT: Nawaytu 'l-arbā'īn, nawaytu 'l-'itikāf, nawaytu 'l-khalwa, nawaytu 'l-'uzla, nawaytu 'r-riyāda, nawaytu 's-sulūk, lillāhi ta'ala fī hādhā 'l-masjid (or fī hādha al-jāmi').		النية: نَوَيْتُ الأَرْبَعِين، نَوَيْتُ الاعتكاف نَوَيْتُ الخَلْوَة نَوَيْتُ العُزْلَة، نَوَيْتُ الرِياضة نَوَيْتُ السُلوك، لله تَعالى في هَذَا المسجد

INTENTION:

I intend the forty (days of seclusion); I intend seclusion in the mosque; I intend seclusion; I intend isolation; I intend discipline (of the ego); I intend to travel in God's Path; I intend to fast for the sake of God in this mosque.

ADABU 'Ṭ-ṬARĪQĀH		ادب الطريقة
THE GRAND TRANSMITTED INVOCATION (AD-DU'AU 'L-MĀTHŪR) OF SULṬĀN AL-AWLĪYĀ (see page 242)		الدعاء المأثور عن سلطان الأولياء
KHATMU 'L-KHWAJAGĀN (see page 179)		ختم الخواجكان مع الذكر
MAWLID		قراءة المولد الشريف
ṢALĀTU 'Ṭ-ṬASĀBĪḤ		صلاة التسابيح اربع ركعات
Fasting its day (and it is desired to present a sacrifice to God).		صيام نهاره (يستحب تقديم القرابين شكرا لله)

Practices on Night of Ascension		ادب ليلة الإسراء والمعراج
On the night preceding the 27th day of Rajab (Laylat al-Isrā' wa 'l-Mi'rāj), considered by many to be the night in which the Prophet ﷺ was invited to the Divine Presence, observe the following:		
NĪYYAT: Nawaytu 'l-arbā'īn, nawaytu 'l-'itikāf, nawaytu 'l-khalwa, nawaytu 'l-'uzla, nawaytu 'r-riyāda, nawaytu 's-sulūk, lillāhi ta'ala fī hādhā 'l-masjid (or fī hādha al-jāmi').		النية: نَوَيْتُ الأَرْبَعِين، نَوَيْتُ الاعتكاف، نَوَيْتُ الخَلْوَة، نَوَيْتُ العُزْلة، نَوَيْتُ الرِياضَة، نَوَيْتُ السُلوك لله تَعالى في هَذَا المسجد

INTENTION:

I intend the forty (days of seclusion); I intend seclusion in the mosque; I intend seclusion; I intend isolation; I intend discipline (of the ego); I intend to travel in God's Path; I intend to fast for the sake of God in this mosque.

ADABU 'Ṭ-ṬARĪQAH		ادب الطريقة
THE GRAND TRANSMITTED INVOCATION (AD-DU'AU 'L-MĀTHŪR) OF SULṬĀN AL-AWLIYĀ (see page 242)		الدعاء المأثور عن سلطان الأولياء
KHATMU 'L-KHWAJAGĀN (see page 179)		خَتْم الخواجكان مع الذكر
MAWLID		قراءة المولد الشريف
ṢALĀTU 'Ṭ-ṬASĀBĪḤ		صلاة التسابيح اربع ركعات

ṢALĀTU 'SH-SHUKR & QUNŪT INVOCATION		صلاة الشكر ركعتين مع دعاء القنوت
IHDĀ (SEE PAGE 172)		الإهداء
DU'A AND AL-FĀTIḤĀ		الدعاء الفاتحة
It is desired to fast the 27th and to make a sacrifice in thankfulness to God and to fast on the last day of Rajab.		ويستحب صيام اليوم ٢٧ وان يستحب تقديم القرابين شكرا لله وصيام آخر يوم من شهر رجب

Practices of the 15th of Shaban (nisf Sha'bān)		ادب ليلة النصف من شهر شعبان
Adab aṭ-Ṭarīqah		ادب الطريقة
Reading of Sūrah Yasīn three times; first with the intention of long life in Islam and faith (imān), second with the intention to ward off affliction from one's self and from the nation of Muhammad ﷺ; and the third time with the intention of receiving one's sustenance without reliance on men.		قراءة يس ثلاث مرات، المرة الاولى بنية طول العمر بالإسلام والإيمان، والمرة الثانية بنية دفع البلاء عنه وعن الامة المحمدية ، والمرة الثلاثة بنية الرزق والإستغناء عن الناس
After every reading recite: Allāhumma yā Dhāl-Manni lā yamannu 'alayhi aḥad, yā Dhāl-Jalāli wa 'l-Ikrām yā Dhāṭ-Ṭūli wa 'l-An'ām. Lā ilāha illa Anta. Ṭaharal-Aji'īn wa Jāru 'l-mutaji'īn wa Amānu 'l-khā'ifīn. Allāhumma in kunta katabtanī 'indaka fī ummi 'l-Kitābi shaqīyan aw maḥrūman aw maṭrūdan aw muqataran 'alayya min ar-rizq famḥu-llāhumma bi-faḍlika shaqāwatī wa ḥurmāni wa ṭurdī wa iqtāra rizqī wa thabitnī 'indaka fī ummi 'l-kitābi sa'īdan wa marzūqan li 'l-khayrāti fa-innaka qulta wa qawluku 'l-ḥaqq fī kitābik al-munzal 'ala lisāni nabīyyika 'l-mursal: yamḥullāhu mā yashā'u wa yuthbitu wa 'indahu Ummu 'l-Kitāb. Ilāhī bi 't-tajallī al-ā'aẓami fī lalayti 'n-niṣfi min shahri sha'bāni 'l-mu'aẓami 'l-mukarrami 'llatī yufraqu fīhā kullu amrin ḥakīmin wa yubram, an takshifa 'annā min al-balā'i mā na'lamu wa mā lā na'lamu wa mā Anta bihi ā'alamu innaka Anta al-A'azzu 'l-Akram. Wa ṣalla-Allāhu 'alā sayyidinā Muḥammadin wa 'alā ālihi wa ṣāḥbihi wa sallam.		و بعد كل مرة تدعوا بهذا الدعاء: اللهم يا ذا المن لا يمن عليه احد يا ذا الجلال والإكرام يا ذا الطول والأنعام، لا إله إلا أنتَ ظهر اللاجئين وجار المستجيرين وامان الخائفين اللهم ان كنت كتبتني عندك في ام الكتاب شقيا أو محروما أو مطرودا أو مقترا عليّ من الرزق فامح اللهم بفضلك شقاوتي وحرماني وطردي واقتار رزقي وثبتني عندك في ام الكتاب سعيدا ومرزوقا للخيرات فانكَ قلت وقولك الحق في كتابك المنزل على لسان نبيك المرسل يمحوا الله ما يشاء ويثبت وعنده ام الكتاب. إلهي بالتجلي الأعظم في ليلة النصف من شهر شعبان المعظم المكرم التي يفرق فيها كل امر حكيم ويبرم ان تكشف عنا من البلاء ما نعلم وما لا نعلم وما أنتَ به اعلم إنكَ أنتَ الأعز الأكرم.

<table>
<tr><td></td><td></td><td>وصلى الله على سيدنا محمد وعلى آله وصحبه وسلم.</td></tr>
<tr><td colspan="3">O God, Tireless Owner of Bounty. O Owner of Sublimity, Honor, Power, and Blessings. There is no god except You, the Support of refugees and Neighbor of those who seek nearness, Guardian of the fearful. O God, if you have written in Your Book that I be abject, deprived, banished, and tight-fisted, then erase O God, through Your bounty, my misery, deprivation, banishment, and stinginess and establish me with you as happy, provided with blessings in the Mother of Books, for surely Your Promise in Your Revealed Book on the tongue of Your Messenger is true. God blots out or confirms what He pleases, and with Him is the Mother of Books. My God, by the Great Manifestation of the Night of the middle of the Noble Month of Sha'bān in which every affair of wisdom is made distinct and authorized, remove from us calamities—those we know and those we do not know, and Thou knowest best—for surely You are the Most Mighty, the Most Generous. May God bless Muhammad and his Family and Companions.</td></tr>
<tr><td>One then invokes God with the Grand Transmitted Supplication of Sulṭan al-'Awliyā (see page 242) if it is easy, after each recitation, or if not, one time after the three recitations.</td><td></td><td>وتدعو بالدعاء الأعظم المأثور عن سلطان الأولياء اذا تيسر بعد كل مرة، وإلا تدعو به مرة واحدة بعد القراءة الثالثة</td></tr>
<tr><td>KHATMU 'L-KHWAJAGĀN
(see page 179)</td><td></td><td>ختم الخواجكان مع الذكر</td></tr>
<tr><td>ṢALĀTU 'Ṭ-ṬASĀBĪḤ</td><td></td><td>صلاة التسابيح اربع ركعات</td></tr>
<tr><td>ṢALĀTU 'SH-SHUKR
two rakats with Qunūt.</td><td></td><td>صلاة الشكر ركعتين مع دعاء القنوت</td></tr>
</table>

ṢALĀTU 'T-TAHAJJUD After 'Ishā, complete 100 raka'ts of Ṣalāt at-Tahajjud. In the first raka'h after the Fātiḥah recite Sūrat al-Ikhlāṣ twice and in the second, once.		صلاة تجهد ثم بعد صلاة العشاء تجتهد ان تكمل ١٠٠ ركعة تقرأ في الركعة الأولى بعد الفاتحة سورة الاخلاص مرتين تقرأ في الركعة الثانية بعد الفاتحة اخلاص الشريفة مرة
FASTING You are to fast its day and make a sacrifice to Allāh as a ransom for yourself and your family and distribute it to the needy.		الصيام ثم تصوم نهارها وتقدم قربان إلى الله فداء عنك وعن أهلك وتوزعه على الفقراء المساكين

<table>
<tr>
<td>The Grand Transmitted Supplication
From Sulṭan al-'Awliyā, Mawlānā ash-Shaykh 'Abd-Allāh al-Fā'iz ad-Dāghestānī, may God sanctify his secret.</td>
<td></td>
<td>الدعاء الأعظم المأثور
لسلطان الأولياء مولانا الشيخ عبد الله الفائز الدغستاني</td>
</tr>
<tr>
<td>Bismillāhi 'r-Raḥmāni 'r-Raḥīm.
Allāhumma ṣalli 'alā Muḥammadin an-Nabī il-mukhtār 'adada man ṣalla 'alayhi min al-akhyār, wa 'adada man lam yuṣalli 'alayhi min al-ashrār, wa 'adada qaṭarāti 'l-amṭār, wa 'adada amwāji 'l-biḥār, wa 'adada 'r-rimāli wa 'l-qifār, wa 'adada awrāqi 'l-ashjār, wa 'adada anfāsi 'l-mustaghfirīna bi 'l-ashār, wa 'adada akmāmi 'l-athmār, wa 'adada mā kāna wa mā yakūnu ila yawmi 'l-ḥashri wa 'l-qarār, wa ṣalli 'alayhi mā ta'āqabu 'l-laylu wa 'n-nahāru wa ṣalli 'alayhi mā 'khtalafu 'l-malawān wa ta'āqabu 'l-'asrān wa karrara 'l-jadīdān wa 'staqbal al-farqadān, wa balligh rūḥahu wa arwāhi āhli baytihi minnā taḥīyyatan wat-taslīm wa 'alā jamī'i 'l-anbīyā'i wa 'l-mursalīn wa 'l-ḥamdu lillāhi Rabbi 'l-'alamīn.</td>
<td></td>
<td>بسم الله الرحمن الرحيم
اللهم صل على محمد النبي المختار عدد من صلى عليه من الاخيار ، وعدد من لم يصل عليه من الاشرار، وعدد قطرات الامطار، وعدد امواج البحار، وعدد الرمال والقفار، وعدد اوراق الاشجار ، وعدد انفاس المستغفرين بالاسحار، وعدد اكمام الاثمار، وعدد ما كان وما يكون إلى يوم الحشر والقرار، وصل عليه ما تعاقب الليل والنهار، وصل عليه ما اختلف الملوان وتعاقب العصران وكرر الجديدان واستقبل الفرقدان، وبلّغ روحه وأرواح أهل بيته منا تحية وتسليم وعلى جميع الأنبياء والمرسلين والحمد لله رب العالمين.</td>
</tr>
<tr>
<td colspan="3">In the name of God, the Beneficent, the Merciful.

God, bless Muḥammad, the Chosen Prophet on the number of those who pray on him among the righteous and on the number of those who did not pray on him among the wicked; and on the number of the drops of the rain and on the number of waves of the oceans and on the number of the grains of sand and the wastelands, on the number of the leaves of the trees and on the number of the breaths of those who seek Your forgiveness by morning and on the number of the rinds of fruit and on the number of what was and what is until the Day of Gathering and Verdict.

And Bless him (O God), as the turning of nights and days and bless him as long as the colors alternate and with the changing of time, and with the return of things renewed and with the constancy of diversity.</td>
</tr>
</table>

And convey from us to his soul and the soul of his family, greetings and salutations and on all the prophets and messengers. And all Praise is due to God.

Allāhumma ṣalli ʻalā Muḥammad wa ʻalā āli Muḥammadin bi ʻadadi kulli dharratin alfa alfa marrah. Allāhumma ṣalli ʻalā Muḥammadin wa ʻalā āli Muḥammadin wa ṣaḥbihi wa sallim. Subūḥun quddūsun rabbunā wa rabbu ʼl-malāʼikati wa ʼr-Rūḥ, Rabbighfir wa ʼrḥam wa tawājaz ʻamma tʻalamu innaka Anta ʼl-Aʻazzu ʼl-Akram.	اللهم صل على محمد وعلى آل محمد بعدد كل ذرة الف الف مرة. اللهم صل على محمد وعلى آله وصحبه وسلم، سبوح قدوس ربنا ورب الملائكة والروح، رب اغفر وارحم وتجاوز عما تعلم إنكَ أنتَ الأعز الأكرم.

O God bless Muḥammad and the Family of Muḥammad of the number of the atom a thousand times over. O God bless Muḥammad and the Family of Muḥammad and His Companions and grant them peace. Glory and Holiness belongs to our Lord, Lord of the angels and the Holy Spirit. O our Lord forgive and have mercy and pardon of what You know (best), for You are surely the Most Mighty, Most Honorable.

Bismillāhi ʼr-Raḥmāni ʼr-Raḥīm. Allāhumma innī astaghfiruka min kulli mā tubtu ʻanhu ilayka thumma ʻudtu fīhi. Wa astaghfiruka min kulli mā āradtu bihi wajhaka fakhālaṭani fīhi la laysa fīhi raḍāʻuk. Wa astaghfiruka li ʼn-niʻam ʼillatī taqawwaytu bihā ʻalā mʻaṣīyatik. Wa astaghfiruka min adh-dhunūb ʼillati lā yʻalamuhā ghayruka, wa lā yaṭaliʻu ʻalayhā aḥadun siwāk wa lā tasaʻūhā illa raḥmatika, wa lā tunjī minhā illa maghfiratuka wa ḥilmuka. Lā ilāha illa Anta subḥānaka innī kuntu min aẓ-ẓālimīn.	بسم الله الرحمن الرحيم اللهم اني استغفرك من كل ما تبت عنه اليك ثم عدت فيه، واستغفرك من كل ما اردت به وجهك فخالطني فيه ما ليس فيه رضائك. واستغفرك للنعم التي تقويت بها على معصيتك، واستغفرك من الذنوب التي لا يعلمها غيرك ولا يطلع عليها احد سواك ولا تسعها الا رحمتك ولا تنجي منها الا مغفرتك وحلمك لا اله الا أنتَ سبحانك اني كنت من الظالمين.

In the name of Allah, the All-Beneficent, the All-Merciful

O Allah, I ask forgiveness of You for everything for which I repented to You then returned to. And I ask forgiveness of You for everything I displeased You with and all that concerns me with which You are displeased. And I ask forgiveness of You for the favors which I used for increasing my disobedience towards You. And I ask forgiveness of You for the sins which no one knows except You and no one sees except You and nothing encompasses except Your Mercy and nothing delivers from except Your forgiveness and clemency. There is no god except You

<table>
<tr><td colspan="2">alone. Glory be to You! Indeed I was an oppressor to myself.</td></tr>
<tr><td>Allāhumma innī astaghfiruka min kulli ẓulmin ẓalamtu bihi ʿībāduka fa ayyamā ʿabdan min ʿibādika aw ʾamatin min imāʾika ẓalamtu fī badanihi aw ʿirdhihi aw mālihi fʾāṭihi min khazāʿinak ʾillati lā tanquṣ, wa asʿaluka an tukrimanī bi raḥmatik ʾillati wasiʿat kulla shayʾin wa lā tuhīnanī bi ʿadhābika wa tʿuṭianī mā asʿaluka fa innī ḥaqīqun bi-raḥmatika ya Arḥam ar-rāḥimīn. Wa ṣalla-Allāhu ʿalā sayyidinā Muḥammadin wa ālihi wa ṣāḥbihi ajmāʿīn wa lā ḥawla wa lā quwwata illa billāhi ʾl-ʿAliyyi ʾl-ʿAẓīm.</td><td>اللهم اني استغفرك من كل ظلم ظلمت به عبادك فايما عبد من عبادك أو أمة من امائك ظلمت في بدنه أو عرضه أو ماله فأعطه من خزائنك التي لا تنقص وأسألك ان تكرمني برحمتك التي وسعت كل شيء ولا تهينني بعذابك وتعطيني ما أسألك فاني حقيق برحمتك يا ارحم الراحمين. وصلى الله على سيدنا محمد وآله وصحبه أجمعين، ولا حول ولا قوة الا بالله العلي العظيم.</td></tr>
<tr><td colspan="2">O God, I ask forgiveness of You for the injustice I committed against Your servants. Whatever of Your male or female servants whom I have hurt, physically or in their dignity or in their property give them of Your bounty which lacks nothing. And I ask You to honor me with Your mercy which encompasses all things. Do not humble me with Your punishment but give me what I ask of You, for I am in great need of Your mercy, O Most Merciful of the merciful. May God send blessings upon Muḥammad and upon all his companions. And there is no power and no might except in God the Most High, the Exalted.</td></tr>
<tr><td>Bismillāhi ʾr-Raḥmāni ʾr-Raḥīm.
Bismillāhi ʾn-Nūr, nūrun ʿalā nūr, alḥamdulillāhi ʾlladhī khalaq as-samawāti wa ʾl-arḍ wa jaʿala aẓ-ẓulumāti wa ʾn-nūr wa anzala at-tawrāta ʿalā jabali ʾṭ-Ṭūri fī kitābin masṭūr.
Wa ʾl-ḥamdulillāhi ʾlladhī hūwa bil-Ghanī madhkūr wa bi ʾl-ʿizzi wa ʾl-Jalāl mashhūr, wʾ alḥamdulillāhi ʾlladhī khalaq as-samāwāti wa ʾl-arḍ wa jaʿala ʾẓ-zulumāti wa ʾn-nūr thumma ʾlladhīna kafarū bi-rabbihim yaʿdilūn. Kāf, Hā, ʿAyn, Ṣād. Ḥā, Mīm, ʿAyn, Sīn, Qāf. Īyāka nʿabudu wa Īyāka nastaʿīn. Yā Ḥayyu Yā Qayyūm. Allāhu laṭīfun</td><td>بسم الله الرحمن الرحيم
بسم الله النور، نور على نور والحمد لله الذي خلق السموات والارض وجعل الظلمات والنور وانزل التوراة على جبل الطور في كتاب مسطور ، والحمد لله الذي هو بالغنى مذكور بالعز والجلال مشهور، والحمد لله الذي خلق السموات والارض وجعل الظلمات والنور ثم الذين كفروا بربهم يعدلون، كهيعص حمعسق اياك نعبد واياك نستعين يا حي يا قيوم، الله لطيف بعباده</td></tr>
</table>

bi 'ibādihi yarzuqū man yashā'u wa Hūwa 'l-Qawiyyu 'l-'Azīz. Yā Kāfī kulla shay'in ikfinī waṣrif 'anī kulla shay'in innaka Qādirun 'alā kulli shay'in bi-yadik al-khayr innaka 'alā kulli shay'in Qadīr.		يرزق من يشاء وهو القوي العزيز، يا كافي كل شيء اكفني واصرف عني كل شيء إنكَ قادر على كل شيء بيدك الخير إنكَ على كل شيء قدير

In the name of God, the All-Beneficent, the All-Merciful.

In the name of God, the Source of Light, Light upon Light. All praise is due to God who hath created the heavens and the earth. He created the darkness and the light and hath revealed the Torah on Mount Tūr in a Composed Book. All praise is due to God who created the heavens and the earth and created the darkness and the light.

> *"Yet those who reject Faith hold (others) as equal, with their Guardian-Lord."* (6:1)

> *Kāf, Hā, 'Ayn, Ṣād. Ḥā, Mīm, Sīn, Qāf. "You alone do we worship and You alone do ask for help."* (1:4)

O Ever-Living One, O Self-subsisting One.

> *"Gracious is Allah to His servants: He gives Sustenance to whom He pleases: and He has power and can carry out His Will."* (42:19)

O Giver of all, provide me and turn from me everything that harms me. Surely You are capable over all things. In Your hands is all good and You have power over all things.

Allāhumma ya Kathīr an-nawāli wa yā Dā'im al-wiṣāli wa yā Ḥusna 'l-fi'āli wa yā Razzāq al-'ibādi 'alā kulli ḥāl.		اللهم يا كثير النوال ويا دائم الوصال ويا حسن الفعال ويا رازق العباد على كل حال.

O God, the One who Grants plenty, O One of the Abiding Connection, O Doer of Good, O Provider of Your servants in every state.

Allāhumma in dakhala ash-shaku fī īmānī bika wa lam ā'alam bihi tubtu 'anhu wa aqūlu lā ilāha ill-Allāh Muḥammadur-Rasūlullāh ﷺ.		االلهم إن دخل الشك في إيماني بك ولم أعلم به تبت عنه وأقول لا إله إلا الله محمد رسول الله ﷺ.

O God, if doubt has entered my belief in You, and of which I was unaware, I repent from it and say: There is no god except God, Muḥammad ﷺ is the Prophet of God.

Allāhumma in dakhal ash-shakka wa 'l-kufr fī tawḥīdī īyāka wa lam ā'alam bihi tubtu 'anhu wa aqūlu lā ilāha ill-Allāh Muḥammadur-Rasūlullāh ﷺ.		اللهم إن دخل الشك والكفر في توحيدي اياك ولم أعلم به تبت عنه وأقول لا إله إلا الله محمد رسول الله ﷺ.

O God, if doubt and disbelief entered my affirmation of Your Oneness, and of which I was unaware, I repent from it and say: There is no god except God, Muḥammad ﷺ is the Prophet of God.		
Allāhumma in dakhala ash-shubhata fī m'arifati īyāka wa lam ā'alam bihi tubtu 'anhu wa aqūlu lā ilāha ill-Allāh Muḥammadur-Rasūlullāh ﷺ.		اللهم إن دخلت الشبهة في معرفتي اياك ولم أعلم به تبت عنه وأقول لا إله إلا الله محمد رسول الله ﷺ.
O God, if doubt enters my realization of You, and of which I was unaware, I repent from it and say: There is no god except God, Muḥammad ﷺ is the Prophet of God.		
Allāhumma in dakhal al-'ujb wa 'r-riyā' wa 'l-kibrīyā wa 's-sum'atu fī 'ilmī wa lam ā'alam bihi tubtu 'anhu wa aqūlu lā ilāha ill-Allāh Muḥammadur-Rasūlullāh ﷺ.		اللهم إن دخل العجب والرياء والكبرياء والسمعة في علمي ولم أعلم به تبت عنه وأقول لا إله إلا الله محمد رسول الله ﷺ.
O God, if vanity, affected piety, arrogance and infamy affected me and of which I was unaware, I repent from it and say: There is no god except God, Muḥammad ﷺ is the Prophet of God.		
Allāhumma in jara 'l-kadhiba 'alā lisānī wa lam ā'alam bihi tubtu 'anhu wa aqūlu lā ilāha ill-Allāh Muḥammadur-Rasūlullāh ﷺ.		اللهم إن جرى الكذب على لساني ولم أعلم به تبت عنه وأقول لا إله إلا الله محمد رسول الله ﷺ.
O God, if lies run upon my tongue, of which I was unaware, I repent from it and say: There is no god except God, Muḥammad ﷺ is the Prophet of God.		
Allāhumma in dakhala an-nifāq fī qalbī min adh-dhunūbi 's-saghā'iri wa 'l-kabā'iri wa lam ā'alam bihi tubtu 'anhu wa aqūlu lā ilāha ill-Allāh Muḥammadur-Rasūlullāh ﷺ.		اللهم إن دخل النفاق في قلبي من الذنوب الصغائر والكبائر ولم أعلم به تبت عنه وأقول لا إله إلا الله محمد رسول الله ﷺ
O God, if hypocrisy entered my heart from the minor and major sins, and of which I was unaware, I repent from it and say: There is no god except God, Muḥammad ﷺ is the Prophet of God.		
Allāhumma mā asdayta ilayya min khayrin wa lam ashkuruka wa lam ā'alam bihi tubtu 'anhu wa aqūlu lā ilāha ill-Allāh Muḥammadur-Rasūlullāh ﷺ.		اللهم ما اسديت إليّ من خير ولم أشكرك ولم أعلم به تبت عنه وأقول لا إله إلا الله محمد رسول الله ﷺ.
O Allāh, from what You have granted me of all that is good and for which I had		

<table>
<tr><td colspan="3">not thanked You, and I was unaware of it, I repent from it and say: There is no god except God, Muḥammad ﷺ is the Prophet of God.</td></tr>
<tr><td>Allāhumma mā qadarta lī min amrin wa lam arḍāhu wa lam ā'alam bihi tubtu 'anhu wa aqūlu lā ilāha ill-Allāh Muḥammadur-Rasūlullāh ﷺ.</td><td></td><td>اللهم ما قدرت لي من أمر ولم أرضه ولم أعلم به تبت عنه وأقول لا إله إلا الله محمد رسول الله ﷺ.</td></tr>
<tr><td colspan="3">O God, whatever You have destined for me in matters which I did not accept, and of which I was unaware, I repent from it and say: There is no god except God, Muḥammad ﷺ is the Prophet of God.</td></tr>
<tr><td>Allāhumma mā an'amta 'alayya min n'imatin fa-'aṣaytuka wa ghafaltu 'an shukrika wa lam ā'alam bihi tubtu 'anhu wa aqūlu lā ilāha ill-Allāh Muḥammadur-Rasūlullāh ﷺ.</td><td></td><td>اللهم ما انعمت من نعمة فعصيتك وغفلت عن شكرك ولم أعلم به تبت عنه وأقول لا إله إلا الله محمد رسول الله ﷺ.</td></tr>
<tr><td colspan="3">O God, from what You had conferred upon me of bounty for which I neglected to thank You, and of which I was unaware, I repent from it and say: There is no god except God, Muḥammad ﷺ is the Prophet of God.</td></tr>
<tr><td>Allāhumma mā mananta bihi 'alayya min khayrin fa lam āḥmaduka 'alayhi wa lam ā'alam bihi tubtu 'anhu wa aqūlu lā ilāha ill-Allāh Muḥammadur-Rasūlullāh ﷺ.</td><td></td><td>اللهم ما مننت به علي من خير فلم أحمدك عليه ولم أعلم به تبت عنه وأقول لا إله إلا الله محمد رسول الله ﷺ.</td></tr>
<tr><td colspan="3">O God, whatever You have bestowed on me of goodness and I did not praise You for it, and of which I was unaware, I repent from it and say: There is no god except God, Muḥammad ﷺ is the Prophet of God.</td></tr>
<tr><td>Allāhumma ma ḍayyatu min 'umrī wa lam tarḍa bihi tubtu 'anhu wa aqūlu lā ilāha ill-Allāh Muḥammadur-Rasūlullāh ﷺ.</td><td></td><td>اللهم ما ضيعت من عمري ولم ترض به وتبت عنه وأقول لا إله إلا الله محمد رسول الله ﷺ.</td></tr>
<tr><td colspan="3">O God, whatever I have wasted from my allotted lifetime which You were not pleased, I repent from it and say: There is no god except God, Muḥammad ﷺ is the Prophet of God.</td></tr>
<tr><td>Allāhumma bimā awjabta 'alayya min al-naẓari min maṣnū'ātika fa-ghafaltu 'anhu wa lam ā'alam bihi tubtu 'anhu wa aqūlu lā ilāha ill-Allāh Muḥammadur-Rasūlullāh ﷺ.</td><td></td><td>اللهم بما اوجبت عليّ من النظر في مصنوعاتك فغفلت عنه ولم أعلم به تبت عنه وأقول لا إله إلا الله محمد رسول الله ﷺ.</td></tr>
<tr><td colspan="3">O God, of what You have imposed upon me in the observation of the creation of</td></tr>
</table>

<table>
<tr><td colspan="3">Your design and of which I was heedless, and I was unaware of it, I repent from it and say: There is no god except God, Muḥammad ﷺ is the Prophet of God.</td></tr>
<tr><td>Allāhumma mā qaṣartu ʻanhu āmālī fī rajāʼika wa lam āʻalam bihi tubtu ʻanhu wa aqūlu lā ilāha ill-Allāh Muḥammadur-Rasūlullāh ﷺ.</td><td></td><td>اللهم ما قصرت عنه آمالي في رجائك ولم أعلم به تبت عنه وأقول لا إله إلا الله محمد رسول الله ﷺ.</td></tr>
<tr><td colspan="3">O God, from whatever fell short of my hope in my turning to You, and of which I was unaware, I repent from it and say: There is no god except God, Muḥammad ﷺ is the Prophet of God.</td></tr>
<tr><td>Allāhumma māʻtamadtu ʻalā aḥadin siwāka fī ʼsh-shadāʼidi wa lam āʻalamu bihi tubtu ʻanhu wa aqūlu lā ilāha ill-Allāh Muḥammadur-Rasūlullāh ﷺ.</td><td></td><td>اللهم ما اعتمدت على احد سواك في الشدائد ولم أعلم به تبت عنه وأقول لا إله إلا الله محمد رسول الله ﷺ.</td></tr>
<tr><td colspan="3">O God, from placing dependence on other than You in the face of calamities, and of which I was unaware, I repent from it and say: There is no god except God, Muḥammad ﷺ is the Prophet of God.</td></tr>
<tr><td>Allāhumma mā astanaʻtu li-ghayrika fiʼsh-shadāʼidi wa ʼn-nawāʼibi wa lam āʻalam bihi tubtu ʻanhu wa aqūlu lā ilāha ill-Allāh Muḥammadur-Rasūlullāh ﷺ.</td><td></td><td>اللهم ما استعنت بغيرك في الشدائد والنوائب ولم أعلم به تبت عنه وأقول لا إله إلا الله محمد رسول الله ﷺ.</td></tr>
<tr><td colspan="3">O God, in what I had sought assistance from other than You in calamities and misfortune, and of which I was unaware, I repent from it and say: There is no god except God, Muḥammad ﷺ is the Prophet of God.</td></tr>
<tr><td>Allāhumma in zalla lisānī bis-suʼāli li-ghayrika wa lam āʻalam bihi tubtu ʻanhu wa aqūlu lā ilāha ill-Allāh Muḥammadur-Rasūlullāh ﷺ.</td><td></td><td>اللهم إن زلّ لساني بالسؤال لغيرك ولم أعلم به تبت عنه وأقول لا إله إلا الله محمد رسول الله ﷺ.</td></tr>
<tr><td colspan="3">O God, if my tongue has slipped by askng other than You and I was unaware of it, I repent from it and say: There is no god except God, Muḥammad ﷺ is the Prophet of God.</td></tr>
<tr><td>Allāhumma mā ṣaluḥa min shānī bi-faḍlika faraʼituhu min ghayrika wa lam āʻalam bihi tubtu ʻanhu wa aqūlu lā ilāha ill-Allāh Muḥammadur-Rasūlullāh ﷺ.</td><td></td><td>اللهم ما صَلُح من شأني بفضلك فرأيته من غيرك ولم أعلم به تبت عنه وأقول لا إله إلا الله محمد رسول الله ﷺ.</td></tr>
<tr><td colspan="3">O God, whatever was rectified in my affairs through Your Grace and I saw it coming from other than You, and I was unaware of it, I repent from it and say: There is no god except God, Muḥammad ﷺ is the Prophet of God.</td></tr>
</table>

Allāhumma bi-ḥaqqi lā ilāha ill-Allāh wa bi-ʿizzatih		اللهم بحق لا إله إلا الله وبعزته
O God, by the right of lā ilāha ill-Allāh and its Might;		
Wa bi-ḥaqqi ʾl-ʿarshi wa ʿaẓamatihih		و بحق العرش وعظمته
And by the right of the Throne and its grandeur;		
Wa bi-ḥaqqi ʾl-kursī wa saʿatih		و بحق الكرسي وسعته
And by the right of the Chair and its vastness;		
Wa bi-ḥaqqi ʾl-qalami wa jariyatihi		و بحق القلم وجَرَيَتِه
And by the right of the Pen and its motion;		
Wa bi-ḥaqqi ʾl-lawḥi wa ḥafaẓatih		و بحق اللوح وحفظته
And by the right of the Tablet and its preservation;		
Wa bi-ḥaqqi ʾl-mīzāni wa khifatih		و بحق الميزان وخفته
And by the right of the Scale and its accuracy;		
Wa bi-ḥaqqi ʾṣ-Ṣirāṭi wa riqqatihi		و بحق الصراط ورقته
And by the right of the Bridge and it narrowness;		
Wa bi-ḥaqqi Jibrīl wa amānatihi		و بحق جبريل وامانَته
And by the right of Jibrīl and his trust;		
Wa bi-ḥaqqi Riḍwān wa jannatih		و بحق رضوان وجنته
And by the right of Riḍwān and his paradise;		
Wa bi-ḥaqqi Mālik wa zabānīyatih		و بحق مالك وزبانيته
And by the right of Mālik and his angels of punishment;		
Wa bi-ḥaqqi Mīkāʾīl wa shafqatih		و بحق ميكائيل وشفقته
And by the right of Mīkāʾīl and his compassion;		
Wa bi-ḥaqqi Isrāfīl wa nafkhatih		و بحق اسرافيل ونفخته
And by the right of Isrāfīl and his blowing (of the Trumpet);		
Wa bi-ḥaqqi ʿAzrāʾīl wa qabḍatih		و بحق عزرائيل وقبضته

And by the right of ʻAzrāʼīl and his seizing (of the soul in death);		
Wa bi-ḥaqqi Ādam wa ṣafwatih		و بحق آدم وصفوته
And by the right of Ādam and his purity;		
Wa bi-ḥaqqi Shuʻayb wa nubūwwatih		و بحق شعيب ونبوته
And by the right of Shuʻayb and his prophethood;		
Wa bi-ḥaqqi Nūḥ wa safīnatih		و بحق نوح وسفينته
And by the right of Nūḥ and his vessel;		
Wa bi-ḥaqqi Ibrāhīm wa khullatih		و بحق ابراهيم وخلّته
And by the right of Ibrāhīm and his Friendship (to God);		
Wa bi-ḥaqqi Isḥāq wa dīyānatih		و بحق اسحاق وديانته
And by the right of Isḥaq and his belief;		
Wa bi-ḥaqqi Ismāʻīl wa fidyatih		و بحق اسماعيل وفديته
And by the right of Ismāʻīl and his ransom;		
Wa bi-ḥaqqi Yūsuf wa ghurbatih		و بحق يوسف وغربته
And by the right of Yūsuf and his estrangement;		
Wa bi-ḥaqqi Mūsā wa āyātih		و بحق موسى وآياته
And by the right of Mūsa and his signs;		
Wa bi-ḥaqqi Hārūn wa ḥurmatih		و بحق هارون وحرمته
And by the right of Hārūn and his sanctity;		
Wa bi-ḥaqqi Hūd wa haybatih		و بحق هود وهيبته
And by the right of Hūd and his Veneration;		
Wa bi-ḥaqqi Ṣāliḥ wa nāqatih		و بحق صالح وناقته
And by the right of Ṣāliḥ and his she-camel;		
Wa bi-ḥaqqi Lūṭ wa jīratih		و بحق لوط وجيرته
And by the right of Lūṭ and his guests;		
Wa bi-ḥaqqi Yūnus wa daʻwatih		و بحق يونس ودعوته

And by the right of Yūnus and his invocation;		
Wa bi-ḥaqqi Dānyāl wa karāmatih		و بحق دنيال وكرامته
And by the right of Danyāl and his miracles;		
Wa bi-ḥaqqi Zakariyā wa ṭahāratih		و بحق زكريا وطهارته
And by the right of Zakariyā and his purity;		
Wa bi-ḥaqqi 'Isā wa sīyāḥatih		و بحق عيسى وسياحته
And by the right of 'Isa and his wandering;		
Wa bi-ḥaqqi sayyidinā Muḥammadin ﷺ wa shafā'atih		و بحق سيدنا محمد(ص) وشفاعته
And by the right of Our Master Muḥammad and his Intercession;		
An taghfir lanā wa li-wālidīynā wa li-'ulamā'inā wa an tākhudha bi-yadī wa t'utīyanī su'āli wa tubalighanī āmālī wa an taṣrifa 'anī kulla man 'aādānī bi-raḥmatika yā Arḥamu 'r-Rāhimīn, wa taḥfaẓnī min kulli sū'in, lā ilāha illa Anta, subḥānaka innī kuntu min aẓ-ẓālimīn.		ان تغفر لنا ولوالدينا ولعلمائنا وان تأخذ بيدى وتعطيني سؤالي وتبلغني آمالي وان تصرف عني كل من عاداني برحمتك يا ارحم الراحمين وتحفظني من كل سوء لا إله إلا أنتَ سبحانك إني كنت من الظالمين
That You forgive us, our parents and our scholars. And to take me by the hand and to grant me my asking and deliver me to my goals. And fend off all those who harm me, by Your mercy, O the Most Merciful of those who give mercy. And to protect me from every vice. There is no god except You, Glory be to You! Surely I have been a wrong-doer.		
Yā Ḥayyu, yā Qayyūm. Lā ilāha illa Anta, yā Allāh, astāghfiruka wa atūbu ilayk. Fastajabnā lahu wa najaynāhu min al-ghamm wa kadhālika nanjī al-mu'minīn wa ḥasbuna-llāhu wa n'ima 'l-wakīl ḥasbī Allāhu lā ilāha illa hūwa 'alayhi tawakkaltu wa Hūwa rabbu 'l-'Arshi 'l-'Aẓīm wa lā ḥawlah wa lā quwwata illa billāhi 'l-'Aẓīm.		يا حي يا قيوم لا إله إلا أنتَ يا الله استغفر ك واتوب إليك فاستجبنا له ونجيناه من الغم وكذلك ننجي المؤمنين. وحسبنا الله ونعم الوكيل حسبي الله لا إله إلا هو عليه توكلت وهو رب العرش العظيم ولا حول ولا قوة إلا بالله العلي العظيم
O Living, O Eternal there is no god except You. O Allāḥ, I seek forgiveness in You and I turn to You, So We listened to him: and We delivered him from distress: and thus do We deliver those who have faith. God is enough for us, the best Disposer of affairs; God sufficeth me: there is no god but He: On Him is my		

<table>
<tr><td colspan="2">trust,- He the Lord of the Throne (of Glory) Supreme!" And there is no strength, nor power except by God, The High, The Mighty.</td></tr>
<tr><td>Wa ṣalla-Allāhu ʻalā sayyidinā Muḥammad wa ʻalā ālihi wa ṣāḥbihi wa sallim ajmāʻīn. subḥānā rabbika rabbi ʼl-ʻIzzati ʻamā yaṣifūn wa salāmun ʻalā ʼl-mursalīn wa ʼl-ḥamdulillāhi rabbi ʼl-ʻālamīn.</td><td>و صلى الله على سيدنا محمد وعلى آله وصحبه وسلم أجمعين. سبحان ربك رب العزة عما يصفون وسلام على المرسلين والحمد لله رب العالمين.</td></tr>
<tr><td colspan="2">May God bless our master Muḥammad, His Family and Companions altogether. Glory to Allah, the Lord of the Throne: (High is He) above what they attribute to Him! And Peace on the Messengers and all Praise is due to the Lord of the worlds.</td></tr>
<tr><td>Bismillāhi ʼr-Raḥmāni ʼr-Raḥīm.
Allāhumma innī as'aluka bi mushāhadati asrāri ʼl-muḥibbīn wa bi ʼl-khalwati ʼllatī khaṣaṣta bihā sayyid al-mursalīn ḥīna asrayta bihi laylat as-sābʻi wa ʼl-ʻishrīn an tarḥam qalbī al-ḥazīn wa tujīb dʻawatī yā Akram al-Akramīn yā Arḥamar-Rāḥimīn. Wa ṣalla-Allāhu ʻalā sayyidinā Muḥammadin wa ʻalā ālihi wa ṣāḥbihi wa sallim ajmāʻīn.</td><td>بسم الله الرحمن الرحيم.
ثم نقول اللهم اني أسألك بمشاهدة اسرار المحبين وبالخلوة التي خصصت بها سيد المرسلين حين اسريت به ليلة السابع والعشرين ان ترحم قلبي الحزين وتجيب دعوتي يا أكرم الأكرمين يا ارحم الراحمين وصلى الله على سيدنا محمد وآله وصحبه أجمعين.</td></tr>
<tr><td colspan="2">In the name of God, the Beneficent, the Merciful.
O God, surely I beseech You by the witnessing of the secrets of the Lovers and the reclusion which you hath specified with the Master of Messengers when You raised Him on the Night of the 27th. And to pity by depressed heart and to answer my plea, O Most Generous of those who show generosity, O Most Merciful of those who show mercy. May God bless our master Muḥammad, His Family and all his Companions and greet them with peace.</td></tr>
<tr><td>Bismillāhi ʼr-Raḥmāni ʼr-Raḥīm.
Lā illāha ill-Allāh Muḥammadu Rasūlullāh yā Raḥmān yā Raḥīm yā Mustaʻan yā Allāh yā Muḥammad ṣalla-Allāhu ʻalayhi wa sallam. Yā Abā Bakr, yā ʻUmar, yā ʻUthmān, yā ʻAlī, yā Ḥasan, yā Ḥusayn, yā Yahyā; yā Ḥalīm, yā Allāh, wa lā ḥawlah wa lā quwwata illa billāhi ʼl-ʻAliyyi ʼl-ʻAẓīm.</td><td>بسم الله الرحمن الرحيم
لا إله إلا الله محمد رسول الله يا رحمن يا رحيم يا مستعان يالله يا محمد صلى الله عليه وسلم، يا أبا بكر يا عمر يا عثمان يا علي يا حسن يا حسين يا يحي يا حليم يا الله ولا حول ولا قوة إلا بالله العلي العظيم.</td></tr>
<tr><td colspan="2">In the name of God, the Beneficent, the Merciful.</td></tr>
</table>

There is no god except God, Muḥammad is the Messenger of God; O Merciful, O Beneficent One, O Musta'ān, O God; O Muḥammad peace and blessings be upon him. O Abū Bakr; O 'Umar; O 'Uthmān; O 'Alī; O Ḥasan; O Ḥusayn; O Yaḥyā; O Forbearing One, O God. There is no power and no strength save in God, All-High and Almighty.		
Astaghfirullāh dhul-jalāli wa 'l-Ikrām min jamī'i 'dh-dhunūb wa 'l-āthām. Āmīn.		استغفر الله ذو الجلال والإكرام من جميع الذنوب والآثام آمين.
I seek forgiveness in God, the Possessor of Majesty and Honor, from every sin and transgression. Amen.		

Ramadan Salatu-t-Tarawih		التراويح في رمضان
2 OR 4 RAK'ATS SUNNAH		صلاة السنة ٢ أو ٤ ركعات
4 RAK'ATS FARḌ 'ISHĀ		صلاة العشاء
2 RAK'ATS SUNNAH		وبعدها ركعتين السنة البعدية
INTENTION Intend to fast the obligatory fast of the next day, then intend Ṣalāt at-Tarāwīḥ (20 rak'ats).		ينوي الصيام ثم ينوي لصلاة التراويح قائلا: نويت ان اصلي ٢٠ ركعات صلاة التراويح لله تعالى رب العالمين
After each four rak 'ats sit and read 3 times Sūratu 'l-Ikhlāṣ, followed by the following: liqā'ullāh yurjā fīṣ-ṣīyām wa nūru qalbī fī 'l-qīyām, ta'al-Allāh dhul 'arshi'l majīd aṣ-Ṣalātu jāmi'a Ṣalātu't-tarāwīḥ athāb akumullāh. An-nabī yashfa'u liman yuṣalli 'alayh. Allāhumma ṣalli 'alā Muḥammadin wa 'alā Muhammdin wa sallam. Allāhumma innā nas'aluka'l-jannata wa na'udhu bika min an-nār.		و بعد كل ٤ ركعات اقرأ سورة الاخلاص ٣ مرات أو قل: لقاء الله يرجى في الصيام ونور القلب في القيام تعالى الله ذو العرش المجيد، الصلاة الجامعة صلاة التراويح أثابكم الله، النبي يشفع لمن يصلي عليه. اللهم صل على سيدنا محمد وعلى آل سيدنا محمد . اللهم إنا نسألك الجنّة ونعوذ بك من النار
ṢALĀTU 'T-TARĀWĪH. (20 RAK'ATS)		صلاة التراويح (٢٠ ركعات)
ṢALĀTU 'L-WITR (3 RAK'ATS)		صلاة الوتر (٣ ركعات)
Then recite: 'alā Rasūlinā 'ṣ-ṣalawāt and recitations following Ṣalāt al-'Ishā.		على رسولنا الصلوات
ĀMAN AR-RASŪLU (see page 169) 2:285- 286		آمَنَ الرَّسُولُ
SŪRATU 'L-FĀTIHĀ		الفاتحة

Notes to the Guidebook

Voluntary Worship

In the approach to the Divine Presence, the seeker must build his or her divine aspect based on the spirit of the holy hadith:

> *...My servant draws not near to Me with anything more loved by Me than the religious duties I have enjoined upon him, and My servant continues to draw near to Me with supererogatory works so that I shall love him. When I love him I am his hearing with which he hears, his seeing with which he sees, his hand with which he strikes and his foot with which he walks...*[275]

The shaykhs of the most distinguished Naqshbandi Way have ordered the seeker at the level of the People of Determination and the Prepared to adopt himself or herself to practices of the Prophet ﷺ in daily worship, in particular:

- observing all the *Sunan* prayers accompanying the obligatory ones (*farā'id*).
- observing the night vigil (*tahajjud*).
- additionally observing the following prayers:
    - **Ṣalātu 'l-Ishrāq** – shortly after sunrise.
    - **Ṣalātu 'd-Duḥā** – two sets of four rak'at sets in the time between mid-morning and Ṣalāt aẓ-Ẓuhr.
    - **Ṣalātu'l-Awwābīn** – three sets of two rak'ats after Ṣalāt al-Maghrib.

Special Practices

These notes address unusual or special practices. All the practices are based on the *Sunnah* of the Prophet ﷺ and explanations of their special benefits can be found in traditional references.

The following notes are meant to clarify some of the practices which occur in the preceding pages. The perfection of them has come to us from our Master Shaykh Muhammad Nazim al-Haqqani al-Naqshbandi (may God continually raise his station). If there is any imperfection in

---

[275] Related by Abu Hurayrah in *Sahih al-Bukhari*.

this text, however, it comes from us, and may God be Merciful with us and forgive us.

Note: The Shaykh uses the *miswāk* (natural toothstick) before every ritual action, and before every Qur'ān reading.

Sunan Prayers

The Prophet ﷺ said:

A house will be built in paradise for every Muslim who offers twelve rak'ats of optional prayers other than the obligatory prayers in one day and a night, seeking the pleasure of God.[276]

Thus we observe Mawlana Shaykh Nazim does not neglect one *Sunnah* prayer, whether "emphasized" (*mu'akkadah*) or voluntary rak'ats (*nāfilah*) observed by the Prophet at one time or another.

Prayer	Preceding Sunnah	Preceding Nafl	Following Sunnah	Following Nafl
Ṣalātu 'l-Maghrib	2 rak'ats	None	2 rak'ats	6 rak'ats (al-awwābīn)
Ṣalātu 'l-'Ishā	2 rak'ats	2 rak'ats	2 rak'ats 3 rak'ats (al-witr)	2 rak'ats
Ṣalātu 'l-Fajr	2 rak'ats	None	None	None
Ṣalātu 'ẓ-Ẓuhr	2 rak'ats	2 rak'ats	2 rak'ats	2 rak'ats
Ṣalātu 'l-'Aṣr	2 rak'ats	2 rak'ats	None	None

Note: In the Hanafī school the two rak'ats *Sunnah* and two rak'ats of *Nāfilah* preceding Ṣalātu 'ẓ-Ẓuhr, al-'Aṣr and al-'Ishā are combined in four rak'ats, whereas in the Shafi'i school they are separate.

[276] Narrated by Muslim.

Salatu-l-Maghrib

The two rak'ats *Sunnah* prayer before the obligatory (*farḍ*) prayer are a "non-emphasized *Sunnah*" (*sunnah ghayr mu'akkadah*). They were quickly prayed by the Sahaba ﷺ of the Prophet ﷺ after hearing the *adhān* of Ṣalāt al-Maghrib. We find hadith on this practice in some of the traditional hadith collections, and referenced by Imam Suyuti. The Prophet ﷺ never prevented the Companions from doing this and, therefore, it is considered a *Sunnah*, based on what the Prophet ﷺ did, what the Prophet ﷺ said, and what the Prophet ﷺ approved of (i.e., did not specifically forbid). It is mentioned that many of the great Sufi shaykhs maintained this practice, including Imam Ghazali.

Salatu-l-Janazah

The funeral prayer for those absent persons who have died without anyone praying over them is a daily *fard kifāyah,* a practice which only one member of the community is obliged to perform. Like the two *Sunnah* rak'ats before Ṣalātu 'l-Maghrib, we know that the great shaykhs made this a daily practice. The prayer is performed standing, facing the *Qiblah.*

Abu Hurayrah ﷺ narrated:

The Prophet ﷺ announced to the people the death of the Negus (al-Najāshī) on the same day that he died, then he came outside with them to the (open air) place of prayer and said, "God is greatest!" four times.

Salatu-l-Awwabin

The 2-2-2 rak'at Ṣalātu 'l-Awwābīn refers to those who turn frequently in prayer to their Lord. They constitute six rak'ats of two rak'ats each with a *taslīm* (*as-salām 'alaykum wa raḥmatullāh* to the right and left, at the end), between every two rak'ats.

Your Lord is best aware of what is in your minds. If you are righteous, then lo! He was ever Forgiving unto those who turn (unto Him) (awwābīn*)"* (17:25).

Anas bin Malik ﷺ related that the verse, *"Who forsake their beds to cry unto their Lord in fear and hope, and spend of what we have bestowed on them."*

(32:16) means, "The supererogatory prayer between the sunset and evening."[277]

The Prophet of God ﷺ said:

Whoever prays ten (supererogatory) rak'at between the sunset and evening prayers, a castle will be built for him in Paradise.[278]

The Prophet ﷺ said:

Whoever forsakes his sleep between the sunset and evening prayers, two palaces are built for him in Paradise between which is the distance of one year's travel. They contain enough trees to cover the people of both East and West in fruit." [279]

Abd Allah ibn Umar and Ibn al-As ﷺ said:
Ṣalāt al-Awwābīn is [in] the gap between the sunset and evening prayers until the time people spring to the prayer.[280]

Salatu-l-Witr

The *qunūt* prayer is inserted in the third rak'at after reading al-Fātiḥ a and a sūra from the Qur'ān (the Shaykh usually reads Sūratu 'l-Ikhlāṣ), and before the *ruk'u*, or bowing. According the the Hanafī school, after you have finished reading, raise your hands to your ears—as you would to begin the prayer—and say the *takbīr, Allāhu akbar* and continue with the *du'ā* (supplication) indicated in the text. After reciting the *du'ā*, go into *ruk'u*, then continue as in a normal prayer sequence. In the Shafi'i school the supplication is made in the standing position after *ruk'u*.

Ṣalātu 'l-witr is prayed as three rak'ats in the Hanafi school but in the Shafi'i it is broken into two rak'ats Ṣalātu 'sh-shaf' and one rak'at Ṣalātu 'l-witr.

---

[277] Abu Dawud from Qatadah and Ikrimah.

[278] Related from Muhammad ibn al-Hajaj or Ibn Abi 'l-Hajaj from Abd al-Karim. Note: 2 rak'ats before the obligatory prayers, 2 Sunnah, and 6 Ṣalātu 'l-Awābīn is 10 rak'ats total.

[279] Ath-Thalabi reported it *marfu'an* from Ibn Umar. Commenting on this hadith, Imam al-Quturbi said, "This is the prayer of Awwābīn and it is the heedlessness of the negligent (that miss it) and there are supplications that are accepted and not rejected between the sunset and evening prayers."

[280] *Mawqufan* from Ibn Umar by Ibn Abi Shaybah in his *Musannaf* (2:14 #5922) and from Abd Allah ibn Amr ibn al-As by Ibn al-Mubarak in *al-Zuhd* (p. 445)

Salatu-l-Fajr

The congregational morning prayer is a major pillar of the daily devotions.

While reading Sūrat Yā Sīn Mawlana Shaykh Nazim pauses to recite the words *Ṣalla-Allāhu 'alayhi wa sallam,* as "Yā Sīn" is one the names of the Prophet ﷺ.

After reciting Verse 36:58, he says, r*azaqanā Allāh* (God grant it to us!).

After reciting Verse 36:59, he says, *a'ādhanā Allāh* (God protect us!).

The pauses in the recitation of the 99 names of God are not fixed. The Shaykh frequently changes the places of these pauses in his recitations.

Salatu-l-Ishraq

One should try to stay awake until the actual rising of the sun and then perform the two *Sunnah* rak'ats of *Ishrāq* five to ten minutes after it has risen. Most scholars believe the hadiths about this prayer refer to Ṣalātu 'ḍ-Ḍuḥā, defining its earliest and preferred times.

Al-Qurtubi relates in his exegesis from Ibn Abbas ﵁ who said:

> I used to pass by the verse, "*at eventide and at break of day (ishrāq),*"[281] but I didn't know what it was until Umm Hani related to me that the Messenger of God ﷺ made supplication for ablution, then performed the ablution, and then prayed the Ḍuhā prayer. He ﷺ then said, 'O Umm Hani, this is the Ishrāq prayer.'"

About this prayer the Prophet ﷺ also said:

> *He who prays Fajr in congregation then sits and remember God until the sun rises and then prays two rak'ats its reward will be like that of Hajj and Umrah, complete and not missing anything [and he repeated it thrice]!*[282]

Salatu-d-Duha

Ṣalātu 'ḍ-Ḍuḥā consists of two sets of four rak'at sets in the time between mid-morning and Ṣalātu'ẓ-Ẓuhr. The Prophet ﷺ said:

---

[281] *Lo! We subdued the hills to hymn the praises (of their Lord) with him [David] at nightfall and sunrise.* (38:18)

[282] Imam an-Nawawi recorded it in his *Adhkar* from Anas. At-Tirmidhi narrated and said it was good.

> *In the morning, charity is due on every joint bone of the body of everyone of you. Every utterance of God's glorification (i.e., saying Subḥānallāh) is an act of charity; and every utterance of His Praise (i.e., saying Alḥamdulillāh) is an act of charity; and every utterance of the Phrase of Oneness (i.e. lā ilāha ill-Allāh) is an act of charity and every utterance of declaration of His Greatness (i.e., saying Allāhu akbar) is an act of charity; and enjoining good is an act of charity, and forbidding iniquity is an act of charity, and two rak'at Duḥā prayers which one performs in the forenoon is equal to all this (in reward).*[283]

Imam an-Nawawi in *al-Maqasid* said none of the people of *sainthood* reached high levels except by adhering firmly to the two prayers: Ṣalātu - Ḍuḥā and Ṣalātu 'l-Awwābīn.

---

[283] Narrated by Muslim.

Explanations and Procedures

In the following prayers, to keep track of any given number of recitations, it is permitted to lightly press one finger of each hand in turn, in whatever position they are (i.e., crossed or hanging at the sides). However, the *an-Najāt* and *Tasbīḥ* prayers are for the People of Determination and the Prepared; these prayers are not for beginners.

Salatu-n-Najat

The Prophet ﷺ said:

> *When it is the last third of the night, our Lord, the Blessed, the Superior, descends every night to the heaven of the world and says, "Is there anyone who invokes Me tha I may respond to his invocation; Is there anyone who asks Me for something that I may give (it to) him; Is there anyone who asks My forgiveness that I may forgive him?"*[284]

One should get up at least one hour before Fajr since it is at this time that the gate of the Mercy of God, Who is Powerful and Sublime, is opened and the time when the great shaykhs look at their murīds. One should get up and perform ablution and perform two rak'ats of *Taḥīyyatu 'l-wuḍu* and then stand up, facing the *Qiblah* and ask that God, Exalted and Glorious, to purify oneself from the anger of one's *nafs* and, with this intention, one should then recite *Yā Ḥalīm* 100 times, and then one should seek protection from one's external and internal enemies, and from both heavenly and earthly misfortune, reciting *Yā Ḥafīẓ* 100 times.

Whoever wishes to reach the station of the People of Determination must keep up these practices. Our shaykhs tell us about the importance of this time and its virtues, saying: "If a person gets up one hour before Fajr and does nothing, not even praying, not even making *tasbīḥ*, but gets up to drink something, such as coffee or tea, or eat a morsel of food, then he must also be raised with the vigilant people (*ahlu 's-sahar*)."

---

[284] Bukhari.

Ṣalātu 'n-Najāt, the Prayer of Salvation, is prayed according to the following steps:

In the first rak'at read Sūratu 'l-Fātiḥah as usual.		الفاتحة الشريفة
This is followed by reading the Verse of the Throne (2:255) and (3:18-19), and (3:26-27).		
ĀYATU 'L-KURSĪ (THE VERSE OF THE THRONE) CHAPTER 2, VERSE 255 Allāhū lā ilāha illa Hūwa 'l-Ḥayyu 'l-Qayyūm, lā tākhudhuhū 's-sinatun wa lā nawm, lahū mā fis-samāwāti wa mā fil-arḍ. Man dhā-ladhī yashfa'u 'indahū illā bi idhniḥ ya'lamu mā bayna aydīhim wa mā khalfahum wa lā yuḥīṭunā bi-shay'im min 'ilmihi illā bimā shā'. Wasi'a kursīyyuhu 's-samāwāti wa 'l-arḍa, wa lā ya'uduhū ḥifẓuhuma, wa Hūwa 'l-'Alīyyu 'l-'Aẓīm. Ṣadaq-Allāhu 'l-'Aẓīm.		آية الكُرْسي البقرة ٢ اللهُ لا إلهَ إلا هُوَ الحيُّ القيُّوم لا تأخُذُهُ سِنَةٌ ولا نَوْمٌ لَهُ ما في السماوات وما في الأرْضِ من ذا الذي يَشْفَعُ عِنْدَهُ إلا بإذْنِه يَعْلَمُ ما في بَيْنَ أيدِيهم وما خَلفَهُم ولا يُحيطونَ بِشَيْءٍ من عِلْمِه إلا بما شاء وَسِعَ كُرْسِيُّهُ السَّماواتِ والأرْضَ ولا يَؤُدُّهُ حِفْظُهُما وهُوَ العَليُّ العَظيمُ
God, there is no god but He, the Living, the Everlasting. Slumber seizes Him not, neither sleep; to Him belongs all that is in the heavens and the earth. Who is there that shall intercede with Him save by His leave? He knows what lies before them, and they comprehend not anything of His knowledge save such as He wills. His Throne comprises the heavens and the earth; the preserving of them oppresses Him not; He is the All-High, the Almighty.		
CHAPTER 3, VERSE 18-19 Shahid-Allāhu annahū lā ilāha illa Hū. Wa 'l-malā'ikatu wa ūlu 'l-'ilmi qā'iman bil-qisṭ. Lā ilāha illa Hū al-'Azīzu 'l-Ḥakīm. Inna 'd-dīna 'ind Allāhi 'l-islām.		سورة آل عمران ١٨–١٩ شَهِدَ اللهُ أَنَّهُ لا إله إلا هُوَ والمَلائكةُ وأُولُو العِلْمِ قائمًا بالقِسْطِ لا إله إلا هُوَ العَزيزُ الحَكيمُ إنَّ الدينَ عِنْدَ الله الإسْلام
God bears witness that there is no god but He—and the angels and men of		

<table>
<tr><td colspan="2">knowledge—upholding justice; there is no god but He, the All-Mighty, the All-Wise. The religion with God is Islam.</td></tr>
<tr><td>CHAPTER 3, VERSE 26-27
Qul 'illāhumma Mālik al-mulki. Tu'tī 'l-mulka man tasha'u wa tanzi'u 'l-mulka mimman tashā'u wa tu'izzu man tashā'u wa tudhillu man tashā'u, bi yadika 'l-khayr, innaka 'alā kulli shay'in qadīr. Tūliju 'l-layla fī 'n-nahāri wa tūliju nahāra fī 'l-layl, wa tukhriju 'l-ḥāyya min al-mayyiti, wa tukhriju 'l-mayyita min al-ḥāyy, wa tarzuqu man tashā'u bi ghayri ḥisāb.</td><td>سورة آل عمران ٢٦–٢٧
قل اللَّهُمَّ مالكُ المُلْك تؤْتي المُلْكَ من تشاء وتَنْزِع المُلْكَ ممَّن تشاء وتُعِزُّ من تشاء وتُذِلُّ من تشاءُ بِيَدِكَ الخَيْرُ إنَّكَ على كُلِّ شيءٍ قدير تُولِجُ اللَّيْل في النَّهارِ وتُولِجُ النهارَ في اللَّيلِ وتُخْرِجُ الحيَّ من الميِّتِ وتُخْرِجُ الميِّتَ من الحيِّ وتَرْزُقُ من تشاءُ بِغَيْرِ حساب</td></tr>
<tr><td colspan="2">Say: O God, Master of the Kingdom, Thou givest the Kingdom to whom Thou wilt, and seizest the Kingdom from whom Thou wilt, Thou exaltest whom Thou wilt, and Thou abasest whom Thou wilt; in Thy hand is the good; Thou art over all things Powerful. Thou makest the night to enter into the day, and Thou makest the day to enter into the night, Thou bringest forth the living from the dead, and Thou bringest forth the dead from the living, and Thou providest for whomsoever Thou wilt without reckoning.</td></tr>
<tr><td>In the second rak'at, read the Fātiḥ a.</td><td>تقرأ في الركعة الثانية بعد الفاتحة الشريفة</td></tr>
<tr><td>SŪRATU 'L-IKHLĀṢ (11 TIMES).</td><td>سورة الاخلاص (١١ مرات)</td></tr>
<tr><td>After completing the taslīm (final salām right and left), go into prostration with the intention of asking God to rid your heart of all envy.</td><td>بعد التسليم من الصلاة
تدعوا بهذا الدعاء:</td></tr>
<tr><td>DU'A
Yā Rabbī, kamā tākul un-nāru 'l-ḥataba hākadha yākulu 'amalīyy jamī'an al-ḥasadu mu'tasila fīyya fa khallișnī minh yā Rabbī wa khallișnī ayḍan 'an il-ghadab an-nafsānī wa 'an nafs iṭ-ṭifl il-madhmuma, wa 'an il-akhlāq idh-dhamīma wa baddil yā Rabbī akhlāqī jamī'an ila akhlāqin ḥamīdatin wa af'ālin ḥasana.</td><td>دعاء:
يا ربِّي كما تأكُلُ النارُ الحَطَبَ هَكَذا الحَسَدُ المُتَأَصِّلُ فيَّ يأكل جَميع أعْمالي. يا ربِّي خَلِّصْني منه ومنَ الغضبِ النَّفْساني ومن نَفْسِ الطِّفْلِ المَذْمُومة ومن الأَخْلاقِ الذميمة ويا ربِّي بَدِّلْ كُلَّ أخْلاقي إلى أخْلاقٍ حَميدة وأفْعالٍ حَسَنة</td></tr>
<tr><td colspan="2">O my Lord! Just as fire consumes firewood, in the same way the envy which is</td></tr>
</table>

rooted in me consumes all my actions. Purify me, O my Lord, from it and purify me, too, from the anger of my ego. Rid me as well, O my Lord, of the blameworthy ego of the child and reprehensible manners. And, O my Lord, change all my manners to laudable manners and into good actions.

Salatu-t-Tasabih

It is narrated that Ibn Abbas use to pray ṣalāt at-tasbīḥ every Jumū'ah.[285]		
These are four rak'ats prayed with a taslīm between them. This prayer can be done in two ways, but we have included only the one the Shaykh uses (with the taslīm at the end of the fourth rak'at). The tasbīḥ which is recited during this prayer is:		
Subḥānallāhi wa 'l-ḥamdulillāhi wa lā illāha ill-Allāh wallāhu akbar.		سبحان الله والحمد لله ولا إله إلا الله والله أكبر
Glory be to God! Praise be to God! There is no god but God, and God is Greatest.		
At the end of every set of 10 or 15 tasbīḥs the Shaykh adds: wa lā ḥawla wa lā quwwata illa billāhi 'l-'Alīyyi 'l-'Āẓīm.		و لا حول ولا قوة إلا بالله العليّ العظيم
There is no power and no strength save in God, All-High and Almighty.		
The total number of tasbīḥs recited is 300, with 75 in each rak'at. Also, the tasbīḥs is added to the regular parts of the prayer. We have observed the Shaykh using the following method:		

WHEN TASBIḤ IS RECITED	NUMBER OF TIMES
After reciting the Thanā', before Sūratu 'l-Fātiḥah	15
After reciting Sūratu 'l-Fātiḥah and two Sūratu 'l-Ikhlāṣ	10
In ruk'u, (bowing position)	10
In qiyām (standing position), after the ruk'u	10
In the first sajda (prostration)	10
In jalsa (sitting position), after the first sajda	10
In the second sajda	10
Sub-total for first rak'at	75
The second rak'at is performed as above (no tasbīḥs is	75

285 Abu Dawud, Bin Majah, Ibn Kuzaymah and al-Hakim narrated it. **It is in al-Iraqi's recension whom al-Aqili and others graded sound.**

recited in the final jalsa, only tashahhud)	
The third rak'at is performed as above	75
The fourth rak'at is performed as above (no tasbīḥs are recited in the final jalsa, only tashahhud)	75

Conduct of Pilgrimage - Hajj

God says:

And complete the Ḥajj or 'Umrah in the service of Allah. But if ye are prevented (From completing it), send an offering for sacrifice, such as ye may find, and do not shave your heads until the offering reaches the place of sacrifice. And if any of you is ill, or has an ailment in his scalp, (Necessitating shaving), (He should) in compensation either fast, or feed the poor, or offer sacrifice; and when ye are in peaceful conditions (again), if any one wishes to continue the 'umrah on to the Ḥajj, He must make an offering, such as he can afford, but if he cannot afford it, He should fast three days during the Ḥajj and seven days on his return, Making ten days in all. This is for those whose household is not in (the precincts of) the Sacred Mosque. And fear Allah, and know that Allah Is strict in punishment. For Ḥajj are the months well known. If any one undertakes that duty therein, Let there be no obscenity, nor wickedness, nor wrangling in the Ḥajj. And whatever good ye do, (be sure) Allah knoweth it. And take a provision (With you) for the journey, but the best of provisions is right conduct. So fear Me, o ye that are wise. (2:196-197).

And proclaim the Pilgrimage among men: they will come to thee on foot and (mounted) on every kind of camel, lean on account of journeys through deep and distant mountain highways; That they may witness the benefits (provided) for them, and celebrate the name of God, through the Days appointed, over the cattle which He has provided for them (for sacrifice): then eat ye thereof and feed the distressed ones in want. (22:27-38)

This section contains a summarized version of the Ḥajj/Umrah rites. The intent here behind this section is not to detail each aspect of the Ḥajj/'Umrah, but is to present the spiritual aspects of the niyyah and recitations at various point in the pilgrimage. However, to observe the Ḥajj correctly it is essential to follow the instructions and details that your Ḥajj guide directs you to do.

Obligations of Hajj According to the Four Schools

ḤANAFĪ	SHAFI'Ī	MĀLIKĪ	ḤANBALĪ
Iḥrām.	Iḥrām.	Iḥrām.	Iḥrām.
Spending a day at 'Arafah	Spending a day at 'Arafah.	Spending a day at 'Arafah.	Spending a day at 'Arafah.
Sa'ī between Ṣafā and Marwah.	Sa'ī between Ṣafā and Marwah.	Sa'ī between Ṣafā and Marwah.	Sa'ī between Ṣafā and Marwah.
Circumambulation. Ṭawāf al-Ifāḍah which is done at the Yawm an-Naḥr - the day of sacrifice - on returning from Minā. (Iḥrām is a prerequisite for the validity of Ṭawāf.)	Circumambulation. Ṭawāf al-Ifāḍah which involves seven rounds of the Ka'bah.	Circumambu-lation. Ṭawāf al-Ifāḍah which involves seven rounds of the Ka'bah.	Circumambu-lation. Ṭawāf al-Ifāḍah which involves seven rounds of the Ka'bah.
	Clipping some of the pilgrim's hair or shaving it all.		
	Close sequence of most rites of Ḥajj, e.g. Iḥrām must proceed all other rites and standing at 'Arafah must proceed Ṭawāf .		

Restrictions of *Ihram*

Sexual intercourse and all matters leading to it such as kissing, caresses or talking with one's spouse about intercourse or related sexual matters.
Violating the limits ordained by Allah and disobeying His orders.
Disputing, arguing or fighting with servants, companions or others.
Wearing any sewn clothes which fit the body
It is forbidden for the Muḥrim to wear clothes dyed with a scented material that lingers with him wherever he goes. He is forbidden from using perfume on body,

clothes or hair.
Abū Ḥanīfa and ath-Thawrī held that a Muḥrim may contract a marriage but he is forbidden to consummate it.
There is a consensus among the scholars that, in the state of Iḥrām, the Muḥrim is forbidden to clip his nails without any genuine excuse.
It is forbidden for a Muḥrim to cover his head with any normal headcover.
There is consensus among the scholars that hunting is forbidden to the Muḥrim even if he does not actually slaughter the animal

Summarized Steps of Hajj

On the pre-noon of the eighth Dhul-Ḥijjah enter into Iḥrām from your place and perform ghusl (total washing) if it is possible and put on the Iḥrām cloths and repeat the Talbīyah
Set out and stay at Minā to pray Ẓuhr, 'Aṣr, Maghrib, 'Isha and Fajr prayers. Every prayer comprising of four rak'ats is to be shortened to two rak'ats only.
At 'Arafah perform Ẓuhr and 'Aṣr obligatory prayers in combination for travelers; each prayer shortened to two rak'ats. Stay there until sunset and implore God frequently facing the Qiblah.
When the sun sets, march from 'Arafah to Muzdalifah. Once at Muzdalifah you should pray Maghrib, Isha and Fajr prayers. Stay there to implore God until sunrise. If you are weak and are not able to walk and mingle with the crowd, you may go to Minā at late night. However the 49 stones must be collected by you or someone on your behalf. When the sun is about to rise, walk from Muzdalifah to Minā; when you arrive at Minā, do the following:

A:	Stone Jamarat al-'Aqabah which is the Stoning Site located nearest to Makkah. You have to throw seven pebbles, one by one, pronouncing Takbīr (Allāhu Akbar!) at every throw and say:	
	raghman li 'sh-Shaytan riḍan li 'r-Raḥmān 3 times, bismillāh Allāhu akbar!	رغماً للشيطان رضاً للرحمن ٣ مرات بسم الله الله اكبر.
	In opposition to Satan, seeking God's good pleasure and satisfaction; God is greater!	
B:	Slaughter a sacrificial animal, eat from its meat and distribute the rest to the poor. The slaughtering of a sacrificial animal is obligatory on the one doing Ḥajj Tamattu' or Ḥajj Qirān (combined 'Umrah and Ḥajj).	
C:	Shave or shorten the hair of your head. Shaving is recommended (women	

should shorten their hair equal to a fingertip length). The order of the three above-mentioned acts is: first, throwing the pebbles, second, slaughtering the sacrificial animal and third to shave or shorten the hair of the head. There is no harm if the order is interchanged. After completion of the above mentioned three acts, you can put on your normal clothes and do all the acts prohibited during the Ḥajj with the exception of sexual intercourse.

Then go to Makkah with the intention to perform Ṭawāf al-Ifāḍah (Ṭawāf al-Ḥajj) and to perform Sa'ī between Ṣafā and Marwah (Sa'ī al-Ḥajj).

When you reach Makkah, do circumambulation (Ṭawāf) of the Ka'bah seven times starting from the corner of Ḥajaru 'l-Aswad (the Black Stone) and finishing by it. One then prays two rak'ats behind Maqām Ibrahīm, if possible.

After the performance of two rak'ats, go to the hillock of Ṣafā to perform Sa'ī seven times commencing from Ṣafā and ending at Marwah.

After completion of Ṭawāf and Sa'ī, go back to Minā in order to spend the two nights of 11th and 12th of Dhul-Ḥijjah. By completion of Ṭawāf al-Ifāḍah, every act prohibited for the pilgrim during the Ḥajj time now becomes lawful including sexual intercourse.

On the days of 11th and 12th of Dhul-Ḥijjah, after the sun declines, throw the pebbles at the three Stoning Sites (Jamarahs). Start with the furthest from Makkah and then the middle one and finally Jamarat al-'Aqabah. Throw seven pebbles at each Stoning Site and pronounce the Takbīr every time a stone is thrown. After throwing at the first and the middle Stoning Site, implore God facing the Qiblah; it is a must that throwing of the stones in these two days (i.e. 11th and 12th) be after zawāl (noon).

When you complete throwing the pebbles on the 12th of Dhul-Ḥijjah, you may go out of Minā before sunset. If you want to delay going out it is better to spend the night of the 13th of Dhul-Ḥijjah at Minā and repeat throwing pebbles at the three Stoning Sites after the sun reaches its noon peak (zawāl) as before.

If you want to go back home, you have to perform a Farewell Circumambulation (Ṭawāf al-Wida') (seven turns around the Ka'bah). There is no Ṭawāf al-Wida' enjoined on a woman in the post-partum state or one in her menses.

Umrah – Summary of Steps

'Umrah technically means paying a visit to Ka'bah, performing circumambulation (Ṭawāf) around it, walking between Ṣafā and Marwah seven times (Sā'ī). A performer of 'Umrah puts off his Iḥrām by having his hair shaved or cut.

If you want to perform 'Umrah, make the intention (niyyah) for 'Umrah, first perform ghusl (shower). Next put on the Iḥrām clothes. Pray two rakats Sunnatu 'l-Iḥrām. Then pronounce the Talbīyah.

When you reach Makkah, do circumambulation (Ṭawāf) of the Ka'bah seven times for

'Umrah starting from the corner of Ḥajar al-Aswad (the Black Stone) and finishing by it. One then prays two rak'ats behind Maqām Ibrahīm, if possible.

After the performance of two rak'ats, go to the hillock of Ṣafā to perform Sa'ī seven times commencing from Ṣafā and ending at Marwah.

After completion of Sa'ī you may shorten your hair. By this, your 'Umrah is complete and you may disengage from Iḥrām clothes and put on normal clothes.

Hajj and *Umrah* - Detailed Steps

Here we present details of some but not all aspects of the rites of Ḥajj and 'Umrah for which the shaykhs of the Naqshbandi Way have given particular recitations and or methodologies, to be observed in addition to all the normal steps performed by the pilgrim in following his or her particular madhhab and the guide assigned to his or her group.

PREPARATION FOR ḤAJJ

Imam Nawawī said according to the consensus of scholars it is from the adab of Ḥajj, that the essential intention of Ḥajj is to repent. Such repentance has the following conditions:

1. to leave all manner of sins;
2. to never return to these sins;
3. to regret the sins you have committed;
4. to ask forgiveness of anyone you have harmed, upset or made angry. If you owe someone money but you are unable pay them back at the time, you should inform them of your intention to make Ḥajj and give them a faithful promise to repay them in the future.
5. to write a will, since one does not knows if he will return from Ḥajj alive;
6. to use only money from licit means (ḥalāl) to go for Ḥajj, as God said:

> *O ye who believe! Give of the good things which ye have (honourably) earned, and of the fruits of the earth which We have produced for you, and do not even aim at getting anything which is bad, in order that out of it ye may give away something, when ye yourselves would not receive it except with closed eyes.* (2:267)

Abu Hurayra reported God's Messenger as saying:

> *O people, God is Good and He therefore, accepts only that which is good. And God commanded the believers as He commanded the Messengers by saying: "O Messengers, eat of the good things, and do good deeds; verily I am aware of what you do." (23:51). And He said, "O those who believe, eat of the good things that We gave you." (2:172)*

> *He then made a mention of a person who travels far and wide, his hair dishevelled and covered with dust. He lifts his hand towards the sky (to makes supplication), "O Lord, O Lord," whereas his diet is unlawful, his drink is unlawful, and his clothes are unlawful and his nourishment is unlawful. How then can his supplication be accepted?*

The meaning of this is that when going for Ḥajj, you must only use only licit means and leave all that is forbidden and repent from it, as God ordered: *"O ye who believe! Turn to God with sincere repentance."* (66: 8).

The pilgrim visits his family, neighbors and friends, informs them he is leaving and asks them to pray for him.

One states the intention to go for Ḥajj before the 8th of Dhul-Ḥijjah, or before arriving at the location (al-mīqāt) for dressing in the Iḥrām, whichever comes first. Intention should normally be made before starting one's trip, or at least one hour by plane from arrival at Jeddah. If coming by land from outside the Ḥijāz, it is recommended to make intention before setting out.

Before you enter into travel, take a shower and pray two rak'ats niyyatu 'l-Ḥajj, according to the Prophet ﷺ who said, "The best that a servant can put behind him when he travels to take care of his family, are two rak'ats that he prays before he sets forth on his travel; they which will be like his deputy during his absence [calipha]."[286]

If more than two are travelling together should choose one among them as a leader, according to the hadith:

> *If three are travelling let them choose one as leader.*[287]

Make intention to undertake a great deal of supplication (du'a) and to give generously in the way of God for the poor, for the Prophet ﷺ said:

> *Spending (on others) in Ḥajj is like giving in the way of God: one dirham is rewarded seven hundred-fold."*[288]

Ihram

Types of Iḥrām

For men, Iḥrām consists of two pieces of white, un-sewn and plain cloth; for women no special form of dress is required.

There are three types of Iḥrām:

---

[286] Ibn Abi Shaybah from Miqdad (*mursal*).

[287] Ibn Majah from Abu Hurayra.

[288] Narrated by Ahmad from Ibn Burayda.

1. Ifrād (single) One intends only the Ḥajj and maintains Iḥrām up to the Day of Sacrifice. No offering is required from the mufrid.
2. Qirān (combined) One intends the Ḥajj and 'Umrah combined. 'Umrah is done and Ḥajj is followed immediately in the same Iḥrām. Only after pelting the Jamrah of al-'Aqabah, and shaving the hair for men or trimming the hair (men and women) can the pilgrim take off Iḥrām. The condition is to slaughter an animal, or if one is unable, to fast three days during Ḥajj and seven upon returning home.
3. Tamattu' (interrupted) One intends 'Umrah and Ḥajj separately. One performs 'Umrah in Iḥrām, then return to a normal state and dress and remains like that until the Yawm al-tarwīyya, which is the 8th of Dhul-Ḥijjah, when he again dresses in Iḥrām from the mīqāt with the intention of Ḥajj and performs the Ḥajj. After fulfilling the Ḥajj rituals, one should offer a sacrificial animal.

INTENTION

Correct intention is crucial when putting on Iḥrām for Ḥajj or 'Umrah. The intention is made based on the type of Ḥajj/'Umrah being performed.

1. Ḥajj Ifrād One says: Allāhuma innī nawaytu al-Ḥajja, fa-yassirhu lī wa taqabalhu minnī.		نية الحج: اللهم إني نَوَيتُ الحج فيسره لي وتقبله مني
O God I intend to make the pilgrimage so make it easy for me and accept it from me.		
2. 'Umrah For 'Umrah alone one says: Allāhuma innī nawaytu al-'Umrata, fa-yassirhā lī wa taqabalhā minnī.		نية العمرة: اللهم إني نويتُ العمرة فيسرها لي وتقبلها مني
O God I intend to make the lesser pilgrimage so make it easy for me and accept it from me.		
3. Qirān For Ḥajj and 'Umrah combined one says: Allāhuma innī nawaytu al-'umrata wal-Ḥajja, fa-yassirhumā lī wa taqabalhumā minnī.		نية الحج والعمرة: اللهم إني نويتُ الحج والعمرة فيسرهما لي وتقبلهما مني

O God I intend to make both the lesser pilgrimage and the greater pilgrimage so make them both easy for me and accept them both from me.

One then says: Nawaytu 'l-arbā'īn, nawaytu 'l-'itikāf, nawaytu 'l-khalwah, nawaytu 'l-'uzlah, nawaytu 'r-riyāda, nawaytu 's-sulūk, lillāhi ta'alā al-'Adhīm.	نَويتُ الأربعين، نويتُ الاعتكاف نويتُ الخلوة نَوَيتُ العُزْلة، نَويتُ الرياضة نويتُ السُلوك، لله تعالى

For the sake of blessing (barakah) I intend the forty (days of seclusion); I intend isolation; I intend discipline (of the ego); I intend to travel in God's Path; for the sake of God, the Exalted.

I am intending to perform Ḥajj on behalf of myself and my family and on behalf of the entire Nation of the Prophet ﷺ. If God with His Favor, honors me by accepting my Ḥajj, I gift the rewards of this worship (faḍīlat), to the Prophet ﷺ, to all 124,000 prophets and messengers, to the Sahabah, to the saints, to Imam Mahdi and to my Shaykh. I am sharing all the rewards that He is granting me in His Mercy with the entire Nation of the Prophet ﷺ, without leaving one person behind.

TALBĪYAH Recite three times: Labaik allāhumma labaik, labaika lā sharīka laka labaik. Then: Inna al-ḥamda w'an-ni'mata laka wal-mulk, lā sharīka laka labaik.	التلبية لبيك اللهم لبيك لبيك لا شريك لك لبيك، إن الحمد والنعمة لك والملك لا شريك لك

At Your service O my God, at your service. At Your service, there is no partner to You, at Your service. Verily all praise, and all bounty belongs to You, as does the Kingdom. There is no partner to You, at Your service.

Then sit and recite the Naqshbandi Adab up to the first Ihdā. (see page 165)

ABANDONING ANGER AND SMOKING

Then from that time onwards, do not speak unnecessarily. Two things must be avoided at all costs during Ḥajj: anger and smoking. Anger must be abandoned completely. Know that that there will be a lot of testing to see if you have truly eliminated anger. Know that God, His Angels, the Prophet ﷺ and the inheritors of the Prophet ﷺ the awliya and the Abdāl are observing you. Even on the last moment of your pilgrimage, you might face a disliked situation that incites your anger, so you must be careful. If your anger emerges; if you complain or fight, your Ḥajj will be

<table>
<tr><td colspan="2">brought to nought, so beware of anger.</td></tr>
<tr><td colspan="2">Anger in Ḥajj is utterly unacceptable. If you sense that you are likely to get angry, do not go for Ḥajj, but rather work to eliminate this bad characteristic from yourself.</td></tr>
<tr><td colspan="2">Avoid smoking.</td></tr>
<tr><td>CONDUCT OF TRAVEL
As soon as you enter the vehicle of travel recite:
100x Bismillāhi 'r-Raḥmāni 'r-Raḥīm. Dhālika taqdīru 'l-'Azīzi 'l-'Alīm (36:38)</td><td>ادب السفر
(١٠٠ مرة) بِسْمِ اللهِ الرَّحْمنِ الرَّحِيمِ. ذَلِكَ تَقْدِيرُ الْعَزِيزِ الْعَلِيمِ</td></tr>
<tr><td colspan="2">In the name of God the Beneficent, the Merciful. That is the decree of (Him), the Exalted in Might, the All-Knowing.</td></tr>
<tr><td colspan="2">From that time on, occupy the time on your journey with whatever comes to your heart of dhikr, praise of the Prophet ﷺ, reading Quran, reading Dalā'il al-Khayrāt or making any kind of glorification (tasbīḥ) until you reach your destination.
When one approaches Madīnah (if flying, this is about an hour and a half before arriving at Jeddah), you pay respect towards the Prophet ﷺ by praising and seeking his intercession to accept you to be from his Ummah, and to facilitate your Ḥajj and your Visitation (ziyārah) to him. Then call upon the Men of God (rijālullāh) of Makkah and Madīnah to support you in that intention, as mentioned in the hadith that the Prophet said:
If one of you loses something or seeks help or a helper (ghawth), and he is in a land where there is no-one to befriend, let him say: "O servants of God, help me! (yā 'ibād Allāh, aghithūnī), for verily God has servants whom he does not see.[289]</td></tr>
<tr><td colspan="2">Praise the Prophet ﷺ excessively one hour before landing, five hundred or one thousand times continuously until you reach your first entry point or destination in Ḥijāz.</td></tr>
<tr><td colspan="2">When you reach the entry point (the airport at Jeddah or the border, if coming by land), you will go through some formalities after which your guide will take you to either Makkah or Madīnah depending on your date of arrival.</td></tr>
<tr><td colspan="2">CONDUCT OF ARRIVAL IN MAKKAH</td></tr>
<tr><td colspan="2">When you arrive in Makkah, proceed directly to the accommodations assigned to</td></tr>
</table>

[289] Abu Yala, Ibn al-Sani, and Tabarani in *al-Mujam al-kabir*. Al-Haythami said in *Majma al-zawaid* (10:132): "The men in its chain of transmission have been declared reliable despite weakness in one of them."

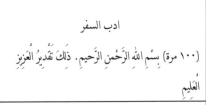

you, whether it be a hotel room, a room in a house or any other form of lodging. Do not fight with other members of your Ḥajj group by demanding special treatment or accommodations, but rather go directly to whatever accommodations have been assigned to you or is available.

If you are tired rest. Then shower (ghusl), pray two rak'ats, then proceed to Masjid al-Ḥarām for making 'Umrah, if you are doing Ḥajj tamattu'. Intend to make your 'Umrah immediately after you enter Masjid al-Ḥarām.

Before entering the Sanctuary (ḥaram), recite a greeting for the Ka'bah:

GREETING KA'BAH	تحية الكعبة
Allāhumma anta 's-Salām wa minka 's-salām wa ilayka yā'ūdu 's-salām, fa ḥayyinā Rabbanā bi 's-salām, wa adkhilnā 'l-Jannata bi luṭfika wa karamika wa jūdika dāraka, dār as-salām. Tabārakta Rabbanā wa tā'alayta, yā Dhal-Jalāli wa 'l-Jamāli wal-Baqā'i wa 'l-'Aẓamati wa 'l-Ikrām. Kulluna laka 'abdun. Wa aḥaqqu mā yaqūl al-'abd Allāhumma lā māni'a limā āa'ṭayta, wa lā mu'ṭiya limā man'ata wa lā rādda limā qaḍayta, wa lā yanfa'u dhāl-jaddi minka al-jaddu. Rabbī lā ḥawla wa lā quwwata illa billāhi 'l-'Alīyyi 'l-'Aẓīm.	اللهم أنت السلام ومنك السلام وإليك يعود السلام فحينا ربنا بالسلام وادخلنا الجنة بلطفك وكرمك وجودك دارك دار السلام. تباركت ربنا وتعاليت يا ذا الجلال والجمال والبقاء والعظمة الإكرام. كلنا لك عبد, واحق ما يقول العبد اللَّهُمَّ لا مانع لما أعطيتَ ولا مُعْطي لما مَنَعْتَ ولا رادَّ لما قَضيتَ ولا يَنْفَعُ ذا الجدّ منك الجَدُّ رَبّي لا حَوْلَ ولا قُوَّةَ إلا بالله العَليّ العَظيم.

O God! You are Peace and from You comes Peace. Blessed and lofty are You, O Lord of Majesty and Bounty. There is no god but God, He is One, no partner has He. His is the Kingdom and His is all praise, and He is over all things Powerful. We have heard and obeyed. Your forgiveness, O our Lord! And to Thee is the end of all journeys. All of us are servants to You, and the most true of what a servant may say is: O God! No one can disallow the one to whom You are giving, and there is no giver, to the one whom You have denied. And there is no refusing Your decree. Riches and good fortune will not profit the possessor thereof with You (for nothing will profit him but acting in obedience to You). My Lord, there is no power and no strength save in God, All-High and Almighty.

That is greeting for Makkah and the Ka'bah. You ask the spiritual servants of God, His angels and the inheritors of the Prophet ﷺ to direct you as you perform your ¤ajj/

'Umrah. When you enter, it is recommended to enter from the Bāb us-salām – the Gate of Peace. Bāb us-salām is below where adhān is called, as you enter the Ḥaram, there is a line of sight direct to the Ka'bah where you recite greetings to the Ka'bah, raising your two hands towards the Ḥajar al-Aswad or if it is possible to approach it without scuffling, one should do so and kiss it, otherwise raise both hands towards it and say:		
Face the Ḥajar al-Aswad and say: Bismillāh Allāhu Akbar (3 times) As-salāmu 'alayki yā Ka'batallāh		بسم الله الله اكبر (٣ مرات) السلام عليك يا كعبة الله
Peace be upon you, O Ka'bah of God.		
As-salāmu 'alayka yā Baytallāh		السلام عليك يا بيت الله
Peace be upon you, O House of God.		
If God wants, you will hear the Ka'bah return the greeting to you, as many saints hear. If you have not yet reached that level, the Ka'bah will return your greeting but you will not hear anything.		
Tawaf al-Qudum		
Before 'Umrah or Ḥajj, the Ṭawāf al-qudūm is required (wājib). First make intention, depending on whether doing Ḥajj or 'Umrah:		
Intention (Ḥajj) Nawaitu Ṭawāf al qudūm.		نَوَيتُ طوف القدوم
I intend the preliminary circumambulation.		
Intention ('Umrah) Nawaitu Ṭawāf al 'umrāh.		نَوَيتُ طواف العمرة
I intend the circumambulation of the lesser pilgrimage.		
Raise hands towards the Black Stone and say: Bismillāh, Allāhu Akbar three times.		بسم الله الله أكبر (٣ مرات)
During circumambulation talbīyah is not done, until after complete sā'ī.		
When in front of the door of the Ka'bah say: Allāhumma innal bayta baytuk, wal-ḥaramu ḥaramuk, wal-amnu amnuk wa hadhā maqāmu 'l-'ā'idha bika min an-nār.		امام باب الكعبة: اللهم إنّ البيت بيتك والحرم حرمك والأمن أمنك وهذا مقام العائذ بك من النار

O God, this house is Thy house, this sacred territory is Thy sacred territory, this security is Thy security, and this is the place for one who seeks protection with Thee against the hell fire.

(ii) At the corner of the second wall by the opening of the ḥijr (semi-circular wall): Allāhumma innī ʻaūdhu bika min ash-shakki wa 'sh-shirki wa 'sh-shiqāqi wa 'n-nifāqi wa sū 'il-akhlāqi wa sū 'il-munqalabi fil āhli wal-māli wal-walad.	(ب) امام باقي الجدار من باب الكعبة: اللهم أعوذ بك من الشك والشرك والشقاق والنفاق وسوء الأخلاق وسوء المنقلب في الأهل والمال والولد .

O God I take refuge in You from doubt, from ascribing partners to You, from discord, hypocrisy, evil traits, and bad turns of fortune in family, property and children.

(iii) While passing the second wall, in front of the drainspout of Mercy (mīzāb ar-raḥmah): Allāhumma aẓillanī fee ẓillika yauma lā ẓilla illā ẓilla ʻarshik. Wasqinī bi-kā'si sayyidinā Muḥammadin sallallāhu ʻalaihi wa sallam, sharbatan hanī'atan ma-rī'atan lā azmā'u bʻadahā abadan yā dhal jalāli wal-ikrām.	(ج) عند الجدار الثاني: اللهم أظلني في ظلك يوم لا ظل إلا ظل عرشك واسقني بكأس سيدنا محمد صلى الله عليه وسلم شربة هنيئة مريئة لا أظمأ بعدها أبدا، يا ذا الجلال والإكرام.

O God, put me under Thy shadow on the day when there will be no shadow except the shadow of Thy Throne and give me to drink from the cup of our master Muhammad a delicious and sating drink after which I shall never get thirsty, O Thou full of Majesty and Bounty.

(iv) When crossing the third wall between the third corner and the Yamānī corner (and according to whether it is during the Ḥajj or the ʻUmrah): Allāhum ʻajʻalhu Ḥajjan mabrūrā/ (ajʻalhā ʻumratam-mabrūra) wa dhanban maghfūran wa sāʻīyan mashkūrān wa tijāratan lan tabūra yā ʻAzīzu yā Ghafūr.	(د) عند الجدار الثالث حسب الحج او العمرة: اللهم اجعله حجا مبرورا (أو عمرة مبرورة) وذنبا مغفورا وسعيا مشكورا وتجارة لن تبور يا عزيز يا غفور

O God, make that this be a Ḥajj/ʻUmrah which is accepted, with (my) sin which is pardoned, an accepted work, a commerce which is not lost, O Thou the Powerful, the Forgiving.

When one reaches the Yamānī corner do not kiss it, but touch it if possible and then

<table>
<tr><td colspan="3">kiss one's hand.</td></tr>
<tr><td>(v) While crossing the fourth wall:
Rabbanā ātinā fid-dunyā ḥasanatan wa fī 'l-ākhirati ḥasanatan wa qinā 'adhāb an-nār.</td><td></td><td>(هـ) عند الجدار الرابع:
ربنا آتنا في الدنيا حسنة وفي الآخرة حسنة وقنا عذاب النار.</td></tr>
<tr><td colspan="3">O our Lord, give us good in this world and good in the Hereafter, and protect us from the punishment of the hell fire.</td></tr>
<tr><td colspan="3">Once one reaches the Black Stone a single round (ṭawāf) has been completed. It is Sunnah for men to trot in the first three rounds and to bare their right shoulders, except in the Farewell Ṭawāf. However if this means leaving any women without menfolk to accompany, this should not be done, or some men should remain with the women.</td></tr>
<tr><td colspan="3">After completing the circumambulation until you finish seven turns (ṭawāf), reciting what you are able of the above invocations then you go to Bāb al-Multazam and make du'a there. If it is difficult due to crowds, do not fight, but step back and go to Maqām Ibrāhīm and from far away make the invocation. Then pray two raka'at at Maqām Ibrāhīm. It is often not possible for ladies to pray there, so they should pray two raka'ats in the ladies section.</td></tr>
<tr><td colspan="3">Sai</td></tr>
<tr><td colspan="3">Then you go to do Sa'ī. At this portion of 'Umrah/Ḥajj one should keep in mind the struggle of Lady Hajar, searching desperately for water for her baby, the Prophet Isma'īl.</td></tr>
<tr><td>CONDUCT OF SA'Ī</td><td></td><td>ادب السعي</td></tr>
<tr><td>Begin saying:
Bismillāhi 'r-Raḥmāni 'r-Raḥīm
In the name of God the Beneficent, the Merciful.</td><td></td><td>بِسْمِ اللهِ الرَّحْمنِ الرَّحِيمِ</td></tr>
<tr><td colspan="3">Then invoke God (du'a):
Ya Rabbī, Ya Allāh, I am making Sa'ī I am seeking the means of support through the Prophet ﷺ and the inheritors of his spiritual states, the saints. O God, if You favor me by accepting my 'Umrah/Ḥajj, all the rewards that I receive I will share with all your servants on this earth.</td></tr>
<tr><td colspan="3">After completing Sa'ī, present your 'Umrah, or Ḥajj to the Presence of the Prophet ﷺ, by saying, "Ya Rasulullāh, I performed that 'Umrah/Ḥajj by trying to follow your</td></tr>
</table>

footsteps, I am requesting that it be accepted and be changed from imitational to real worship and that you O Prophet of God, present it to the Presence of God."

You then ask from God whatever you want for this life and the hereafter.

You return to your lodging if you are making 'Umrah.

In the case of Ḥajj at-Tamattu', after completing the 'Umrah, the pilgrim trims his or her hair, showers, and changes into everyday clothes.

These steps complete the 'Umrah portion of the Ḥajj at-Tamattu'. All restrictions of the Iḥrām are temporarily lifted. The pilgrim waits until the 8th of Dhul-Ḥijjah to start the rites of Ḥajj and return to Iḥrām.

INTENTION AND IḤRĀM FOR ḤAJJ TAMATTU'

If doing Ḥajj at-Tamattu', on the 8th of Dhul-Ḥijjah, the pilgrim pronounces a new intention (nīyyah) at the place to perform Ḥajj. There is no need to go to the mīqāt for this. The pilgrim changes into Iḥrām in the prescribed manner and proceeds to Minā soon after the Fajr Prayers.

Then perform the rites of Ḥajj, by going to 'Arafah, Minā and Muzdalifa and Minā and observing all the details following one's Ḥajj guide.

Standing at Arafah

> *It is no crime in you if ye seek of the bounty of your Lord (during pilgrimage). Then when ye pour down from (Mount) Arafah, celebrate the praises of God at the Sacred Monument, and celebrate His praises as He has directed you, even though, before this, ye went astray.* (2:198).

There is consensus among Muslim scholars that spending the Day of 'Arafah is the most important part of Ḥajj.

'Abd ar-Raḥmān bin Ya'mur reported:

> *The Prophet ﷺ ordered an announcer to proclaim, "Ḥajj is 'Arafah...."*

Standing as much as possible is very much recommended, especially around the plains of Jabal ar-Raḥmah (Mount of Mercy) where the Prophet ﷺ delivered his last sermon.

In another hadith, Jābir reported that the Prophet ﷺ said:

> *....And there is no day better in the sight of Allah than the Day of 'Arafah. On this day Allah, the Almighty and the Exalted, descends to the nearest heaven, and He is proud of His slaves on the earth, and says to those in Heaven, "Look at My servants. They have come from far and near, with hair dishevelled and faces covered with dust, to seek My*

mercy, even though they have not seen My chastisement." Far more people are freed from the Hell-fire on the Day of 'Arafah than on any other day.

On that day the pilgrims should spend most of their time reading the Qur'an, making remembrance of God (dhikr), supplication (du'a), praising the Prophet (ṣalawāt) ﷺ, and most importantly asking Allah for forgiveness.

Stoning the *Jamarat*

One pelts the Stoning Sites on the four days of Eid. On the first day you throw seven stones at the Jamarat al-'Aqabah only. On the remaining three days you must throw 21 stones altogether each day, seven at each Jamarah, one-by-one pronouncing the formula below. Some people take the stones and throw them altogether - this is not accepted. Similarly, it is unacceptable to use your slippers or other objects to stone the sites.

Ladies can appoint someone to throw stones for them if the Stoning Sites are very crowded.

CONDUCT OF STONING Take one pebble at a time and with each one say: Raghman li 'sh-shaiṭān, riḍan li 'r-Rahman, 3 times, Bismillāh, Allāhu Akbar. And then throw it at the Jamarah.		ادب الرجم رغماً للشيطان رضاً للرحمن ٣ مرات, بسم الله, الله اكبر.

In opposition to Satan, seeking God's good pleasure and satisfaction; In opposition to Satan, seeking God's good pleasure and satisfaction; God is greater!

Stay at Mina

During one's stay at Minā, the pilgrim should engage in much remembrance (dhikr, tasbiīḥ), praise of the Prophet ﷺ (ṣalawāt), recitation of Qur'an, invocation (du'a) and supererogatory prayers, for God said:

Then pass on at a quick pace from the place whence it is usual for the multitude so to do, and ask for Allah's forgiveness. For Allah is Oft-forgiving, Most Merciful. So when ye have accomplished your holy rites, celebrate the praises of Allah, as ye used to celebrate the praises of your fathers,- yea, with far more Heart and soul. (2:199-200)

And:

Celebrate the praises of Allah during the Appointed Days. But if any one hastens to leave in two days, there is no blame on him, and if any one stays on, there is no blame on him, if his aim is to do right. Then fear Allah, and know that ye will surely be gathered unto Him. (2:203)

And:

O you who believe! Remember Allah with much remembrance. And glorify His praises morning and evening. (33:41-42).

ṬAWĀF AL-WADA'

This is the Ṭawāf of farewell, which is unrelated to either the 'Umrah or Ḥajj. One makes this before leaving with the intention not to return.

This concludes the essential conduct of Ḥajj. Keep in mind this contains only a summarized version of the Ḥajj rites. The main intent here is to present the spiritual aspects of the intention and recitations at various point in the pilgrimage. However, to observe the Ḥajj correctly it is essential to follow the instructions and details that your Ḥajj guide directs you to do.

Zamzam

It is recommended to do much of drinking the water of the well of Zamzam for whatever intention one wishes, religious or other-worldly, as the Prophet ﷺ said, *"The water of Zamzam is for whatever it is drunk for."*[290]

It is Sunnah to face the Ka'bah standing while drinking, to breathe three times and say, "Bismillāh" each time one drinks and "alḥamdulillāh," drinking one's fill of it. People often take bottles of Zamzam water home from pilgrimage to share as a blessing (barakah) with family and friends. The same adab is observed when drinking it.

The Prophet ﷺ is reported to have said that the Earthly Ka'bah is the diametrically opposite of the mosque of the angels underneath the Throne of God, (and so exactly so that if one were to throw a stone from there, it would fall on the top of the Ka'bah on earth).[291] The scholar Ibn Kathīr reports that there is a particular Ka'bah at each of the seven heavens, each for the use of the inhabitants of that heaven.[292] He adds the name of the Ka'bah at the seventh heaven is Bait al-Ma'mūr, the Celebrated House, and that the earthly Ka'bah is at exactly the point below this heavenly Ka'bah.[293]

---

[290] Keller, *Reliance of the Traveler*, j11.6 (3), p. 349.

[291] *Bukhari*.

[292] Ibn Kathir, *Al-Bidayah wa al-nihayah*, 1, 163.

[293] Ibn Kathir, *Tafsir*, on surah 52, verse 4.

The Bait al-Ma'mūr was originally in the place where the Ka'bah stands today, sent down from Paradise by God, and built as the first house by Adam with the help of angels.[294] God ordered Adam to circumambulate it, as the angels turn about the Throne of the Merciful. At the time of Noah's flood, the House was raised up to the heavens, and the Prophet ﷺ saw the angels circumambulating it when he was taken to the heavens on the Night of Ascension.[295]

The Prophet Abraham was ordered by God to rebuild the Ka'bah with the help of his son, Prophet Ismail, and the archangel Gabriel brought out the only remaining stone from the original Ka'bah, the Black Stone, which had been ensconced within Mount Abu Qubais above Makkah since the time of the flood.[296]

It is recommended to look at the Ka'bah, for it is the locus of the Divine Gaze, and it is said that God sends down one hundred and twenty mercies day and night upon the House of God: sixty for those circumambulating; forty for those praying there and twenty for those looking at it.[297]

Significance of the Black Stone

The Black Stone - Ḥajaru 'l-Aswad - was sent down from heaven and the angels put it in the Ka'bah in the time of Adam, before he made the first circumambulation.[298] On the Day of Judgement it will bear witness for all those who have performed Ḥajj or 'Umrah.

When you say Allāhu Akbar 3x, each time you make Ṭawāf, remember that the maqām of the Black Stone (Ḥajaru 'l-aswad) is a sacred place. That stone has life and it greets those visiting it, so greet it with full reverence. For that reason the Prophet ﷺ kissed the Black Stone.

It is reported that when 'Umar ibn al-Khaṭṭāb ؓ performed pilgrimage and embraced the (Black) Stone, he said, "I know by God that you are a stone which neither harms nor benefits, and had I not seen God's Messenger embrace you, I would not have embraced you."

However, 'Alī ibn Abī Ṭālib ؓ said to him, "Abū Hafs, do not say this, for God's Messenger ﷺ did not embrace it (the Black Stone) save for wisdom he knew: It has

---

294 Al-Kisai, Muhammad ibn Abdullah, *Qisas al-anbiya: Tales of the Prophets* (Kazi, 1997) p. 62.

295 Adil, Hajjah Amina, *Lore of Light*, volume 1, p. 167.

296 Adil, Hajjah Amina, *Lore of Light*, volume 1, p. 22, 23.

297 Keller, *Reliance of the Traveler*, j11.6 (2), p. 349.

298 Adil, Hajjah Amina, *Lore of Light*, volume 1, p. 22.

two eyes and two lips and possesses a keen tongue that testifies for those who fulfill their obligations to it."[299]

An authentic narration states that the Black Stone shall appear with two eyes and a tongue on the Day of Resurrection.[300]

Significance of *Sai*

The story is related in Qiṣas al-Anbīyā that Prophet Abraham ﷺ took Lady Hagar (Hājar) and the baby Ishmael to the Sacred valley at Bakkah (now Makkah), near the Ka'bah of Adam ﷺ, which had been destroyed by the Flood of Noah ﷺ. Prophet Abraham told Lady Hagar, "Remain here with my child, for thus I have been commanded." "Upon whom shall I rely?" asked Lady Hagar. "Upon your Lord," answered Prophet Abraham, who then turned to the right and the left, but seeing no one called upon God:

> *O our Lord! I have made some of my offspring to dwell in a valley without cultivation, by Thy Sacred House; in order, O our Lord, that they may establish regular Prayer: so fill the hearts of some among men with love towards them, and feed them with fruits: so that they may give thanks.* (14:37)

When the heat became unbearable, Lady Hagar saw a tree where the Well of Zamzam was destined to be, over which she suspended a robe to shade them from the heat of the sun. as they had finished the water in the jug they had with them and were thirsty, Hagar did not know what to do. First she ran in the direction of the hillock Ṣafā in search of water, and then towards the hillock Marwāh, crying, "Our God, do not destroy us by thirst!"

Then [archangel] Gabriel ﷺ descended to them bearing tidings of relief, whereupon she went to Ishmael, who was scratching the earth with his finger; there the well of Zamzam sprang up, and she fell down prostrate in thanks to God. Lady Hagar said, "It is abundant water [Zamzam in her language]," from which the well took its name. Then she gathered stones around the spring lest it the water flow away. Prophet Muhammad ﷺ explained that had she not done that, the water would have flowed across the face of the earth from east to west.

Later a caravan approached from Yemen headed for Syria. When they saw birds

---

[299] Reported by Imam Ghazali, *Ihya ulum ad-din*, and, Hajjah Amina Adil, *Lore of Light*, volume 1, p.24, with additional wording.

[300] Narrated by Tirmidhi, Ibn Majah, Ahmad, al-Darimi, Ibn Hibban (#3711-3712), and others.

hovering above Lady Hagar and the child, they were perplexed and said, "Birds hover only over water and inhabited places." Drawing near, they found Hagar and baby Isma'īl beside a well of sweet water. After some discussion, Lady Hagar gave them permission to draw water and they came with their flocks and people and settled there, and eventually Isma'īl married a noble woman from their tribe. Lady Hagar died and it is said she was buried by the Ka'bah, in the semi-circular area known as Hijr - Isma'īl, where the Prophet Ishmael ﷺ was later buried as well.[301]

In one narration Lady Hagar, when she was running in search of water between Ṣafā and Marwāh, heard a voice and called out: "O you whose voice you have made me hear! If there is a ghawth (help/helper) with you (then help me)!" and an angel appeared at the spot of the spring of Zamzam."[302]

DAILY ṬAWĀF

When you enter the Sacred Mosque, it is preferred to make a Ṭawāf as it is the greeting for the Ka'bah (Taḥīyyatul Ka'bah). Use the same steps mentioned above, leaving out the wording "al-qudūm" from the intention. If it is not possible to do the Ṭawāf, pray first, and when it is less crowded make Ṭawāf if you are able.

When you leave the Sacred Mosque, it is not necessary to make Ṭawāf.

SHOPPING AND DAILY ACTIVITY

During pilgrimage it is permitted to shop, but one should not spend excessive time doing so. Similarly, excessive time should not be spent in restaurants and coffee shops. Rather, keep oneself busy in praying, remembrance (dhikr) and praise of the Prophet (ṣalawāt) ﷺ.

Holy Places of Visitation in Makkah

JANNAT AL-MU'ALLA

Also known as al-Ḥājūn, this is a general cemetery in existence from before the time of the Prophet ﷺ and in which his first wife, the Mother of the Believers (Umm al-mu'minīn) Sayyida Khadījat al-Kubrā ؓ is buried. Buried there too are many member of the Family of the Prophet ﷺ, his Companions, Successors, Successors of the Successors, saints and scholars. The Prophet ﷺ used to visit it frequently. It is the second holiest graveyard after al-Baqi' in Madīnah.

Those buried here include:

[301] Al-Kisai, Muhammad ibn Abdullah, *Qisas al-anbiya: Tales of the Prophets*, (Kazi, 1997) p. 152.

[302] *Bukhari.*

Grave of 'Abd Manāf: Great, great-grandfather of the Holy Prophet ﷺ

Grave of Hāshim: Great-grandfather of the Holy Prophet ﷺ

Grave of 'Abd al-Muṭṭalib: Grandfather of the Holy Prophet ﷺ, who raised him in his early childhood.

Grave of Sayyidah Āmina bint Wahb: Mother of the Holy Prophet ﷺ who died when he was only 5 years old. According to another source, Sayyidah Āmina is buried in Abwā (between Makkah and Madīna)

Grave of Sayyidinā 'Abd Allāh ibn 'Abd al-Muṭṭalib: The blessed father of our Holy Prophet ﷺ, who died and was buried in Madīna. Later his body was disinterred and found to be intact. It was transferred to Makkah and buried in Jannat al-Mu'alla.

Grave of Abū Ṭālib: The uncle of the Prophet ﷺ who raised him after the passing of his grandfather 'Abd al-Muṭṭalib. He was father of 'Alī ibn Abī Ṭālib, Ja'far and 'Aqīl.

Grave of Khadīja: First wife of the Holy Prophet ﷺ and mother of his daughters.

Grave of Qāsim: son of the Holy Prophet ﷺ who died in his infancy.

MASJID AL-JINN

A group of Jinn were passing by, when they heard the Prophet ﷺ reciting the Holy Quran. They were so moved that they came to the Prophet ﷺ, repented and accepted Islam. A masjid was later built at the location and named Masjid al-Jinn.

CAVE OF THAWR

During the Hijrah the Prophet ﷺ stayed here for three days during the Migration from Makkah. The miraculous incident took place here, in which a spider spun a web and a pigeon laid eggs at the mouth of this cave causing the trackers sparing the Prophet ﷺ and his companion Abū Bakr aṣ-Ṣiddīq from being found and harmed by the pursuing Makkans.

CAVE OF HIRĀ

The cave in which the Prophet ﷺ used to seclude himself before the first revelation, and in which the first revelation, the Surah "The Clot" was revealed to him by the archangel Gabriel.

MOUNT OF MERCY (JABAL RAḤMAH)

This is a mountain in the plain of 'Arafah. It is highly recommended to pray two rak'at Prayer of Need (ḥājah) here.

MUZDALIFAH Pilgrims on Ḥajj are required to spend the night here. It is here they collect 70 pebbles for lapidating the pillars representing Satan in Minā.
MINĀ This is a city that comes to existence for three days during the year. All pilgrims are required to spend the night in Minā, to stone the three pillars representing Satan each day and to sacrifice an animal for the sake of God, whose meat is distributed to the indigent. Men must shave their heads or cut their hair, while women are required only to cut the hair.
MASJID KHAYF It is highly recommended to pray six rak'at of prayer in this Masjid in Minā and that has great reward as it is said that many prophets of God prayed here.
MASJID HUDAYBĪYYAH This is the location where the Prophet ﷺ gave a special initiation (baya') to the Companions that were with him seeking to make pilgrimage, after Quraysh captured our master 'Uthmān ibn 'Affān and held him.

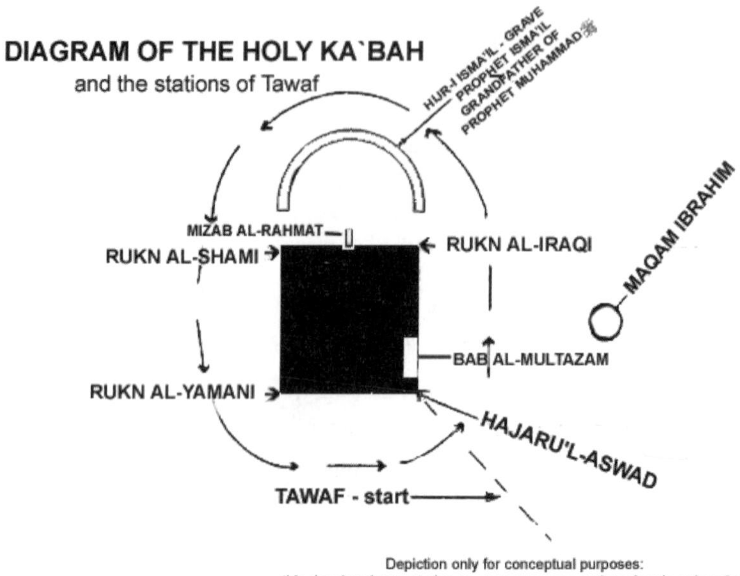

Depiction only for conceptual purposes:
this drawing does not give an accurate presentation of scale or location

Visiting Madinat al-Munawwarah

The merits of Madīnah, of prayer in Madīnah, of visiting the Masjid al-Nabawī, of living in Madīnah, of not cutting trees there, etc. are all based on the fact that the Prophet ﷺ is there.

Thus in Madīnah, you must keep even more respect than in Makkah, because there you are in the presence of the Prophet ﷺ. Make continuous ṣalawāt in your heart, in unison with fellow pilgrims if you are on a bus, until you reach Madīnah. Whether you enter Madīnah by bus or by plane, after you clear the checkpoints, you will travel four or five miles before you begin to see the Sanctuary of the Prophet's Holy Mosque (ḥaram) in the distance. When you do, ask permission from the Prophet ﷺ to enter into his territory.

Significance of the Prophet's Mosque and Grave

In Islam, the Prophet's Mosque is second in rank with regard to merit and status in God's sight. The same applies to the reward for the worshipers and those heading there.

The Prophet ﷺ said:

> Do not undertake a journey, but to one of the three Mosques: the Sacred Mosque, this Mosque of mine, and Al-Aqsā Mosque.[303]

It has been narrated that performing prayers in the Prophet's Mosque is of great merit and reward when the Prophet ﷺ said, "A prayer in this Mosque of mine is a thousand times more excellent than a prayer in any other mosque except the Sacred Mosque (in Mecca)."[304]

The Prophet ﷺ said:

> Between my Grave and my Pulpit lies a grove from the groves of Paradise.[305]

The Blessed Grove of Paradise, known as Rawḍatu 'sh-Sharīfah, is the space in the mosque which lies between the pulpit and the Room in which the Prophet ﷺ is buried.

Ibn 'Umar ؓ related that the Prophet ﷺ said:

> Whoever comes to me as a visitor, with nothing in his heart except the

---

[303] Bukhari, Muslim, Tirmidhi, al-Nasai, Abu Dawud, Ibn Majah, Ahmad, al-Darimi.

[304] al-Bazzar authentic (sahih).

[305] Bukhari and Muslim.

intention to visit me, it is an obligation on me to be his intercessor on Judgment Day.[306]

Anas ﷺ narrates: God's Messenger ﷺ said:

He who visits me in Madīna counting on his visit to me (muḥtasiban), I will be his witness and intercessor on the Day of Judgment.[307]

It is written in large script on the Rawḍah the famous hadith:

Whoever visits my grave, my intercession is obligatory for him.[308]

The Prophet ﷺ said:

Whoever invokes blessings on me at my grave, I hear him, and whoever invokes blessings on me from afar, I am informed about it.[309]

Abū Hurayra ﷺ said, "I heard the Prophet ﷺ say:

Jesus عليه السلام will descend as an arbitrator and just judge and sincere Imam and he will follow the pilgrimage or the one with 'Umrah, or with intention to do both, and he will come to my grave, reciting greetings on me and I will respond to him."[310]

---

[306] Tabarani in *al-Awsat* and *al-Kabir* with a chain containing Maslama ibn Salim, and by al-Daraqutni in his *Amali* and by Ibn al-Sakan in his *Sunan al-Sihah* as stated by al-Shirbini in *Mughni al-Muhtaj* (1:512).

[307] Mentioned by Ibn al-Jawzi in *Muthir Al-Gharam Al-Sakin Ila Ashraf Al-Amakin.*

[308] Arabic: *man zāra qabrī wajabat lahu shafaatī.* Narrated from Ibn Umar by al-Daraqutni in his *Sunan* (2:278 #194), Abu Dawud al-Tayalisi in his *Musnad* (2:12), al-Dulabi in *al-Kuna wa al-Asma* (2:64), al-Khatib in *Talkhis al-Mutashabih fi al-Rasm* (1:581), Ibn al-Dubaythi in *al-Dhayl ala al-Tarikh* (2:170), Ibn Abi al-Dunya in *Kitab al-Qubur*, al-Bayhaqi in *Shuab al-Iman* (3:490), al-Hakim al-Tirmidhi in *Nawadir al-Usul* (p. 148), al-Haythami (4:2), al-Subki in *Shifa al-Siqam* (p. 12-14), Abu al-Shaykh, Ibn Adi in *al-Kamil* (6:235, 6:351), al-Uqayli in *al-Duafa* (4:170), and Ibn Hajar who indicated its grade of *hasan* in *Talkhis al-Habir* (2:266) as it is strengthened by other hadiths which both he and al-Haythami mention.

[309] Abu al-Shaykh cites it in *Kitab al-Salat ala al-nabi* (Jala al-afham p. 22), and Ibn Hajar says in *Fath al-Bari* (6:379): "Abu al-Shaykh cites it with a good chain (*sanad jayyid*)." Bayhaqi mentions it in *Hayat al-anbiya* and *Shuab al-iman* (2:218 #1583) with ublightuhu in the end.

[310] Al-Hakim narrated it and graded it authentic (595/2), and al-Dhahabi concurred.

[311] Abu Hurayra in Abu Dawud (Manasik #2039) with a sound chain; Ibn Asakir, *Mukhtasar Tarikh Dimashq* 2:407; Ahmad, *Musnad* 2:527; Abu Nuaym, *Akhbar Asbahan* 2:353; Ibn al-Najjar, *Akhbar al-Madina* p. 145; Bayhaqi, *Shuab al-iman* #4161; Haythami, *Majma al-zawaid* 10:162; Ibn Kathir, *Tafsir* 6:464; al-Mundhiri, *al-Targhib wa al-tarhib* 2:499; *Talkhis al-habir* 2:267.

[312] in *Anba al-adhkiya bi hayat al-anbiya*

So it is very important to stand before the door of the grave of the Prophet ﷺ with utmost reverence, feeling the greatness of the Seal of Messengers, invoking God with whatever words come to the heart, keeping in mind the verse:

> *We sent not a messenger, but to be obeyed, in accordance with the will of God. If they had only, when they were unjust to themselves, come unto thee and asked God's forgiveness, and the Messenger had asked forgiveness for them, they would have found God indeed Oft-returning, Most Merciful.* (4:64)

One must keep in mind the hadith from Abū Hurayra ؓ where the Prophet ﷺ said:

> *No one greets me except God has returned my soul to me so that I can return his greetings.*[311]

And 'Abd Allāh ibn Mas'ud ؓ said: God's Messenger ﷺ said, *"God has angels that roam the earth bringing me the greetings of my nation."*

> *The eminent scholar Imām aṣ-Ṣuyūti said that what is meant here by returned my soul is permanently, and not temporarily*[312] *In other words, God does not return the Prophet's ﷺ soul and take it back, then return it again and then take it back again, but He has returned it to him permanently. Thus the Prophet ﷺ is alive permanently without interruption or lapse. Consider this, at every moment there is someone sending him greetings to the Prophet ﷺ, so there is no time in which his soul is absent.*

HOW THE OTTOMAN SULTAN WOULD CLEAN THE RAWḌAH

Our master Shaykh Nazim relates that in the time of the Ottomans, the Sultan would come from Anatolia himself during the time of Hajj. Approaching the Blessed Hujratu 'sh-Sharifah crawling he would await the sign of his acceptance: the doors of the Hujrah would open of themselves. Still crawling, he would enter with perfect manners and proceed to dust and clean the room. Then, with fresh rose oil from roses grown especially for this purpose in Isparta, he would wash the surface of the grave and its floor. For the Ottoman sultans, this was the highest honor, and for their honoring the God's Messenger, God honored them with steadfast rule, respect and dignity before the world for over 500 years. Today the Blessed Rawḍah has not been cleaned in many years and the dust has been left to accumulate inside the maqām.

Etiquette in the Rawdah

A visitor should not raise his voice in the Mosque as a sign of politeness with the Messenger of God's ﷺ. Lowering one's voice is also a sign of obedience to the words of the Almighty God:

O ye who believe! Raise not your voices above the voice of the Prophet, nor speak aloud to him in talk, as ye may speak aloud to one another, lest your deeds become vain and ye perceive not. Of those who lower their voices in the presence of God's Messenger, their hearts has God tested for piety: for them is forgiveness and a great reward. (49:2-3)

This is a warning to those who raise their voices in the presence of God's Messenger, that God will render their deeds vain and void and will not reward them.

It has been narrated that Abū Bakr aṣ-Ṣiddīq ﷺ used to say, "There should be no raising of voices in the presence of a prophet, whether dead or alive."

Hearing the sound of a tent peg or a nail being hammered in the neighboring houses, 'A'ishah ﷺ dispatched them a messenger saying, "Do not hurt God's Messenger ﷺ."

'Umar bin al-Khaṭṭāb ﷺ heard two men raising their voices in the Mosque of the Prophet ﷺ. At this he asked them, "Where do you come from?" They answered, "From Ṭāif." Thereupon he said, "Had you been from Madīnah, I would have punished you. No voice should be raised in this Mosque of ours."

Qāḍī 'Iyād expresses the consensus of Muslims that the site of the Prophet's grave is the holiest site on earth.[313] Thus the visitation to the Prophet ﷺ (ziyārah) is of crucial importance to every believer, and to pray in the masjid of the Prophet ﷺ is also very important. The Prophet ﷺ said, "Between my grave and my pulpit lies a grove from the groves of Paradise."[314]

CONDUCT OF ENTERING THE MOSQUE OF THE HOLY PROPHET ﷺ

When you enter al-Ḥaram ash-Sharīf, take your miswāk and make Sunnat al-istiyāk saying, Allāhumma ṭāhir qalbī min ash-shirki wa 'n-nifāq (O God, purify my heart from the lesser association with You and from hypocrisy). For men it is preferred to enter from Bāb ar-Rahmah (Door of Mercy), the door of Sayyidinā Abū Bakr ﷺ, Bāb as-Salām (Door of Peace), Bāb Jibrīl ﷺ (Door of Archangel Gabriel), Bāb Fāṭimata 'z-Zahrah ﷺ (Door of Fāṭima, daughter of the Prophet ﷺ). For women there is no choice, they have to enter through one special door. Before entering stand still and recite greetings on the Prophet ﷺ and his caliphs, his children, the Sahaba of the Prophet ﷺ and on awlīyāullāh, especially your shaykh, in the following manner:

Aṣ-ṣālatu was-salāmu 'alayka yā Sayyidī yā Rasūlullāh		الصلوة والسلام عليك يا رسول الله

Blessings and peace be upon you, O Prophet of God.

---

[313] in *al-Shifa,* in the chapter on visiting the Prophet.

[314] Bukhari and Muslim.

Aṣ-ṣālatu was-salāmu ʻalayka yā Ḥabīballāh		الصلوة والسلام عليك يا حبيب الله
Blessings and peace be upon you, O Beloved of God.		
As-salāmu ʻalayka yā Sayyidinā Abā Bakr aṣ-Ṣiddīq		السلام عليك يا سيدنا أبا بكر الصديق
Peace be upon you, O our master Abū Bakr aṣ-Ṣiddīq.		
As-salāmu ʻalayka yā Sayyidinā ʻUmar al-Fārūq		السلام عليك يا سيدنا عمر الفاروق
Peace be upon you, O our master ʻUmar al-Fārūq.		
As-salāmu ʻalayka yā Sayyidinā ʻUthman wa yā Sayyidinā ʻAlī		السلام عليك يا سيدنا عثمان وسيدنا علي
Peace be upon you, O our master ʻUthman and our master ʻAlī.		
As-salāmu ʻalayki yā Sayyidatinā Fāṭimat az-Zahrah		السلام عليك يا سيدتنا فاطمة الزهرة
Peace be upon you, O our Lady Fāṭimat az-Zahrah.		
As-salāmu ʻalaykum yā Āhla-Jannati ʼl-Baqʻi		السلام عليكم يا يا اهل جنة البقيع
Peace be upon you, O inhabitants of the Garden of Baqʻi.		
As-salāmu ʻalayka yā Sayyidinā Ḥamzah		السلام عليك يا سيدنا حمزة
Peace be upon you, O our master Ḥamzah.		
As-salāmu ʻalaykum yā Shuhadā Uḥud.		السلام عليكم يا شهداء احُد
Peace be upon you, O martyrs of Uḥud.		
You then enter the Prophet's Mosque with your right foot saying: Aʻudhū billāhi ʼl-ʻAẓīm wa wajhihi ʼl-karīm wa sulṭānahu ʼl-qadīm min ash-shayṭāni ʼr-rajīm. Allāhuma ʼftaḥ abwāba raḥmatik. I seek refuge with the Mighty God. I seek protection in His Generous Countenance and His Everlasting Authority against the cursed Devil. In the Name of God. O God! Bless Muhammad and his family. O God! Forgive my sins, and open the gates of Your mercy to me.[315]		إذا وصلت إلى المسجد النبوي فقدم رجلك اليمين عند دخوله وقل أعوذ بالله العظيم ووجهه الكريم وسلطانه القديم من الشيطان الرجيم اللهم افتح لي أبواب رحمتك.

[315] Ibn Majah, Tirmidhi, Ahmad.

One then says: Nawaitu 'l-arbā'īn, nawaytu 'l-'itikāf, nawaytu 'l-khalwah, nawaytu 'l-'uzlah, nawaytu 'r-riyāda, nawaytu 's-sulūk, lillāhi ta'alā al-'Adhīm fī ḥarami 'n-Nabi ﷺ. Then enter the Mosque.	نويتُ الأربعين، نويتُ الاعتكاف، نويتُ الخلوة نويتُ العُزلة، نويتُ الرياضة نويتُ السلوك لله تعالى في حَرَم النبي صلى الله عليه وسلم

For the sake of blessings (barakah) I intend the forty (days of seclusion); I intend isolation; I intend discipline (of the ego); I intend to travel in God's Path; for the sake of God, the Exalted in the Holy Place of the Prophet ﷺ.

If it is not possible to visit the Prophet ﷺ immediately because it is crowded, or it is time for congregational prayer, then pray two rak'at greeting the Mosque (taḥiyyat al-masjid). However, if you are able to do so, go directly to make your visit. When you visit the Prophet ﷺ, try to enter from the door of Sayyidinā Abū Bakr ؓ or Bāb as-Salām, opposite the grave. Move all the way across the space to arrive at the Prophet's ﷺ Muwājihatu 'sh-Sharīfah. If you are coming at the time of prayer, enter the Mosque from any door, pray first with the congregation, then make your visit to the Prophet ﷺ after finishing the prayers.

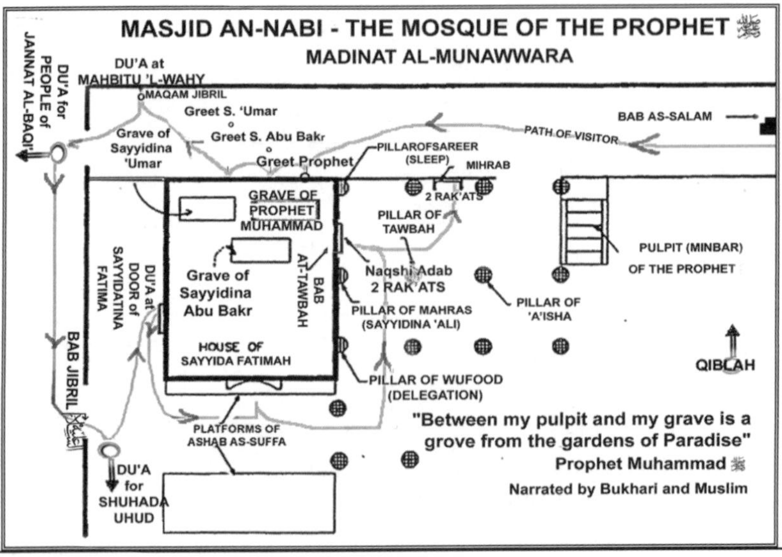

CONDUCT OF ZIYĀRAH

At the Muwājihatu 'sh-Sharīfah face the holy grave of the Prophet ﷺ. Be careful, as many people mistakenly think that the first door with a hole is the door of the Prophet ﷺ. The first two doors, with two small holes, contain nothing. The one in the middle which has a large hole and two small holes is the grave of Sayyidinā Muhammad ﷺ and directly behind his grave, at his feet is the grave of Sayyidinā Abu Bakr ؓ; Sayyidinā Umar ؓ is buried at the feet of Sayyidinā Abu Bakr ؓ.

Greeting the Prophet ﷺ

Stand in front of the middle door a bit far away behind where there are two pillars, and say:

O Prophet of God, I came to your presence, please accept me.		
Aṣ-ṣālatu was-salāmu 'alayka yā Sayyidī yā Rasūlullāh		السلام عليك يا سيدنا أبا بكر الصديق
Blessings and Peace be upon you, O Prophet of God.		
Aṣ-ṣālatu was-salāmu 'alayka yā Ḥabīballāh		السلام عليك يا سيدنا عمر الفاروق
Blessings and Peace be upon you, O Beloved of God.		
Aṣ-ṣālatu was-salāmu 'alayka yā Shāfi'an li 'l-muslimīn		الصلوة والسلام عليك يا شافعاً للمسلمين
Blessings and Peace be upon you, O Intercessor of the Muslims.		
Aṣ-ṣālatu was-salāmu 'alayka yā Rasūla rabbi' l-'alamin		الصلوة والسلام عليك يا رسول رب العالمين
Blessings and Peace be upon you, O Messenger of the Lord of the Worlds.		
Then add to that whatever comes to your heart of greetings to the Prophet ﷺ.		
Testification of Faith (Shahāda) 3 times: ash-hadu an lā ilāha illa-Allāh wa ash-hadu anna Muḥammadan 'abduhu wa rasūluh;		كَلِمةُ الشَّهادتين (٣ مرات) أَشْهَدُ أَنْ لا إله إلا الله وأَشْهَدُ أَنَّ مُحَمَّدًا عَبْدُهُ ورَسُولُهُ
I testify that there is no god but God and I testify that Muḥmmad is His Servant and Messenger.		

The first Testification of Faith (Shahādah) is for one's self, bringing to mind the Presence of the Prophet ﷺ and saying in one's heart, "Yā Sayyidī Yā Rasūlullāh, you are my witness; Allah is my witness; all angels are my witness; all Ṣaḥābah are my witness; all Prophets are my witness; everyone in creation is my witness; and my

<table>
<tr><td colspan="3">Shaykh is my witness," then pronounce the Shahādah, for you are renewing your Islam. Then pronounce the second Shahādah on behalf of yourself, your parents, your children, your family, your brothers and sisters, your relations, friends and neighbors and all Muslim people. The third Shahādah is on behalf of unbelievers with the intention that they become believers.</td></tr>
<tr><td>Istighfār: 3x Istighfārullāh</td><td></td><td>أستغفر الله (٣ مرات)</td></tr>
<tr><td colspan="3">I ask forgiveness of God.
The first Istighf□r is for yourself; the second is for your family and for whoever asked you to pray (make du‘□) for them and the third is for the Community of the Prophet ﷺ.</td></tr>
<tr><td>Yā Rabbī, yā Allāh, kam ẓahara minnī min adh-dhunūbi wa 'l-ma'āṣīyy ẓāhiran wa bāṭinan wa sirran min ẓuhūrī fī 'ālami 'd-dunyā ilā yawminā hādha, raj'atu 'ani 'l-jamī'i bi 't-tawbati wa 'l-istighfār wa as'aluka an taghfira lī bi-jāhi Nabīyyika Muḥammad.</td><td></td><td>يا ربي يا الله، كم ظهر مني من الذنوب والمعاصي ظاهرا وباطنا وسرا من عهد ايجاد ذرتي وروحي ودخول روحي إلى جسمي وظهوري من العدم إلى الوجود وظهوري في عالم الدنيا إلى يومنا هذا، رجعت عن الجميع اليك بالتوبة والإستغفار وأسألك ان تغفر لي يا الله بجاه نبيّك</td></tr>
<tr><td colspan="3">O My Lord, O God, from the day of my appearance in creation until our day, how much of disobedience has appeared from me spiritually or physically - I am regretting them all coming and asking forgiveness and repentance, and I am asking you to forgive me for the sake of the Prophet.</td></tr>
<tr><td>Kamā qāl Allāhu ta'ala fīl-Qur'ān:
wa mā arsalnā min rasūlin illā liyuṭā'a bi-idhnillāhi wa law annahum idh dhalamū anfusahum jā'ūka fastaghfarū'llāha wastaghfara lahumu 'r-rasūlu la-wajadū'llāha tawwāban rahīmān.</td><td></td><td>كما قال الله تعالى في القرآن:
وَمَا أَرْسَلْنَا مِن رَّسُولٍ إِلاَّ لِيُطَاعَ بِإِذْنِ اللّهِ وَلَوْ أَنَّهُمْ إِذ ظَّلَمُواْ أَنفُسَهُمْ جَآؤُوكَ فَاسْتَغْفَرُواْ اللّهَ وَاسْتَغْفَرَ لَهُمُ الرَّسُولُ لَوَجَدُواْ اللّهَ تَوَّاباً رَّحِيماً</td></tr>
<tr><td colspan="3">As God said in the Holy Quran:
We sent not a messenger, but to be obeyed, in accordance with the will of God. If they had only, when they were unjust to themselves, come unto thee and asked God's forgiveness, and the Messenger had asked forgiveness for them, they would have found</td></tr>
</table>

God indeed Oft-returning, Most Merciful. (4:64)		
Then you invoke God, asking for whatever you need or desire, seeking a good life for yourself, your family and for your Shaykh, for the Muslims in general, and mercy and peace for all mankind.		
Then you move on (it is not necessary to move physically) to give greetings to Sayyidinā Abu Bakr as-Siddiq ﷺ. Follow the same adab as with the Prophet ﷺ. Then move on to give greetings to Sayyidinā 'Umar ﷺ, again following the same adab. Then, before leaving, give greetings in your heart to to Sayyidinā 'Uthman ﷺ, Sayyidinā 'Alī ﷺ, all the Companions, all 124,000 prophets and messengers, all 124,000 saints because their souls too, have a spiritual presence in that holy place. Finally, send greetings to Sayyidinā al-Ḥasan ﷺ and Sayyidinā al-Ḥusain ﷺ.		
As-salāmu 'alayka yā Sayyidinā Abā Bakr aṣ-Ṣiddīq		السلام عليك يا سيدنا أبا بكر الصديق
Peace be upon you, O our master Abā Bakr aṣ-Ṣiddīq.		
As-salāmu 'alayka yā Sayyidinā 'Umar al-Fārūq		السلام عليك يا سيدنا عمر الفاروق
Peace be upon you, O our master 'Umar al-Fārūq.		
As-salāmu 'alayka yā Sayyidinā 'Uthmān wa yā Sayyidinā 'Alī		السلام عليك يا سيدنا عثمان وسيدنا علي
Peace be upon you, O our master 'Uthmān and our master 'Alī.		
As-salāmu 'alaykum yā aṣḥāb an-Nabī		السلام عليكم يا اصحاب النبي
Peace be upon you, O Companions of the Prophet.		
As-salāmu 'alaykum yā awlīyā'ullāh.		السلام عليكم يا أولياء الله
Peace be upon you, O saints of God.		
Then, on the right side before the exit door is a large wall covered with ceramic ornamention/calligraphy. There is the Maḥbitu 'l-waḥī, where Gabriel ﷺ used to come to bring revelation to the Prophet. In the past, one could make a turn inside, but it is now blocked with a fence, so you have to go outside. But before you go outside, make du'ā at the Maḥbitu 'l-waḥī. From this station, you face Qiblah and say:		
Ya Rabbi' l-'izzati wa 'l-'aẓamati wa 'l-jabarūt.		يا رب العزة والعظيمة الجبروت
O Lord of Honor and Greatness, Imposer of Thy Will.		
As-salāmu 'alayka yā Sayyidinā Jibrīl.		السلام عليك يا سيدنا جبريل

Peace be upon you, O our master Gabriel.		
As-salāmu 'alayka yā Sayyidinā Mikā'īl.		السلام عليك يا سيدنا ميكائيل
Peace be upon you, O our master Michael.		
As-salāmu 'alayka yā Sayyidinā Izrā'īl.		السلام عليك يا سيدنا عزرائيل
Peace be upon you, O our master Izra'īl.		
As-salāmu 'alayka yā Sayyidinā Isrāfīl.		السلام عليك يا سيدنا اسرافيل
Peace be upon you, O our master Isrāfīl.		
As-salāmu 'alayka yā Sayyidinā Riḍwān.		السلام عليك يا سيدنا رضوان
Peace be upon you, O our master Riḍwān.		
As-salāmu 'alayka yā Sayyidina Mālik.		السلام عليك يا سيدنا مالك
Peace be upon you, O our master Mālik.		
As-salāmu 'alaykum yā Malāi'kati 's-samāwati al-'aẓīm.		السلام عليكم يا ملائكة السموات والأرض
Peace be upon you, O Angels of the Tremendous Heavens.		
As-salāmu 'alaykum yā Malā'ikati 'l-karībiyyūn.		السلام عليكم يا ملائكة الكريبون
Peace be upon you, O Cherubim.		
As-salāmu 'alaykum yā Ḥamalat ul-'Arsh.		السلام عليكم يا حملة العرش
Peace be upon you, O our master O Bearers of the Throne.		
As-salāmu 'alaykum yā Malā'ikati Anwārillāh		السلام عليكم يا ملائكة انوار الله
Peace be upon you, O Angels of God's Light.		
You beseech God there saying: 'Yā Rabbī for the sake of the Prophet ﷺ, for the sake of his Sahaba and his caliphs; for the sake of Mahdī and for the sake of all saints, Yā Rabbī Yā Allāh□", and then invoke God in du'a for whatever you like.		
And then after reciting these greetings to the angels you make whatever du'a you like, and then pray two rak'at. You exit from that door, at which point you will be facing Jannat al-Baq'i. You make a Fatiha for all who are buried there. You go left and go down, then enter the door of Sayyidatina Fāṭimatu 'z-Zahrā ؓ and go left in there to an empty area, just before reaching the Platforms of Aṣḥāb aṣ-Ṣuffah. It is reported historically that the angels have transferred Sayyidatina Fāṭimat az-Zahra ؓ from		

Jannat al-Baq'i to this grave. So you approach the grave and say:		
As-salāmu 'alaykī ya Sayyidatanā Fāṭimata 'z-zahrā.		السلام عليك يا سيدتنا فاطمة الزهرة
Peace be upon you, O our Lady ā Fāṭimata 'z-zahrā.		
As-salāmu 'alaykī yā Umi 'l-Ḥasani wa 'l-Ḥusain		السلام عليك يا سيدتنا أم الحسن والحسين
Peace be upon you, O mother of al-Ḥasan and al-Ḥusain.		
As-salāmu 'alaykī yā Sayyidata nisā'i āhli 'l-jannah.		السلام عليك يا سيدة نساء أهل الجنة
Peace be upon you, O Noble Chief of the ladies of the People of Paradise.		
You then go around and come to the Blessed Garden (Rawḍat ash-Sharīfah) if you are able. If you are not able to, you come anywhere adjacent to Rawḍat ash-Sharīfah. There is Bāb at-Tawbah which is the last closet of Quran's, near the Rawḍah. Try to reach there, but if you cannot stand at a distance, face the Qiblah and say:		
Law kāna laka yā Rabbī bābayni āḥadahumā mukhaṣaṣṣun lit-tā'ibīna min 'ibādika al-mu'minīn wal-ākharu lit-tā'ibīna min 'ibādika al-mudhinibīn. Ji'tuka yā Allāh naḥwu bābik alladhī yaḥtāju an yadkhula minhu 'ibāduka al-mudhinibīn. Wa innanī uqirru wa āa'tarif annahu yajibu an ujaddida islāmī wa īmānī min hādha 'l-bāb iẓhāran li 'l-'ajzi.		لو كان لك ياربي بابين احدهما مخصص للتائبين من عبادك المؤمنين والأخر للتائبين من عبادك المذنبين، جئتك يا الله نحو بابك الذي يحتاج ان يدخل منه عبادك المذنبين وانني اقر واعترف انه يجب ان اجدد إسلامي وإيماني من هذا الباب إظهاراً للعجز.
O my Lord, O God, I am coming to your door, the door of repentance. Yā Rabbi, if you had two doors for Your servant to enter through; one for the believers from Your servants and one for the sinner from Your servants, I am coming to You from the door that the sinner needs to come through and I am declaring that believing that this is the only door for me to come through. I am saying to you that I have to renew my faith from this door to show humility and helplessness.		
Recite Shahādah three times and the remainder of the adab of the Naqshbandi Order, leaving out the dhikr. This will take from ten minutes. Following the adab pray two rak'at, and then to invoke God seeking whatever you like.		

DAILY CONDUCT

It was the custom of Mawlana Shaykh Nazim to perform these devotions a half-hour after Fajr prayer, when it would be less crowded. During the Ḥajj season, however, it is always crowded. Still, there are some times that are better than others. One of these is the period after Duḥā (mid-day), until the time of Ẓuhr prayer (9 a.m. to noon). The other is the period between Ẓuhr and 'Aṣr prayers, because people then go to eat and take an afternoon nap. During that time, ladies—but not men—can enter the Rawḍah, so this is the best time for them to perform these devotions.

It is recommended to visit the Prophet ﷺ every day as long as you are staying in Madīnah. For those with a higher level of aspiration, it is strongly advised to make one ziyārah of Prophet ﷺ in the morning and one in the evening.

The murīd should try to hold fast to as much as of the above aspects of adab as possible, but should not worry if some parts of it are missed.

Finally keep in mind you must control your ego as much as possible. If you get angry quickly take a shower and ask forgiveness from God and seek the Prophet's ﷺ asking forgiveness on your behalf.

FAREWELL VISITATION

When the time comes for you to leave Madīnah, on your last day in the city, you make ziyārah and you ask permission from the Prophet ﷺ to travel.

Perform the Farewell Visitation of the Prophet ﷺ (ziyāratu 'l-wada') and then you set forth.

Holy Places of Visitation in Madinah

SEEKING BLESSINGS BY MEANS OF PLACES THE PROPHET ﷺ VISITED (TABARRUK)

Abū Burdā ؓ narrated:

> When I came to Madīnah, I met 'Abd Allāh bin Salām. He said, "Will you come to me so that I may serve you with sawiq (i.e. powdered barley) and dates, and let you enter a (blessed) house in which the Prophet entered?. . ."

Thus to visit any location where the Prophet's ﷺ blessed feet touched the earth, was touched by his holy hand or his breath entered is to take blessings. For that reason, the entire earth of Madīnah, its air and its water are blessed.

The Prophet of God ﷺ, invoked:

> *O God! Make us love Madīnah as much as we love Mecca or even more. Make it sound and bless us in its sa' and its mudd (units of measure used in Madīnah)...*[316]

As the Prophet ﷺ asked God's Blessings on the city and its fruits, then Madīnah must be full of blessing, as his supplication is an or answered prayer (du'a mustajāb). Therefore, it is common practice for pilgrims to purchase dates from Madīnah for the blessings, and to bring them back home to share among those who could not make the pilgrimage. It is said that there remain living some of the date palms planted by the Holy Prophet ﷺ himself.

THE GRAVEYARD BAQI' AL-GHARQAD

The term Baqi' signifies soft land void of stones. This is the sort of land in which graves are commonly dug. Madīnah has several places of that sort, such as: Baqi' of al-Zubair, Baqi' of al-Khail, and others.

God's Messenger went out frequently at night to visit Baqi' al-Gharqad and to pray for its dwellers. He used to say, "Peace be upon you, O abode of Believers" or "Peace be upon the believing men and women dwelling here. May Allah grant mercy to those from among us who passed away and those who are to come after us. Certainly, Allah willing, we will join you."[317]

It has been narrated that the Prophet ﷺ said:

> *I am the first person for whom the earth will split asunder on the Day of Judgment. This means that I am the first to be resurrected. Then, I, Abū Bakr and 'Umar will head for the people of Baqi' who will be resurrected and followed by the people of Mecca. Thereupon, I will be resurrected between the Two Mosques.*[318]

About ten thousand Companions have been buried in Madīnah ﷺ.

It is desirable that one go daily to the cemetery of Baqi', but particularly on Friday; before the visit, one should first pronounce greetings on the Prophet ﷺ.

When one arrives at Baqi', say:

as-Salāmu 'alaykum dāra qawmin		السَّلَامُ عَلَيْكُمْ دَارَ قَوْمٍ مُؤْمِنِينَ وَإِنَّا إِنْ شَاءَ اللهُ بِكُمْ

[316] *Muwatta,* Book 45, Number 45.4.14.

[317] Muslim, An-Nasai, Ahmad, Ibn Majah.

[318] Tirmidhi.

mu'minīna wa innā inshā-Allāhu bikum lāhiqūn, Allāhumma ighfir li āhli Baqi' al-gharqad, Allāhumma ighfir lanā wa lahum.		لَلَاحِقُونَ اللّٰهُمَّ اغْفِرْ لِأَهْلِ بَقِيعِ الْغَرْقَدِ اللّٰهُمَّ اغْفِرْ لَنَا وَلَهُمْ

Peace be upon ye, abode of the believing folk. And indeed we will soon be meeting with ye. O God forgive the people of Baqi' al-gharqad, O God forgive us and them.

Then he visits the visible graves there, such as that of Ībrahīm, 'Uthmān, al-'Abbās, al-Ḥasan the son of 'Alī, 'Alī the son of al-Ḥusayn, Muḥammad ibn 'Alī, Ja'far ibn Muḥammad, and others ؓ. The last stop would be the grave of Safīyya ؓ, the Aunt of God's Messenger ﷺ;. It has been established in numerous sound hadiths that there is merit in the graves of the Baqi' and in visiting them.

THE QUBĀ MOSQUE

It was the first mosque to be built in Madīnah. God praised this Mosque and those who maintained it:

> *There is a Mosque whose foundation was laid from the first day on Piety; it is more worthy of thy standing forth [for Prayer] therein. In it are men who love to be purified, and God loveth those who make themselves pure.* (9:108)

> *Thereupon, the Prophet ﷺ said to them, "What is the good thing you are performing in this Mosque that Allah has so highly praised you?" They said, "We use both stone and water for purification."*[319]

> *It has been narrated that the Prophet ﷺ used to ride his camel and visit Qubā every Saturday and Monday. The Prophet ﷺ said, "Whoever performs ablution at home, then comes to Qubā Mosque to perform Prayer therein, will get the reward as for 'Umrah."*[320]

> *It has also been reported that the Prophet ﷺ said, "Whoever prays in Qubā Mosque on Monday and Thursday is given the reward as for 'Umrah."*[321]

It is recommended to visit the well of Ārīs, which is located by the mosque of Qubā, and drink from its water and perform ablution with it.

It is desirable that one visit all the sites of significance in Islam. There are approximately thirty such places, and they are known to the inhabitants of Madīnah. The pilgrim should visit as many as he can.

---

[319] Tirmidhi, Abu Dawud, Ibn Majah, Ahmad.

[320] Bukhari and Muslim.

[321] Tirmidhi, Ibn Majah, Ahmad.

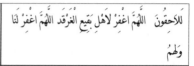

SEVEN MOSQUES

Masjid Qiblatain: In this mosque, God directed Prophet Muhammad ﷺ, who was in the middle of prayers along with his Companions, to turn his face from Islam's first Qiblah (Baitu 'l-Maqdis) towards the Ka'bah in Masjid al-Ḥarām in the verse:

> *"Verily! We have seen the turning of your face towards the heaven. Surely, We shall turn you to a Qiblah that shall please you, so turn your face in the direction of al-Masjid al-Ḥarām...."* (2:144).

That is why this mosque is known as a mosque with two Qiblas.

Masjid Jum'ah: This mosque was built at a place where the Prophet offered his first Jum'ah prayer in Madīnah.

Masjid Ghamāmah: This mosque is not far from Masjid an-Nabī. The Prophet ﷺ used to offer his the prayers of the two Eids here. Once the Prophet ﷺ led prayer for rain (istasqā) in it and suddenly clouds appeared and it started raining, hence the name ghamāma (clouds).

Masjid Fatima, Masjid Abū Bakr, Masjid Umar Farūq and Masjid 'Alī: These four mosques are near Masjid Ghamāmah.

BADR

The plain and dune of Badr is 32 kilometers southwest of Madīnah where the first battle between 313 Muslims and 1,000 Quraish of Makkah took place in 624 A.D. The Muslims had 70 camels and two horses whereas the Quraish had a cavalry of 200 horses and 700 camels. They were superior in weapons as well, but Muslims were victorious because they were strong in morale and strategy due to the presence of the Holy Prophet's ﷺ leadership.

UḤUD MOUNTAIN

About seven kilometers to the north of Madīnah, the famous battle of Uḥud was fought here. Sayyidina Hamza ؓ, the Holy Prophet's uncle and other companions are buried at the foot of the mountain.

It is reported that the Prophet ﷺ said, "Uḥud is a mountain which loves us and we love it."[322]

---

[322] Muslim.

SALA'A MOUNTAIN This is the site for the battle of the Trench was fought in 5 A.H. Now there are six mosques at this location.
WATER-WELLS OF THE PROPHET ﷺ It is a blessing to visit the wells where the Prophet ﷺ used to perform ablution and wash. There are seven such wells.
Additionally the visitor can ask the muṭawaf to assist you in Madīnah to visit the seven mosques, the many cemeteries, wells and other locations of historical significance.

Quranic Readings

Surah Ya Sin (36)		سورة يس
The Messenger of God ﷺ said: *Everything has a heart and the heart of the Qur'ān is Yā Sīn. And whoever reads Yā Sīn God will write for him as if he had read the Qur'ān ten times.*[323] Abū Hurayrah (ra) related that the Prophet ﷺ said: *Who reads Yā Sīn at night, desiring only the Face of God, God forgives him therein.*[324]		
Read after Ṣalāt al-Fajr.		
Bismillāhi 'r-Raḥmāni 'r-Rahīm		بسم الله الرحمن الرحيم
In the Name of Allah, the Most Beneficent, the Most Merciful.		
1. Yā Sīn		يس
Yā Sīn.		
2. Wa 'l-qur'āni 'l-ḥakīm		وَالْقُرْآنِ الْحَكِيمِ
By the wise Quran,		
3. Innaka la-mina 'l-mursalīn		إِنَّكَ لَمِنَ الْمُرْسَلِينَ
Lo! thou art of those sent		
4. 'alā ṣirāṭin mustaqīm		عَلَى صِرَاطٍ مُسْتَقِيمٍ

---

[323] Ad-Darimī, at-Tirmidhī and al-Bayhaqī in his *Shuab* all from Anas.

[324] Ad-Darimī, Abū Yala, at-Tabarani in his *Awsat,* and al-Bayhaqī in his *Shuab,* all from Abu Hurayrah.

On a straight path,		
5. Tanzīla 'l-'Azīz 'r-Raḥīm		تَنزِيلَ الْعَزِيزِ الرَّحِيمِ
A revelation of the Mighty, the Merciful,		
6. Li-tundhira qawman mā undhira ābāū'hum fa-hum ghāfilūn		لِتُنذِرَ قَوْمًا مَّا أُنذِرَ آبَاؤُهُمْ فَهُمْ غَافِلُونَ
That thou mayst warn a folk whose fathers were not warned, so they are heedless.		
7. Laqad haqqa 'l-qawlu 'alā aktharihim fa-hum lā yu'minūn		لَقَدْ حَقَّ الْقَوْلُ عَلَى أَكْثَرِهِمْ فَهُمْ لاَ يُؤْمِنُونَ
Already hath the word proved true of most of them, for they believe not.		
8. Inna ja'alnā fī 'anāqihim aghlālan fa-hīya ila 'l-adhqāni fa-hum muqmaḥūn		إِنَّا جَعَلْنَا فِي أَعْنَاقِهِمْ أَغْلاَلاً فَهِيَ إِلَى الأَذْقَانِ فَهُم مُّقْمَحُونَ
Lo! we have put on their necks carcans reaching unto the chins, so that they are made stiff necked.		
9. Wa ja'alnā min bayni aydīhim saddan wa min khalfihim saddan fa-aghshaynāhum fa-hum lā yubṣirūn		وَجَعَلْنَا مِن بَيْنِ أَيْدِيهِمْ سَدًّا وَمِنْ خَلْفِهِمْ سَدًّا فَأَغْشَيْنَاهُمْ فَهُمْ لاَ يُبْصِرُونَ
And We have set a bar before them and a bar behind them, and (thus) have covered them so that they see not.		
10. Wa sawā'un 'alayhim ā-andhartahum am lam tundhirhum lā yu'minūn		وَسَوَاء عَلَيْهِمْ أَأَنذَرْتَهُمْ أَمْ لَمْ تُنذِرْهُمْ لاَ يُؤْمِنُونَ
Whether thou warn them or thou warn them not, it is alike for them, for they believe not.		
11. Innamā tundhiru mani 'ttaba'a 'dh-		إِنَّمَا تُنذِرُ مَنِ اتَّبَعَ الذِّكْرَ وَخَشِيَ الرَّحْمَن بِالْغَيْبِ فَبَشِّرْهُ

dhikra wa khashīya 'r-Raḥmāna bi 'l-ghaybi fa-bashshirhu bi-maghfiratin wa ajrin karīm		بِمَغْفِرَةٍ وَأَجْرٍ كَرِيمٍ
Thou warnest only him who followeth the Reminder and feareth the Beneficent in secret. To him bear tidings of forgiveness and a rich reward.		
12. Inna naḥnu nuḥyī 'l-mawta wa naktubu mā qaddamū wa āthārahum wa kulla shay'in aḥṣaynāhu fī imāmin mubīn		إِنَّا نَحْنُ نُحْيِي الْمَوْتَىٰ وَنَكْتُبُ مَا قَدَّمُوا وَآثَارَهُمْ وَكُلَّ شَيْءٍ أَحْصَيْنَاهُ فِي إِمَامٍ مُبِينٍ
Lo! We it is Who bring the dead to life. We record that which they send before (them), and their footprints. And all things We have kept in a clear register.		
13. W 'adrib lahum mathalan aṣḥāba 'l-qarīyati idh jā'ahā 'l-mursalūn		وَاضْرِبْ لَهُمْ مَثَلًا أَصْحَابَ الْقَرْيَةِ إِذْ جَاءَهَا الْمُرْسَلُونَ
Coin for them a similitude: The people of the city when those sent (from Allah) came unto them;		
14. Idh arsalnā ilayhimu 'thnayni fa-kadhdhabūhuma fa 'azzaznā bi-thālithin fa qālū innā ilaykum mursalūn		إِذْ أَرْسَلْنَا إِلَيْهِمُ اثْنَيْنِ فَكَذَّبُوهُمَا فَعَزَّزْنَا بِثَالِثٍ فَقَالُوا إِنَّا إِلَيْكُمْ مُرْسَلُونَ
When We sent unto them twain, and they denied them both, so We reinforced them with a third, and they said; Lo! we have been sent unto you.		
15. Qālū mā antum illa basharun mithlunā wa mā anzala 'r-Raḥmānu min shay'in in antum illa takdhibūn		قَالُوا مَا أَنْتُمْ إِلَّا بَشَرٌ مِثْلُنَا وَمَا أَنْزَلَ الرَّحْمَٰنُ مِنْ شَيْءٍ إِنْ أَنْتُمْ إِلَّا تَكْذِبُونَ
They said: Ye are but mortals like unto us. The Beneficent hath naught revealed. Ye do but lie!		
16. Qālū rabbunā ya'lamu inna ilaykum la-mursalūna		قَالُوا رَبُّنَا يَعْلَمُ إِنَّا إِلَيْكُمْ لَمُرْسَلُونَ

<table>
<tr><td colspan="3">They answered: Our lord knoweth that we are indeed sent unto you,</td></tr>
<tr><td>17. Wa mā ʻalaynā illa ʼl-balāghu ʼl-mubīn</td><td></td><td>وَمَا عَلَيْنَا إِلَّا الْبَلَاغُ الْمُبِينُ</td></tr>
<tr><td colspan="3">And our duty is but plain conveyance (of the message).</td></tr>
<tr><td>18. Qālū innā taṭayyarnā bikum laʼin lam tantahū la-narjumannakum wa la-yamassannakum minnā ʻadhābun alīm</td><td></td><td>قَالُوا إِنَّا تَطَيَّرْنَا بِكُمْ لَئِن لَّمْ تَنتَهُوا لَنَرْجُمَنَّكُمْ وَلَيَمَسَّنَّكُم مِّنَّا عَذَابٌ أَلِيمٌ</td></tr>
<tr><td colspan="3">(The people of the city) said: We augur ill of you. If ye desist not, we shall surely stone you, and grievous torture will befall you at our hands.</td></tr>
<tr><td>19. Qālū ṭaʼirukum maʻakum aʼin dhukkirtum bal antum qawmun musrifūn</td><td></td><td>قَالُوا طَائِرُكُم مَّعَكُمْ أَئِن ذُكِّرْتُم بَلْ أَنتُمْ قَوْمٌ مُّسْرِفُونَ</td></tr>
<tr><td colspan="3">They said: Your evil augury be with you! Is it because ye are reminded (of the truth)? Nay, but ye are froward folk?</td></tr>
<tr><td>20. Wa jāʼa min aqsa ʼl-madīnati rajulun yasʻa qāla yā qawmi ʼittabiʻū ʼl-mursalīn</td><td></td><td>وَجَاءَ مِنْ أَقْصَى الْمَدِينَةِ رَجُلٌ يَسْعَى قَالَ يَا قَوْمِ اتَّبِعُوا الْمُرْسَلِينَ</td></tr>
<tr><td colspan="3">And there came from the uttermost part of the city a man running. He cried: O my people! Follow those who have been sent!</td></tr>
<tr><td>21. ʼIttabiʻū man lā yasʼalukum ajran wa-hum muhtadūn</td><td></td><td>اتَّبِعُوا مَن لَّا يَسْأَلُكُمْ أَجْرًا وَهُم مُّهْتَدُونَ</td></tr>
<tr><td colspan="3">Follow those who ask of you no fee, and who are rightly guided.</td></tr>
<tr><td>22. Wa-mā līya lā ʻabudu ʼl-ladhī faṭaranī wa ilayhi turjaʻūn</td><td></td><td>وَمَا لِيَ لَا أَعْبُدُ الَّذِي فَطَرَنِي وَإِلَيْهِ تُرْجَعُونَ</td></tr>
<tr><td colspan="3">For what cause should I not serve Him Who hath created me, and unto Whom ye will</td></tr>
</table>

be brought back?		
23. A'attakhidhu min dūnihi ālihatan in yuridni 'r-Raḥmānu bi-ḍurrin lā tughni 'annī shafā'atuhum shay'an wa lā yunqidhūn		ءَأَتَّخِذُ مِن دُونِهِ آلِهَةً إِن يُرِدْنِ الرَّحْمَن بِضُرٍّ لاَّ تُغْنِ عَنِّي شَفَاعَتُهُمْ شَيْئًا وَلاَ يُنقِذُونِ
Shall I take (other) gods in place of Him when, if the Beneficent should wish me any harm, their intercession will avail me naught, nor can they save?		
24. Innī idhan lafī ḍalālin mubīn		إِنِّي إِذًا لَّفِي ضَلاَلٍ مُّبِينٍ
Then truly I should be in error manifest.		
25. Innī āmantu bi-rabbikum fa 'sma'ūn		إِنِّي آمَنتُ بِرَبِّكُمْ فَاسْمَعُونِ
Lo! I have believed in your Lord, so hear met		
26. Qīla 'dkhuli 'l-jannata qāla ya layta qawmī ya'lamūna		قِيلَ ادْخُلِ الْجَنَّةَ قَالَ يَا لَيْتَ قَوْمِي يَعْلَمُونَ
It was said (unto him): Enter Paradise. He said: Would that my people knew		
27. Bi-mā ghafara lī rabbī wa ja'alanī mina 'l-mukramīn		بِمَا غَفَرَ لِي رَبِّي وَجَعَلَنِي مِنَ الْمُكْرَمِينَ
With what (munificence) my Lord hath pardoned me and made me of the honored ones!		
28. Wa-mā anzalnā 'alā qawmihi min ba'dihi min jundin mina 's-samā'i wa mā kunnā munzilīn		وَمَا أَنزَلْنَا عَلَى قَوْمِهِ مِن بَعْدِهِ مِنْ جُندٍ مِّنَ السَّمَاء وَمَا كُنَّا مُنزِلِينَ
We sent not down against his people after him a host from heaven, nor do We ever send.		
29. In kānat illa ṣayḥatan waḥidatan fa		إِن كَانَتْ إِلاَّ صَيْحَةً وَاحِدَةً فَإِذَا هُمْ خَامِدُونَ

idhā hum khāmidūn		
It was but one Shout, and lo! they were extinct.		
30. Yā ḥasratan ʻalā 'l-ʻibadi ma yā'tīhim min rasūlin illa kānū bihi yastahzi'ūn		يَا حَسْرَةً عَلَى الْعِبَادِ مَا يَأْتِيهِم مِّن رَّسُولٍ إِلَّا كَانُوا بِهِ يَسْتَهْزِئُونَ
Ah, the anguish for the bondmen! Never came there unto them a messenger but they did mock him!		
31. Alam yaraw kam ahlaknā qablahum mina 'l-qurūni annahum ilayhim la yarjiʻūn		أَلَمْ يَرَوْا كَمْ أَهْلَكْنَا قَبْلَهُم مِّنَ الْقُرُونِ أَنَّهُمْ إِلَيْهِمْ لَا يَرْجِعُونَ
Have they not seen how many generations We destroyed before them, which Indeed return not unto them;		
32. Wa in kullun lammā jamīʻūn ladayna muḥḍarūn		وَإِن كُلٌّ لَّمَّا جَمِيعٌ لَّدَيْنَا مُحْضَرُونَ
But all, without exception, will be brought before Us.		
33. Wa āyatun lahumu 'l-arḍu 'l-maytatu aḥyaynāhā wa akhrajnā min-hā ḥabban fa minhu ya'kulūn		وَآيَةٌ لَّهُمُ الْأَرْضُ الْمَيْتَةُ أَحْيَيْنَاهَا وَأَخْرَجْنَا مِنْهَا حَبًّا فَمِنْهُ يَأْكُلُونَ
A token unto them is the dead earth. We revive it, and We bring forth from it grain so that they eat thereof;		
34. Wa jaʻalnā fī-hā jannātin min nakhīlin wa ʻanābin wa fajjarnā fī-hā mina 'l-ʻuyūn		وَجَعَلْنَا فِيهَا جَنَّاتٍ مِّن نَّخِيلٍ وَأَعْنَابٍ وَفَجَّرْنَا فِيهَا مِنَ الْعُيُونِ
And We have placed therein gardens of the date palm and grapes, and We have caused springs of water to gush forth therein.		
35. Li yā'kulū min thamarihi wa mā		لِيَأْكُلُوا مِن ثَمَرِهِ وَمَا عَمِلَتْهُ أَيْدِيهِمْ أَفَلَا يَشْكُرُونَ

<table>
<tr><td>ʻamilathu aydīhim afalā yashkurūn</td><td></td><td></td></tr>
<tr><td colspan="3">That they may eat of the fruit thereof, and their hand made it not. Will they not, then, give thanks?</td></tr>
<tr><td>36. Subḥāna ʼl-ladhī khalaqa ʼl-azwāja kullahā mimmā tunbitu ʼl-arḍu wa min anfusihim wa mimmā lā yaʻlamūn</td><td></td><td>سُبْحَانَ الَّذِي خَلَقَ الْأَزْوَاجَ كُلَّهَا مِمَّا تُنبِتُ الْأَرْضُ وَمِنْ أَنفُسِهِمْ وَمِمَّا لَا يَعْلَمُونَ</td></tr>
<tr><td colspan="3">Glory be to Him Who created all the sexual pairs, of that which the earth groweth, and of themselves, and of that which they know not!</td></tr>
<tr><td>37. Wa āyatun lahumu ʼl-laylu naslakhu minhu ʻn-nahāra fa-idhā hum muẓlimūn</td><td></td><td>وَآيَةٌ لَّهُمُ اللَّيْلُ نَسْلَخُ مِنْهُ النَّهَارَ فَإِذَا هُم مُّظْلِمُونَ</td></tr>
<tr><td colspan="3">A token unto them is night. We strip it of the day, and lo! they are in darkness.</td></tr>
<tr><td>38. Wa ʼsh-shamsu tajrī li-mustaqarrin lahā dhālika taqdīru ʼl-ʻazīzi ʼl-alīm</td><td></td><td>وَالشَّمْسُ تَجْرِي لِمُسْتَقَرٍّ لَّهَا ذَٰلِكَ تَقْدِيرُ الْعَزِيزِ الْعَلِيمِ</td></tr>
<tr><td colspan="3">And the sun runneth on unto a resting place for him. That is the measuring of the Mighty, the Wise.</td></tr>
<tr><td>39. Wa ʼl-qamara qaddarnāhu manāzila ḥattā aʻāda ka ʼl-ʻurjūni ʼl-qadīm</td><td></td><td>وَالْقَمَرَ قَدَّرْنَاهُ مَنَازِلَ حَتَّىٰ عَادَ كَالْعُرْجُونِ الْقَدِيمِ</td></tr>
<tr><td colspan="3">And for the moon We have appointed mansions till she return like an old shrivelled palm leaf.</td></tr>
<tr><td>40. Lā ʼsh-shamsu yanbaghī lahā an tudrika ʼl-qamara wa lā ʼl-laylu ṣābiqu ʼn-nahāri wa kullun fī falakin yasbaḥūn</td><td></td><td>لَا الشَّمْسُ يَنبَغِي لَهَا أَن تُدْرِكَ الْقَمَرَ وَلَا اللَّيْلُ سَابِقُ النَّهَارِ وَكُلٌّ فِي فَلَكٍ يَسْبَحُونَ</td></tr>
<tr><td colspan="3">It is not for the sun to overtake the moon, nor doth the night outstrip the day. They float each in an orbit.</td></tr>
<tr><td>41. Wa āyatun lahum annā ḥamalnā</td><td></td><td>وَآيَةٌ لَّهُمْ أَنَّا حَمَلْنَا ذُرِّيَّتَهُمْ فِي الْفُلْكِ الْمَشْحُونِ</td></tr>
</table>

dhurrīyyatahum fī 'l-fulki 'l-mashḥūn		
And a token unto them is that We bear their offspring in the laden ship,		
42. Wa khalaqnā lahum min mithlihi mā yarkabūn		وَخَلَقْنَا لَهُم مِّن مِّثْلِهِ مَا يَرْكَبُونَ
And have created for them of the like thereof whereon they ride.		
43. Wa in nashā' nughriqhum fa-lā ṣarīkha lahum walā hum yunqadhūn		وَإِن نَّشَأْ نُغْرِقْهُمْ فَلا صَرِيخَ لَهُمْ وَلا هُمْ يُنقَذُونَ
And if We will, We drown them, and there is no help for them, neither can they be saved;		
44. Illa raḥmatan minnā wa matā'an ilā hīn		إِلا رَحْمَةً مِّنَّا وَمَتَاعًا إِلَى حِينٍ
Unless by mercy from Us and as comfort for a while.		
45. Wa idha qīla lahumu 'ttaqū mā bayna aydīkum wa mā khalfakum la'allakum turḥamūn		وَإِذَا قِيلَ لَهُمُ اتَّقُوا مَا بَيْنَ أَيْدِيكُمْ وَمَا خَلْفَكُمْ لَعَلَّكُمْ تُرْحَمُونَ
When it is said unto them: Beware of that which is before you and that which is behind you, that haply ye may find mercy (they are heedless).		
46. Wa mā tā'tīhim min āyatin min āyāti rabbihim illā kānū 'anhā m'uridīn		وَمَا تَأْتِيهِم مِّنْ آيَةٍ مِّنْ آيَاتِ رَبِّهِمْ إِلا كَانُوا عَنْهَا مُعْرِضِينَ
Never came a token of the tokens of their Lord to them, but they did turn away from it!		
47. Wa idhā qīla lahum anfiqū mimmā razaqakum-ullāhu qāla 'l-ladhīna kafarū lil-ladhīna amanū anuṭ'imu man law yashā'u 'llāhu aṭ'amahu in antum illā fī		وَإِذَا قِيلَ لَهُمْ أَنفِقُوا مِمَّا رَزَقَكُمُ اللَّهُ قَالَ الَّذِينَ كَفَرُوا لِلَّذِينَ آمَنُوا أَنُطْعِمُ مَن لَّوْ يَشَاءُ اللَّهُ أَطْعَمَهُ إِنْ أَنتُمْ إِلا فِي ضَلَالٍ مُّبِينٍ

ḍalālin mubīn		
And when it is said unto them: Spend of that wherewith Allah hath provided you. those who disbelieve say unto those who believe: Shall we feed those whom Allah, if He willed, would feed? Ye are in naught else than error manifest.		
48. Wa yaqūlūna matā hadhā 'l-w'adu in kuntum ṣādiqīn		وَيَقُولُونَ مَتَى هَذَا الْوَعْدُ إِن كُنتُمْ صَادِقِينَ
And they say: When will this promise be fulfilled, if ye are truthful?		
49. Ma yanẓurūna illa ṣayḥatan waḥidatan ta'khudhuhum wa hum yakhiṣṣimūn		مَا يَنظُرُونَ إِلَّا صَيْحَةً وَاحِدَةً تَأْخُذُهُمْ وَهُمْ يَخِصِّمُونَ
They await but one Shout, which will surprise them while they are disputing.		
50. Fa-lā yastaṭī'ūna tawṣiyatan wa lā ila āhlihim yarji'ūn		فَلَا يَسْتَطِيعُونَ تَوْصِيَةً وَلَا إِلَى أَهْلِهِمْ يَرْجِعُونَ
Then they cannot make bequest, nor can they return to their own folk.		
51. Wa nufikha fī 'ṣ-ṣūri fa idhā hum mina 'l-ajdāthi ila rabbihim yansilūn		وَنُفِخَ فِي الصُّورِ فَإِذَا هُم مِّنَ الْأَجْدَاثِ إِلَى رَبِّهِمْ يَنسِلُونَ
And the trumpet is blown and lo! from the graves they hie unto their Lord,		
52. Qālū yā waylanā man ba'athanā min marqadinā hadhā mā wa'ada 'r-Raḥmānu wa ṣadaqa 'l-mursalūn		قَالُوا يَا وَيْلَنَا مَن بَعَثَنَا مِن مَّرْقَدِنَا هَذَا مَا وَعَدَ الرَّحْمَنُ وَصَدَقَ الْمُرْسَلُونَ
Crying: Woe upon us! Who hath raised us from our place of sleep? This is that which the Beneficent did promise, and the messengers spoke truth,		
53. In kānat illa ṣayḥatan waḥidatan fa idhā hum jamī'un ladaynā muḥḍarūn		إِن كَانَتْ إِلَّا صَيْحَةً وَاحِدَةً فَإِذَا هُمْ جَمِيعٌ لَّدَيْنَا مُحْضَرُونَ

It is but one Shout, and behold them brought together before Us!		
54. Fa 'l-yawma lā tuẓlamu nafsun shay'an wa lā tujzawna illa mā kuntum t'amalūn		فَالْيَوْمَ لَا تُظْلَمُ نَفْسٌ شَيْئًا وَلَا تُجْزَوْنَ إِلَّا مَا كُنْتُمْ تَعْمَلُونَ
This day no soul is wronged in aught; nor are ye requited aught save what ye used to do.		
55. Inna aṣḥāba 'l-jannati 'l-yawma fī shughulin fākihūn		إِنَّ أَصْحَابَ الْجَنَّةِ الْيَوْمَ فِي شُغُلٍ فَاكِهُونَ
Lo! those who merit paradise this day are happily employed,		
56. Hum wa azwājuhum fī ẓilālin 'ala 'l-arā'iki muttaki'ūn		هُمْ وَأَزْوَاجُهُمْ فِي ظِلَالٍ عَلَى الْأَرَائِكِ مُتَّكِئُونَ
They and their wives, in pleasant shade, on thrones reclining;		
57. La-hum fī-hā fākihatun wa lahum mā yadda'ūna		لَهُمْ فِيهَا فَاكِهَةٌ وَلَهُمْ مَا يَدَّعُونَ
Theirs the fruit (of their good deeds) and theirs (all) that they ask;		
58. Salāmun qawlan min rabbin raḥīm		سَلَامٌ قَوْلًا مِنْ رَبٍّ رَحِيمٍ
The word from a Merciful Lord (for them) is: Peace!		
59. W 'amtāzū 'l-yawma ayyuhā 'l-mujrimūn		وَامْتَازُوا الْيَوْمَ أَيُّهَا الْمُجْرِمُونَ
But away for ye, O ye guilty, this day!		
60. Alam a'ahad ilaykum yā banī ādama an lā t'abudū 'sh-shayṭāna innahu lakum 'adūwwun mubīn		أَلَمْ أَعْهَدْ إِلَيْكُمْ يَا بَنِي آدَمَ أَنْ لَا تَعْبُدُوا الشَّيْطَانَ إِنَّهُ لَكُمْ عَدُوٌّ مُبِينٌ

Did I not charge you, O ye sons of Adam, that ye worship not the devil Lo! he is your open foe!		
61. Wa ani'budūnī hadhā ṣirāṭun mustaqīm		وَأَنْ اعْبُدُونِي هَذَا صِرَاطٌ مُّسْتَقِيمٌ
But that ye worship Me? That was the right path.		
62. Wa laqad aḍalla minkum jibillan kathīran afalam takūnū t'aqilūn		وَلَقَدْ أَضَلَّ مِنكُمْ جِبِلًّا كَثِيرًا أَفَلَمْ تَكُونُوا تَعْقِلُونَ
Yet he hath led astray of you a great multitude. Had ye then no sense?		
63. Hadhihi jahannamu 'l-latī kuntum tūa'dūn		هَذِهِ جَهَنَّمُ الَّتِي كُنتُمْ تُوعَدُونَ
This is hell which ye were promised (if ye followed him).		
64. Iṣlawhā 'l-yawma bi-mā kuntum takfurūn		اصْلَوْهَا الْيَوْمَ بِمَا كُنتُمْ تَكْفُرُونَ
Burn therein this day for that ye disbelieved.		
65. Al-yawma nakhtimu 'alā afwāhihim wa tukallimuna aydīhim wa tashhadu arjuluhum bi-mā kānū yaksibūn		الْيَوْمَ نَخْتِمُ عَلَى أَفْوَاهِهِمْ وَتُكَلِّمُنَا أَيْدِيهِمْ وَتَشْهَدُ أَرْجُلُهُم بِمَا كَانُوا يَكْسِبُونَ
This day We seal up mouths, and hands speak out and feet bear witness as to what they used to earn.		
66. Wa law nashā'u la-ṭamasnā 'ala ā'ayunihim fa-stabaqū 'ṣ-ṣirāṭa fa-anna yubṣirūn		وَلَوْ نَشَاء لَطَمَسْنَا عَلَى أَعْيُنِهِمْ فَاسْتَبَقُوا الصِّرَاطَ فَأَنَّى يُبْصِرُونَ
And had We willed, We verily could have quenched their eyesight so that they should struggle for the way. Then how could they have seen?		

<table>
<tr><td>67. Wa law nasha'u la-masakhnāhum 'ala makānatihim fa-mā istaṭā'ū muḍīyyan wa lā yarji'ūn</td><td></td><td>وَلَوْ نَشَاء لَمَسَخْنَاهُمْ عَلَى مَكَانَتِهِمْ فَمَا اسْتَطَاعُوا مُضِيًّا وَلَا يَرْجِعُونَ</td></tr>
<tr><td colspan="3">And had We willed, We verily could have fixed them in their place, making them powerless to go forward or turn back.</td></tr>
<tr><td>68. Wa man nu'ammirhu nunakkis-hu fī 'l-khalqi afalā y'aqilūn</td><td></td><td>وَمَنْ نُعَمِّرْهُ نُنَكِّسْهُ فِي الْخَلْقِ أَفَلَا يَعْقِلُونَ</td></tr>
<tr><td colspan="3">He whom We bring unto old age, We reverse him in creation (making him go back to weakness after strength). Have ye then no sense?</td></tr>
<tr><td>69. Wa mā 'allamnāhu 'sh-sh'ira wa mā yanbaghī lahu in Huwa illa dhikrun wa qur'ānun mubīn</td><td></td><td>وَمَا عَلَّمْنَاهُ الشِّعْرَ وَمَا يَنْبَغِي لَهُ إِنْ هُوَ إِلَّا ذِكْرٌ وَقُرْآنٌ مُبِينٌ</td></tr>
<tr><td colspan="3">And we have not taught him (Muhammad) poetry, nor is it meet for him. This is naught else than a Reminder and a Lecture making plain,</td></tr>
<tr><td>70. Li-yundhira man kāna ḥayyan wa yaḥiqqa 'l-qawlu 'ala 'l-kāfirīn</td><td></td><td>لِيُنْذِرَ مَنْ كَانَ حَيًّا وَيَحِقَّ الْقَوْلُ عَلَى الْكَافِرِينَ</td></tr>
<tr><td colspan="3">To warn whosoever liveth, and that the word may be fulfilled against the disbelievers.</td></tr>
<tr><td>71. Awa lam yaraw annā khalaqnā la-hum mimmā 'amilat aydīna ana'āman fa-hum lahā mālikūn</td><td></td><td>أَوَلَمْ يَرَوْا أَنَّا خَلَقْنَا لَهُمْ مِمَّا عَمِلَتْ أَيْدِينَا أَنْعَامًا فَهُمْ لَهَا مَالِكُونَ</td></tr>
<tr><td colspan="3">Have they not seen how We have created for them of Our handiwork the cattle, so that they are their owners,</td></tr>
<tr><td>72. Wa dhallalnāhā la-hum fa-minhā rakūbuhum wa minhā yā'kulūn</td><td></td><td>وَذَلَّلْنَاهَا لَهُمْ فَمِنْهَا رَكُوبُهُمْ وَمِنْهَا يَأْكُلُونَ</td></tr>
<tr><td colspan="3">And have subdued them unto them, so that some of them they have for riding, some</td></tr>
</table>

for food?		
73. Wa la-hum fīhā manāfi'u wa mashāribu afalā yashkurūn		وَلَهُمْ فِيهَا مَنَافِعُ وَمَشَارِبُ أَفَلَا يَشْكُرُونَ
Benefits and (divers) drinks have they from them. Will they not then give thanks?		
74. Wat-takhadhū min dūni 'l-lāhi alihatan la'allahum yunṣarūn		وَاتَّخَذُوا مِن دُونِ اللَّهِ آلِهَةً لَّعَلَّهُمْ يُنصَرُونَ
And they have taken (other) gods beside Allah, in order that they may be helped.		
75. Lā yastaṭī'ūna naṣrahum wa hum lahum jundun muḥḍarūn		لَا يَسْتَطِيعُونَ نَصْرَهُمْ وَهُمْ لَهُمْ جُندٌ مُّحْضَرُونَ
It is not in their power to help them; but they (the worshippers) are unto them a host in arms.		
76. Falā yaḥzunka qawluhum innā n'alamu mā yusirrūna wa mā y'ulinūn		فَلَا يَحْزُنكَ قَوْلُهُمْ إِنَّا نَعْلَمُ مَا يُسِرُّونَ وَمَا يُعْلِنُونَ
So let not their speech grieve thee (O Muhammad). Lo! We know what they conceal and what proclaim.		
77. Awa lam yara 'l-insānu annā khalaqnāhu min nuṭfatin fa-idhā Huwa khaṣīmun mubīn		أَوَلَمْ يَرَ الْإِنسَانُ أَنَّا خَلَقْنَاهُ مِن نُّطْفَةٍ فَإِذَا هُوَ خَصِيمٌ مُّبِينٌ
Hath not man seen that We have created him from a drop of seed? Yet lo! he is an open opponent.		
78. Wa ḍaraba lanā mathalan wa nasīya khalqahu qāla man yuḥyī 'l-'iẓāma wa hīya ramīm		وَضَرَبَ لَنَا مَثَلًا وَنَسِيَ خَلْقَهُ قَالَ مَن يُحْيِي الْعِظَامَ وَهِيَ رَمِيمٌ
And he hath coined for Us a similitude, and hath forgotten the fact of his creation, saying: Who will revive these bones when they have rotted away?		

<table>
<tr><td>79. Qul yuḥyīhā ’l-ladhī anshā’ahā āwwala marratin wa Huwa bi kulli khalqin ‘alīm</td><td></td><td>قُلْ يُحْيِيهَا الَّذِي أَنشَأَهَا أَوَّلَ مَرَّةٍ وَهُوَ بِكُلِّ خَلْقٍ عَلِيمٌ</td></tr>
<tr><td colspan="3">Say: He will revive them Who produced them at the first, for He is Knower of every creation,</td></tr>
<tr><td>80. Al-ladhī ja‘ala lakum mina ’sh-shajari ’l-akhḍari nāran fa idhā antum minhu tūqidūn</td><td></td><td>الَّذِي جَعَلَ لَكُم مِّنَ الشَّجَرِ الْأَخْضَرِ نَارًا فَإِذَا أَنتُم مِّنْهُ تُوقِدُونَ</td></tr>
<tr><td colspan="3">Who hath appointed for you fire from the green tree, and behold! ye kindle from it.</td></tr>
<tr><td>81. Awa laysa ’l-ladhī khalaqa ’s-samawāti wa ’l-arḍa bi-qādirin ‘alā an yakhluqa mithlahum balā wa Huwa ’l-Khallāqu ’l-‘Alīm</td><td></td><td>أَوَلَيْسَ الَّذِي خَلَقَ السَّمَاوَاتِ وَالْأَرْضَ بِقَادِرٍ عَلَى أَنْ يَخْلُقَ مِثْلَهُم بَلَى وَهُوَ الْخَلَّاقُ الْعَلِيمُ</td></tr>
<tr><td colspan="3">Is not He Who created the heavens and the earth Able to create the like of them? Aye, that He is! for He is the All Wise Creator,</td></tr>
<tr><td>82. Innamā amruhu idhā arada shay’an an yaqūla lahu kun fa-yakūn</td><td></td><td>إِنَّمَا أَمْرُهُ إِذَا أَرَادَ شَيْئًا أَنْ يَقُولَ لَهُ كُنْ فَيَكُونُ</td></tr>
<tr><td colspan="3">But His command, when He intendeth a thing, is only that he saith unto it: Be! and it is.</td></tr>
<tr><td>83. Fa subḥāna ’l-ladhī bi-yadihi malakūtu kulli shay’in wa ilayhi turja‘ūn</td><td></td><td>فَسُبْحَانَ الَّذِي بِيَدِهِ مَلَكُوتُ كُلِّ شَيْءٍ وَإِلَيْهِ تُرْجَعُونَ</td></tr>
<tr><td colspan="3">Therefore glory be to Him in Whose hand is the dominion over all things! Unto Him ye will be brought back.</td></tr>
</table>

<table>
<tr><td>Surat al-Mulk: Kingship (67)</td><td></td><td dir="rtl">سورة الملك</td></tr>
<tr><td colspan="3">The Prophet ﷺ said:

There is a chapter of the Book which only has thirty verses which will intercede for a man on the Day of Rising, bring him out of the Fire and cause him to enter the Garden. It is the chapter Tabārak (i.e. al-Mulk).[325]

Ibn Masud ﷺ related that the Messenger of God ﷺ said:

The chapter Tabārak, is the preventer from the punishment of the grave.[326]</td></tr>
<tr><td colspan="3">To be read after Ṣalāt aẓ-Ẓuhr and after Ṣalāt al-'Ishā</td></tr>
<tr><td>Bismillāhi 'r-Raḥmāni 'r-Rahīm</td><td></td><td dir="rtl">بِسْمِ اللهِ الرَّحْمٰنِ الرَّحِيمِ</td></tr>
<tr><td colspan="3">In the Name of Allah, the Most Beneficent, the Most Merciful.</td></tr>
<tr><td>1. Tabāraka 'l-ladhī bi-yadihi 'l-Mulku wa Huwa 'alā kulli shay'in qadīr</td><td></td><td dir="rtl">تَبَارَكَ الَّذِي بِيَدِهِ الْمُلْكُ وَهُوَ عَلَى كُلِّ شَيْءٍ قَدِيرٌ</td></tr>
<tr><td colspan="3">Blessed is He in Whose hand is the Sovereignty, and He is Able to do all things.</td></tr>
<tr><td>2. Al-ladhī khalaqa 'l-mawta wa 'l-ḥayāta li-yabluwakum ayyukum aḥsanu 'amala wa Huwa 'l-'Azīzu 'l-Ghafūr.</td><td></td><td dir="rtl">الَّذِي خَلَقَ الْمَوْتَ وَالْحَيَاةَ لِيَبْلُوَكُمْ أَيُّكُمْ أَحْسَنُ عَمَلًا وَهُوَ الْعَزِيزُ الْغَفُورُ</td></tr>
<tr><td colspan="3">Who hath created life and death that He may try you, which of you is best in conduct; and He is the Mighty, Forgiving,</td></tr>
<tr><td>3. Al-ladhī khalaqa saba'a samāwātin ṭibāqan mā tarā fī khalqi 'r-Raḥmāni min tafāwutin farji'i 'l-baṣara hal tarā min</td><td></td><td dir="rtl">الَّذِي خَلَقَ سَبْعَ سَمَاوَاتٍ طِبَاقًا مَّا تَرَى فِي خَلْقِ الرَّحْمَنِ مِن تَفَاوُتٍ فَارْجِعِ الْبَصَرَ هَلْ تَرَى مِن فُطُورٍ</td></tr>
</table>

[325] Narrated by at-Tirmidhi and Ahmad.

[326] Ibn Mardawayh from ibn Masud.

fuṭūr		
Who hath created seven heavens in harmony. Thou (Muhammad) canst see no fault in the Beneficent One's creation; then look again: Canst thou see any rifts?		
4. Thumma 'rji'i 'l-baṣara karratayni yanqalib ilayka 'l-baṣaru khāsi'an wa Huwa ḥasīr		ثُمَّ ارْجِعِ الْبَصَرَ كَرَّتَيْنِ يَنقَلِبْ إِلَيْكَ الْبَصَرُ خَاسِأً وَهُوَ حَسِيرٌ
Then look again and yet again, thy sight will return unto thee weakened and made dim.		
5. Wa-laqad zayyanna 's-samā ad-dunyā bi maṣābīḥa wa ja'alnāha rujūman li 'sh-shayāṭīni wa ā'atadnā la-hum 'aḍāba 's-sa'īr		وَلَقَدْ زَيَّنَّا السَّمَاءَ الدُّنْيَا بِمَصَابِيحَ وَجَعَلْنَاهَا رُجُومًا لِّلشَّيَاطِينِ وَأَعْتَدْنَا لَهُمْ عَذَابَ السَّعِيرِ
And verily We have beatified the world's heaven with lamps, and We have made them missiles for the devils, and for them We have prepared the doom of flame.		
6. Wa lil-ladhīna kafarū bi-rabbihim 'adhābu jahannama wa bi'sa 'l-maṣīr		وَلِلَّذِينَ كَفَرُوا بِرَبِّهِمْ عَذَابُ جَهَنَّمَ وَبِئْسَ الْمَصِيرُ
And for those who disbelieve in their Lord there is the doom of hell, a hapless journey's end!		
7. Idhā ulqū fīhā sami'ū lahā shahīqan wa hīya tafūr		إِذَا أُلْقُوا فِيهَا سَمِعُوا لَهَا شَهِيقًا وَهِيَ تَفُورُ
When they are flung therein they hear its roaring as it boileth up,		
8. Takādu tamayyazu mina 'l-ghayẓi kullamā ulqīya fīhā fawjun sa'alahum khazanatuhā alam yā'tikum nadhīr		تَكَادُ تَمَيَّزُ مِنَ الْغَيْظِ كُلَّمَا أُلْقِيَ فِيهَا فَوْجٌ سَأَلَهُمْ خَزَنَتُهَا أَلَمْ يَأْتِكُمْ نَذِيرٌ
As it would burst with rage. Whenever a (fresh) host flung therein the wardens thereof ask them: Came there unto you no warner?		

<table>
<tr><td>9. Qālū balā qad jā'anā nadhīrun fa-kadhdhabnā wa qulnā mā nazzala-Allāhu min shay'in in antum illa fī ḍalālin kabīr</td><td></td><td>قَالُوا بَلَىٰ قَدْ جَاءَنَا نَذِيرٌ فَكَذَّبْنَا وَقُلْنَا مَا نَزَّلَ اللَّهُ مِن شَيْءٍ إِنْ أَنتُمْ إِلَّا فِي ضَلَالٍ كَبِيرٍ</td></tr>
<tr><td colspan="3">They say: Yea, verily, a warner came unto us; but we denied and said: Allah hath naught revealed; ye are in nought but a great error.</td></tr>
<tr><td>10. Wa qālū law kunnā nasma'u aw n'aqilu mā kunnā fī aṣḥābi 's-sa'īr</td><td></td><td>وَقَالُوا لَوْ كُنَّا نَسْمَعُ أَوْ نَعْقِلُ مَا كُنَّا فِي أَصْحَابِ السَّعِيرِ</td></tr>
<tr><td colspan="3">And they say: Had we been wont to listen or have sense, we had not been among the dwellers in the flames.</td></tr>
<tr><td>11. F'atarafū bi-dhanbihim fasuḥqan li aṣḥabi 's-sa'īr</td><td></td><td>فَاعْتَرَفُوا بِذَنبِهِمْ فَسُحْقًا لِّأَصْحَابِ السَّعِيرِ</td></tr>
<tr><td colspan="3">So they acknowledge their sins; but far removed (from mercy) are the dwellers in the flames.</td></tr>
<tr><td>12. Inna 'l-ladhīna yakhshawna rabbahum bi 'l-ghaybi la-hum maghfiratun wa ajrun kabīr</td><td></td><td>إِنَّ الَّذِينَ يَخْشَوْنَ رَبَّهُم بِالْغَيْبِ لَهُم مَّغْفِرَةٌ وَأَجْرٌ كَبِيرٌ</td></tr>
<tr><td colspan="3">Lo! those who fear their Lord in secret, theirs will be forgiveness and a great reward.</td></tr>
<tr><td>13. Wa asirrū qawlakum awi 'jharū bihi innahu 'alīmun bi-dhāti 'ṣ-ṣudūr</td><td></td><td>وَأَسِرُّوا قَوْلَكُمْ أَوِ اجْهَرُوا بِهِ إِنَّهُ عَلِيمٌ بِذَاتِ الصُّدُورِ</td></tr>
<tr><td colspan="3">And keep your opinion secret or proclaim it, lo! He is Knower of all that is in the breasts (of men)</td></tr>
<tr><td>14. Alā y'alamu man khalaqa wa Huwa 'l-Latīfu 'l-Khabīr</td><td></td><td>أَلَا يَعْلَمُ مَنْ خَلَقَ وَهُوَ اللَّطِيفُ الْخَبِيرُ</td></tr>
<tr><td colspan="3">Should He not know what He created? And He is the Subtile, the Aware.</td></tr>
</table>

<table>
<tr><td>15. Huwa ’l-ladhī ja‘ala lakumu ’l-arḍa dhalūlan fa-mshū fī manākibihā wa kulū min rizqihi wa ilayhi ’n-nushūr</td><td></td><td>هُوَ الَّذِي جَعَلَ لَكُمُ الأَرْضَ ذَلُولاً فَامْشُوا فِي مَنَاكِبِهَا وَكُلُوا مِن رِّزْقِهِ وَإِلَيْهِ النُّشُورُ</td></tr>
<tr><td colspan="3">He it is Who hath made the earth subservient unto you, so walk in the paths thereof and eat of His providence. And unto Him will be the resurrection (of the dead)</td></tr>
<tr><td>16. A-amintum man fī ’s-samā’i an yakhsifa bikumu ’l-arḍa fa-idhā hīya tamūr</td><td></td><td>أَأَمِنتُم مَّن فِي السَّمَاءِ أَن يَخْسِفَ بِكُمُ الأَرْضَ فَإِذَا هِيَ تَمُورُ</td></tr>
<tr><td colspan="3">Have ye taken security from Him Who is in the heaven that He will not cause the earth to swallow you when lo! it is convulsed?</td></tr>
<tr><td>17. Am amintum man fī ’s-samā’i an yursila ‘alaykum ḥāṣiban fa-sa-t‘alamūna kayfa nadhīr</td><td></td><td>أَمْ أَمِنتُم مَّن فِي السَّمَاءِ أَن يُرْسِلَ عَلَيْكُمْ حَاصِبًا فَسَتَعْلَمُونَ كَيْفَ نَذِيرِ</td></tr>
<tr><td colspan="3">Or have ye taken security from Him Who is in the heaven that He will not let loose on you a hurricane? But ye shall know the manner of My warning.</td></tr>
<tr><td>18. Wa-laqad kadhdhaba ’l-ladhīna min qablihim fa-kayfa kāna nakīr</td><td></td><td>وَلَقَدْ كَذَّبَ الَّذِينَ مِن قَبْلِهِمْ فَكَيْفَ كَانَ نَكِيرِ</td></tr>
<tr><td colspan="3">And verily those before them denied, then (see) the manner of My wrath (with them!)</td></tr>
<tr><td>19. Awa lam yaraw ila aṭ-ṭayri fawqahum ṣāffātin wa yaqbidna mā yumsikuhunna illa ar-raḥmānu innahu bi-kulli shay’in basīr.</td><td></td><td>أَوَلَمْ يَرَوْا إِلَى الطَّيْرِ فَوْقَهُمْ صَافَّاتٍ وَيَقْبِضْنَ مَا يُمْسِكُهُنَّ إِلاَّ الرَّحْمَنُ إِنَّهُ بِكُلِّ شَيْءٍ بَصِيرٌ</td></tr>
<tr><td colspan="3">Have they not seen the birds above them spreading out their wings and closing them? Naught upholdeth them save the Beneficent. Lo! He is Seer of all things.</td></tr>
<tr><td>20. Amman hadha ’l-ladhī Huwa jundun lakum yanṣurukum min dūni ’r-Raḥmān</td><td></td><td>أَمَّنْ هَذَا الَّذِي هُوَ جُندٌ لَّكُمْ يَنصُرُكُم مِّن دُونِ الرَّحْمَنِ إِنِ الْكَافِرُونَ إِلاَّ فِي غُرُورٍ</td></tr>
</table>

ini 'l-kāfirūna illa fī ghurūr		
Or who is he that will be an army unto you to help you instead of the Beneficent? The disbelievers are in naught but illusion.		
21. Amman hadha 'l-ladhī yarzuqukum in amsaka rizqahu bal lajjū fī 'utuwwin wa nufūr		أَمَّنْ هَٰذَا الَّذِي يَرْزُقُكُمْ إِنْ أَمْسَكَ رِزْقَهُ بَل لَّجُّوا فِي عُتُوٍّ وَنُفُورٍ
Or who is he that will provide for you if He should withhold His providence? Nay, but they are set in pride and frowardness.		
22. Afa-man yamshī mukibban 'alā wajhihi ahdā amman yamshī sawiyyan 'alā ṣirāṭin mustaqīm		أَفَمَن يَمْشِي مُكِبًّا عَلَىٰ وَجْهِهِ أَهْدَىٰ أَمَّن يَمْشِي سَوِيًّا عَلَىٰ صِرَاطٍ مُّسْتَقِيمٍ
Is he who goeth groping on his face more rightly guided, or he who walketh upright on a beaten road?		
23. Qul Huwa 'l-ladhī anshā'akum wa ja'ala lakumu 's-sam'a wa 'l-abṣāra wa 'l-af'idata qalīlan mā tashkurūn		قُلْ هُوَ الَّذِي أَنشَأَكُمْ وَجَعَلَ لَكُمُ السَّمْعَ وَالْأَبْصَارَ وَالْأَفْئِدَةَ قَلِيلًا مَّا تَشْكُرُونَ
Say (unto them, O Muhammad): He it is Who gave you being, and hath assigned unto you ears and eyes and hearts. Small thanks give ye!		
24. Qul huwa 'l-ladhī dharā'kum fī 'l-arḍi wa ilayhi tuḥsharūn		قُلْ هُوَ الَّذِي ذَرَأَكُمْ فِي الْأَرْضِ وَإِلَيْهِ تُحْشَرُونَ
Say, He it is Who multiplieth you in the earth, and unto Whom ye will be gathered.		
25. Wa yaqūlūna matā hadha 'l-wa'adu in kuntum ṣādiqīn		وَيَقُولُونَ مَتَىٰ هَٰذَا الْوَعْدُ إِن كُنتُمْ صَادِقِينَ
And they say: When (will) this promise (be fulfilled), if ye are truthful?		
26. Qul innamā 'l-'ilmu 'inda -llāhi wa		قُلْ إِنَّمَا الْعِلْمُ عِندَ اللَّهِ وَإِنَّمَا أَنَا نَذِيرٌ مُّبِينٌ

innamā anā nadhīrun mubīn		
Say: The knowledge is with Allah only, and I am but a plain warner;		
27. Fa-lammā ra'awhu zulfatan sī'at wujūhu 'l-ladhīna kafarū wa qīla hadha 'l-ladhī kuntum bihi tadda'ūn		فَلَمَّا رَأَوْهُ زُلْفَةً سِيئَتْ وُجُوهُ الَّذِينَ كَفَرُوا وَقِيلَ هَذَا الَّذِي كُنتُم بِهِ تَدَّعُونَ
But when they see it nigh, the faces of those who disbelieve will be awry, and it will be said (unto them): This is that for which ye used to call		
28. Qul arā'aytum in ahlakanīy-allāhu wa man ma'īya aw raḥimanā fa-man yujīru 'l-kāfirīna min 'adhābin alīm		قُلْ أَرَأَيْتُمْ إِنْ أَهْلَكَنِيَ اللَّهُ وَمَن مَّعِيَ أَوْ رَحِمَنَا فَمَن يُجِيرُ الْكَافِرِينَ مِنْ عَذَابٍ أَلِيمٍ
Say (O Muhammad): Have ye thought: Whether Allah causeth me (Muhammad) and those with me to perish or hath mercy on us, still, who will protect the disbelievers from a painful doom?		
29. Qul Huwa 'r-Raḥmānu āmannā bihi wa 'alayhi tawakkalnā fa-sat'alamūna man Huwa fī ḍalālin mubīn		قُلْ هُوَ الرَّحْمَٰنُ آمَنَّا بِهِ وَعَلَيْهِ تَوَكَّلْنَا فَسَتَعْلَمُونَ مَنْ هُوَ فِي ضَلَالٍ مُّبِينٍ
Say: He is the Beneficent. In Him we believe and in Him we put our trust. And ye will soon know who it is that is in error manifest.		
30. Qul arā'ytum in aṣbaḥa mā'ūkum ghawran fa-man yā'tīkum bi mā'in ma'īn		قُلْ أَرَأَيْتُمْ إِنْ أَصْبَحَ مَاؤُكُمْ غَوْرًا فَمَن يَأْتِيكُم بِمَاءٍ مَّعِينٍ
Say: Have ye thought: If (all) your water were to disappear into the earth, who then could bring you gushing water?		

Surat an-Naba: The Event (78)			سورة النبأ
Abd Allāh bin Qais ﵁ said: *I asked Anas ﵁ about the measure of the prayer of the Prophet ﷺ. Then he called for one of his sons and he prayed with us the noon and afternoon prayer and read: "Whereof do they question one another?"*[327]			
To be read after Ṣalāt al-'Aṣr			
Bismillāhi 'r-Raḥmāni 'r-Rahīm			بِسْمِ اللهِ الرَّحْمٰنِ الرَّحِيمِ
In the Name of Allah, the Most Beneficent, the Most Merciful.			
1. 'amma yatasā'alūna			عَمَّ يَتَسَاءَلُونَ
Whereof do they question one another?			
2. 'ani 'n-nabā'i 'l-'aẓīm			عَنِ النَّبَإِ الْعَظِيمِ
(It is) of the awful tidings,			
3. Alladhī hum fīhi mukhtalifūn			الَّذِي هُمْ فِيهِ مُخْتَلِفُونَ
Concerning which they are in disagreement.			
4. Kallā sa-y'alamūna			كَلَّا سَيَعْلَمُونَ
Nay, but they will come to know!			
5. Thumma kalla say'alamūn.			ثُمَّ كَلَّا سَيَعْلَمُونَ
Nay, again, but they will come to know!			
6. Alam naj'ali 'l-arḍa mihādan			أَلَمْ نَجْعَلِ الْأَرْضَ مِهَادًا

[327] Al-Bayhaqī related it in his *Sunan*.

Have We not made the earth an expanse,		
7. Wa 'l-jibāla awtādan		وَالْجِبَالَ أَوْتَادًا
And the high hills bulwarks?		
8. Wa khalaqnākum azwāja		وَخَلَقْنَاكُمْ أَزْوَاجًا
And We have created you in pairs,		
9. Wa ja'alnā nawmakum subātan		وَجَعَلْنَا نَوْمَكُمْ سُبَاتًا
And have appointed your sleep for repose,		
10. Wa ja'alnā 'l-layla libāsan		وَجَعَلْنَا اللَّيْلَ لِبَاسًا
And have appointed the night as a cloak,		
11. Wa ja'alnā 'n-nahāra ma'āsha		وَجَعَلْنَا النَّهَارَ مَعَاشًا
And have appointed the day for livelihood.		
12. Wa banaynā fawqakum sab'an shidādan		وَبَنَيْنَا فَوْقَكُمْ سَبْعًا شِدَادًا
And We have built above you seven strong (heavens),		
13. Wa ja'alnā sirājan wa h-hāja		وَجَعَلْنَا سِرَاجًا وَهَّاجًا
And have appointed a dazzling lamp,		
14. Wa anzalnā mina 'l-m'uṣirāti mā'an thajjājan		وَأَنْزَلْنَا مِنَ الْمُعْصِرَاتِ مَاءً ثَجَّاجًا
And have sent down from the rainy clouds abundant Water,		
15. Li nukhrija bihi ḥabban wa nabātan		لِنُخْرِجَ بِهِ حَبًّا وَنَبَاتًا

Thereby to produce grain and plant,		
16. Wa jannātin alfāfa.		وَجَنَّاتٍ أَلْفَافًا
And gardens of thick foliage.		
17. Inna yawma 'l-faṣli kāna mīqāta;		إِنَّ يَوْمَ الْفَصْلِ كَانَ مِيقَاتًا
Lo! the Day of Decision is a fixed time,		
18. Yawma yunfakhu fī 'ṣ-ṣūri fatā'tūna afwājan		يَوْمَ يُنفَخُ فِي الصُّورِ فَتَأْتُونَ أَفْوَاجًا
A day when the trumpet is blown, and ye come in multitudes		
19. Wa futiḥati 's-samā'u fa-kānat abwāban		وَفُتِحَتِ السَّمَاءُ فَكَانَتْ أَبْوَابًا
And the heaven is opened and becometh as gates		
20. Wa suyyirati 'l-jibālu fakānat sarāba.		وَسُيِّرَتِ الْجِبَالُ فَكَانَتْ سَرَابًا
And the hills are set in motion and become as a mirage.		
21. Inna jahannama kānat mirṣādan		إِنَّ جَهَنَّمَ كَانَتْ مِرْصَادًا
Lo! Hell lurketh in ambush,		
22. Li 'ṭ-ṭāghīna ma-āba		لِّلطَّاغِينَ مَآبًا
A home for the rebellious		
23. Lābithīna fīhā aḥqāban		لَّابِثِينَ فِيهَا أَحْقَابًا
They will abide therein for ages.		
24. Lā yadhūqūna fīhā bardan wa lā		لَّا يَذُوقُونَ فِيهَا بَرْدًا وَلَا شَرَابًا

sharāban		
Therein taste they neither coolness nor (any) drink		
25. Illā ḥamīman wa ghassāqan		إِلَّا حَمِيمًا وَغَسَّاقًا
Save boiling water and a paralyzing cold:		
26. Jazā'an wifāqa		جَزَاءً وِفَاقًا
Reward proportioned (to their evil deeds).		
27. Innahum kānū la yarjūna ḥisāba		إِنَّهُمْ كَانُوا لَا يَرْجُونَ حِسَابًا
For lo! They looked not for a reckoning;		
28. Wa kadhdhabū bi āyātinā kidhdhāba		وَكَذَّبُوا بِآيَاتِنَا كِذَّابًا
They called Our revelations false with strong denial.		
29. Wa kulla shay'in aḥṣaynāhu kitāba		وَكُلَّ شَيْءٍ أَحْصَيْنَاهُ كِتَابًا
Everything have We recorded in a Book.		
30. Fa-dhūqū fa-lan nazīdakum illā 'adhāba.		فَذُوقُوا فَلَن نَّزِيدَكُمْ إِلَّا عَذَابًا
So taste (of that which ye have earned). No increase do We give you save of torment.		
31. Inna li 'l-muttaqīna mafāzan		إِنَّ لِلْمُتَّقِينَ مَفَازًا
Lo! for the duteous is achievement		
32. ḥadā'iqa wa a'anāban		حَدَائِقَ وَأَعْنَابًا
Gardens enclosed and vineyards,		
33. Wa kawā'iba atrāban		وَكَوَاعِبَ أَتْرَابًا

And maidens for companions,		
34. Wa kā'san dihāqa		وَكَأْسًا دِهَاقًا
And a full cup.		
35. Lā yasma'ūna fīhā laghwan wa lā kidhdhāba		لَا يَسْمَعُونَ فِيهَا لَغْوًا وَلَا كِذَّابًا
There hear they never vain discourse, nor lying		
36. Jazā'an min rabbika 'atā'an ḥisāba		جَزَاءً مِّن رَّبِّكَ عَطَاءً حِسَابًا
Requital from thy Lord a gift in payment		
37. Rabbi 's-samāwāti wa 'l-arḍi wa mā baynahuma 'r-Raḥmāni lā yamlikūna minhu khiṭāba		رَبِّ السَّمَاوَاتِ وَالْأَرْضِ وَمَا بَيْنَهُمَا الرَّحْمَنِ لَا يَمْلِكُونَ مِنْهُ خِطَابًا
Lord of the heavens and the earth, and (all) that is between them, the Beneficent; with Whom none can converse.		
38. Yawma yaqūmu 'r-rūḥu wa 'l-malā'ikatu ṣaffan lā yatakallamūna illa man adhina lahu 'r-Raḥmānu wa qāla ṣawāba		يَوْمَ يَقُومُ الرُّوحُ وَالْمَلَائِكَةُ صَفًّا لَا يَتَكَلَّمُونَ إِلَّا مَنْ أَذِنَ لَهُ الرَّحْمَنُ وَقَالَ صَوَابًا
On the day when the angels and the Spirit stand arrayed, they speak not, saving him whom the Beneficent alloweth and who speaketh right.		
39. Dhalika 'l-yawmu 'l-ḥaqqu fa-man shā'a 'ttakhadha ilā rabbihi ma'āba		ذَلِكَ الْيَوْمُ الْحَقُّ فَمَن شَاءَ اتَّخَذَ إِلَى رَبِّهِ مَآبًا
That is the True Day. So whoso will should seek recourse unto his Lord.		
40. Innā andharnākum 'adhāban qarīban yawma yanẓuru 'l-mar'u mā qaddamat		إِنَّا أَنذَرْنَاكُمْ عَذَابًا قَرِيبًا يَوْمَ يَنظُرُ الْمَرْءُ مَا قَدَّمَتْ يَدَاهُ وَيَقُولُ

yadāhu wa yaqūlu 'l-kāfiru yā laytanī kuntu turābā.		الْكَافِرُ يَا لَيْتَنِي كُنتُ تُرَابًا
Lo! We warn you of a doom at hand, a day whereon a man will look on that which his own hands have sent before, and the disbeliever will cry: "Would that I were dust!"		

<table>
<tr><td>Surat As-Sajdah: The Prostration (32)</td><td></td><td>سورة السجدة</td></tr>
<tr><td colspan="3">Ibn Umar ﷺ related that the Prophet ﷺ said:

Whoever reads tabārak alladhī bi-yaddihi 'l-Mulk (Surat al-Mulk) and Alif. Lām. Mīm. Tanzīl... (Surat as-Sajdah) between the sunset prayer and the later of the night prayer is like he who stood in prayer during the Night of Power.[328]</td></tr>
<tr><td colspan="3">To be read after Ṣalāt al-Maghrib</td></tr>
<tr><td>Bismillāhi 'r-Raḥmāni 'r-Rahīm</td><td></td><td>بِسْمِ اللهِ الرَّحْمٰنِ الرَّحِيمِ</td></tr>
<tr><td colspan="3">In the Name of Allah, the Most Beneficent, the Most Merciful.</td></tr>
<tr><td>1. Alif lām mīm</td><td></td><td>الم</td></tr>
<tr><td colspan="3">Alif. Lām. Mīm.</td></tr>
<tr><td>2. Tanzīlu 'l-kitābi lā rayba fīhi min rabbi 'l-'ālamīn</td><td></td><td>تَنزِيلُ الْكِتَابِ لَا رَيْبَ فِيهِ مِن رَّبِّ الْعَالَمِينَ</td></tr>
<tr><td colspan="3">The revelation of the Scripture whereof there is no doubt is from the Lord of the Worlds.</td></tr>
<tr><td>3. Am yaqūlūna 'ftarāhu bal huwa 'l-ḥaqqu min Rabbika li-tundhira qawman mā atāhum min nadhīrin min qablika la'allahum yahtadūn</td><td></td><td>أَمْ يَقُولُونَ افْتَرَاهُ بَلْ هُوَ الْحَقُّ مِن رَّبِّكَ لِتُنذِرَ قَوْمًا مَّا أَتَاهُم مِّن نَّذِيرٍ مِّن قَبْلِكَ لَعَلَّهُمْ يَهْتَدُونَ</td></tr>
<tr><td colspan="3">Or say they: He hath invented it? Nay, but it is the Truth from thy Lord, that thou mayst warn a folk to whom no warner came before thee, that haply they may walk aright.</td></tr>
</table>

[328] Ibn Mardawayh related it from Ibn Umar.

4. Allāhu 'l-ladhī khalaqa 's-samāwāti wa 'l-arḍa wa mā baynahumā fī sittati ayyāmin thumma 'stawa 'ala 'l-'arsh. mā lakum min dūnihi min walīyyin wa lā shafī'in afalā tatadhakkarūn		اللَّهُ الَّذِي خَلَقَ السَّمَاوَاتِ وَالْأَرْضَ وَمَا بَيْنَهُمَا فِي سِتَّةِ أَيَّامٍ ثُمَّ اسْتَوَى عَلَى الْعَرْشِ مَا لَكُم مِّن دُونِهِ مِن وَلِيٍّ وَلَا شَفِيعٍ أَفَلَا تَتَذَكَّرُونَ
Allah it is Who created the heavens and the earth, and that which is between them, in six Days. Then He mounted the throne. Ye have not, beside Him, a protecting friend or mediator. Will ye not then remember?		
5. Yudabbiru 'l-amra mina 's-sama'i ila 'l-arḍi thumma y'aruju ilayhi fī yawmin kāna miqdāruhu alfa sanatin mimmā ta'uddūn		يُدَبِّرُ الْأَمْرَ مِنَ السَّمَاءِ إِلَى الْأَرْضِ ثُمَّ يَعْرُجُ إِلَيْهِ فِي يَوْمٍ كَانَ مِقْدَارُهُ أَلْفَ سَنَةٍ مِّمَّا تَعُدُّونَ
He directeth the ordinance from the heaven unto the earth; then it ascendeth unto Him in a Day, whereof the measure is a thousand years of that ye reckon.		
6. dhalika 'ālimu 'l-ghaybi wa 'sh-shahādati 'l-'Azīzu 'r-Raḥīm		ذَلِكَ عَالِمُ الْغَيْبِ وَالشَّهَادَةِ الْعَزِيزُ الرَّحِيمُ
Such is the Knower of the invisible and the visible, the Mighty, the Merciful,		
7. Alladhī aḥsana kulla shay'in khalaqah, wa bada'a khalqa 'l-insān min ṭīn		الَّذِي أَحْسَنَ كُلَّ شَيْءٍ خَلَقَهُ وَبَدَأَ خَلْقَ الْإِنسَانِ مِن طِينٍ
Who made all things good which He created, and He began the creation of man from clay;		
8. Thumma ja'ala naslahu min sulālatin min mā'in mahīn		ثُمَّ جَعَلَ نَسْلَهُ مِن سُلَالَةٍ مِّن مَّاءٍ مَّهِينٍ
Then He made his seed from a draught of despised fluid;		
9. Thumma sawwāhu wa nafakha fīhi min rūḥihi wa ja'ala lakumu 's-sam'a wa		ثُمَّ سَوَّاهُ وَنَفَخَ فِيهِ مِن رُّوحِهِ وَجَعَلَ لَكُمُ السَّمْعَ وَالْأَبْصَارَ

<table>
<tr><td>'l-abṣāra wa 'l-af'idata qalīlan mā tashkurūna</td><td></td><td>وَالْأَفْئِدَةَ قَلِيلًا مَّا تَشْكُرُونَ</td></tr>
<tr><td colspan="3">Then He fashioned him and breathed into him of His spirit; and appointed for you hearing and sight and hearts. Small thanks give ye!</td></tr>
<tr><td>10. Wa qālū a'idhā ḍalalnā fī 'l-arḍi a-inna lafī khalqin jadīd bal hum bi liqā'i rabbihim kāfirūn</td><td></td><td>وَقَالُوا أَئِذَا ضَلَلْنَا فِي الْأَرْضِ أَئِنَّا لَفِي خَلْقٍ جَدِيدٍ بَلْ هُم
بِلِقَاءِ رَبِّهِمْ كَافِرُونَ</td></tr>
<tr><td colspan="3">And they say: When we are lost in the earth, how can we then be recreated? Nay but they are disbelievers in the meeting with their Lord.</td></tr>
<tr><td>11. Qul yatawaffākum malaku 'l-mawti 'l-ladhī wukkila bikum thumma ila rabbikum turja'ūn</td><td></td><td>قُلْ يَتَوَفَّاكُم مَّلَكُ الْمَوْتِ الَّذِي وُكِّلَ بِكُمْ ثُمَّ إِلَى رَبِّكُمْ
تُرْجَعُونَ</td></tr>
<tr><td colspan="3">Say: The angel of death, who hath charge concerning you, will gather you, and afterward unto your Lord ye will be returned.</td></tr>
<tr><td>12. Wa law tarā idhi 'l-mujrimūna nākisū ru'ūsihim 'inda rabbihim rabbanā abṣarnā wasam'inā farj'inā n'amal ṣāliḥan innā mūqinūn.</td><td></td><td>وَلَوْ تَرَى إِذِ الْمُجْرِمُونَ نَاكِسُو رُؤُوسِهِمْ عِندَ رَبِّهِمْ رَبَّنَا
أَبْصَرْنَا وَسَمِعْنَا فَارْجِعْنَا نَعْمَلْ صَالِحًا إِنَّا مُوقِنُونَ</td></tr>
<tr><td colspan="3">Couldst thou but see when the guilty hang their heads before their Lord, (and say): Our Lord! We have now seen and heard, so send us back; we will do right, now we are sure.</td></tr>
<tr><td>13. Wa-law sh'inā la ataynā kulla nafsin hudāha wa lākin ḥaqqa 'l-qawlu minnī la-amla-anna jahannama mina 'l-jinnati wa 'n-nāsi ajma'īn</td><td></td><td>وَلَوْ شِئْنَا لَآتَيْنَا كُلَّ نَفْسٍ هُدَاهَا وَلَكِنْ حَقَّ الْقَوْلُ مِنِّي
لَأَمْلَأَنَّ جَهَنَّمَ مِنَ الْجِنَّةِ وَالنَّاسِ أَجْمَعِينَ</td></tr>
<tr><td colspan="3">And if We had so willed, We could have given every soul its guidance, but the word from Me concerning evil doers took effect: that I will fill hell with the jinn and mankind together.</td></tr>
</table>

<table>
<tr><td>14. Fa-dhūqū bimā nasīytum liqā'a yawmikum hadhā innā nasīnākum wa dhūqū 'adhāba 'l-khuldi bimā kuntum ta'amalūn</td><td></td><td>فَذُوقُوا بِمَا نَسِيتُمْ لِقَاءَ يَوْمِكُمْ هَٰذَا إِنَّا نَسِينَاكُمْ وَذُوقُوا عَذَابَ الْخُلْدِ بِمَا كُنتُمْ تَعْمَلُونَ</td></tr>
<tr><td colspan="3">So taste (the evil of your deeds). Forasmuch as ye forgot the meeting of this your day, lo! We forget you. Taste the doom immortality because of what ye used to do.</td></tr>
<tr><td>15. Innamā y'uminu bi āyātinā 'l-ladhīna idhā dhukkirū bihā kharrū sujjadan wa sabbaḥū bi-ḥamdi rabbihim wa hum lā yastakbirūn</td><td></td><td>إِنَّمَا يُؤْمِنُ بِآيَاتِنَا الَّذِينَ إِذَا ذُكِّرُوا بِهَا خَرُّوا سُجَّدًا وَسَبَّحُوا بِحَمْدِ رَبِّهِمْ وَهُمْ لَا يَسْتَكْبِرُونَ</td></tr>
<tr><td colspan="3">Only those believe in Our revelations who, when they are reminded of them, fall down prostrate and hymn the praise of their Lord, and they are not scornful,</td></tr>
<tr><td>16. Tatajāfā junūbuhum 'ani 'l-maḍāji'i yad'ūna rabbahum khawfan wa ṭama'an wa mimmā razaqnāhum yunfiqūn</td><td></td><td>تَتَجَافَىٰ جُنُوبُهُمْ عَنِ الْمَضَاجِعِ يَدْعُونَ رَبَّهُمْ خَوْفًا وَطَمَعًا وَمِمَّا رَزَقْنَاهُمْ يُنفِقُونَ</td></tr>
<tr><td colspan="3">Who forsake their beds to cry unto their Lord in fear and hope, and spend of what we have bestowed on them.</td></tr>
<tr><td>17. Falā t'alamu nafsun mā ukhfiya lahum min qurrati 'ayunin jazā'an bi-mā kānū y'amalūn</td><td></td><td>فَلَا تَعْلَمُ نَفْسٌ مَّا أُخْفِيَ لَهُم مِّن قُرَّةِ أَعْيُنٍ جَزَاءً بِمَا كَانُوا يَعْمَلُونَ</td></tr>
<tr><td colspan="3">No soul knoweth what is kept hid for them of joy, as a reward for what they used to do.</td></tr>
<tr><td>18. Afa-man kāna m'uminan kaman kāna fāsiqan lā yastawūn</td><td></td><td>أَفَمَن كَانَ مُؤْمِنًا كَمَن كَانَ فَاسِقًا لَّا يَسْتَوُونَ</td></tr>
<tr><td colspan="3">Is he who is a believer like unto him who is an evil liver? They are not alike.</td></tr>
<tr><td>19. Ammā 'l-ladhīna āmanū wa 'amilū 'ṣ-ṣāliḥāti fa-lahum jannatu 'l-mā'wā</td><td></td><td>أَمَّا الَّذِينَ آمَنُوا وَعَمِلُوا الصَّالِحَاتِ فَلَهُمْ جَنَّاتُ الْمَأْوَىٰ نُزُلًا</td></tr>
</table>

<table>
<tr><td>nuzulan bimā kānū y‘amalūn</td><td></td><td>بِمَا كَانُوا يَعْمَلُونَ</td></tr>
<tr><td colspan="3">But as for those who believe and do good works, for them are the Gardens of Retreat, a welcome (in reward) for what they used to do.</td></tr>
<tr><td>20. Wa ammā ’l-ladhīna fasaqū fa-mā’wāhumu ’n-nāru kullamā arādū an yakhrujū minhā u‘īdū fīhā wa qīla lahum dhūqū ‘adhāba ’n-nāri ’l-ladhī kuntum bihi tukadhdhibūn</td><td></td><td>وَأَمَّا الَّذِينَ فَسَقُوا فَمَأْوَاهُمُ النَّارُ كُلَّمَا أَرَادُوا أَن يَخْرُجُوا مِنْهَا أُعِيدُوا فِيهَا وَقِيلَ لَهُمْ ذُوقُوا عَذَابَ النَّارِ الَّذِي كُنتُم بِهِ تُكَذِّبُونَ</td></tr>
<tr><td colspan="3">And as for those who do evil, their retreat is the Fire. Whenever they desire to issue forth from thence, they are brought hack thither. Unto them it is said: Taste the torment of the Fire which ye used to deny.</td></tr>
<tr><td>21. Wa la-nudhīqannahum mina ’l-‘adhābi ’l-adna dūna ’l-‘adhabi ’l-akbari la‘allahum yarji‘ūn</td><td></td><td>وَلَنُذِيقَنَّهُمْ مِنَ الْعَذَابِ الْأَدْنَى دُونَ الْعَذَابِ الْأَكْبَرِ لَعَلَّهُمْ يَرْجِعُونَ</td></tr>
<tr><td colspan="3">And verily We make them taste the lower punishment before the greater, that haply they may return.</td></tr>
<tr><td>22. Wa man aẓlamu mim-man dhukkira bi āyāti rabbihi thumma ā‘arada ‘anha innā mina ’l-mujrimīna muntaqimūn</td><td></td><td>وَمَنْ أَظْلَمُ مِمَّن ذُكِّرَ بِآيَاتِ رَبِّهِ ثُمَّ أَعْرَضَ عَنْهَا إِنَّا مِنَ الْمُجْرِمِينَ مُنتَقِمُونَ</td></tr>
<tr><td colspan="3">And who doth greater wrong than he who is reminded of the revelations of his Lord, then turneth from them. Lo! We shall requite the guilty.</td></tr>
<tr><td>23. Wa laqad ataynā mūsā ’l-kitāba falā takun fī miryatin min liqā’ihi wa ja‘alnāhu hudan libanī isrā’īl</td><td></td><td>وَلَقَدْ آتَيْنَا مُوسَى الْكِتَابَ فَلَا تَكُن فِي مِرْيَةٍ مِّن لِّقَائِهِ وَجَعَلْنَاهُ هُدًى لِّبَنِي إِسْرَائِيلَ</td></tr>
<tr><td colspan="3">We verily gave Moses the Scripture; so be not ye in doubt of his receiving it; and We appointed it a guidance for the Children of Israel.</td></tr>
<tr><td>24. Wa ja‘alnā minhum a’immatan</td><td></td><td>وَجَعَلْنَا مِنْهُمْ أَئِمَّةً يَهْدُونَ بِأَمْرِنَا لَمَّا صَبَرُوا وَكَانُوا بِآيَاتِنَا</td></tr>
</table>

yahdūna bi amrinā lammā ṣabarū wa kānū bi āyātinā yūqinūn		يُوقِنُونَ
And when they became steadfast and believed firmly in Our revelations, We appointed from among them leaders who guided by Our command.		
25. Inna rabbaka huwa yafṣilu baynahum yawma 'l-qiyāmati fīmā kānū fīhī yakhtalifūn		إِنَّ رَبَّكَ هُوَ يَفْصِلُ بَيْنَهُمْ يَوْمَ الْقِيَامَةِ فِيمَا كَانُوا فِيهِ يَخْتَلِفُونَ
Lo! thy Lord will judge between them on the Day of Resurrection concerning that wherein they used to differ.		
26. Awa lam yahdi lahum kam ahlaknā min qablihim mina 'l-qurūni yamshūna fī masākinihim inna fī dhalika la-āyātin afalā yasma'ūn		أَوَلَمْ يَهْدِ لَهُمْ كَمْ أَهْلَكْنَا مِن قَبْلِهِم مِّنَ الْقُرُونِ يَمْشُونَ فِي مَسَاكِنِهِمْ إِنَّ فِي ذَٰلِكَ لَآيَاتٍ أَفَلَا يَسْمَعُونَ
Is it not a guidance for them (to observe) how many generations He destroyed before them, amid whose dwelling places they do walk? Lo, therein verily are portents! Will they not then heed?		
29. Awa lam yaraw annā nasūqu 'l-mā'a ila 'l-arḍi 'l-juruzi fanukhriju bihi zar'an t'akulu minhu an'āmuhum wa anfusuhum afalā yubṣirūn		أَوَلَمْ يَرَوْا أَنَّا نَسُوقُ الْمَاءَ إِلَى الْأَرْضِ الْجُرُزِ فَنُخْرِجُ بِهِ زَرْعًا تَأْكُلُ مِنْهُ أَنْعَامُهُمْ وَأَنفُسُهُمْ أَفَلَا يُبْصِرُونَ
Have they not seen how We lead the water to the barren land and therewith bring forth crops whereof their cattle eat, and they themselves? Will they not then see?		
30. Wa yaqūlūn matā hadha 'l-fatḥu in kuntum ṣādiqīn		وَيَقُولُونَ مَتَىٰ هَٰذَا الْفَتْحُ إِن كُنتُمْ صَادِقِينَ
And they say: When cometh this victory (of yours) if ye are truthful?		
31. Qul yawma 'l-fatḥi lā yanfa'u 'l-ladhīna kafarū īmānuhum walā hum		قُلْ يَوْمَ الْفَتْحِ لَا يَنفَعُ الَّذِينَ كَفَرُوا إِيمَانُهُمْ وَلَا هُمْ يُنظَرُونَ

yunẓarūn		
Say (unto them): On the day of the victory the faith of those who disbelieve (and who then will believe) will not avail them, neither will they be reprieved.		
32. Fā'arid 'anhum w 'antaẓir innahum muntaẓirūn		فَأَعْرِضْ عَنْهُمْ وَانتَظِرْ إِنَّهُم مُّنتَظِرُونَ
So withdraw from them (O Muhammad), and await (the event). Lo! they also are awaiting (it)		

Index

G

H

I

J

K

L

M

Y

Z